LINCOLN'S
RISE TO POWER

THE REPUBLICAN NOMINEE POSES FOR CAMPAIGN
PORTRAITS

(*Portrait of Lincoln Taken in Springfield, June, 1860, by Alexander
Hesler, Chicago*)

WILLIAM BARINGER

LINCOLN'S RISE TO POWER

W I T H   I L L U S T R A T I O N S

BOSTON · LITTLE, BROWN AND COMPANY · 1937
Republished 1976
Scholarly Press, Inc., 22929 Industrial Drive East
St. Clair Shores, Michigan 48080

973.7092
L736 b-a
1976

"To a party it is more important that its nominee should be a good candidate than that he turn out a good President."

LORD BRYCE

"Root would make the best President, but Taft the best candidate."

THEODORE ROOSEVELT

Preface

SOME years ago the writer had occasion, while serving his novitiate in historiography, to write a brief account of Lincoln's nomination as background for a study of campaign methods in the day when politics was the national sport. To his astonishment he discovered that in all the five-mile shelf of Lincoln literature (speaking in hyperbole) there was no satisfactory account of Lincoln's meteoric rise to power. Some writers told one part of the story, some another, and glaring errors were noticeable in the most celebrated works. Also, the dramatic quality of the story seemed to merit the telling for its own sake, as an absorbing novel is important. At the earliest opportunity, therefore, the present volume was undertaken.

It is hardly necessary to point out the importance in Lincoln biography of the nomination of May, 1860. Without it, he could not have been President in the time of great national crisis. One well-known Lincoln writer (Frank B. Carpenter, the artist) called the nomination "the central event of his life," marveling that historians had paid so little attention to it. In fact, knowledge of the truth about Lincoln's entrance upon the large stage of history has declined as the Emancipator's historic stature has grown with each passing year. The myth-making trend has made him a superman whose elevation to high authority was inevitable; he has become a folk hero of America, comparable to gods of antiquity like Osiris, Apollo, Adonis. One recent writer has characterized him as "a man nominated at Chicago as the undisputed leader of his party." Another concludes: "He [Lincoln] has more ability to stand alone than any other public man

of the time. He is the lodestar, drawing to him a whole people who
feel that perhaps he alone is able to lead the way through these
troublous times." This point of view absolutely blocks an understanding of the man.

In writing the following pages, the writer does not claim to have
used "all available material." No Lincoln student could make that
affirmation without, to say the least, prevarication. The present work,
however, is firmly grounded in original material, much of it previously unused by any writer, and no significant Lincoln work, old or
new, has escaped examination.

The writer wishes to express his thanks to the following institutions: Library of the University of Illinois; Illinois Historical Survey, Urbana, Illinois; Urbana Free Library; Illinois State Historical
Library, Springfield, Illinois; Abraham Lincoln Association, Springfield; Newberry Library, Chicago; Harper Memorial Library, University of Chicago; Chicago Historical Society; Library of Congress;
Historical Society of Pennsylvania, Philadelphia; Indiana State
Library, Indianapolis; Lincoln National Life Foundation, Fort
Wayne, Indiana.

Many friends have given generously of their time and judgment.
Miss May Lantz, Miss Louise Eyman, and Mr. Howard J. Caquelin
gave valuable aid in determining the reaction of the lay reader to
the book. Professional services were rendered by Miss Flora Michel-
mann; Miss Mary H. Webster, secretary to the late Lorado Taft;
Mr. H. W. Fay, custodian of the Lincoln Tomb; and Dr. Harry E.
Pratt, executive secretary of the Abraham Lincoln Association. The
writer considers himself extremely fortunate in having had the
assistance of two outstanding authorities in the field: Professor
James G. Randall of the University of Illinois, and Mr. Paul M.
Angle of the Illinois State Historical Library. Both gave encouragement as the book was undertaken; both read the manuscript and gave
it the benefit of their broad knowledge and seasoned scholarship.
Blame for all deficiencies must rest on

                                                    W. E. B.

Chronology

June 16, 1858	Illinois Republican Convention nominates Lincoln for United States Senator.
	Lincoln delivers the "house divided" speech.
July 9	Stephen A. Douglas opens his campaign, Chicago.
July 10	Lincoln replies, Chicago.
July 31	Douglas and Lincoln complete negotiations for seven joint debates.
August 21	First debate, Ottawa.
August 27	Second debate, Freeport.
September 15	Third debate, Jonesboro.
September 18	Fourth debate, Charleston.
October 7	Fifth debate, Galesburg.
October 13	Sixth debate, Quincy.
October 15	Seventh debate, Alton.
November 2	Election Day. Douglas Democrats elected to the Legislature, 54; Lincoln Republicans, 46.
November 4	*Illinois Gazette,* Lacon, Illinois, nominates Lincoln for President.
November 5	Mass meeting at Sandusky, Ohio, nominates Lincoln for President.
November 10	Cincinnati *Gazette* prints letter nominating a Republican ticket for 1860: For President, Abraham Lincoln, For Vice President, John P. Kennedy.
November 11	Chicago *Daily Democrat* suggests Lincoln for Governor, President, or Vice President.
November 19	Olney (Ill.) *Times* declares its support of "Abram Lincoln for President in 1860."

December 21 *or* 30	Jesse W. Fell advises Lincoln to seek the 1860 Republican nomination for President.
January 5, 1859	Douglas re-elected.
January 6	Illinois Republican leaders caucus in Springfield, discuss Lincoln's possible candidacy.
January 25	Lincoln speaks at Burns Centenary banquet, Springfield.
February 11	Lincoln delivers lecture, Jacksonville.
February 21	Lincoln lectures, Springfield.
March 1	Lincoln speaks at Chicago Republican jubilee banquet.
March 17	Rockford (Ill.) *Republican* nominates Lincoln for Vice President.
April 6	Lincoln writes a political speech by letter to Jefferson Birthday Committee, Boston.
April 8	Lincoln attends meeting of Illinois Republican Central Committee, Bloomington.
May 30	Lincoln becomes secret owner of the *Illinois Staats-Anzeiger*, Springfield.
July 4	Lincoln speaks at Independence Day rally, Atlanta, Illinois.
August 13	Lincoln addresses citizens of Council Bluffs, Iowa.
September 16	Lincoln delivers two speeches at Columbus, Ohio.
September 17	Lincoln speaks at Dayton, Hamilton, Cincinnati.
September 19	Lincoln speaks at Indianapolis.
September 30	Lincoln delivers two speeches in Milwaukee.
October 1	Lincoln speaks in Beloit and Janesville, Wisconsin.
October 14	Lincoln speaks at Clinton, Illinois, as Republicans celebrate victory in October elections.
October 15	Lincoln speaks as Springfield Republicans celebrate.
October 27	Lincoln speaks in support of John M. Palmer, Republican candidate for Congress, Springfield.
October 31 *circa*	Leaders of the Pennsylvania Cameron machine approach Lincoln as a potential running mate for Senator Cameron. Cameron-Lincoln ticket widely discussed in the press.
November 4	Lincoln speaks at Mechanicsburg, Illinois.
December 1	Lincoln speaks at Elwood, Kansas.
December 2	Lincoln speaks at Troy, Doniphan, Atchison, Kansas.

December 3	Lincoln speaks at Leavenworth.
December 19	Lincoln sends copies of the 1858 debates to Ohio Republicans for publication as a campaign document.
December 20 *circa*	Lincoln writes his autobiography, for campaign purposes.
December 21	Chicago awarded the Republican National Convention.
January 12, 1860	The Young Men's Republican Club of Springfield becomes the Lincoln Club. *Illinois State Journal*, Springfield, endorses Lincoln for President.
January 25 *circa*	Illinois Republican chiefs meet in secret caucus, Springfield; agree to support Lincoln for President.
February 16	Chicago *Press and Tribune* endorses Lincoln for President.
February 27	Lincoln speaks at Cooper Institute, New York City.
February 28–March 10	Lincoln tours New England.
March 3	Lincoln wins first official Party endorsement as candidate for President as the Wayne County (Ill.) Republican Convention declares for him.
May 9	Illinois Republican Convention meets at Decatur, salutes Lincoln as "The Rail Candidate for President."
May 10	Illinois delegates instructed to vote as a unit for Lincoln for President.
May 12	Lincoln headquarters opened in Chicago.
May 16	Republican Convention opens.
May 17	Platform adopted.
May 18	Lincoln nominated on third ballot.
May 19	Lincoln officially notified of his nomination.
May 23	Lincoln writes his formal acceptance.
November 6	Lincoln elected.

Contents

Illustrations

LINCOLN'S
RISE TO POWER

☆   ☆   ☆   ☆

Foreword

THAT God rules in the affairs of men is as certain as any truth of physical science. On the great moving Power which is from the beginning hangs the world of the senses and the world of thought and action. . . . Kings are lifted up or thrown down, nations come and go, republics flourish and wither, dynasties pass away like a tale that is told; but nothing is by chance, though men, in their ignorance of causes, may think so. The deeds of time are governed, as well as judged, by the decrees of eternity." [1]

These were words of George Bancroft. He was explaining why Abraham Lincoln had been chosen in 1860 to guide the United States of America in the hour of greatest peril to its national unity, as he began his eulogy of the late lamented War President. In front of the speaker curved the benches of the House of Representatives, where sat the combined Houses of Congress and official dignitaries representing the nations of the world, on February 12, 1866. The Abraham Lincoln memorial services were in progress. Bancroft, distinguished historian and able politician, knew politics and history too well to say directly that the Almighty made Lincoln President. But such was the impression he was careful to make as he commenced his encomium.

In the pre-relativity days of 1866, when the healthy skepticisms of modern science were yet infants, emotional Americans were anxious to conceive of Lincoln as something more than human, and they welcomed Eulogist Bancroft's innuendo. Not so David Davis,[2] Bancroft

---

[1] George Bancroft, *Abraham Lincoln: A Tribute,* pp. 3–4.
[2] William H. Herndon and Jesse W. Weik, *Abraham Lincoln,* Vol. II, p. 227*n.*

went on to say that Lincoln's administrative policies were frequently unsteady and confused; the historian made outright errors, such as his statement that Lincoln's knowledge of literature was so slim that he knew only one poet, Shakespeare. And David Davis must have laughed in his sleeve when he heard Bancroft suggest that the Almighty was the prime mover in making Lincoln President. He knew better; and history must accept his version in place of George Bancroft's interpretation. For if we let authentic facts speak out and examine the complete story of Lincoln's rise to the Presidency (so far as the evidence allows us to know it) there can be no dissent from this — that Lincoln was made President by the vicissitudes of politics, by events quite mundane, in no way divine, by contacts and agreements which observers who do not understand the hard necessities of political life might well deem corrupt.

CHAPTER I

Building a Reputation

ONE DAY in late December 1859 a very tall, thin, rawboned man with dark intellectual face, homely with roughhewn features, mop of uncombed dark hair and careless dress, sat cogitating in his dingy law office in Springfield, Illinois. His expression was thoughtful, melancholy, as he thought back over the fifty years of his life and tried to fathom what the next year would hold for him. He was, in a way, a candidate for his Party's next presidential nomination. But his knowledge of himself and of current politics was too solid to allow him to take this ambition very seriously. Several political associates had been urging that he make the race for the 1860 Republican nomination, one of whom had repeatedly asked the giant politician for the details of his private life, to be used in introducing the new candidate to the nation. Abraham Lincoln was complying with that request, and taking a faltering step toward a presidential nomination, when he composed and sent to Jesse W. Fell his concise, intimate autobiography.

The gaunt, homely man sat writing at his desk that December day not because he expected to be President, but because he expected some day to be United States Senator from Illinois.[1] He nourished the presidential gossip because he knew that to be talked of for the Presidency would make the coveted Senatorship easier to grasp. Politics

---

[1] Helen Nicolay, *Personal Traits of Abraham Lincoln*, p. 125. A. Lincoln to Gen. Welsh, of New York, Oct. 25, 1860; in Paul M. Angle, *Lincoln, 1854–1861*, p. 356.

works that way. In the presidential gossip which preceded the 1860 campaign, one John M. Read, Republican jurist of Pennsylvania, was, like Abraham Lincoln, being mentioned as a possible Republican candidate for President. But when the Republican convention met at Chicago, Read received one vote on the first ballot. Then the prestige of that lone vote multiplied like the progeny of an oyster. Years passed; the story grew with repetition until Read was known as a man who could have been President but for the perfidy of Simon Cameron.[1] Soon a so-called "reliable reference work" on historic Americans was telling how "he received sixty votes at the Chicago convention of 1860, but withdrew in favor of Abraham Lincoln." [2] Twice had Abraham Lincoln failed by a narrow margin to make himself "the Senator from Illinois." Next time he did not expect to lose. As a man who reputedly "nearly became President," it would be easy for Lincoln to capture that senatorial seat the next time an opportunity should present itself.

Had this tall politician been a practitioner under the parliamentary system of government, where leadership of a Party comes after long years of faithful political labor, he would certainly not have been dallying with the notion that he might become his Party's national leader. Many other politicians had far greater claims on that choicest favor of the Republican Party. In American politics, however, leaders are chosen under the convention system. One career may be made, another broken, overnight, in the heat of a national convention. Alert citizens who, like Abraham Lincoln, lived in the year of grace 1859, saw in the convention history of the preceding fifteen years an undertow of opportunism which with striking regularity pulled down seasoned Party leaders and set up dark horses, military heroes, innocuous compromise figures. For career men, the legislative and administrative masters of the nation, the trend was thoroughly depressing. For able politicians like Abraham Lincoln, strong in their local bailiwicks but holding no responsible position, it was hope.

One day in the early summer of the preceding twelvemonth of 1858, when the Party was still young in years but no longer young in

[1] *Appleton's Cyclopaedia of American Biography,* Vol. V, p. 199.
[2] *Lamb's Biographical Dictionary of the United States,* Vol. VI, p. 425.

strength, there occurred an interesting incident in point. Scheduled to meet on June 16, at Springfield, was the Republican Convention of the state of Illinois. From all corners of the state leaders swarmed to the capital, enthusiastically ready to marshal their strength for a turbulent campaign. Into Springfield from St. Louis puffed a tiny train bearing many delegates and news of a straw vote.

These delegates from southwestern Illinois had relieved the monotony of their journey across the hot, treeless prairie, by heartily talking politics. There were many important aspects to be discussed. For one, there was Douglas — the whole dramatic tale of how that stentorian little man, the outstanding Democrat of the nation since Martin Van Buren's retirement, had been denied his Party's nomination in 1856 in favor of the inoffensive "Old Public Functionary," Buchanan; how President Buchanan had heeded the advice of his Party's Southern faction in shaping his Administration's policies and spurned the Northerner, Douglas; how Douglas had, quite recently, publicly broken with his Party's titular leader, the President, because the Administration refused to permit settlers in the Kansas Territory to vote slavery in or out as it pleased them, in forming the government under which they would join the Union.

Even more exciting was the surprisingly stout opposition Senator Douglas had encountered in his own state in the person of Abraham Lincoln, of Springfield. When Douglas and Lincoln were rising young lawyer-politicians, one a Democrat, the other a Whig, they had been frequent opponents in debating society and in provincial politics. Douglas went early to Washington and steadily advanced. Lincoln went to the national capital late, and his record in the House of Representatives was so unfortunate that after one term he half retired from politics. Douglas, become nationally famous as "the Little Giant," induced Congress in 1854 to pass the Kansas-Nebraska Act, a measure which brought political revolution because it deprived the free North of its legislative safeguards against encroachments of the slave system. The North turned against Douglas in audible indignation; vast numbers of his former Democratic followers became Anti-Nebraska men. Among those roused to vigorous opposition was Abra-

ham Lincoln. Still calling himself a Whig, moribund though that
Party was, he took up the forensic cudgels against the Little Giant
and popular sovereignty. In the autumn of 1854 Douglas came home
to justify his acts and repair the Party schism. When he spoke in
Springfield in October, Lincoln made reply with a brilliant address
which constituted his "first great speech." [1] Two weeks later Douglas
and Lincoln met again at Peoria. In 1857, when Douglas returned to
justify popular sovereignty in the light of the Dred Scott decision, the
two men met again as oratorical opponents.

Douglas, obliged now to stand for re-election to the Senate, stood in
grave danger of defeat. Lincoln, his logical opponent, was to be named
at the imminent State Convention as the Republican choice for United
States Senator.

Having thus covered the key factors of Illinois politics, these
Springfield-bound politicians had inevitably reached an absorbing
subject. Who would the next President be, should their Party win?
Someone had suggested a presidential poll of the train; so a straw vote
had been taken with this result [2]:

William H. Seward	139	S. P. Chase	6
John C. Freemont [sic]	32	W. H. Bissell	2
John McLean	13	Scattering	26
Lyman Trumbull	7		

Those who thought Abraham Lincoln might be in the running were
so few that the St. Louis correspondent who reported this vote vouch-
safed him no mention by name.

On that lovely summer day of June 16, 1858, Springfield was full
of jubilating, confident Republicans, their hopes raised to new heights
by the enduring Democratic split. Ninety-five counties had passed
resolutions requesting that Abraham Lincoln be the Party's choice
for Senator. [3] Opening speeches glowed with confidence and enthusi-

[1] Albert J. Beveridge, *Abraham Lincoln, 1809–1858*, Vol. II, p. 195. Paul M. Angle,
"*Here I Have Lived,*" p. 212.
[2] *Missouri Republican,* June 24, 1858; in E. E. Sparks (ed.), *The Lincoln-Douglas Debates of 1858,* p. 24.
[3] Arthur C. Cole, *Era of the Civil War,* p. 163.

asm and delegates yelled lustily. When nominations came in the order
of business, careful strategy was followed. Chicago's delegation carried in a banner: COOK COUNTY IS FOR ABRAHAM LINCOLN. Roars
of approval "fairly shook" the State House. Another wave of applause
greeted the resolution: "Resolved, that Abraham Lincoln is the first
and only choice of the Republicans of Illinois for the United States
Senate, as the successor of Stephen A. Douglas." Unanimous adoption
was a mere formality.

That evening the Convention reassembled and listened to its candidate's acceptance address. What they heard was the celebrated
"house divided" speech. For the important occasion Lincoln had ready
the fourth oration of his anti-Douglas series. On this work the author
had lavished all his power as a politician and writer; for months he
had been thinking, writing, revising, trimming. The result was a brilliant speech which pleased Lincoln and his radical law partner, William H. Herndon,[1] but which moved all his other close political
friends to say that Lincoln's remarks, if delivered as written, would
place him in a position far too radical, too close to abolitionism. Said
Herndon, "Lincoln, deliver that speech as read and it will make you
President." Lincoln, weighing these comments, made reply to the
Cassandras. "The time has come when these sentiments should be
uttered; and if it is decreed that I should go down because of this
speech, then let me go down linked to the truth — let me die in the
advocacy of what is just and right." [2] In the light of that future event
which is the subject of this history, Herndon's remark about the Presidency must not be regarded as prophecy. As a highly competent politician he knew that nobody was ever made President by producing
fine speeches. Rather, what Billy Herndon did was pay his hero the
highest possible compliment by saying that the author of so great a
speech deserved to be made President.

When, as Senatorial nominee, "the angular and homely clad Lincoln
arose by the table in the Hall of the House of Representatives on that

[1] Paul M. Angle (ed.), *Herndon's Lincoln*, pp. 324–325.
[2] Angle, *Herndon's Lincoln*, p. 326.

June night, and stood before the cheering multitude, . . . great events, still in the future, were to make his words historic." [1] He read his speech from manuscript, slowly, gravely.

If we could first know where we are, and whither we are tending, we could better judge what to do, and how to do it. We are now far into the fifth year since a policy was initiated with the avowed object and confident promise of putting an end to slavery agitation. Under the operation of that policy, the agitation has not only not ceased, but has constantly augmented. In my opinion, it will not cease until a crisis shall have been reached and passed. "A house divided against itself cannot stand." I believe this government cannot endure permanently half slave and half free. I do not expect the Union to be dissolved — I do not expect the house to fall — but I do expect it will cease to be divided. It will become all one thing, or all the other. Either the opponents of slavery will arrest the further spread of it, and place it where the public mind shall rest in the belief that it is in the course of ultimate extinction; or its advocates will push it forward till it shall become alike lawful in all the states, old as well as new, North as well as South.

With this philosophic introduction, the nominee made a forceful argument, based on history, to demonstrate that slavery had always expanded and would continue to spread unless firmly resisted by stern political opposition. He proclaimed Douglas' popular sovereignty a false protection. True, said Lincoln, "he is a very great man . . . and the largest of us are very small ones. Let this be granted. But 'a living dog is better than a dead lion.' Judge Douglas, if not a dead lion for this work, is at least a caged and toothless one. How can he oppose the advances of slavery? His avowed mission is impressing the 'public heart' to care nothing about it."

Our cause, then, must be intrusted to, and conducted by its own undoubted friends — those whose hands are free, whose hearts are in the work — who do care for the result. The result is not doubtful. We shall not fail — if we stand firm we shall not fail. Wise councils may accelerate or mistakes delay it, but sooner or later the victory is sure to come. [2]

Impressed, the Illinois Republican press made the speech their

[1] Beveridge, Vol. II, p. 576.
[2] *Illinois State Journal*, Springfield, Ill., June 18, 1858. John G. Nicolay and John Hay (eds.), *Complete Works of Abraham Lincoln*, Vol. III, pp. 1–15.

text for the campaign. It became a campaign document, and the New York *Tribune* printed the speech in full, with cordial praise as an effort "compact and forcible, concise and admirable." Though other newspapers outside the state paid little attention to Lincoln's speech,[1] national attention would soon be his, for his "house divided" speech was the mighty opening gun in the greatest fight Lincoln had ever made, a Homeric conflict that was to create the greatest single force in the metamorphosis of Abraham Lincoln from the Illinois "literary statesman" into a specimen of that ubiquitous figure in American history, the "presidential possibility."

In Washington, when Senator Douglas heard of Lincoln's nomination, he said: "I shall have my hands full. He is the strong man of his party — full of wit, facts, dates — and the best stump speaker, with his droll ways and dry jokes, in the West." Soon the Little Giant was back from Washington ready to open his fight. In Chicago, on July 9, Douglas made reply to Lincoln's speech. When the Little Giant in 1854 had returned home after fathering the Kansas-Nebraska Act, bells were tolled in Chicago and flags hung at half-mast. Now along his homeward route crowds gathered to do him honor, vociferously welcoming the "conquering hero." Chicago gave him a greeting reminiscent of the "triumphs" which Republican Rome staged to honor victorious captains.[2] Douglas, conveyed to the Tremont House through dense, roaring crowds, stepped out on the balcony and spoke extempore to the huge open-air audience of more than twelve thousand which clogged the street below and milled about in torchlit, flickering semidarkness. Against a lively background of cheering, the short, massive, deep-voiced man with great head, heavy black hair, piercing dark eyes, told his clamorous partisans why he had broken with the Administration. All his public acts, he said, were explained by his devotion to the "great principle of self-government." Lincoln, sitting near by, an alert observer, heard himself referred to as "an intelligent, honorable gentleman." Cried Douglas, "Whatever issue I may have with him will be of principle and not involving personal-

[1] Beveridge, Vol. II, p. 585.
[2] Sparks, *Lincoln-Douglas Debates,* pp. 30–35.

ities. [Cheers.]" The speaker proceeded to attack the honorable gentleman's "house divided" beliefs, calling that doctrine an erroneous notion which invited "a war of sections — a war of extermination." Lincoln's belief meant uniformity in the domestic institutions of all states, argued Douglas. Had not the nation's founders left regulation of domestic institutions to the several states? Slavery, a domestic institution, must be controlled by individual states, like police regulations and marriage laws. Lincoln's vaunted uniformity, hammered Douglas, could only be had by "merging the rights and sovereignty of the states in one consolidated empire . . . with the uniformity of despotism reigning triumphant throughout the length and breadth of the land ["hear," "hear," "bravo," and great applause]."

Leaping to the attack with his favorite plea for white supremacy, the Little Giant argued against Negro equality. Cried he: "This government . . . is founded on a white basis. [Great applause.] It was made by the white man, for the white man, to be administered by white men. [Cheers.]" Members of any "inferior race" should have all rights "consistent with the safety of society" but "each state must decide for itself the nature and extent of these rights."

The throng became so excited that at one point they cheered and whooped while a band played and fireworks exploded; the speaker had to stop until the demonstration was spent. When Douglas at last finished, loud calls for Lincoln went up. Lincoln announced that next evening he would speak. Partisans lingered long, shouting for Douglas and shooting fireworks.

The Republican Chicago *Journal* commented that Douglas had spoken [1] —

in his usual style — dispensing "soft-soap" quite freely, setting himself forth as a hero of no common order, and indulging even more than ordinarily in that inexorable habit of misrepresentation, and prevarication which appears in political matters to have become a sort of second nature to him.

He . . . very falsely imputed to Mr. Lincoln this doctrine of "negro equality," while the fact is that Mr. Lincoln has no more to do with . . .

[1] In Sparks, p. 37.

the question of placing negroes on an equality with white men, than Douglas has to do with the Americanizing of the Hottentots or the Fejee Islanders.

Lincoln the next night, not at all intimidated by Douglas' popularity, made reply from the same balcony. When Lincoln's form emerged, towering, stooping, ungainly, a storm of cheers broke out and continued until the speaker asked for quiet. His speech was a detailed attack on his opponent's arguments. He spent much time shooting holes in what Douglas had said the night before, displaying great perspicacity in seeking out the weaknesses of his opponent's armor, great force in pointing them out to his crowd.

"Popular sovereignty!" Lincoln exclaimed. "Everlasting popular sovereignty! [Laughter and continued cheers]. . . . What is it? Why, it is the sovereignty of the people!" What effrontery in Judge Douglas to think he had invented that doctrine. Lincoln repeated the equality clause of the Declaration of Independence. "There is the origin of popular sovereignty. [Loud applause.]" In the battle in Congress against the proslavery Lecompton Constitution of Kansas, the effective opposition came not from Douglas but from the Republican members, Lincoln pointed out — almost losing his temper at hecklers who kept yelling up through the night from the jammed streets that Douglas must have the credit for defeating Lecomptonism.

Repeating the moot portion of his "house divided" speech, Lincoln declared that Douglas had twisted the meaning of the Biblical passage. Lincoln insisted he had pointed out what *would* happen to the Union, not what he *wanted* to happen. He had not even said that he wished slavery placed in the course of ultimate extinction. "I do say so now, however. [Applause.] " True, as Douglas said, the Union had "endured eighty-two years half slave and half free," but only because the public all that time thought slavery a dying institution. Lincoln confessed he had always hated slavery, but had done so quietly "until this new era of the introduction of the Nebraska bill began. I always *believed* that everybody was against it, and that it was in course of ultimate extinction." The Constitution's framers had thought so, and had put a period to the slave trade and excluded slavery from new territory. Americans who resisted slavery's spread were following the founders of the Union. Free state citizens have no right to meddle with slavery in the slave states, said Lincoln; a hundred times he had said that, regardless of Douglas' charges to the contrary.

Douglas had likewise misconstrued his position, said the speaker, on regulation of local institutions. How on earth, Lincoln exclaimed, could Douglas infer from Lincoln's doctrines that he favored "general consolidation of all the local institutions of the various states?" Each state could do as it liked in all matters "that interfere with the rights of no other state." How could Douglas infer that because Lincoln wished to halt slavery's spread, he therefore demanded that Illinois interfere with the cranberry laws of Indiana? Douglas erred in regarding "this matter of keeping one sixth of the population of the whole nation in a state of oppression and tyranny . . . as . . . only equal to the question of the cranberry laws of Indiana," but "a vast portion of the American people" regarded slavery as no such small thing, rather considering it "a vast moral evil."

The Republican Party must not, cried Lincoln the practical politician, help re-elect Douglas. In this "mighty issue . . . upon which hang the destinies of the nation, it is nothing to you — nothing to the mass of the people . . . whether or not Judge Douglas or myself shall ever be heard of after this night." But "if you indorse him, you tell him you do not care whether slavery be voted up or down . . . [A voice "Hit him again."]"

No one denies that the government was meant for white men, the orator went on. Whites and blacks would not marry in the territories if blacks were kept out, Lincoln remarked, a blow which brought "immense applause" and a call for "Three cheers for Lincoln!" Three mighty hurrahs agitated the night air.

Lincoln swept to a powerful conclusion with a brilliant eulogy of the Declaration of Independence.

Douglas' doctrine of inferior races did not stop with the Negro. Appealing directly to the Germans, whose arrival in a body had caused a sensation, Lincoln cried, "You Germans are not connected" with the Declaration of Independence, in Douglas' view; and he hinted that the Germans might be called an "inferior race" soon, under Douglas' doctrine. "If that Declaration is not the truth, let us get the statute-book in which we find it, and tear it out! Who is so bold as to do it? If it is not true, let us tear it out. [Cries of "No, no."] Let us stick to it, then. [Cheers.] " Let the principle that all men are created equal be as nearly reached as possible. "If we cannot give freedom to every creature, let us do nothing that will impose slavery upon any other creature. [Applause.] Let us then turn this government back into the channel in which the framers of the Constitution originally placed it. . . . Let us discard all this quibbling about this man and the other man, this race and that race and the other race being inferior . . . and unite as one people throughout this land, until we shall once more stand up declaring that all men are created equal." [1]

The sheer oratory of this closing passage spellbound the throng, and as the orator ceased a hurricane of cheers rang out. Lincoln had struck a fighting chord which filled Republicans with boisterous confidence. Illinois' leading Republican papers published the speech in full and praised it as an "overwhelming refutation" of Douglas' position. Too, Eastern newspapers gave Lincoln's speech as much space as they did Douglas', and predicted defeat for the Little Giant because he was obliged to fight both the Buchanan machine and the rising Republican Party.[2]

So with these two eloquent addresses the campaign on which the eyes of the country were focused, because the famous Douglas was fighting for his political life against two potent foes, was off to a hot start. For some days the two candidates remained in Chicago, conferring with committees and preparing the canvass; then the campaign moved south. Douglas traveled in a gaudily bannered private car, accompanied by his beautiful wife, his secretary, stenographers, and a flock of Democratic politicians. Lincoln went north from Springfield to hear Douglas at Bloomington,[3] for his Party strategists

[1] *Complete Works of Lincoln*, Vol. III, pp. 19-52.
[2] Beveridge, Vol. II, pp. 608-609, p. 627. G. D. Davis, "Factional Differences in the Democratic Party in Illinois, 1854-1858," pp. 173-183.
[3] Angle, *Lincoln, 1854-1861*, p. 237.

decided that Lincoln ought to follow his opponent closely. At Joliet a flat car mounted with a brass cannon was hitched to the Senator's train. Douglas took this along whenever possible throughout the canvass, its reverberating booms announcing to the citizenry of towns ahead the thrilling news that Douglas was coming.

At Bloomington the Little Giant made a night speech in the Court House square. Upon his arrival, his artillery was answered in kind; and the town, Republican though it was, greeted him with decorations, crowds, cheers. His address was a more forceful presentation of the arguments he made at Chicago; at once it became a Democratic campaign document and received wide circulation. Lincoln's powerful Chicago speech caused no change in Douglas' arguments. Lincoln stood with the crowd as Douglas harangued them. When the Little Giant closed the throng called for Lincoln more noisily than they had cheered the speaker. Reluctantly Lincoln climbed on the stand, declining to speak because the meeting was Douglas', but promising to return soon.[1]

The Douglas car moved toward Springfield, Lincoln on the same train. The two candidates made a striking contrast: the dashing, well-tailored Douglas, traveling with retainers; the solitary Lincoln, with weather-beaten top hat, old carpetbag, in black alpaca trousers and long loose black coat, very dusty. In Springfield the Douglas partisans outdid themselves to welcome the Little Giant, festooning a grove north of town with elaborate decorations. Rain had spoiled the gala effect, but a great crowd nevertheless assembled, muddy-footed under dripping trees. Douglas delivered the same arguments he had offered at Chicago and Bloomington, a bit more powerfully put. The crowd received them vociferously, and a pamphlet edition was soon printed and scattered. Douglas papers reported the meeting a complete success; Republican sheets chronicled a complete failure.

That evening in the Hall of the House of Representatives the Republicans held their counter-demonstration. Lincoln's speech offered no new arguments, but he made much of the disadvantages under which his Party was fighting the battle, contrasting the position and

---

[1] Bloomington *Pantagraph*, July 17, 1858; in Sparks, p. 51.

prospects of Douglas with his own lack of position, noting the legislative apportionment law as giving the Democrats a long lead. Lincoln made the crowd laugh heartily many times by his amusing thrusts. He ridiculed Douglas' opposition to what the Little Giant called Lincoln's "monstrous revolutionary doctrines." Was popular sovereignty the doctrine Douglas was "going to spend his life for? Does he expect to stand up in majestic dignity, and go through his *apotheosis* and become a god, in the maintaining of a principle which neither man nor mouse in all God's creation is opposing?" The orator was irritated by Douglas' declaration that Lincoln's "house divided" speech (the moot pasage of which Lincoln again repeated) meant war. Douglas was unfair in saying so. "I have often expressed an expectation to die, but I have never expressed a wish to die"; Lincoln thus put his position so forcefully that the lowest moron in the audience could not mistake his meaning, however heartily rabid Douglasites might disagree. He re-emphasized his position that the Declaration of Independence meant that blacks were the equals of whites, not in all things, but in their right to "life, liberty, and the pursuit of happiness." He said, in poetic rhythms: "All I ask for the negro is that if you do not like him, let him alone. If God gave him but little, that little let him enjoy." Republican papers said Lincoln's speech "completely demolished Mr. Douglas." The Douglas press plumbed its capacity for contempt.

Douglas planned a campaign so strenuous that it called for a speech almost every day and covered the whole state. His itinerary was published; whereupon Lincoln and his committee drew up parallel plans. Lincoln would camp along the Douglas trail. Democrats were angry at these tactics, hotly remarking that in no other way could Lincoln secure crowds.[1] Obviously, it was in rather bad taste. Worse, for political purposes, it placed Lincoln definitely in the rôle of underdog. Several Republicans advised that Lincoln strategically abandon the defensive by challenging Douglas to conduct the canvass by joint debates. Late in July Lincoln yielded to the pressure, and after conferences in Chicago with Norman Judd,

---

[1] Sparks, pp. 55–57. George Fort Milton, *The Eve of Conflict*, pp. 328–329.

the powerful Republican state chairman, and other strategists, sent Judd to Douglas with a letter proposing that the two candidates "divide time and address the same audiences." [1] Lincoln was reluctant to challenge Douglas for vanity's sake; he thought his speeches better than those of Douglas and that he could therefore manage without the challenge, in the making of which he recognized the pre-eminence of Douglas. He had hoped Douglas would challenge him.[2] Lincoln's offer was, however (forgetting his feelings) an astute move. Douglas did not welcome such a contest, for he had nothing to gain in fame, while a series of debates would advertise Lincoln to the nation. The Senator wanted to beg off on the ground that his campaign was already planned, but he knew that Republicans would brand him a coward if he dodged Lincoln's challenge. So he compromised and wrote to Lincoln suggesting a debate at a town in each congressional district except those of Chicago and Springfield, where both had already spoken.

While this diplomacy was going on the two candidates were stumping in central Illinois.[3] At Clinton, Douglas delivered an afternoon speech with Lincoln as one of his auditors. That evening Lincoln made reply. A Douglas reporter sketched a Dickensian scene of the afternoon rally.[4]

Lincoln was present during the delivery of the speech, sitting immediately in front of Senator Douglas, but rendered invisible from the stand by a gentleman in green goggles, whom he used as a shield and cover. After Senator Douglas had concluded, and the cheers which greeted him ceased, green goggles rose and proposed three cheers for Lincoln, which were given by about ten men who stood immediately around him. Mr. Lincoln then gradually lengthened out his long, lank proportions until he stood upon his feet, and with a desperate attempt at looking pleasant, said that he would not take advantage of Judge Douglas' crowd, but would address "sich" as liked to hear him in the evening at the Court House. Having made this announcement in a tone and with an air of a perfect "Uriah Heep," pleading his humility, and asking for forgiveness of

[1] Lincoln to Douglas, July 24, 1858; in Sparks, p. 59.
[2] Lincoln to Douglas, July 29, 1858; in Sparks, pp. 68–69. Chicago *Journal*, July 27, 1858; Peoria *Transcript*, July 29, 1858; in Sparks, pp. 61, 63.
[3] Angle, *Lincoln, 1854–1861*, p. 239.
[4] Sparks, pp. 57–58.

Heaven for his enemies, he stood washing his hands with invisible soap in imperceptible water, until his friends, seeing that his mind was wandering, took him in charge, and bundled him off the ground.

Lincoln, upon receiving Douglas' reply to the challenge, accepted; the two men met and arranged the terms of seven debates, to begin at Ottawa on August 21.

The Illinois press, already excited over the campaign, became more so as the personal rivalry sharpened. Lincoln's papers said Douglas had dodged, in narrowing the debates to a mere seven; Democrat journals retorted that Lincoln had at last acquired crowds honorably by arranging to speak with Douglas.[1]

The debates arranged, weeks remained before the first one would take place at Ottawa. Douglas campaigned steadily, speaking almost every day, while Lincoln stayed at home two weeks, planning the campaign and writing letters to numerous politicians.[2] Then on August 12 Lincoln opened his active campaign by speaking at Beardstown, following Douglas as the Little Giant's campaign moved northward on the Illinois River, speaking on the same day or the next, sometimes arriving as the Douglas meeting was going on. Republicans annoyed Douglas by greeting Lincoln with a demonstration.

As the two candidates moved up the river toward Ottawa, speaking at Beardstown, Havana, Peoria, and several smaller towns, the contest grew perceptibly warm. For political reasons Lincoln had persuaded himself that all available evidence pointed to Douglas' guilt as a conspirator to extend slavery when he created the Kansas-Nebraska Act; and he had twice in the early campaign publicly charged Douglas with conspiracy, first by inference, in the "house-divided" speech, then directly, in his second Springfield speech, still with the reservation that he did not *know* of a conspiracy, but inferred it from the evidence.[3] Douglas knew (as the historian does) that these charges were libelous and politically dangerous mis-

---

[1] Sparks, pp. 60–66.
[2] William E. Barton, *Life of Abraham Lincoln*, Vol. I, pp. 501–502. Angle, *Lincoln, 1854–1861*, pp. 240–241. Milton, *Eve of Conflict*, pp. 331–333.
[3] Lincoln's Freeport speech; Sparks, p. 158.

representation; but he at first disregarded them as beneath notice.
Then, when he heard Lincoln pointing to his opponent's silence on
the conspiracy issue as proof of guilt and learned that Lyman Trumbull had harangued fiercely in Chicago about Douglas the traitor to
the North, the Little Giant exploded. At Clinton he made a direct
denial. At Beardstown he roared that Lincoln's charge was "an infamous lie." [1] Senator Douglas paid his disrespects to Senator Trumbull by labeling him a "miserable, craven-hearted wretch." Next day
Lincoln was met at the Beardstown wharf by two bands and forty
horsemen, and escorted to a large meeting where he spoke for two
hours. He repeated the conspiracy charges at length and dared Douglas to deny them. [2]

Following Douglas up the river to Havana, Lincoln next day
heard that Douglas in his Havana speech had called him "a liar, a
coward, a wretch and a sneak," that the Senator must have been
drunk to say such a thing. Replying on the following day, Lincoln
talked about hearing that Douglas had been "a little excited, nervous
(?) perhaps, and that he said something about fighting . . . a personal encounter between himself and me." Humorously Lincoln
pointed out the complete absurdity of any fistic display: a fight would
prove nothing except that "it might establish that Judge Douglas is
a more muscular man than myself," or *vice versa*. "But this subject
is not referred to in the Cincinnati platform, nor in either of the
Springfield platforms." Besides, "he and I are about the best friends
in the world." When Douglas talked about fighting he was merely
"trying to excite — well, let us say enthusiasm against me on the part
of his audience. And, as I find he was tolerably successful in this,
we will call it quits." [3]

The two continued northward, each haranguing receptive crowds
with the same speech he had used at Chicago and Springfield. At
Lewistown and Peoria both had large audiences and elaborate receptions. On the twentieth they were near Ottawa, ready for a dra-

[1] Milton, pp. 333–335.
[2] Horace White; in Herndon and Weik, *Abraham Lincoln*, Vol. II, pp. 95–101.
Beveridge, Vol. II, pp. 642–643.
[3] White; in Herndon and Weik, Vol. II, pp. 102–103.

matic arrival at the scene of the first joint debate. The sun rose on an animated scene of mass migration as holiday-making farmers poured towards town in every sort of conveyance, stirring great clouds of dust on every road. Special trains brought crowds from nearly every large town in Illinois. All morning the throng gathered — gay with floats, parading delegations, banners and mottoes; noisy with bands, fife and drum corps, booming cannon; until by noon the bunting-bedecked town seethed with people. Lincoln arrived in a special train loaded with shouting Republicans, listened to a tumultuous welcome by a dense crowd, drove off, surrounded by bands, in a motto-plastered carriage at the head of a parade. Douglas reached town accompanied by a long, brilliant cavalcade of horsemen who met his grand four-horse carriage a few miles out. Cannon thundered, cheers and blaring bands agitated the dusty air as more than ten thousand people packed into the public square for the afternoon debate. The crowd swarmed upon the lumber platform. A half-hour's skirmish cleared the stand for speakers, committees, reporters; but some interlopers remained perched on the wooden awning, and presently part of it came crashing down on the heads of the Douglas committee. Looking imperiously out upon the milling throng, so large that many were out of earshot, Douglas spoke for an hour, hammering at the political sincerity of Lincoln and striving mightily to convince everybody that the Republican party and abolitionism were identical. Every few minutes loud noises of approbation, comments humorous and sharp from the crowd, interrupted the speaker. Lincoln rose to reply, and cheers went up so loud that for several minutes he could not speak. He denied in detail Douglas' various charges of political crookery, and made his telling arguments against Douglas' representation that Republicanism meant race equality and war between North and South. He reasserted his conspiracy charge, inviting Douglas to prove that he was not a conspirator or at best a tool of conspirators to extend slavery, recalled some embarrassing incidents in the political history of Douglas, many times making the crowd laugh and cheer loud and long. Douglas in his half-hour rejoinder placed back upon Lincoln the charge of political chicanery, called the conspiracy talk "an infamous lie" and lost his temper over it amid confusion and interruptions, for in this northern region the crowd was overwhelmingly for Lincoln. Both candidates had given a powerful stump performance; each smote the other with terrific verbal blows while maintaining a show of mutual respect.[1]

The debate over, in the noisy confusion of departure several excited Republicans grabbed Lincoln and carried him off on their shoulders, paraded to their embarrassed hero's lodgings behind a band at the head of an impromptu parade, marchers singing patriotic songs. Correspondents of leading Eastern papers, on hand to report Douglas (not Lincoln), wrote long accounts of the theatrical contest, dwelling on the striking contrasts between the two warriors — their political principles, their fame, their appearance: Douglas "a short, thickset, burly man, with large, round head, heavy hair, dark complexion, and fierce, bull-dog look"; Lincoln "very tall, slender and angular, awkward even in gait and attitude. His face is sharp, large-featured and unprepossessing. His eyes are deep-set under heavy brows, his forehead is high and retreating, and his hair is dark and heavy. In repose, I must confess that 'Long Abe's' appearance is *not* comely. But stir him up and the fire of his genius plays on every feature. His eye glows and sparkles; every lineament, now so ill-formed, grows brilliant and expressive, and you have before you a man of rare power and of strong magnetic personality. He *takes* the people every time, and there is no getting away from his sturdy good sense, his unaffected sincerity and the unceasing play of his good humor, which accompanies his close logic and smooths the way to conviction. Listening to him on Saturday, calmly and unprejudiced, I was convinced that he had no superior as a stump-speaker. He is clear, concise and logical, his language is eloquent and at perfect command. He is altogether a more fluent speaker than Douglas, and in all the arts of debate fully his equal." [2] So said a Republican reporter from New York.

[1] Sparks, pp. 86–124.
[2] Chester P. Dewey of the New York *Evening Post;* in Herndon and Weik, Vol. II, pp. 105–107.

Illinois newspapers resolutely warped their elaborate accounts of the Ottawa debate according to their politics. Douglas papers told about the "funereal" tone of Lincoln parades, how Douglas' attack and thunderous reception had left Lincoln so weak he had to be carried from the stand. Lincoln sheets chronicled the events which left Douglas crushed and his followers gloomy.[1] The Chicago *Times* headlined: —

Joint Discussion at Ottawa. — Lincoln Breaks Down. — Enthusiasm of the People! — The Battle Fought and Won. — Lincoln's Heart Fails Him! — Lincoln's Legs Fail Him! — Lincoln's Tongue Fails Him! — Lincoln's Arms Fail Him! — Lincoln Fails All Over!! — The People Refuse to Support Him! — The People Laugh At Him! — Douglas the Champion of the People! — Douglas Skins the "Living Dog." — The "Dead Lion" Frightens the Canine. — Douglas "Trotting" Lincoln Out. — Douglas "Concludes" on Abe.

The Illinois press commented endlessly on this opening debate, and papers all over the country discussed it. A St. Louis correspondent noted that "Lincoln may as well hang up his hat, take a back seat, and wait until 1860," when Lincoln might get into the Senate because Douglas would be President and out of Lincoln's way. The *Illinois State Register* of Springfield acidly observed that the scene of Lincoln "with his long arms about his carrier's shoulders, his long legs dangling nearly to the ground, while his long face was an incessant contortion to wear a winning smile that succeeded in being only a ghastly one," would make a study for a Hogarth. The Chicago *Journal* suggested that "since the flailing Senator Douglas received at Ottawa," his friends should "address him as the late Mr. Douglas."

The second debate was scheduled for six days later at Freeport. In the interim both candidates spoke separately at several towns, and Lincoln made important strategic plans. At Ottawa Douglas had attacked him with seven specific questions concerning Republican doctrine, which he put off answering until the next debate. Douglas denounced Lincoln violently because he did not answer at Ottawa. Having planned his replies, Lincoln wrote out four questions to put

[1] Sparks, pp. 124–145.

to Douglas. The second was to be historic: "Can the people of a United States Territory, in any lawful way, against the wish of any citizen of the United States, exclude slavery from its limits prior to the formation of a State Constitution?" He showed these questions to his advisers, who objected to the second, knowing that Douglas would reply affirmatively, thereby appealing to the strong antislavery sentiment and strengthening himself in Illinois, perhaps enough to win re-election. Lincoln refused to be persuaded that his strategy was bad, expecting a different result. An interesting story has Lincoln waiving his friends' objections by saying prophetically, "I am after larger game; the battle of 1860 is worth a hundred of this." This would be more impressive had the story been told before instead of after Lincoln became a presidential nominee.

Of course Douglas would answer "Yes." Many times, without antagonizing the South, he had expounded the theory that unfriendly legislation can exclude slavery, whatever the implications to the contrary in the Dred Scott decision. But now the fire-eaters were coming to fear, and the Administration was openly opposing, this Douglas doctrine. Lincoln planned to run Douglas in a corner with the question, not because of any effect the answering would have on the 1860 battle, but to widen the split in Illinois between the Douglas and the Buchanan factions of the Democracy. His political eye was fixed resolutely on the senatorial election of November 2, 1858, not on any 1860 prospect.[1]

At Freeport the crowd was even larger than at Ottawa, numbering fully fifteen thousand despite weather turned cold and dismal. This region too was vigorously Republican, and thousands came long distances to witness the great event. Railroads offered excursion rates and special trains during the whole series. Douglas, arriving the night before, had been welcomed by a pretentious torchlight procession, tumult of cheers, booming cannon. When Lincoln arrived by train next day the streets around the station were packed with Republicans who shouted themselves hoarse when Lincoln's form,

[1] Beveridge, Vol. II, pp. 655–658. White, in Herndon and Weik, Vol. II, p. 109. Sparks, pp. 203–206. Cole, *Era of the Civil War*, pp. 171–173.

"tall and ungainly with a lean face, homely and sorrowful looking," emerged. Artillery roared and a bannered parade led by a band escorted him to the Brewster House through dense, clamorous crowds, where he responded to the usual speech of welcome. When Lincoln rode to the speaking stand in a lumbering prairie schooner loaded with exuberant farmers, the crowd cheered him for flattering them with this democratic gesture. Douglas, richly and flamboyantly dressed in the "plantation style," decided to walk at the head of his noisy procession instead of riding in an ornate carriage Democrats had ready. He would show that after all he was one of the common people too. Again a scuffle was required to clear the stand before the celebrities could get on.

The lank orator began by carefully replying to each of Douglas' questions at considerable length and with great skill. Then he leveled his own questions at Douglas, who sat on the tiny platform nonchalantly puffing a cigar. Loud applause surged up as he read out each question. After an extended and telling attack on Douglas for his objectionable methods as campaigner and conspirator, which made the crowd time and again roar with delight, Lincoln sat his lean frame down, exclaimed, "Go on, Judge Douglas," and Douglas began. He called Lincoln's questions absurd, based on nothing but Lincoln's "curiosity," and then made his famous reply to Lincoln's second question: —

I answer emphatically, as Mr. Lincoln has heard me answer a hundred times from every stump in Illinois, that in my opinion the people of a Territory can, by lawful means, exclude slavery from their limits prior to the formation of a State Constitution. [Enthusiastic applause.] Mr. Lincoln knew that I had answered that question over and over again. He heard me argue the Nebraska bill on that principle all over the state in 1854, in 1855, and in 1856, and he has no excuse for pretending to be in doubt as to my position on that question. It matters not what way the Supreme Court may hereafter decide as to the abstract question whether slavery may or may not go into a Territory under the Constitution, the people have the lawful means to introduce it or exclude it as they please, for the reason that slavery cannot exist a day or an hour anywhere, unless it is supported by local police regulations. ["Right, right."]

Dealing contemptuously with the other questions, but carefully answering them, Douglas wondered if Lincoln had more questions. "As soon as he is able to hold a council with his advisers, Lovejoy, Farnsworth, and Fred Douglass, he will frame and propound others." The crowd laughed. Lincoln, large-minded enough to appreciate a laugh on himself, joined in the mirth and said that with the aid of those Abolitionists he hoped to devise three more questions, to make him even with Douglas. Here Douglas loosed a lengthy diatribe against the supposed "racial equality" implications of Republican doctrine. As he talked along, repeating the phrase "Black Republican" as often as he could, hoots and yells of "White, white," mingled with cheers, rose from the multitude. The scene reached a highly dramatic pitch as Douglas ran on contemptuously and at great length concerning the iniquities of Republican principles and corrupt practices of the Party, the crowd heckling him steadily until he burst out, "I have seen your mobs before, and defy your wrath. [Tremendous applause.]" On he went in bitterly hostile language, using every argument he could think of that might injure Lincoln, frequently indulging in the misrepresentation typical of political forensics. Again calling the conspiracy charge "an infamous lie" and demonstrating its falsity by pointing to history, his time was up. Lincoln's half-hour he spent directly attacking Douglas' scathing remarks about corruption in the Trumbull election of 1855 and about the general faithlessness of Republican politicians, reminding the crowd that not long ago Douglas had tried to make "the great 'Black Republican' party . . . the tail of his new kite," but now was "crawling back into his old camp." The applauding host roared "Go on, go on" as Lincoln's time expired.[1]

This virile struggle had become the cynosure of the nation's eyes, and no wonder, for it had rapidly become "more heated and theatrical than any political contest ever waged in the country." [2] Horace Greeley's special correspondent wrote [3]: —

1 Sparks, pp. 148–211.
2 Beveridge, Vol. II, p. 654.
3 New York *Tribune,* Sept. 9, 1858; in Sparks, p. 201.

On both occasions Lincoln made the best impression. He is an earnest, fluent speaker, with a very good command of language, and he ran the Judge so hard that the latter quite lost his temper.

Douglas is no beauty, but he certainly has the advantage of Lincoln in looks. Very tall and awkward, with a face of grotesque ugliness, he presents the strongest possible contrast to the thick set, burly bust and short legs of the Judge. They tell this story of Lincoln in Southern Illinois, where he resides:

Being out in the woods hunting, he fell in with a most truculent looking hunter, who immediately took a sight on him with his rifle.

"Halloo!" says Lincoln. "What are you going to do, stranger!"

"See here, friend; the folks in my settlement told me if ever I saw a man uglier than I was, then I must shoot him; and I've found him at last."

"Well," said Lincoln, after a good look at the man, "shoot away; for if I am really uglier than you are, I don't want to live any longer!"

But you will see him in Washington, and then you can form your own opinion of his looks. We mean to send him there.

While the debaters exchanged blows, Republican orators of every caliber hammered at Douglas from every stump. Buchanan papers and Lincoln papers of Illinois battered away at the common opponent with type-lines which fairly smoked and headlines that flamed, while Douglas sheets gave as good as they got. The two warriors, in their debates, invented little but used their tried and trusted weapons in dexterous attack and counterattack.

The next debate, more than two weeks away, was scheduled for Jonesboro, far south in Illinois. Lincoln's managers were worried after the Freeport affair, afraid that Douglas' answer to that important question would attract votes away from Lincoln while having little effect on the Democratic split.[1] Both candidates, traveling steadily through central Illinois, spoke nearly every day, Sunday excepted, to a clamorous gathering in some important town.[2] At Clinton when he got off the train Lincoln was chased out of town so that enthusiastic Republicans could escort him back to town in

[1] White, in Herndon and Weik, Vol. II, p. 110. Beveridge, Vol. II, p. 671.
[2] Milton, pp. 345–346.

proper ceremony. At Bloomington he had a first-class crowd and reception. On two days, September 6 and 7, Lincoln appeared before cheering crowds at Monticello, Mattoon, and Paris. Heading south, he appeared at four towns on the way to Jonesboro, where he met Douglas again "in the heart of Egypt." [1]

This region was rocky and backward, the town small and "ancient," the weather hot, languorous, the people not much interested in the debate. And the candidates had competition; Donati's comet was passing over. The night before the debate, Lincoln and Horace White of the Chicago *Press and Tribune* sat for over an hour in front of their hotel, gazing up at the flaming meteor's long tail. On the fifteenth, few more than a thousand people came, nearly all of them Democrats, Buchanan Democrats at that, and the two orators got a modicum of cheers. Lincoln had only a corporal's guard to escort him to a grove near town, while Douglas' friends managed a parade with the usual accouterments. Lincoln made a superb defense against Douglas' charge that Republican beliefs grew progressively less "black," less radical, as Republican speakers moved south in Illinois. He made two strong points before this hostile audience. Looking down a long past and forward to a long future, he vigorously denied his opponent's constant preachment that popular sovereignty and continuance of the North and South's labor differences were simply an extension of the principles upon which the Fathers founded the Republic.

DOUGLAS: "He tells you that this Republic cannot endure permanently divided into Slave and Free States, as our Fathers made it. He says that they must all become Free or all become Slave . . ., or this Government cannot last. Why can it not last, if we will execute the Government in the same spirit and upon the same principles upon which it was founded?"

LINCOLN: "I say that Judge Douglas and his friends have changed [slavery] from the position in which our fathers originally placed it.

[1] White, in Herndon and Weik, Vol. II, pp. 111–118. Angle, *Lincoln, 1854–1861*, pp. 244–246. Barton, *Lincoln*, Vol. I, p. 503.

I say, in the way our fathers originally left the slavery question, the institution was in the course of ultimate extinction, and the public mind rested in the belief that it *was* in the course of ultimate extinction. . . . But Judge Douglas and his friends have broken up that policy, and placed it upon a new basis, by which it is to become national and perpetual. All I have asked or desired anywhere is that it should be placed back again upon the basis that the fathers of our Government originally placed it upon."

Lincoln's second strong point was a powerful attack on the inconsistencies of the Dred Scott decision and Douglas' unfriendly legislation. "I hold that the proposition that slavery cannot enter a new country without police regulations is historically false." The Supreme Court in its Dred Scott decision ruled that "the Constitution of the United States guarantees property in slaves in the Territories." How then could a man hold public office, on his oath to support the Constitution, and pass legislation unfriendly to slave property, without violating that oath? To clinch this point Lincoln asked Douglas a fifth question: if slaveholders of a Territory should demand Congressional legislation to protect their slave property, would Douglas vote for or against such legislation?

Douglas' reply was an evasion: "I answer him that it is a fundamental article of the Democratic creed that there should be non-interference and non-intervention by Congress with slavery in the States or Territories." The Senator strove mightily to cover his dodge by explaining lengthily how Lincoln had evaded some of Douglas' questions.[1]

Reporting the Jonesboro bout, the Lincoln press chided Douglas for delivering "the same old speech." The Douglas press headlined, "Douglas Triumphs over All!" But impartial observers noted that Lincoln had gained.[2] A Kentucky paper described Lincoln's speeches: "They are searching, scathing, stunning. They belong to what some one has graphically styled the *tomahawking* species."[3]

---

[1] Sparks, pp. 214–259.
[2] New York *Evening Post*, Sept. 22, 1858; in Sparks, p. 262.
[3] Louisville *Journal;* in Sparks, p. 266.

Next day the two moved north to Centralia, site of the State Fair. Speaking was barred, but when Lincoln or Douglas appeared on the grounds a swarm of admirers clustered round. Two days later came the fourth debate, at Charleston. No Jonesboro apathy appeared in this old Whig country. Lincoln's admirers outdid themselves to welcome the boy who rose from the ranks. Across Charleston's dusty Main Street hung a giant banner with a big painting in carnival poster style: "Old Abe" as he supposedly looked driving a pioneer's wagon through town when he came to Illinois twenty-eight years past. The banner's reverse side stated dogmatically that Lincoln would carry Coles County. Democratic posters denied it. One local Delacroix represented "Old Abe" bludgeoning the Little Giant to earth; when Douglas saw this one he became hopping mad. Here and there a patch of building was visible beneath trappings of flags and symbols. A Democratic dauber sketched the Living Dog's party with a domestic scene entitled "Negro Equality," in which a white man stood beside a negro woman, their negro offspring trailing the couple.

Lincoln and Douglas traveled ten dusty miles from Mattoon to Charleston under flamboyant escort. In Lincoln's long cavalcade rolled a huge wagon decked out with festoons of blue and white bunting, leaves, flowers, "containing thirty-two young ladies, representing the thirty-two States of the Union, and carrying banners to designate the same."

Following this, was one young lady on horseback holding aloft a banner inscribed, "Kansas — I will be free." As she was very good-looking, we thought that she would not remain free always. The muses had been wide awake also, for, on the side of the chariot, was the stirring legend:
    "Westward the star of empire takes its way;
    The girls link-on to Lincoln, as their mothers did to Clay."

Thirty-one young men on horseback followed the girls.

The Douglas procession was likewise a formidable one. He, too, had his chariot of young ladies. . . . The two processions stretched an almost interminable distance along the road, and were marked by a moving cloud of dust.[1]

Greater than at Freeport was the crowd and pageantry, several carloads coming over from Indiana. Lincoln talked about Negro equality. Somebody had asked him that morning, he related, "whether I was really in favor of producing a perfect equality between the negroes and white people. [Great laughter.] . . . I will say, then, that I am not, nor ever have been, in favor of bringing about in any way the social and political equality of the white and black races [applause]." The throng roared with laughter when Lincoln declared that neither he nor his friends needed a law to prevent their marrying black women, but if Douglas and his friends required such a law, the candidate in mock solemnity pledged himself to stand by the existing state law prohibiting black-white marriages. Then Lincoln spent the rest of his time aiding and abetting Trumbull's unrestrained conspiracy charges against Douglas. His speech was loaded with fearfully dull congressional detail, but the crowd did not seem to mind.

Douglas in his reply accused Lincoln and Trumbull of avoiding the issues of the day by harping on the conspiracy myth, which he angrily demonstrated to be a myth by pointing in detail to his own record and that of Trumbull in the Senate, to the facts in the creation of the Kansas-Nebraska Act and the Dred Scott decision, which showed no connection between the two.

"I have exposed these facts to Mr. Lincoln, and yet he will not withdraw his charge of conspiracy. I now submit to you whether you can place any confidence in a man who continues to make a charge when its utter falsity is proven by the public records." Cried he, "This great Free-soil Abolition party" — what an organization! They do not even use the same name in different parts of Illinois. "What object have these Black Republicans in changing their name in every county? ["To cheat people."] . . . Their principles in the north

---

[1] White, in Herndon and Weik, Vol. II, p. 121. Sparks, p. 320.

are jet-black [laughter], in the center they are in color a decent mulatto [renewed laughter], and in lower Egypt they are almost white [shouts of laughter]. . . . And here let me recall to Mr. Lincoln the scriptural quotation which he has applied to the Federal Government, that a house divided against itself cannot stand, and ask him how does he expect this Abolition party to stand when in one half of the state it advocated a set of principles which it has repudiated in the other half? [Laughter and applause.]" Closing, Douglas dwelt on his own firm opposition to negro citizenship and demanded that Lincoln declare "whether or not he is opposed to negroes voting and negro citizenship," since he had declared himself opposed to negro equality.

Lincoln stood up, looking out over the dusty, bannered throng as they cheered him heartily. The crowd had applauded when Douglas smote Lincoln solidly by asking why he spent his whole hour making Trumbull's speech. So in his half-hour the Republican candidate made haste to talk about issues. He emphatically stated his opposition to Negro citizenship, but, cried he, the nation must put slavery "back upon the basis where our fathers placed it [applause]; . . . restrict it forever to the old states where it now exists. [Tremendous and prolonged cheering; cries of "that's the doctrine"; "good, good," etc.] Then the public mind *will* rest in the belief that it is in the course of ultimate extinction. That is one way of putting an end to the slavery agitation. [Applause.]" Douglas and his friends would preserve peace by spreading slavery over all the nation if the North would let them. Lincoln's closing note was a tedious discussion of the conspiracy charge. Nevertheless the crowd liked it.[1]

The turbulent crowd marched back to town and demanded more speeches; so that evening there was oratory in the streets at two great bonfires, one for Republicans, one for Democrats. Reporting the debate, the Chicago *Times* headlined: —

15,000 People on the Ground. — A Field-Day for the Democracy. — Lincoln Full of Trumbull; Delivers Trumbull's Alton Speech; Has Nothing to say for Himself. — Lincoln Retreats from Egypt. — Trum-

[1] Sparks, pp. 267–311.

bull Covers His Flight. — Great Speech by Senator Douglas. Trumbull's Slanders Refuted! — Lincoln's Weakness Exposed!

The Chicago *Press & Tribune* offered a variant version: —

Twelve to Fifteen Thousand Persons Present. — Lincoln Tomahawks His Antagonist with the Toombs Bill. — Great Rout of the Douglasites in the Seventh District. — Killed, Wounded and Missing. — Great Demonstration of the Republican Girls of Charleston, etc., etc., etc.

Resuming their stumping from town to town, Lincoln camped on Douglas' trail again as they spoke in Sullivan, Danville, Urbana; then he moved west, Douglas north, the Living Dog and the Dead Lion converging again at Galesburg two weeks later for the fifth debate. On October 6 a violent storm occurred, and the debate day was cold, raw, windy. Nevertheless the largest crowd of the entire series turned out, people flocking despite the fierce wind from far and near into the charming little college town merrily accoutered for the occasion with banners, bunting, placards, flags, until the place had the exotic aspect of an Oriental bazaar. The howling wind caused a great waving and snapping of decorations and considerable havoc. Partisan signs were blown "pell mell all over town." [1] From Monmouth County came an exuberant Lincoln delegation exhibiting many sensational crayon drawings. One showed Douglas standing reversed on a collapsing platform labeled "Dred Scott." A giant wagon hauled the Monmouth County Glee Club; they loudly sang original songs "ground out by one of their number." Banners of the Macomb Lincoln Club let it be known that "We honor the man who brands the Traitor and Nullifier," "Small-fisted Farmers, Mud Sills of Society, Greasy Mechanics, for A. Lincoln." Another masterpiece displayed in zoölogical juxtaposition "Douglas the dead Lion," "Lincoln the living Dog." Many Democrats named the Living Dog "Spot" for short and for auld lang syne. Best banner of this bumper crop was a painting of a locomotive, "Freedom," bearing swiftly down on Douglas' cotton-laden oxcart. The rushing train whistled "Clear the track for Freedom," and the Little Giant's negro driver shouted in

[1] Galesburg *Democrat*, Oct. 9, 1858; in Sparks, p. 372.

panic, " 'Fore God, Massa, I bleves we's in danger!" On one banner
Douglas had just been catapulted aloft by two cantankerous donkeys,
Popular Sovereignty and Dred Scott, disastrously terminating his
daring straddle act. A Democratic writer said this flowering of Republican art was trumped up: "The Abolitionists, obeying the behests
of their leading men, paraded dirty designs and beastly caricatures."
Preliminary ceremonies went off in grand style with glamorous
escorts into town, reception speeches, presentation of a "beautiful
banner" to each candidate by students of Lombard University.
Horace White said Lincoln's escorting cavalcade was long enough "to
reach around the town and tie in a bow knot."

From the speaker's stand erected against one of the Knox College
buildings, standing beneath the words "Knox College for Lincoln,"
Douglas delivered to the throng of twenty thousand a very brilliant
speech, exactly suited to his task of winning this hostile audience.
Lauding popular sovereignty as "the great fundamental principle
that the people of each State and each Territory of this Union have
the right, and ought to be permitted to exercise the right, of regulat-
ing their own domestic institutions in their own way," he pointed
out in great detail that upon this principle were built the Compromise
of 1850 and the Nebraska Act. Therefore, he had supported them,
and had opposed the Lecompton Constitution. He complained that
the Administration was surreptitiously assisting Lincoln to punish
Douglas for refusing to fall in line. "I never will consent, for the sake
of conciliating the frowns of power, to pledge myself to do that which
I do not intend to perform. I now submit the question to you, as my
constituency, whether I was not right. . . . [An universal "Yes"
from the crowd.] I repeat that I opposed the Lecompton Constitution
because it was not the act and deed of the people of Kansas. . . . I
denied the right of any power on earth, under our system of government, to force a constitution on an unwilling people. ["Hear, hear;
that's the doctrine"; and cheers.]"

The speaker swung into an extended attack on the Republican
Party: —

"Permit me to say to you in perfect good humor, but in all sincerity, that no political creed is sound which cannot be proclaimed fearlessly in every State of this Union. ["That's so," and cheers.] . . .

"Not only is the Republican party unable to proclaim its principles alike in the North and in the South . . . but it cannot even proclaim them in all parts of the same state."

Douglas read out excerpts from Lincoln's Chicago and Charleston speeches which, he was at great pains to convince the crowd, proved that Lincoln declared in favor of Negro equality at Chicago, against it at Charleston. Then he swept to a close of consummate mastery, reiterating his belief in popular sovereignty, unfriendly legislation, white supremacy, in a long passage so brilliant that it must be read entire to appreciate its oratorical magnificence.[1] The throng shouted its homage in nine cheers as he sat down and Lincoln rose. Lincoln knew that the crowd was applauding Douglas' skill, not his principles. Not to be outdone, Lincoln delivered his best speech of the series.[2] He spent much time battering down the specific attacks Douglas had just made, elaborately denying that his own speeches were inconsistent, that Republican doctrine vacillated between Negro equality and Negro subjection according to the necessity of securing votes.

I have all the while maintained that in so far as it should be insisted that there was an equality between the white and black races that should produce a perfect social and political equality, it was an impossibility. This you have seen in my printed speeches, and with it I have said that in their right of "life, Liberty, and the pursuit of happiness," as proclaimed in that old Declaration, the inferior races are our equals. [Long-continued cheering.]

If, as Douglas said, — continued Lincoln, — the Republican Party was sectional because people of the South would not allow Republican principles preached there, was not Douglas himself becoming sectional — "[Great cheers and laughter]" — for "his speeches would not go as current now south of the Ohio River as they have

[1] Sparks, pp. 342–346.
[2] White, in Herndon and Weik, Vol. II, p. 123.

formerly gone there. [Loud cheers.]" He parried another Douglas weapon: "There was nothing of the principle of the Nebraska bill in the Compromise of 1850 at all, — nothing whatever. . . ." Then he eloquently portrayed the "wrong" of slavery. Whereas Douglas saw no wrong in slavery, no difference between "slavery and liberty," caring not if slavery were voted down or up, Lincoln himself discovered slavery "a moral, social, and political evil," and, with due regard for Constitutional rights, desired "a policy that looks to the prevention of it as a wrong, and looks hopefully to the time when as a wrong it may come to an end. [Great applause.]" That was the real difference between Douglas and his friends and the Republicans. After a long passage dealing in personalities, which delighted the vast assemblage, Lincoln made a profound constitutional argument that the Party which produced the Dred Scott decision would presently create a new Dred Scott decision that a state may not exclude slavery, should the people continue that Party in power. This new decision, in the speaker's belief, cried Lincoln, "is just as sure to be made as tomorrow is to come, if that party shall be sustained. ["We won't sustain it"; "Never"; "Never."]" Douglas' arguments were now preparing the public mind for that new decision, "preparing (whether purposely or not) the way for making the institution of slavery national! [Cries of "Yes, yes"; "That's so."]" When the orator finished, the packed acres of people exploded in "three tremendous cheers for Lincoln."

The gist of Douglas' reply was that Lincoln could not have said in Charleston what he had just spoken. "He tells you today that the negro was included in the Declaration of Independence when it asserted that all men were created equal." Here groans, catcalls, noise in general, drowned Douglas' voice until Lincoln appealed for silence. But "how came he to say at Charleston . . . that the negro was physically inferior to the white man, belonged to a different race, and he was for keeping him always in that inferior condition?" Douglas thought he had Lincoln on this point, and kept hammering away, arguing that if Lincoln interpreted the Constitution and laws differently in different localities (borrowing one of Lincoln's Jonesboro points) how could he take an official oath to support the Constitution? Republican doctrines would change the government "from one of laws into that of a mob. . . . I stand by the laws of the land." Finishing in a peroration celebrating the sanctity of the Constitution "as our fathers made it," the laws and the courts, Douglas received furious applause in tribute to such masterly skill.[1]

Correspondents rushed off to their partisan occupation of political reporting. Lincoln's journalists sketched the opponent: he "foamed at the mouth," displaying "the saliva of incipient madness." He glowered "black and repulsive" at the crowd. The Little Giant's journalists limned Lincoln: he was a "most abject picture of wretchedness. . . . His knees knocked together, and the chattering of his teeth could be heard all over the stand. He looked pitiful beyond expression, and curled himself up in a corner." "That scare-crow looking individual. . . ." His argument "descended to the level of the street blackguard." He gazed at Orator Douglas "with a blank stare, as if fascinated." "Behold the white man of Jonesboro and the Dred Scottite of Charleston came forth at Galesburg clothed in the habiliments of Uncle Tom, praying admission of his colored brethren to the rights and privileges of white men. . . . He is the mottled candidate." [2]

Moving toward Quincy, the two politicians spoke separately, daily,[3] then met for the sixth debate on October 13. The day was fine and the crowd again huge, the rally paraphernalia striking and quite Whiggish. Lincoln was greeted heartily and escorted by a gaudy, serpentine procession to the Orville H. Browning residence, where the Quincy Republican ladies presented him with "a beautiful and elegant bouquet." To the usual presentation speech by a local Republican, Lincoln replied gallantly that he was delighted to see the ladies so interested in the campaign. A mixed glee club of young Republicans then lifted up voices in a campaign ballad.[4] Lincoln's opening speech was mainly a vigorous effort to acquit himself of the Douglas

[1] Sparks, pp. 333–372.
[2] Sparks, pp. 376–388.
[3] Angle, *Lincoln, 1854–1861*, pp. 249–250.
[4] Sparks, pp. 435–445.

double-dealing charge. Then he pointedly put aside personalities and
in a superb passage laid bare the fundamental differences between
the opposing doctrines of non-extension and non-intervention. Douglas too recapitulated lengthily, directly charging Lincoln with several
kinds of bad faith and cowardly conduct, then made his usual reply
that the moral right or wrong of slavery is a matter to be decided by
citizens of each state, free from all outside interference: "Let each
state mind its own business and let its neighbors alone, and there
will be no trouble on this question. . . . It does not become Mr.
Lincoln, or anybody else, to tell the people of Kentucky that they have
no consciences, that they are living in a state of iniquity. . . . Better
for him to adopt the doctrine of 'Judge not, lest ye shall be judged.'
["Good," and applause.]"

Lincoln in his rejoinder pointed out as Douglas' main weakness
that he and his friends woefully mistook the historical American attitude toward slavery. He thanked Douglas for declaring his Party's
intentions when he had exclaimed, "Why cannot the nation, part
Slave and part Free, continue as our fathers made it, *forever?*" "I
insist," cried Lincoln, "that our fathers did not make this nation half
Slave and half Free, or part Slave and part Free. [Applause, and
"That's so."] I insist that they found the institution of slavery existing here. . . . They left it so because they knew of no way to get
rid of it at that time. ["Good," "Good," "That's true."]" The great
Democratic error was that that Party had renewed slavery *"upon the
cotton gin basis,"* had refused to let slavery remain "where the
fathers of the Government originally placed it. [Cheers and cries of
"Hurrah for Lincoln"; "Good"; "Good."]" He hit Douglas with
the idea he had been using with telling effect all during the campaign — that a Territorial Legislature is bound to protect slavery
under the Dred Scott interpretation of the Constitution.

Douglas has "sung paeans" to his popular sovereignty, chided Lincoln, until his Supreme Court has "*squatted* his Squatter Sovereignty
out. [Uproarious laughter and applause.] But he will keep up this
species of humbuggery about Squatter Sovereignty. He has at last
invented this sort of *do-nothing* Sovereignty [renewed laughter]

— that the people may exclude slavery by a sort of 'Sovereignty' that is exercised by doing nothing at all. [Continued laughter.] . . . The Dred Scott decision covers the whole ground, and while it occupies it, there is no room even for the shadow of a starved pigeon to occupy the same ground. [Loud cheers and laughter. A voice on the platform — "Your time is almost out." Loud cries of "Go on, go on"; "We'll listen all day."]"

His few remaining minutes he spent presenting again the evidence to acquit himself of Douglas' duplicity charges, and plucking at the conspiracy string.[1] The crowd melted away, hurrahing for their favorite as loudly as weary lungs and hoarse throats permitted.

That evening the Republicans put on a colorful torchlight procession and more speeches, while liquor flowed as readily as oratory. The main speaker was an intellectual and ambitious young German from Wisconsin named Carl Schurz, called to Illinois by the State Central Committee and now on the threshold of a long, brilliant career, one of the most remarkable in American history. In his absorbing *Reminiscences* he has left us a photographic delineation (unfortunately too long to include) of the Quincy debate.[2] He saw the Republican candidate for the first time when Lincoln boarded the Quincy train as admirers crowded about and Lincoln greeted them with ready cordiality. Somebody introduced the lean, Hamletlike German orator, who was taken aback by Lincoln's towering height and impressed by the swarthy, deep-furrowed face, haggard expression, melancholy eyes, rusty, ill-fitting clothing. Having shaken hands with practically everybody, Lincoln sat down with Schurz and began talking to him "like an old acquaintance," discussing the campaign and even asking his new friend's advice. He told stories and talked so familiarly that presently Schurz felt he had known Lincoln for years.

Next day the two debaters and parties were voyaging down the Mississippi to the bannered city of Alton, where on the fifteenth they staged the closing debate. The struggle had been man-killing, and Douglas' deep voice was giving out. Lincoln, however, showed no sign

[1] Sparks, pp. 395–435.
[2] *Reminiscences of Carl Schurz*, Vol. II, pp. 89–96. Carl Schurz to Gerrit Smith, Sept. 14, 1860; Schurz MSS.

of fatigue, his high voice carrying as far as ever. His iron constitution had always defied sickness, but the Little Giant had since childhood suffered one serious illness after another. Douglas began speaking at Alton, jauntily confident still despite his husky, worn voice. Buchanan Democrats were present in force to discomfit him, even heckling him from the speaker's platform. This goaded Douglas to such fury that he struck at the Administration harder than at Lincoln. With terrific power he repeated every charge he had made against the Administration Democrats; he roared that they were traitorously working with Republicans in this campaign. The orator hotly cried that the President opposed him because he had refused to obey executive orders. He had time to attack the Republicans only with his useful argument that the sectional Party was trying to rend the nation merely to gratify ambitions of its leaders.

Lincoln began his hour and a half by telling how pleasant it was to hear Douglas attack Buchanan, the crowd cheering and roaring with laughter. Becoming serious, Lincoln concluded his part in the debates with a summary of the salient doctrines of his campaign appeal. He spent a great deal of time refuting the "beautiful fabrication" of his opponent that he sought "a perfect social and political equality between the white and black races," read from his own speeches and those of Henry Clay to prove that the Republican position on the Negro question was that of the men who founded the Republic. One by one he covered the important points of the controversy: the danger that the Negro might become property, "and nothing but property . . . *in all the States of this Union"*; the necessity of non-extension; slavery's menace to the nation's unity. The real issue of the canvass? "It is the eternal struggle between these two principles — right and wrong — throughout the world. They are the two principles that have stood face to face from the beginning of time, and will ever continue to struggle. The one is the common right of humanity, and the other the 'divine right of kings.' " This speech, one of the most powerful he ever made, constituted an intellectual feat so brilliant it makes the student of oratory fairly gasp.

Douglas rose and brought the great series to a close with a smashing finish. Lincoln had told the crowd, said Douglas contemptuously, that only slavery had ever endangered the Union. What ignorance! The speaker recalled the Nullification trouble (in spite of Lincoln's having specifically excepted it), the New England secession movement during the War of 1812. So the slavery question was in reality no more a real danger to the Union than those other two forces had proved; slavery was being used only to arouse sectional strife. So let each state and territory regulate its own affairs and slavery would be no problem. "I care more for the great principle of self-government . . . than I do for all the negroes in Christendom. [Cheers.] I would not endanger the perpetuity of this Union, I would not blot out the great inalienable rights of the white men, for all the negroes that ever existed. [Renewed applause.]" He told once more how local legislation could prohibit slavery; then, with a ringing appeal to sustain the Constitution, the laws, and the courts, the last of the one hundred and thirty thousand odd words comprising the seven debates was uttered, and the throng voiced its approbation in "perfectly deafening and overwhelming" applause lasting many minutes.[1]

More than two weeks remained before Election Day, and both men separately took the stump again, speaking nearly every day at some important town they had previously missed. Several of Lincoln's crowds were much larger than the Alton gathering, and as November 2 approached Lincoln wrote letters warning his friends to watch out for fraudulent Democratic votes which he believed would be imported to swing doubtful districts on Election Day.[2]

With the finish of the seven joint debates between the Living Dog and the Dead Lion, the press all over the country having reported their words in incredible detail, neutral observers inclined to the opinion that the local politician had gained a forensic edge over his world famous opponent.[3] Each had in the struggle misrepresented the other and both were guilty of evasions. Demagogically, Lincoln

[1] Sparks, pp. 450-496.
[2] Angle, *Lincoln, 1854-1861*, pp. 250-252. Barton, *Lincoln*, Vol. I, p. 595. Sparks, p. 499.
[3] Cincinnati *Gazette*, Oct. 20, 1858; St. Louis *Evening News*, Oct. 16; in Sparks, pp. 508-509.

painted Douglas in proslavery colors, and Douglas retaliated by steadily calling Lincoln an Abolitionist. Though at times the great debates were petty, personal, the words of the orators themselves are better reading than most that has been written about them. At his best, as in the lofty passages of the Alton speech, Lincoln's words in celebration of liberty in government constituted "a solid contribution to the literature of democracy," [1] his expression and thought ranking with John Stuart Mill's famous remarks on liberty. The traditional view that Douglas the political dodger was merely a foil for Lincoln the inspired humanitarian quite collapses when one troubles to read the debates. The Little Giant too had his purple passages. Both candidates labored eloquently for democratic principles against the anti-libertarian tendency of slavery. They differed upon method.[2] The debates probably changed few votes.[3] Who was the cynic who said, "Oratory never changed a vote"?

Late in October, after a speech at Petersburg, Lincoln arrived one hot evening at a flag station west of Springfield to catch a train home. He found another man waiting there, Henry Villard, who was reporting the debates for the New York *Staats-Zeitung*. Several times during the campaign Lincoln had met this brilliant young Bavarian who had arrived in America five years before, at the tender age of eighteen, penniless and quite alone, knowing nobody and no English, to seek his fortune. Villard thought the cause of freedom could best be advanced by re-electing Douglas, and he could not stand Lincoln's stories. Their iron horse was late, and when rain began to fall they scrambled into an empty freight car. They sat on the floor, chatting. Lincoln grew reminiscent, moody, told Villard how he had once clerked in a country store and his highest political ambition had been to secure election to the State Legislature. Chuckling, he said, "since then, of course, I have grown some, but my friends got me into *this* business. I did not consider myself qualified for the United States Senate, and it took me a long time to persuade myself that I was. Now, to be sure, I am convinced that I am good enough for it; but, in

[1] L. E. Robinson, *Abraham Lincoln as a Man of Letters*, p. 60.
[2] H. C. Hubbart, *The Older Middle West*, p. 127.
[3] Schurz, *Reminiscences*, Vol. II, p. 96.

spite of it all, I am saying to myself every day: 'It is too big a thing for you; you will never get it.' Mary insists, however, that I am going to be Senator and President of the United States too." He burst out laughing, shook all over, and exclaimed, "Just think of such a sucker as me as President!"[1]

Next day at Springfield the Republicans gave him a giant rally with all the obstreperous trimmings, and on Monday at Decatur he made his closing speech. Tuesday was Election Day, cold and rainy, but everywhere the excitement of election was intense and there were plenty of fights in the sloppy streets.

A few days before election an Iowa paper predicted [2]: —

What a night next Tuesday will be all over the Union! The whole Nation is watching with the greatest possible anxiety for the result of that day. No state has ever fought so great a battle as that which Illinois is to fight on that day. Its result is big with the fate of our Government and the Union and the telegraph wires will be kept hot with it until the result is known all over the land.

Lincoln spent an unhappy evening at the telegraph office with friends, watching the returns come in. They told of a Republican triumph; but the lot of Lincoln was defeat. Though the Republican state ticket won by a small plurality, and Lincoln's popular vote exceeded Douglas', the Democrats won the Legislature.[3]

Six years later, on another Election Night, President Lincoln told his secretary, John Hay, how the defeated candidate had walked home that gloomy night. "The path had been worn pig-backed and was slippery. My foot slipped from under me, knocking the other out of the way; but I recovered and said to myself, *'It's a slip and not a fall!'* "[4]

Illinois Republicans, holding post mortems, displayed wounded feelings. Of the national Republican leaders, men who were already in the race for the 1860 Republican nomination, only Chase had done

[1] Henry Villard, *Memoirs*, Vol. I, pp. 96–97.
[2] Burlington *State Gazette*, Oct. 29, 1858; in Sparks, p. 533.
[3] Cole, *Era*, p. 179.
[4] *Diary of John Hay;* in Barton, *Lincoln*, Vol. I, p. 403.

anything to help defeat Douglas.[1] John M. Palmer wrote Senator
Trumbull his reactions to what he called the betrayal of Lincoln by
the Eastern Republicans. Their inaction, he exploded, had destroyed
the confidence of Illinois Republicans in their Eastern leaders.[2]
Trumbull heard identical rumblings from Ebenezer Peck of Chicago,
one of the earliest of Illinois Republican leaders [3]: —

Now that Seward, Greely [sic] & Co. have contributed so much to our
defeat, they may expect us in the true christian spirit to return good for
evil — but in this I fear they will find themselves mistaken.

If the vote of Illinois can nominate another than Seward — I hope it
will be so cast.

As the strenuous stumping began in September a Kentucky paper
had pointed to the national significance of the Lincoln-Douglas contest. "The debate in Illinois, between Lincoln and Douglas, is the
ablest and the most important that has ever taken place in any of
the States, on the great question which has so long agitated the
country, elected and defeated Presidential candidates, built up and
broken down parties. It is the opening of the question for 1860." [4]
Then, upon learning that Douglas would continue to occupy a conspicuous place in the Senate despite Buchanan's strenuous opposition, pro-Douglas Democrats of the North barked vociferous demands that he be made the Party's next candidate for President.[5]
Republicans believed "his triumph would render inevitable his nomination for next President at Charleston in 1860. He must either be
nominated or the Democratic party practically retires from the contest, surrendering the Government to the Republicans." [6]

With headlines bugling "DOUGLAS FOR PRESIDENT," editorials lauding his "most wonderful personal" victory over the
Buchanan machine,[7] with Lincoln now so well known to the country

---

[1] Chicago *Democrat*, Nov. 10, 1858; in Sparks, p. 531.
[2] J. M. Palmer to Trumbull, Dec. 9, 1858; Trumbull MSS.
[3] E. Peck to Trumbull, Nov. 22, 1858; Trumbull MSS.
[4] Louisville *Democrat*, Sept. 5, 1858; in Sparks, p. 42.
[5] Louisville *Democrat*, Nov. 23, 1858; in Sparks, p. 538.
[6] New York *Tribune*, Nov. 9, Boston *Daily Advertiser*, Nov. 6, 1858; in Sparks,
pp. 544–546, p. 537.
[7] Sparks, pp. 575–578.

PROMINENT CANDIDATES FOR THE REPUBLICAN PRESIDENTIAL NOMINATION

as the man who had, surprisingly, proved himself quite able to cope with the celebrated Douglas in political combat, it required but a fillip of the imagination to begin thinking about Lincoln as the Republican to pit against Democrat Douglas in the forthcoming presidential contest. In August a Massachusetts paper told how at the outset of the campaign Republicans feared Lincoln would be demolished by Douglas, but "as the canvass progresses their fears disappear; they perceive his ability to cope with the 'Little Giant,' and the success which has attended his forensic efforts have exceeded their most sanguine expectations. The natural consequence of this contest will be to bring Mr. Lincoln more prominently before the people of the country, and if thoughts were made known it would not be surprising to hear that individuals were now calculating his fitness and chances for a more elevated position." [1] Prophetic words!

Likewise sound was the opinion of plain Illinois Republicans that the giant Springfield lawyer had grown to national prominence. Congressman Elihu Washburne of Galena, an old political associate of Lincoln, perusing his mail on Capitol Hill, read: "Lincoln has made a brilliant canvass. He has achieved a national reputation. . . . There is a future for him." [2]

As the debates took the national spotlight Lincoln heard that he was like Byron; he had awakened one morning to find himself famous. But Lincoln's new fame did not mean that his country had come to know him for the man he was. To the general public he remained unknown save as the man who nearly defeated Douglas. Many expressed doubts that Lincoln was the author of the speeches he delivered,[3] so little did the public really comprehend him. One set of biographical facts was well known: the log cabin birth, the "short and simple annals of the poor" childhood and youth. These had been well advertised in the debates.

Far better as a touchstone to Lincoln's character, had the public known, would have been an awareness of the strong literary cast of

[1] Lowell *Journal and Courier*, Aug. 30; in Sparks, p. 518.
[2] A. Miller to E. B. Washburne, Nov. 5, 1858; Washburne MSS.
[3] Ward H. Lamon, *Life of Abraham Lincoln*, p. 420.

his mind.[1] Despite his pittance of formal education, the spark of genius appeared early and never lacked nourishment, exercise. Once Lincoln had learned to write he amused and developed himself by composing simple essays. Then he dabbled with fiction, but was far more interested in verse writing. He wrote poetry as young Napoleon Bonaparte scribbled away at a novel, as the youthful dandy, Disraeli, tried to be the modern Homer, as Karl Marx poured out his youthful genius in verse, as gifted boys have always lived somehow on a plane above their associates because their eyes are fixed on the stars.

Young Lincoln's creative efforts show unquestionably that he could have made himself a front-rank literary man had his environment been conducive.[2] But his uncultured pioneer surroundings naturally led him to express his talents in political activity. Winning office early, he advanced steadily and found satisfaction in mastering the politician's craft, an advancement which stopped, however, when he entered the national arena.

This rift in his career was one of the most important facts of his life. Stung by failure, he entered a quadrennium of semiretirement from active politics, during which he concentrated on improving his personal competence, with the thoroughly practical view of improving his mind until he should be the equal of the ablest men of his day. As he practised law in Springfield or on the circuit, spare hours were spent in fervent study of Shakespeare, of Euclid.[3] In Congress, Lincoln's speeches were dotted with commonplaces and absurdities.[4] But in the summer of 1852 he delivered a eulogy on Henry Clay in which he touched a new height, showing himself approaching greatness as an orator.[5] Two years later, out of a mind newly deepened, sharply perceptive, logical, he soberly wrote his observations on government in a series of fragmentary compositions which are like Baconian essays in their brevity and closely reasoned logic. They show him

---

[1] N. W. Stephenson, *Abraham Lincoln and the Union*, pp. 53–54, p. 131.
[2] Robinson, pp. 15–16. D. K. Dodge, *Lincoln, Master of Words*, p. 21.
[3] *Herndon's Lincoln*, pp. 247–248, p. 257. N. W. Stephenson, *Lincoln*, pp. 61–68.
[4] *Works*, Vol. II, pp. 59–66.
[5] *Works*, Vol. II, pp. 164–167, pp. 172–177.

applying his new learning and foreshadow the precise reasoning of his great speeches.[1]

Thus Lincoln justified his youthful estimate of himself as a man of "greatness"; [2] thus he prepared himself to astonish his countrymen by successfully crossing swords with Stephen A. Douglas.

[1] *Works,* Vol. II, pp. 182–187. Carl Sandburg, *Abraham Lincoln, the Prairie Years,* Vol. I, pp. 472–479.

[2] In his famous letter to Mrs. Orville H. Browning, which reads like a Stevenson story, he used the phrase, "with all my fancied greatness."

☆   ☆   ☆

CHAPTER II

Rumblings

OR DAYS Lincoln drifted along deep in the Slough of Despond. Again he had lost the office on which his heart was set, lost it after a colossal expenditure of energy and huge outlay of time and money. Beneath the cloud of defeat, Lincoln's mind, tired from the strenuous months of campaigning during which he gave public utterance to nearly two million words, must have occupied itself with melancholy political cogitations: Senator Trumbull's term would end in 1860, but of course Trumbull would expect to succeed himself. Nothing but the Senatorship would fit his high ambitions and lead perhaps to political Olympus. Not until 1864, when the term he had lost by so small a margin would expire, could he have another chance to become Senator Lincoln. True, his great success against Douglas had made him beyond dispute the leading Republican of his state, and he could doubtless make himself Governor if he wanted the place.[1] But as Governor, Lincoln perceived, he would perhaps never go higher in politics.

The silver lining to Lincoln's cloud was the fact that the Republicans of Illinois had, since 1856, gained more votes than the Demo-

---

[1] He had been spoken of for the Governorship as early as January, 1856. (Canton *Weekly Register,* Jan. 17, 1856.) The Howells campaign biography said of Lincoln in 1856: "the anti-Nebraska party of the same year offered him the nomination for Governor, but . . . he declined." The subject of these remarks crossed out this sentence, substituting: "The Republican party of 1856 probably would have given him the nomination." W. D. Howells, *Life of Lincoln,* p. 73; corrections in pencil by A. Lincoln.

crats,[1] a victory due in no small measure to Abraham Lincoln. He
had, with his own voice, aided by the national publicity his speeches
had secured, given the electorate a forceful education in conservative,
non-abolitionist Republican ideals. But this was, for Lincoln, only
half a victory. His Party had risen and left him stranded, a defeated
candidate. Billy Herndon was sure his partner lost because fraudulent votes — "thousands of roving, robbing, bloated, pock-marked
Catholic Irish" — were successfully imported to carry doubtful districts. The apportionment of Illinois into legislative districts favored
Douglas, for in general fewer votes were required to elect in a Democratic district than in a Republican.[2] Hence Lincoln's popular majority of about four thousand shrank in the legislative result until
Democratic members numbered fifty-four, Republicans forty-six.[3]

Herndon figured out other reasons for the defeat, and set them
down in a letter to his celebrated friend, Theodore Parker [4]: —

We never got a smile or a word of encouragement outside of Illinois
from any quarter during all this great canvass. The East was for Douglas
by silence. This silence was terrible to us. Seward was against us too. . . .
Crittenden wrote letters to Illinois urging the Americans and Old Line
Whigs to go for Douglas, and so they went "helter-skelter." Thousands of
Whigs dropped us just on the eve of the election, through the influence of
Crittenden. . . .

All the pro-slavery men, north as well as south, went to a man for
Douglas. They threw into this state money and men, and speakers. These
forces and powers we were wholly denied by our Northern and Eastern
friends. . . .

No one of all of these causes defeated Lincoln; . . . it was the combination . . . that "cleaned us out. . . ."

Then the writer made a shrewd prediction: —

Let me say that as Douglas has got all classes to "boil his pot," with
antagonistic material and forces, that there is bound, by the laws of nature, to be an explosion. . . . Look out!

[1] Horace White; in Herndon and Weik, *Abraham Lincoln,* Vol. II, p. 126.
[2] White; in Herndon and Weik, Vol. II, pp. 125–126.
[3] E. E. Sparks, *Debates,* pp. 533–535.
[4] Herndon to Parker, Nov. 8, 1858; in J. F. Newton, *Lincoln and Herndon,* pp. 234–
235.

Two days after the election Lincoln took his pen, intent on scolding Senator Crittenden of Kentucky. Like Herndon, Lincoln was angry with Crittenden because he had given aid and comfort to Douglas by way of repaying the Little Giant for his Lecompton fight. But Lincoln never sent hot letters. With great restraint, he wrote: "The emotions of defeat at the close of a struggle in which I felt more than a merely selfish interest, and to which defeat the use of your name contributed largely, are fresh upon me; but even in this mood I cannot for a moment suspect you of anything dishonorable." [1]

Lincoln's spirits were not elevated by the miscarriage of important campaign strategy he had himself conceived and executed. When Lincoln consulted his managers about asking that important question at Freeport, he had been told that such a move was very risky and might easily prove a boomerang. He had gambled and lost. Douglas' answer had won conservative votes, and Lincoln's hope that the Little Giant's reply would widen the Democratic split had failed to materialize. The Danite faction (so firm was Douglas' grip) voted strong in only two counties.[2] But Lincoln's strategy, a failure in Illinois in 1858, began to operate in national politics in 1859. Then came a forceful vindication of his political acumen, as the elements which Herndon said were ripe for an explosion did explode,[3] breaking in twain the party which for six decades had ruled America.

Lincoln's narrow defeat appears doubly unfortunate when viewed

[1] *Works,* Vol. V, pp. 90–91.
[2] White, in Herndon and Weik, Vol. II, pp. 118–119.
[3] In this connection the following reminiscence of Joseph Medill is of interest: —

Two or three days after the election of 1860, learning that the active workers of the Republican party in the state were calling on Mr. Lincoln in Springfield from all Illinois to congratulate him . . . , I concluded to make the same pilgrimage and went down. . . . I walked up to . . . where Mr. Lincoln was holding his levee in the office of the Secretary of State. He bent his head down to my ear and said in low tones, something like this: "Do you recollect the argument we had on the way up to Freeport two years ago over my question that I was going to ask Judge Douglas about the power of squatters to exclude slavery from territories?" And I replied — that I recollected it very well. "Now," said he, "don't you think I was right in putting that question to him?" I said: "Yes Mr. Lincoln, you were, and we were both right. Douglas' reply to that question undoubtedly hurt him badly for the Presidency but it re-elected him to the Senate at that time as I feared it would."

Lincoln then gave me a broad smile and said — "Now I have won the place that he was playing for." We both laughed and the matter was never again referred to.
— Sparks, pp. 205–206.

in its national significance. Had he forced Douglas out of the Senate, national acclaim would have been his, and probably Senator Lincoln would have been quickly recognized as the choice of the West for the 1860 Republican nomination.[1] Defeat left him in a doubtful position. His great campaign had given him a reputation which would, no doubt, make him the favorite son of Illinois Republicans, but favorite sons usually fall impotent before the moment of nomination arrives. On the other hand, his individual power demonstrated in the debates, gave Lincoln a political background so brilliant that future events might, without exceeding his proved ability, bestow upon him any office within the gift of the people. He had proved his fitness for high office so forcefully that reminiscence writers like Horace White, looking back at Lincoln as he was in November, 1858, have been led to exaggerate [2]: —

I think that this was the most important intellectual wrestle that has ever taken place in this country, and that it will bear comparison with any which history mentions. Its consequences we all know. It gave Mr. Lincoln such prominence in the public eye that his nomination to the Presidency became possible and almost inevitable.

On the eve of Election Day one Jeriah Bonham of Lacon, Illinois, editor of the *Illinois Gazette,* sat thinking about what he should say in his editorial covering the election result. Bonham had for a quarter-century lived in Illinois, had admired Lincoln since he heard him on the stump for Henry Clay in 1844.[3] Bonham saw Lincoln in the Douglas campaign at Peoria when he spoke there, and talked politics with him.[4] Now Lincoln was beaten, and Jeriah Bonham sat pondering great events. Hear him [5]: —

"Though Lincoln could not go to the senate, I felt that there was yet future triumph for him in another field — and that field the Nation.

[1] Beveridge, *Abraham Lincoln,* Vol. II, p. 695.
[2] In Herndon and Weik, Vol. II, p. 131.
[3] Jeriah Bonham, *Fifty Years' Recollections,* pp. 158–159.
[4] Bonham, p. 170.
[5] Bonham, pp. 528–530.

"I felt prophetic; the possibilities of the near future loomed up and flashed on me, when I took my pen to write the result.

"I had no plan. . . . The *Gazette* was just waiting to go to press; only lacked the announcement of the result of the election. I wrote hastily; it seemed to me carelessly, and when completed, ready for the compositor, it ran, exactly . . . as found below, the first editorial ever proposing that Abraham Lincoln should be nominated as the Republican candidate for the Presidency for the canvass of 1860."

Abraham Lincoln for President in 1860

The contest just closed, and the glorious result of yesterday's election, showing by the popular vote that Illinois is redeemed from Democratic domination . . . although the Legislature will be Democratic by reason of the unfair apportionment of the state . . . by a former Democratic Legislature, in gerrymandering the state, . . . thus insuring the election of Democrats to the Legislature and thwarting the will of the people, by securing the reelection to the Senate . . . of Stephen A. Douglas to misrepresent them for six years more from the 4th of March next, instead of Abraham Lincoln, the orator and statesman, whom the popular voice has declared should be entitled to that high office.

To him, the Republican standard-bearer, their chosen leader in the brilliant and glorious contest just closed, we are indebted for this glorious result.

The masterly manner in which he conducted the canvass, both in the joint discussions with Douglas, and his grand speeches made to the people in all parts of the state, has attracted the attention of the whole country and the world to the man that gave utterance to the sublimest truths yet enunciated, as principles now adopted as the future platform of the Republican party, and marks him as the leading statesman of the age, possessing the confidence of the people in his inflexible honesty, and his fitness to lead the people in yet other contests, in which the field will be the nation, and his leadership to conduct the hosts of freedom to victory in 1860. What man now fills the full measure of public expectation as the statesman of to-day and of the near future, as does Abraham Lincoln? And in writing our own preference for him, we believe we but express the wish of a large majority of the people that he should be the standard-bearer of the Republican party for the Presidency in 1860.

We know there are other great names that will be presented for this great honor — names that have a proud prominence before the American people — but in statesmanship Lincoln is the peer of the greatest of them.

There are McLean, Seward, Chase, Bates, Cameron, and possibly others who will be presented before the convention meets, and their friends will urge their claims with all the pertinacity that devoted friendship and political interests may dictate, and their claims as available candidates will be fully canvassed. And possibly they possess all these in an eminent degree; but Abraham Lincoln more so, both as to eminent statesmanship and also availability. . . .

In the next campaign of 1860 the issues are already sharply defined. These will be, as they have been in our state canvass, slavery and slavery extension on the one hand, and freedom and free territory on the other.

Douglas will lead the cohorts of slavery. Lincoln should lead the hosts of freedom in this "irrepressible conflict." Who has earned the proud position as well as he? as he is in himself the embodiment and exponent of our free institutions. These two men have fought the battles over the plains of Illinois. What so proper as their being the champions of the two principles on the national field? — *Illinois Gazette, Nov. 4, 1858*.[1]

Bonham's editorial brought him into discussion with Republican leaders of Marshall County and "personally strong friends of Mr. Lincoln" concerning Lincoln's prospects. "They thought his time 'was not yet,' that the most that could be expected for him in 1860 was to elect him Governor of the state, and through that he would eventually reach the United States Senate, making his record for the Presidency, if ever, some ten to fourteen years ahead — either for

---

[1] The authenticity of this editorial is not absolutely certain, for the original has been lost, and no reference to it has been found in any newspaper of that day. The sole authority is Bonham himself. In the Illinois State Historical Library are the files of the *Illinois Gazette*, fairly complete, but the issues of November 4 and vicinity are missing. I am deeply obligated to Mr. Charles F. Buck, of Lacon, historian of Marshall County, who searched old attics of Lacon, endeavoring to locate a fugitive copy of the *Gazette* of Nov. 4, 1858. Mr. Buck faintly recalls mention of this original Lincoln-for-President editorial by the late W. H. Ford, son of the *Gazette's* publisher in the Lincoln-Douglas period. (C. F. Buck to Author, May 25, 1934.)

Applying the tests of historical evidence, the editorial seems authentic. Internal evidence of the editorial itself does not, as is usual with forgeries, cause it to collapse. The *Gazette* was an obscure paper (Cole, *Era of the Civil War*, p. 462), which explains why other Illinois Republican sheets did not clip Bonham's suggestion. After the press began to give much space to Lincoln's boom, the *Gazette* might be expected to claim credit for having been first. Nothing of the kind appeared during 1859 or after Lincoln's nomination, but this suspicious circumstance is explained by the fact that Bonham in late November 1858 sold out his interest in the *Gazette* (*Illinois State Journal*, Dec. 1, 1858) and went to Chicago. Lastly, Bonham's book is written in a tone of naïve, uncritical patriotism quite incompatible with studied deception. His chapters on Lincoln and Douglas are remarkably accurate for reminiscence. Bonham wrote his *Recollections* in the early '80s. So, if he were ambitious to make his claim

1868 or 1872." [1] Men of greater fame and longer service to the Party, like Seward and Chase, so the opinion naturally ran, would have to be rewarded before Lincoln could become a national leader.

On the morning of November 6, two days after Bonham's editorial appeared, the *Commercial Register* of Sandusky, Ohio, ran the following at the head of its editorial column [2]: —

LINCOLN FOR PRESIDENT

We are indebted to a friend at Mansfield for the following special dispatch:

"MANSFIELD, *Nov. 5th, 1858.*

"EDITOR SANDUSKY REGISTER: — An enthusiastic meeting is in progress here to-night in favor of Lincoln for the next Republican candidate for President.

REPORTER."

The "friend at Mansfield" who reported this item was David Ross Locke,[3] young Mansfield journalist who had met Lincoln at Quincy the day before the debate there and been profoundly impressed. Locke, who during the Civil War was to become famous as the author of the Petroleum V. Nasby letters, from which President Lincoln derived much enjoyment and relaxation, interviewed Lincoln when the candidate arrived in Quincy. He found him in a hotel room, "surrounded by admirers, who," Locke recalls, naïvely exaggerating, "had made the discovery that one who had previously been considered merely a curious compound of genius and simplicity was a really great man." [4] Waiting until the crowd left, Locke presented himself, and Lincoln astonished his visitor by his total lack of formality. The orator removed his shoes, to give his feet "a chance to

---

as an "original Lincoln man" out of whole cloth, he could hardly at that date have been certain that the *Gazette* originals were no longer in existence to expose him.

[1] Bonham, pp. 178–179.

[2] Sparks, pp. 581–582.

D. J. Ryan, "Lincoln and Ohio," *Ohio Arch. and Hist. Quarterly,* Vol. XXXII, pp. 104–105.

C. H. Workman, speech on "Tablet to Abraham Lincoln at Mansfield," *Ohio Arch. & Hist. Quart.,* Vol. XXXIV, pp. 504–510.

Albert Shaw, *Abraham Lincoln, His Path to the Presidency,* p. 217.

[3] W. E. Barton, *President Lincoln,* Vol. I, pp. 44–45.

[4] David R. Locke, in A. T. Rice (ed.), *Reminiscences of Abraham Lincoln by Distinguished Men of His Time,* p. 440.

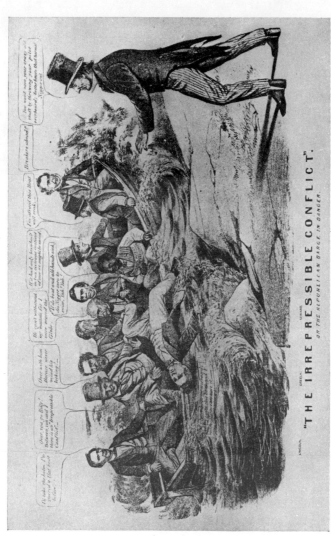

Courtesy New York Public Library

THE REPUBLICAN MUTINY

(Currier and Ives Cartoon)

breathe," he explained, peeled off coat, vest, collar. In comfortable undress, chair tilted back and feet stretched to another chair, the tall homely candidate talked politics seriously with young Locke, who thought he "never saw a more thoughtful face . . . never saw a more dignified face . . . never saw so sad a face. . . . He said wonderfully witty things, but never from a desire to be witty. His wit was entirely illustrative." Lincoln predicted he would carry the state in popular vote, but that Douglas would win the office because of the apportionment — according to David Ross Locke.[1]

Back home in Ohio, Locke conceived the idea of calling a local mass meeting soon after Election Day to boom Lincoln for the Presidency, thereby doing a good turn for himself as a rising young man, and for his hero. What exactly was done at Locke's meeting we do not know, but the aggressive journalist struck off sparks when he sent his dispatch to the Sandusky *Commercial Register* reporting the "enthusiastic meeting" of the night of November 5, 1858. Mansfield had a Republican paper, the *Herald*, which ardently supported the powerful ambition of Salmon P. Chase. Hence Locke sent his story to the Sandusky paper instead of to the local Republican sheet. On November 10 this Chase paper commented on the story of the Mansfield Lincoln meeting [2]: —

"To learn the news of the town, go to the country," is an old saying which, with a slight alteration would read "to learn the news of Mansfield go to Sandusky." Mansfield we know is a large city, and a great many occurrences doubtless take place in it which we never hear of, yet we are inclined to think that a "large and enthusiastic" political meeting would be likely to come to our knowledge. Under these circumstances we are rather disposed to consider the *Register's* Lincoln demonstration somewhat imaginary. The truth is, the *Register* has been hoaxed.

Mr. Lincoln is a popular man in this region of the country, and should he receive the Republican presidential nomination in 1860, he will find the voters of old Richland enthusiastic in his support. It so happens, however, that in Ohio, we have our own standard bearer, "The Noblest Roman of them All," around whom we shall rally until the convention shall decree otherwise. Now is not the time to propose presidential candidates, but

[1] Locke; in Rice, p. 443.
[2] Mansfield *Herald*, Nov. 10, 1858; in Workman, pp. 512–513.

when that time does come, unless we greatly mistake the shaping of events, Ohio will be a unit for her own representative man.

This refutation was so obviously the result of personal politics that no attention whatever was paid to it.[1]

On November 6, the same day that brought into public notice Petroleum Nasby's dispatch from Mansfield, the Cincinnati *Gazette* commented on the Illinois election result in this vein: "The Republicans also, while regretting the defeat of LINCOLN, their gallant leader, will find consolation in the fact that, after all, there is a clear majority of five thousand on the popular vote in his favor. — This affords a reasonable ground of assurance that Illinois will vote for the next Republican candidate for the Presidency. If a man of the Northwest (which now seems to become indispensable) he is likely to carry the state, even against Douglas." [2] This comment contained no mention of Lincoln as a presidential possibility, but the wording happened to convey that suggestion. So suggestive to one Israel Green, druggist and politician of Findlay, Ohio, was the *Gazette's* editorializing that he wrote a letter to the paper. He signed himself "A Member of the Fremont Convention of 1856," called upon the Republican Party to nominate, for its 1860 ticket, Abraham Lincoln for President, John P. Kennedy of Maryland for Vice President. The Cincinnati *Gazette* printed Green's letter on November 10, and presently the New York *Herald* published an acknowledgment of this ticket which had "just been brought out at Cincinnati." [3] Green the druggist-politician had been inspired to essay the rôle of king-maker by his admiration for Lincoln's gallant battle with Douglas.[4] But Green had other irons in the fire. Soon he was writing to his Governor, Salmon P. Chase, advising that Chase need only declare for a protective tariff and secure Pennsylvania's support, to win the nomination and election.[5]

November 10 also brought a brief Lincoln notice in the Chicago *Press & Tribune*. Without comment, in its "Personal and Political"

[1] Workman, pp. 513–515.
[2] Sparks, pp. 581–582.
[3] New York *Herald;* clipped in *Illinois State Journal,* Nov. 19, 1858.
[4] Don C. Seitz, *Lincoln the Politician,* p. 136.
[5] Green to Chase, Jan. 1, 1859; Chase MSS., Library of Congress. Unless otherwise indicated, the Chase MSS. cited herein are those in the Library of Congress.

column, the *Press & Tribune* noted that "The Sandusky *Register* announces the nomination of Abraham Lincoln for the next Presidency, by an enthusiastic meeting at Mansfield, Ohio." For the last item of this "Personal and Political" column, the November 10 issue ran, "The N. Y. *Courier and Enquirer* proposes Mr. Seward for Republican candidate for the Presidency in 1860." Both these stories the *Press & Tribune* repeated in its weekly issue of November 11, which reached far more people than did the daily *Tribune*.[1]

One day after Ohioans had read Israel Green's promise that Lincoln and Kennedy would make a winning team, and Illinoisans saw Lincoln set up as Seward's competitor, inhabitants of "the Sucker state" read more on the same subject in the Chicago *Daily Democrat* — a very long editorial eulogizing Lincoln for his conduct of the late campaign, limning the future in these words [2]: —

We might also state that Mr. Lincoln's name has been used by newspapers and public meetings outside the state in connection with the Presidency and Vice Presidency, so that it is not only in his own state that Honest Old Abe is respected and his many good qualities appreciated. All through the North and in most of the border states he is looked upon as an able statesman and most worthy man, fully competent to fill any post within the gift of the people of this Union.

We, for our part, consider that it would be but a partial appreciation of his services to our noble cause that our next state Republican Convention should nominate him for Governor as unanimously and enthusiastically as it did for Senator . . . and this state should also present his name to the National Republican Convention, first for President, and next for Vice President. We should show to the United States at large that in our opinion, the Great Man of Illinois is Abraham Lincoln, and none other because of the services he has rendered to the glorious cause of liberty and humanity.

Thus was Lincoln publicly proclaimed by one editor as the favorite son of Illinois for the 1860 contest. But it is essential to note that John Wentworth's Chicago *Democrat* regarded the talk about Lincoln for President as purely complimentary, really believing that he

[1] Weekly Chicago *Press & Tribune*, Nov. 11, 1858.
[2] Chicago *Daily Democrat*, Nov. 11, 1858; in Sparks, pp. 586–588.

should be made Governor. This suggestion meant, in bed-rock political fact, a great deal more than appears on the surface. Chicago's two most potent Republicans, John Wentworth and Norman Judd, hated each other like Jew and Nazi. Judd planned to be elected Governor in 1860. Wentworth, the Illinois Machiavelli, was even more anxious to be Senator. This editorial suggestion, therefore, was a subtle machination. If Wentworth could maneuver Lincoln into the gubernatorial chair he could with one stroke discomfit Judd and eliminate Lincoln from senatorial consideration for several years. Wentworth would then be in a vastly improved position from which to fight Trumbull for the Senatorship in 1860.

The incipient Lincoln boom had suddenly become important news in Illinois. When the sun rose again the Chicago *Press & Tribune*, leading Republican newspaper of the West, made it the subject of its lead editorial [1]: —

PRESIDENTIAL

The N. Y. *Times* has come out for Senator Douglas for President in 1860. The *Courier and Enquirer* is out for Seward. The *Herald* advocates the renomination of Buchanan, and advises the Opposition to unite upon Gen. Scott. The *Post* favors the claims of Gov. Chase, or some western man. The N. Y. *Tribune* is non-committal. Wentworth's paper suggests Lincoln for President or Vice President. The PRESS AND TRIBUNE thinks it is premature to name Presidential candidates, as it is impossible to tell what a year may bring forth, and it is nearly two years yet before the great campaign of 1860. Wait patiently until the signs come right.

By another sunup the news of Lincoln's presidential breeze had reached Springfield. Buried in the *Illinois State Journal's* "City Items and Other Matters" column, inconspicuously and without comment, was this [2]: "LINCOLN FOR PRESIDENT. — The *Sandusky* (Ohio) *Register* announces the nomination of Hon. Abraham Lincoln for the next President, by an enthusiastic meeting at Mansfield in that state." For weeks the editorial columns of this paper for which Lincoln had so often written had been full of tributes to Lincoln's Senate fight,

[1] Chicago *Press & Tribune*, Nov. 12, 1858.
[2] *Illinois State Journal*, Nov. 13, 1858.

clipped from Republican papers from every corner of the free states. But when the political editor of the *Journal*, Edward L. Baker, Lincoln's close friend, came upon this news (probably in the *Press & Tribune*) and snipped the editorial scissors, he could not take it seriously and ran the item in an obscure corner. Unfortunately, we do not know what Lincoln's reaction was when he read the Sandusky story in the *Journal*. There is no proof even that he saw it, but he must have, meticulous newspaper reader that he was.

Two days later the *Daily Herald* of Quincy printed a presidential item clipped from the Peoria *Daily Message* [1]: —

Defeat works wonders with some men. It has made a hero of Abraham Lincoln. Two or three Republican journals in different sections of the Union are beginning to talk of him for Vice President, with Seward for President; and a Republican meeting just held in Mansfield, Ohio, raises him a notch higher, by announcing him as its candidate for President. We have no sort of objection to this sort of a programme. . . .

The same day, Chicago's *Press & Tribune* tried to quiet the new presidential gossip with an editorial on [2]

PRESIDENT-MAKING

Our busy Eastern contemporaries who have made Mr. Douglas the candidate of the Democracy, are now busily engaged in fitting the Republicans with an article of the same sort. Some are for Seward, some for Fremont, some for Banks, some for Chase, and two or more of them have nominated Lincoln. We pray these gentlemen to hold their peace, and let the Presidency follow events. . . . When President-making is in order, the Northwest will have something to say. Until then, let us have peace in our ranks. [3]

The *Illinois State Journal* on this same day printed without comment the Chicago *Democrat's* long editorial of November 11. [4] The *Journal* was a morning paper. When Lincoln that morning read this warm (albeit half-sincere) tribute to himself, his spirits went high.

[1] Sparks, p. 582.
[2] Chicago *Press & Tribune*, Nov. 15, 1858.
[3] The Chicago Weekly *Press & Tribune* of Nov. 18, 1858, reprinted both the above *Tribune* editorials on presidential prospects.
[4] *Illinois State Journal*, Nov. 15, 1858.

He sat down and wrote a letter to Norman Judd in which political hope and Lincolnian wit shine once more.[1]

I have the pleasure to inform you that I am convalescent, and hoping these lines may find you in the same improving state of health. Doubtless you have suspected for some time that I entertain a personal wish for a term in the United States Senate; and had the suspicion taken the shape of a direct charge, I think I could not have truthfully denied it. But let the past as nothing be.

For the future, my view is that the fight must go on. . . . We have some hundred and twenty thousand clear Republican votes. That pile is worth keeping together. . . .

Two days after Lincoln wrote his resentful letter to Crittenden he was actively in the practice of law once more,[2] combating disappointment by the old reliable remedy of hard work, and earning sore-needed funds.[3] As political gossip concerning a Lincoln presidential boom began its flaccid stirrings, Lincoln & Herndon were handling numerous law cases,[4] and slowly the defeated candidate's blue devils were sent packing. In spare hours at the office Billy Herndon talked with his melancholy partner about his theory that Douglas, having received aid and comfort from both proslavery and antislavery forces, would soon find himself embarrassed by an explosion. This was convincing, and presently we shall hear Lincoln trying to cheer up other depressed Republicans with the same argument.

One day after writing his cheerful letter to Judd, Lincoln received from the state chairman the melancholy news that their machine was in debt. At once he sent another letter to Judd.[5]

I have been on expenses so long without earning anything that I am absolutely without money now for even household purposes. Still, if you can put in two hundred and fifty dollars for me toward discharging the debt of the committee, I will allow it. . . .

This, with what I have already paid . . . will exceed my subscription of five hundred dollars. This, too, is exclusive of my ordinary expenses

[1] *Works*, Vol. V, pp. 91–92.
[2] Angle, *Lincoln, 1854–1861*, p. 253.
[3] *Herndon's Lincoln*, p. 361.
[4] Angle, pp. 254–255.
[5] *Works*, Vol. V, p. 93.

during the campaign, all of which being added to my loss of time and business, bears pretty heavily upon one no better off in world's goods than I;
but as I had the post of honor, it is not for me to be over nice. You are
feeling badly, — "And this too shall pass away," never fear.

On November 17 the *Weekly Illinois State Journal* (which reached
more people than the daily) again reprinted the Chicago *Democrat's*
boost of Lincoln. Then two days later the *Journal* carried an editorial
which marks a change in the local contemporary view of Lincoln's
prospects [1]: —

CANDIDATES FOR THE PRESIDENCY

Our exchanges of all political complexions are at the present time very
busily engaged in making predictions as to who will be the next nominees
of the respective parties for President. . . . The merit of these predictions
may be estimated by the fact that the last five Presidents, if we except
perhaps Buchanan, were men who were scarcely ever thought of in connection with the Presidency until the conventions assembled which nominated them. As a general thing, the causes which make men conspicuous
for the Presidency a year or two before the nomination, work them clear
into the background by the time the nomination is to be made. What ex-
cites the enthusiasm of one class of partisans aggravates the opposition of
another class, and generally results in a compromise by which the cause
of the troubles in the party is dropped, and a new and unthought of man
taken. . . . Just at this time we think Seward and Douglas the two men
of the nation least likely to be Presidential candidates in 1860.

Certainly this was strange doctrine, this affirming that the real
Party leader practically never gets a presidential nomination. What
was back of it? Adjacent to the closing sentence of this strange editorial, in the next column, was a clipping from the New York
Herald: —

ANOTHER PRESIDENTIAL TEAM. — The following ticket has just been
brought out at Cincinnati: For President, Abraham Lincoln, of Illinois; for
Vice-President, John P. Kennedy, of Maryland — with a platform embracing protection to American industry, the improvement of western rivers
and harbors, and opposition to the extension of slavery by free immigra-
tion into the territories.

[1] *Illinois State Journal,* Nov. 19, 1858.

Thus the *Journal's* politician, Baker, impressed by the numerous mentions, had come to think seriously that Lincoln's presidential chances might after all be good. He determined therefore to give subtle aid to his friend. This he did by rationalizing his natural desire to assist Lincoln and propounding the sophistical theory that a dark horse has a better chance of success than the recognized Party leader.

When Lincoln read the *Journal* that morning its news put him in an ambitious mood. He wrote encouragement to three Party warriors.[1] His message to all was substantially this: —

The fight must go on. The cause of civil liberty must not be surrendered at the end of one or even one hundred defeats; Douglas had the ingenuity to be supported in the late contest both as the best means to break down and to uphold the slave interest. No ingenuity can keep these antagonistic elements in harmony long. Another explosion will soon come.

On this same day of mid-November the few readers of the Olney *Times* saw the streamer "ABRAM LINCOLN FOR PRESIDENT FOR 1860" at the head of the *Times* editorial column.[2] Like Jeriah Bonham's editorial in a paper similarly obscure, this suggestion from Olney caused no reverberations. But as days went by, politicians and voters discovered that the opinions of Petroleum Nasby, Israel Green, and John Wentworth regarding the political future of Abraham Lincoln were being echoed and re-echoed.

Next day Lincoln wrote two more cheer-up letters which have survived. Perhaps he wrote many others, now lost, in this optimistic vein. To. M. M. Inman he said: "The fight must go on — We are right, and can not finally fail — There will be another blow-up in the so-called democratic party before long — "[3] Another went to Dr. C. H. Ray of the *Press & Tribune*. Lincoln had got the ambitious idea of publishing the speeches of himself and Douglas in the late campaign as a capital way to strengthen both himself and his Party.[4] So he asked of Dr. Ray [5]: —

---

[1] *Works*, Vol. V, pp. 94–95. G. A. Tracy, *Uncollected Letters of Lincoln*, pp. 95–96. Emanuel Hertz, *Abraham Lincoln*, Vol. II, p. 735.
[2] F. W. Scott, *Newspapers and Periodicals of Illinois*, p. 266.
[3] Hertz, Vol. II, p. 736.
[4] Lincoln to A. G. Henry, Nov. 19, 1858, *Works*, Vol. V, p. 95.
[5] Hertz, Vol. II, pp. 735–736. *Works*, Vol. XI, p. 111.

I wish to preserve the set of the late debates. . . . Please get 2 copies of each number of your paper . . . and send them to me by express; and I will pay you for the papers and for your trouble. . . .

I believe, according to the letter of yours to Hatch, you are feeling like hell yet. Quit that — you will soon feel better. Another "blow up" is coming; and we shall have fun again. Douglas managed to be supported, both as the best instrument to *put down* and to *uphold* the slave power; but no ingenuity can long keep the antagonism in harmony.

Similarly, in his replies to letters from politicians the defeated candidate steadily counseled that the fight must continue.[1]

Dr. Ray did not reply at once to Lincoln's request for copies of the debates, so on November 30 Lincoln wrote to Henry Whitney asking if he could procure them.[2] Desiring action, Lincoln took no chances of dangerous delay.

On the first day of December Lincoln was pleased to read in Springfield's *Illinois State Register* an editorial which ranked him with Seward as a Party leader and formulator of Party doctrine, placing his "house divided" with Seward's "irrepressible conflict." [3]

A Settler for Seward *

If Illinois Republican journals are to be taken as an index, Mr. Lincoln is to be made a presidential candidate upon the creed which he enunciated here in his June convention speech. . . . Whether this extreme ground will be adopted by the Republicans generally, in a party platform, is a matter of doubt. The resistance to it by a large number of their leading journals, in their commentary upon Seward's speech, is indicative of a warm contest over it. . . . If this contest does not result in their party disintegration, it will, at least, plainly develop, in its controversies, to the people of the country, the "true intent and meaning" of Republicanism, and incur for it that odium which it justly deserves.

The Democracy have only to unite their forces upon their old platform of principle, maintain the rights of the states under the constitution, and the presidential result will be "a settler for Seward," Lincoln and all their fellow aspirants for presidential honors upon a sectional, unconstitutional platform.

[1] *Works*, Vol. V, pp. 96–97. Tracy, p. 96.
[2] Whitney, *Life on the Circuit with Lincoln*, p. 457.
[3] Sparks, pp. 588–589.

A week later the Rockford *Republican* remarked: " 'Long John' suggests that Abram Lincoln would be just the man for Governor two years hence, and unless it should happen that he should be put upon the National ticket for President or Vice President — a very likely circumstance, from present indications — it strikes us that the suggestion is a good one." [1]

Another week, and the *Press & Tribune* clipped a significant editorial from the Reading (Pa.) *Journal*. The Pennsylvania sheet rejoiced that Illinois has "with all the free states (except California) . . . now enrolled on the side of the people, prepared to fight manfully in their behalf." [2]

One word in regard to their standard-bearer in this exciting canvass. Though unsuccessful, Mr. Lincoln has made for himself a reputation as a great statesman and popular debater, as extensive as the country itself. . . . His name, we perceive, has been mentioned in various parts of the country, in connection with the highest post in the gift of the people. A prominent candidate for the Vice Presidency before the Philadelphia Convention in 1856, it is only needed that, at the proper time, his friends should present an unbroken front for the ablest statesman of the West, and the East will delight to honor the man whose integrity and adherence to principle are as proverbial as his mental endowments have been rendered conspicuous in the brilliant canvass through which he has now just passed. [3]

This editorial, which was prophetic as well as rhetorical, the editor of Springfield's *Journal* spotted in the *Press & Tribune* and ran in his paper on the twenty-first, [4] providing Lincoln with welcome evidence that his prospects were not definitely bound down to a "favorite son" status and that before convention time his potential support might possibly be broadened. And he made tentative plans to that end.

On December 11 Lincoln had written to Senator Trumbull a closely reasoned letter on the political situation. [5] Lincoln said he had "not

---

[1] Rockford *Republican*, Dec. 9, 1858.
[2] Chicago *Press & Tribune*, Dec. 16, 1858.
[3] The *Weekly Tribune*, Dec. 23, also carried this.
[4] *Illinois State Journal*, Dec. 21, 1858.
[5] Tracy, pp. 96–98.

the slightest thought" of going to Washington as a representative. As for Douglas, Lincoln was watching him closely.

Since you left, Douglas has gone South, making characteristic speeches, and seeking to reinstate himself in that section. The majority of the democratic politicians of the nation mean to kill him; but I doubt whether they will adopt the aptest way to do it. Their true way is to present him with no new test, let him into the Charleston convention, and then outvote him, and nominate another. In that case, he will have no pretext for bolting the nomination, and will be as powerless as they can wish. On the other hand, if they push a Slave Code upon him, as a test, he will bolt at once, turn upon us, as in the case of Lecompton, and claim that all Northern men shall make common cause in electing him President as the best means of breaking down this Slave power. In that case, the democratic party go into a minority inevitably; and the struggle in the whole North will be, as it was in Illinois last summer and fall, whether the Republican party can maintain its identity, or be broken up to form the tail of Douglas's new kite. . . . The truth is, the Republican principle can in no wise live with Douglas; and it is arrant folly . . . to waste time . . . dallying with him.

Lincoln received a Christmas present from Henry Whitney: the *Tribune* numbers he wanted. On Christmas Day he wrote his thanks. Lincoln was somewhat doubtful that he might find a publisher for the debates, and told Whitney that if the speeches were published he would save a copy for him.[1]

Not many hours of Lincoln's important year remained when he was in Bloomington one day on business.[2] As he left the courthouse that evening he met Jesse W. Fell of Bloomington. Jesse Fell was a remarkable man. Shrewd and able, as a land speculator he was very successful, and he founded the Bloomington *Pantagraph*, a paper which has appeared continuously since that day. He was intellectual as well as shrewd, and, like Billy Herndon, Abraham Lincoln, and Stephen Douglas, read new books and studied new ideas, was actively interested in education and culture. Fell had known Lincoln well since the early 'thirties, the two having boarded together as fellow Whigs at Vandalia while the Legislature met there. In 1856 Fell

[1] Whitney, *Life on the Circuit*, p. 458.
[2] Angle, *Lincoln, 1854–1861*, pp. 260–261.

had helped organize the Illinois Republican Party at the Bloomington Convention, and his speech nominated Lincoln for the Senate
in 1858. Always he was ready to take the stump for his Party.[1] In
the dusk of a December evening, this unusual politician met Lincoln
and steered him into the law office of his brother, Kersey Fell, and
delivered himself of an important idea.

As the two politicians sat among legal papers and bulky, calf-
bound lawbooks, Fell began: "Lincoln, I have been East, as far as
Boston, . . . traveling in all the New England states, save Maine;
in New York, New Jersey, Pennsylvania, Ohio, Michigan and Indiana; and everywhere I hear you talked about. Very frequently I
have been asked, 'Who is this man Lincoln, of your state, now canvassing in opposition to Senator Douglas?' Being, as you know, an
ardent Republican, and your friend, I usually told them, we had in
Illinois, two giants instead of one; that Douglas was the little one,
as they all knew, but that you were the big one, which they didn't
all know.

"But seriously, Lincoln, Judge Douglas being so widely known,
you are getting a national reputation through him, as the result of
the late discussion; your speeches in whole or in part, on both sides,
have been pretty extensively published in the East; you are there
regarded, by discriminating minds, as quite a match for him in debate,
and the truth is, I have a decided impression, that if your popular
history and efforts on the slavery question can be sufficiently brought
before the people, you can be made a formidable, if not a successful,
candidate for the Presidency."

Lincoln answered casually: "Oh, Fell, what's the use of talking of
me for the Presidency, whilst we have such men as Seward, Chase, and
others, who are so much better known . . . and whose names are so
intimately associated with the principles of the Republican Party?
Everybody knows them. Nobody, scarcely, outside of Illinois, knows
me. Besides, is it not, as a matter of justice, due to such men, who
have carried this movement forward to its present status, in spite

[1] F. Morehouse, *Life of Jesse W. Fell*, pp. 19–59.
Barton, *President Lincoln*, Vol. I, p. 60.
Sandburg, Vol. II, pp. 176–178.

of fearful opposition, personal abuse, and hard names? I really think so."

Fell presented strong arguments for his case. "There is much truth in what you say. The men you allude to, occupying more prominent positions, have undoubtedly rendered a larger service in the Republican cause than you have, but the truth is, they have rendered too much service to be available candidates. Placing it on the grounds of personal services, or merit if you please, I concede at once the superiority of their claims. Personal services and merit, however, when incompatible with the public good, must be laid aside. Seward and Chase have both made long records on the slavery question, and have said some very radical things, which, however just and true in themselves, and however much these men may challenge our admiration, . . . would seriously damage them in the contest, if nominated. We must bear in mind, Lincoln, that we are yet in a minority; we are struggling against fearful odds for supremacy; we were defeated on this same issue in 1856, and will be again in 1860, unless we get a great many new votes from what may be called the old conservative parties. These will be repelled by the radical utterances of such men as Seward and Chase.

"What the Republican party wants, to insure success in 1860, is a man of popular origin, of acknowledged ability, committed against slavery aggressions, who has no record to defend, and no radicalism of an offensive character. . . . Your discussion with Douglas has demonstrated your ability, and your devotion to freedom; you have sprung from the humble walks of life . . . ; and if we can only get these facts sufficiently before the people, depend upon it, there is some chance for you. And now, Mr. Lincoln, I come to the business part of this interview. My native state, Pennsylvania, will have a large number of votes to cast for somebody on the question we have been discussing. Pennsylvania doesn't like, over-much, New York and her politicians; she has a candidate, Cameron, of her own, but he will not be acceptable to a larger part of her own people, much less abroad, and will be dropped. Through an eminent jurist and essayist of my native county in Pennsylvania, favorably known throughout the state, I want to get up a well-considered, well-written newspaper article, telling the people who you are, and what you have done, that it may be circulated not only in that state, but elsewhere, and thus help in manufacturing sentiment in your favor.

"I know your public life and can furnish items that your modesty would forbid, but I don't know much about your private history; when you were born, and where, the names and origin of your parents, what you did in early life, what your opportunities for education, etc., and I want you to give me these. Won't you do it?"

Lincoln pooh-poohed the whole idea: "Fell, I admit the force of much that you say, and admit that I am ambitious, and would like to be President; I am not insensible to the compliment you pay me, and the interest you manifest in the matter, but there is no such good luck in store for me as the Presidency . . . ; besides, there is nothing in my early history that would interest you or anybody else; and as Judge Davis says, 'It won't pay.' Good-night." [1]

But Fell was far from discouraged as he watched the giant figure, wrapped in a dilapidated shawl, stalk away into the cold night.

As the new year opened, Lincoln was busy with cases before the Federal Court and the Supreme Court at Springfield.[2] The town was populated with lawyer-politicians appearing at the court sessions and attending sessions of the new Legislature. On the night of January 6 several Republican leaders met in the library of the capital in secret caucus — a meeting important to Lincoln, the surviving details of which are very dim. Lincoln was there, but it is uncertain which other important Illinois Republicans attended. The day before, the Legislature had met in joint session and elected a Senator: Douglas 54, Lincoln 46. When the Republicans met to talk over the defeat, discussion eventually reached the subject of the probability that Lincoln's name would be presented at the next Republican National Convention. Somebody made a speech. "We are going to bring

---

[1] Statement of Jesse W. Fell, in O. H. Oldroyd (ed), *The Lincoln Memorial: Album-Immortelles*, pp. 473–476. Barton, *President Lincoln*, Vol. I, pp. 57–59. L. A. Stevens, "Growth of Public Opinion in the East in Regard to Lincoln Prior to November, 1860," *Transactions*, Ill. State Hist. Soc., 1906, pp. 292–294. S. D. Wakefield, *How Lincoln Became President*, pp. 94–98.

[2] Angle, *Lincoln, 1854–1861*, p. 262.

out Abraham Lincoln as a candidate for President." But Lincoln protested and the caucus broke up without planning an organized movement.[1]

Editorial gossip, coupled with the local pride of machine politics, had thus caused a certain group to talk about Lincoln for President, but Lincoln was not taking this wind of opinion seriously. He was not showing himself willing and anxious to co-operate toward securing a nomination. Unfortunately, we do not know what he really thought about his presidential chances at this date, for nowhere in his writings does he reveal his true reaction. The office he really wanted, expected, was the Senatorship. His aloof attitude toward the presidential gossip, however, could not have been improved upon even if he had seriously believed that in 1860 his name would be on a national ticket. It conformed exactly with the efficient political etiquette in nursing a presidential boom. A profound student of humanity has said, "Mean men must adhere, but great men, that have strength in themselves, were better to maintain themselves indifferent and neutral." [2] A candidate for the exalted presidential office is supposed, to outward view, to be above the wire-pullings of machine politics, is expected to mind his own business, like old Cincinnatus plowing his fields, until the people rise up and demand that he assume leadership and save the nation.

The men who talked about Lincoln for President as the boom began its feeble stirrings were not even sure that Lincoln wanted to be President. Lincoln had publicly scoffed at such an idea as he opened his 1858 campaign. In his Springfield speech of July 17, by way of discrediting the Douglas enthusiasm, he had said: —

Senator Douglas is of world-wide renown. All the anxious politicians of his party . . . have been looking upon him as certainly, at no distant day, to be President. . . . They have seen in his round, jolly, fruitful face, post-offices, land-offices, marshallships, and cabinet appointments, chargé-

[1] Bonham, *Fifty Years' Recollections*, p. 178. Statement of E. M. Haines, in F. F. Browne (ed.), *Every-Day Life of Abraham Lincoln*, pp. 228–229. Whitney, *Life on the Circuit*, pp. 82–83. When Whitney wrote his reminiscences of Lincoln's path to the nomination, about thirty years after the event, he confused the date and work of this indecisive 1859 caucus with a more important one of a year later. *Cf.* p. 142.

[2] Francis Bacon, *Essays*, "Of Faction."

ships and foreign missions, bursting and sprouting out in wonderful exuberance. . . . And as they have been gazing upon this attractive picture so long, they cannot . . . give up the charming hope; but with greedier anxiety they rush about him, sustain him, and give him marches, triumphant entrees, and receptions. . . .

On the contrary, nobody has ever expected me to be President. In my poor, lean, lank face, nobody has ever seen that any cabbages were sprouting out. . . .

Lincoln's self-depreciation provokes the exclamation (in Gilbert and Sullivan manner) "What, nobody?" and the reply, "Hardly anybody!" These "original Lincoln men" knew, as does every close student of politics, that every politician worth his salt hopes that some day he will be "called" to the Presidency. Besides, was not guessing as to the next nominations a favorite intellectual sport in the land of the free? Early President-guessers like Bonham, David Locke, and Israel Green had nothing to lose in presenting their choices. If their guess was wrong, so were the sporting attempts of many others. But if their man won out they could call themselves Warwick, and perhaps realize a fat Government job on their small investment. The game of President-guessing was so popular that many guesses seem incredibly absurd. For instance, in July 1858 the Democratic Chicago *Times* hazarded [1]: Leading Democratic candidates — Senator Hunter, Governor Wise of Virginia, Senator Slidell, Secretary of War Floyd, Alexander H. Stephens of Georgia. The *Times* postponed indefinitely Douglas' chances, "on account of his quarrel with the Administration, and the fact that he is from a Northern state, two circumstances which render his nomination entirely out of the question." Leading Republican candidates — first on the list, Colonel Fremont, "next Mr. Seward, followed by Mr. Crittenden, Gov. Banks, of Mass., Gov. Chase, of Ohio, and Judge McLean." The New York *Herald's* suggestion that the Opposition unite to nominate General Scott, sounds like a joke.

As a matter of fact, of course, Lincoln was ambitious to be President. Legend has it that as an Indiana youngster he had joked that

---

[1] Clipped in Quincy *Whig,* July 21, 1858; in Sparks, p. 43.

some day he would be President.[1] All through his career his writings contain hints here and there that he hopes eventually to climb to the loftiest pinnacle of politics. But with true political skill he refrained during the whole of 1859 from openly confessing his ambition. He steered a perfect course between the Scylla and Charybdis of ambition and indifference, quietly, carefully, cautiously at work on his political fences, steadily building his public reputation by never missing a chance to open his mouth in public.

Political gossip, as the new year opened, shifted from candidates to Congress, with Northern newspapers loaded heavily with discussions concerning the future of Senator Douglas, Republican sheets rejoicing over the disharmony in the Democracy.[2] But Lincoln received valuable publicity in the Republican comments on Douglas' formal re-election to the Senate. When informed of the legislative vote the Little Giant had telegraphed to Springfield's *Register:* "Let the voice of the people rule." This made Republicans snort.[3]

Under ordinary circumstances, the phrase . . . would have been demagogical, but safe; viewed by the light of facts, it is obscure, fishy, and fictitious. It means, "Let the voice of the people rule if it elects me. Let it not rule if it elects Lincoln." We insist that Mr. Douglas must have intended to have his dispatch read in a Pickwickian or negative sense — or else he was not sober when he wrote it. . . .

Lincoln was very busy with law in the opening months of 1859. Thanks to his new fame he had plenty of clients, and the fees he earned soon put him on his feet again financially.[4] But he always had time to speak in public, and in private to pull political wires. On January 25 he went to a banquet celebrating the centenary of the birth of Bobby Burns and made a short speech.[5] On the twenty-ninth he wrote to Trumbull [6]: —

When you can find leisure, write me your present impressions of Doug-

[1] W. H. Lamon, *Lincoln*, p. 68. Arnold, *Life of Abraham Lincoln*, p. 25. C. G. Vannest, *Lincoln the Hoosier*, p. 183. *Lincoln Lore*, no. 262.
[2] Chicago *Press & Tribune. Illinois State Journal*, Jan., Feb., 1859, *passim*.
[3] Chicago *Press & Tribune*, Jan. 11, Jan. 13, 1859.
[4] Angle, *Lincoln, 1854–1861*, pp. 263–275.
[5] *Illinois State Journal*, Jan. 27, 1859.
[6] Tracy, pp. 98–99.

las' movements. Our friends here from different parts of the state, in and out of the Legislature, are united, resolute, and determined; and I think it is almost certain that we shall be far better organized for 1860 than ever before.

Three days later he wrote to a politician with whom he was to have many dealings in the next year and a half, Mark W. Delahay. This chap was an adventurer, a former Illinois Republican who had campaigned with Lincoln,[1] an incompetent lawyer for whom Lincoln had conceived a liking.[2] As editor of a Free State paper at Leavenworth, Kansas, during the Kansas war, he had sent copies of that sheet to Lincoln at Springfield. Now this soldier of fortune was seeking a high place in Kansas politics, and he wanted Lincoln's help. Delahay had recently invited Lincoln to speak in Kansas. Lincoln replied that he would come "some time between this and next summer." Said he, "I should be pleased if I could arrange it so as to meet a Republican mass convention." As to the date, he would be kept home by court sessions for some months but could probably reach Kansas in late May or June.[3]

Next evening, February 2, the Lincolns entertained; "a large party," Orville Browning called the function.[4] Billy Herndon wrote, of his partner's social life: "For fashionable society he had a marked dislike, although he appreciated its value in promoting the welfare of a man ambitious to succeed in politics."

On February 3 Lincoln wrote to Trumbull again. The Senator had complained of an article (allegedly the work of John Wentworth) which was being surreptitiously circulated, directed against Trumbull by trying to stir up bad feeling between Republicans who once were Democrats and those who used to be Whigs. Lincoln said he knew of the canard, but hastened to reassure Trumbull: "Any effort to put enmity between you and me, is as idle as the wind. . . . I beg to assure you . . . that you can scarcely be more anxious to be

[1] Beveridge, Vol. II, p. 556.
[2] Beveridge, Vol. II, p. 308.
[3] Tracy, pp. 99–100.
[4] T. C. Pease and J. G. Randall (eds.), *Diary of Orville Hickman Browning*, Vol. I, p. 349.

sustained two years hence than I am that you shall be so sustained." [1]
Trumbull had grown afraid of Lincoln, perceiving that Lincoln's
fame now exceeded his own.

In spare hours Lincoln had written a lecture, which enjoyed a
successful premiere at Bloomington in April 1858.[2] The golden age
of the American lecture platform was beginning, and the rising
politician saw in lecturing a chance to indulge his literary flair, pick
up some easy money, and perhaps enhance his reputation. February
11, at Jacksonville, before the Phi Alpha Society of Illinois College,
he presented his lecture on "Discoveries, Inventions, and Improvements." [3] His performance was not brilliant. He told the small audience, with rich humor here and there, how in his opinion inventions
came about. He told how Adam made the first invention — "the fig-
leaf apron," how speech was needed, invented. He made the mistake
of attempting a scientific discussion based on unscientific Biblical
material. His analysis was very dull when he told the results of his
original research in the psychology of speech, of writing. Lincoln
rambled on about writing, "the great invention of the world." There
was no thread of sustained interest; he merely dealt out his observations of certain "inventions." His style was in spots so muddled
that the reader wonders where has gone the power of Lincoln the
political orator. When he stopped talking the audience applauded, to
rouse itself from slumber, and went out wondering what the speaker
had been driving at.

On February 21 he gave his lecture another trial, appearing before
the Springfield Library Association. Six weeks later, when he was
in Bloomington on an important case, he was scheduled for another
delivery. But the audience was so small the affair was called off.[4]
This was almost the end of Lincoln's lecture. Unlike Wordsworth,
Lincoln knew when his creations were commonplace, but in this case
he should have known even before the opening performance.[5] He

[1] Tracy, pp. 100–101.
[2] Angle, *Lincoln 1854–1861*, p. 211.
[3] *Works*, Vol. V, pp. 99–113. Angle, p. 267.
[4] Angle, pp. 269–275.
[5] *Herndon's Lincoln*, pp. 362–363.

retained enough faith in his lecture to try it once more next year.[1]

On the night of March 1 Chicago Republicans staged a rally at their headquarters to celebrate their victory in the municipal election held that day. Lincoln, in Chicago on business, made a rousing speech to the jubilators. "The Hall was crowded to its utmost capacity from eight o'clock till eleven. Everybody spoke and everybody shouted."[2] His main point, discussed at considerable length, was a reiteration of his position that the Republican Party must not support Douglas. In his conclusion was the fire of fierce struggle for victory of a great humanitarian cause.[3]

I do not wish to be misunderstood upon this subject of slavery. . . . I suppose it may long exist; and perhaps the best way for it to come to an end peaceably is for it to exist for a length of time. But I say that the spread and strengthening and perpetuation of it is an entirely different proposition. There we should in every way resist it as a wrong, treating it as a wrong, with the fixed idea that it must and will come to an end. If we do not allow ourselves to be allured from the strict path of our duty by such a device as shifting our ground and throwing us into the rear of a leader who denies our first principle . . . then the future of the Republican cause is safe, and victory is assured. You Republicans of Illinois have deliberately taken your ground; you have heard the whole subject discussed again and again; you have stated your faith in platforms laid down in a state convention and in a national convention; you have heard and talked over and considered it until you are now all of opinion that you are on a ground of unquestionable right.

All you have to do is to keep the faith, to remain steadfast to the right, to stand by your banner. Nothing should lead you to leave your guns. Stand together, ready, with match in hand. Allow nothing to turn you to the right or to the left. Remember how long you have been in setting out on the true course; how long you have been in getting your neighbors to understand and believe as you now do. Stand by your principles, stand by your guns, and victory, complete and permanent, is sure at the last.

Lincoln had received a letter from one Thomas J. Pickett of Rock Island, editor of the *Register*, a new Republican paper.[4] Pickett in-

---

[1] Angle, p. 330.
[2] Chicago *Press & Tribune*, March 2, 1859.
[3] *Works*, Vol. V, pp. 114–124.
[4] Chicago *Press & Tribune*, Feb. 12, 1859.

vited Lincoln to deliver his lecture in Rock Island, but was more interested in politics. He wanted to advertise Lincoln, then come out for him for President in his paper. But he made the mistake of asking Lincoln's advice about the Presidency. Lincoln replied (March 5) that business prevented a Rock Island lecture. "In regard to the other matter you speak of, I beg that you will not give it a further mention. Seriously, I do not think I am fit for the Presidency." [1] This engaging attitude of aloof modesty was the correct one for Lincoln, personally, to assume as his boom slowly gathered momentum.

Lincoln could call himself not fit to be President, yet, on the other hand, give thanks that editors were ready to salute him without asking dangerous questions that would make him commit himself, as when he read in the *Illinois State Journal* of January 19 [2]: —

The Marshall (Clark Co.) *Journal* places at the head of its columns: "For President in 1860, ABRAHAM LINCOLN."

But Lincoln was not yet the sole candidate for the "favorite son" position of his state in the 1860 Republican contest. He would not be that until the Illinois Republican machine said so officially in convention. Thirty miles north of Springfield was a village which, six years past, had been named "Lincoln" by the promoters of the new town, in honor of popular Lawyer Lincoln, who was their attorney in the venture of founding the town.[3] So, it would seem, this village should be anxious to do everything in its power to honor its namesake. But in February Springfield's *Journal* reported that the Lincoln *Herald*, in a long editorial, "avows its preference of the HON. LYMAN TRUMBULL as the Republican candidate for President in 1860." [4]

The editor of the Rockford *Republican* had caught the President-guessing fever. But he thought other guessers too far-fetched in talk-

[1] Tracy, p. 104.
[2] *Illinois State Journal,* Jan. 19, 1859; clipped from Chicago *Press & Tribune,* Jan. 10, 1859.
[3] Beveridge, Vol. I, p. 518.
[4] *Illinois State Journal,* Feb. 17, 1859.

ing of Lincoln for President. He preferred a more sensible, less romantic, hypothesis.[1]

ABRAHAM LINCOLN FOR VICE PRESIDENT

Whoever may be thought worthy to receive the distinguished honor of a
nomination for the Presidency by the Republican Party in 1860, we, for
one, are well convinced that ABRAHAM LINCOLN, of Illinois, the true
and tried and noble hearted champion of Free Labor, is to be offered, at
least, the second place on the National ticket. It was apparent in the action
of the last Republican National Convention — in which the claims of the
Northwest to high honor were partially recognized in the handsome vote
extended to Mr. Lincoln, that the public mind was beginning to turn
towards this distinguished gentleman as the representative man of the vast
and important section of the Union lying to the North and Westward of
the Ohio and the Mississippi. . . . If Mr. Lincoln was a strong man before
the country and the Convention two years ago, it is safe to claim now that
a stronger nominee, or more popular man, belonging to the Republican
Party, is not to be found West of the Alleganies. . . .

To our mind, the chief obstacle in the way of his nomination for the
Vice Presidency, lies in the fact, that, all things considered, it is not unlikely but that he may be selected to bear the standard at the very head of
the Republican column — and this, we are persuaded, is the only alternative to which the Republicans of the Northwest will not emphatically
demur.

Lincoln doubtless read this rather chastening suggestion in the
Journal when it was reprinted there two weeks later.

On March 29 the Chicago *Press & Tribune* thought it well to
repeat its caution on premature President-guessing.

PRESIDENT-MAKING

A few of our Republican contemporaries have entered with great zeal
and activity upon President-making. It is a dangerous and thankless business, and the industrious gentlemen who have undertaken to anticipate the
decision of the party will have occasion to learn, before their jobs are accomplished, that their schemes are more perfect in conception than prac-
ticable in execution. The day for the nomination of the Republican
candidate has not yet arrived; and nothing but harm — harm to the

[1] Rockford *Republican*, March 17, 1859.

Republican cause and harm to the candidates unceremoniously thrust forward — can come out of the premature discussion of the presidential question. A session of Congress will intervene between the present and the day of the meeting of the nominating convention; and during that session many new combinations which will materially alter the aspect of affairs, will undoubtedly take place. We beg the friends of the very respectable gentlemen who have been nominated in the newspapers, to hold their hands. The hour and the man will come together. Let them wait in peace.

This is as good a place as any to point out that newspaper editors were indulging in extreme self-flattery when they talked about "President-making." No President was ever made by newspaper hints, suggestions, exhortations, demands. Presidents are made by Party conventions; conventions are made by politicians. True, newspapers exert some control. By talking about Seward, Chase, Lincoln, or some other political chief for President, they built up public opinion in favor of that man for President in the regions where each paper was influential. But the force of public opinion, in Party conventions, is exerted only indirectly, through politicians. And public opinion is so elusive, indecisive a thing that in convention practice political leaders are bothered by it not at all. An exhaustive examination of American convention history would doubtless disclose that public opinion has been flouted as often as followed in the matter of presidential candidates. Politics, like horse racing, is a contest in which the favorite does not always win.

With scissors and paste, Lincoln had completed his scrapbook of his debates with Douglas, and was in correspondence with a publisher, William A. Ross. March 26, as his circuit court season opened, Lincoln sent Ross a long letter telling exactly how he wanted the book made.[1]

Several Boston Republicans that spring conceived the brilliant idea of celebrating Jefferson's birthday as a Republican affair, thereby bringing forcefully to the attention of the electorate the very important fact that not the Democratic Party, which descended from Jefferson himself, but the Republican Party now stood as champion

[1] Tracy, pp. 105–107.

of Jeffersonian principles. Several Republican leaders were invited to attend the celebration at Boston, among them Lincoln. Though unable to leave his law practice, Lincoln wrote a long, careful letter to the committee. He expected his remarks would be published, so the writer said things he thought would do him good politically. He wrote [1] : —

Remembering . . . that the Jefferson party was formed upon its supposed superior devotion to the personal rights of men, holding the rights of property to be secondary only, and greatly inferior, and assuming that the so-called Democracy of to-day are the Jefferson, and their opponents the anti-Jefferson, party, it will be . . . interesting to note how completely the two have changed hands as to the principle upon which they were originally supposed to be divided. The Democracy of to-day hold the liberty of one man to be absolutely nothing, when in conflict with another man's right of property; Republicans, on the contrary, are for both the man and the dollar, but in case of conflict the man before the dollar. . . .

Soberly, it is now no child's play to save the principles of Jefferson from total overthrow in this nation. . . . The principles of Jefferson are the definitions and axioms of free society. And yet they are denied and evaded, with no small show of success. One dashingly calls them "glittering generalities." Another bluntly calls them "self-evident lies." And others insidiously argue that they apply to "superior races." These expressions, differing in form, are identical in object and effect — the supplanting the principles of free government, and restoring those of classification, caste, and legitimacy. . . . All honor to Jefferson — to the man who, in the concrete pressure of a struggle for national independence by a single people, had the coolness, forecast, and capacity to introduce into a merely revolutionary document an abstract truth, applicable to all men and all times, and so to embalm it there that to-day and in all coming days it shall be a rebuke and a stumbling-block to the very harbingers of reappearing tyranny and oppression.

This eloquent letter was read at the dinner and printed widely in the Illinois Republican press.[2] But the *Press & Tribune* complained because Eastern papers, while publishing the less able letters which

[1] Lincoln to H. L. Pierce and others, April 6, 1859, *Works*, Vol. V, pp. 124–127.

[2] Chicago *Press & Tribune*, April 18; *Illinois State Journal*, April 20; *Central Illinois Gazette*, April 20, 1859.

George Boutwell, *Reminiscences of Sixty Years*, Vol. I, p. 250.

Seward, Chase, and Frank Blair, Jr., wrote to the committee, ignored Lincoln's remarks.[1]

A few days after Lincoln wrote his Jefferson letter, the Illinois Republican Central Committee met in Bloomington. Lincoln was not a member, but was in town attending court, and took part in planning the strategy in preparation for the next campaign. A definite plan of close, effective organization was adopted, and Lincoln must have been pleased to see Jesse Fell appointed corresponding secretary of the state machine.[2]

Once a President-guesser got the fever, he was not easily discouraged. Lincoln had another letter from Editor Pickett of Rock Island. He was again asked to lecture there, and Pickett said he was planning to consult Republican editors of Illinois "on the subject of a simultaneous announcement of your name for the Presidency." But Lincoln refused to be persuaded. Still, he was careful not to be the least bit abrupt in waiving Pickett's idea.[3]

> As to the other matter you kindly mention, I must in candor say I do not think myself fit for the Presidency. I certainly am flattered and gratified that some partial friends think of me in that connection; but I really think it best for our cause that no concerted effort, such as you suggest, should be made. Let this be confidential.

In the East, presidential gossip was on the move precisely as it was in Illinois. On April 19 the Cincinnati *Gazette* remarked: "The Springfield *Republican* has decided that the next Republican candidate for the Presidency ought to be either Seward, Banks, or Bates. In the full plentitude of its authority, the paper aforesaid administers a rebuke to the Providence *Journal* . . . for suggesting Gov. Chase for that honor. . . .

"We are no special champions of any presidential candidate, yet we have a very definite opinion that those who advise the nomination of any other than a Western man, are sadly deceived. . . . The Providence *Journal*, too, undoubtedly expresses the predominant

---

[1] April 21, 1859.
[2] Lincoln to G. Koerner, April 11, 1859; in Tracy, pp. 107–108.
[3] Lincoln to Pickett, April 16, 1859, *Works*, Vol. V, pp. 127–128.

sentiment of New England, in so far as it favors some other candidate than Seward." [1]

This palpable anxiety of Western politicians to stop the Seward boom well illustrates the danger of openly seeking a nomination long before convention time; countermovements are thereby fomented. And it shows how astute Lincoln was when he wrote to Pickett, "I really think it best for our cause that no concerted effort, such as you suggest, should be made."

In the small but thriving town of West Urbana (Champaign) was published the *Central Illinois Gazette,* a sheet which proclaimed itself, in a pretentious Gothic streamer: 𝕬𝖓 𝕴𝖓𝖉𝖊𝖕𝖊𝖓𝖉𝖊𝖓𝖙 𝕻𝖆𝖕𝖊𝖗: 𝕯𝖊𝖛𝖔𝖙𝖊𝖉 𝖙𝖔 𝕬𝖌𝖗𝖎𝖈𝖚𝖑𝖙𝖚𝖗𝖊, 𝕰𝖉𝖚𝖈𝖆𝖙𝖎𝖔𝖓, 𝕻𝖔𝖑𝖎𝖙𝖎𝖈𝖘, 𝕿𝖊𝖒𝖕𝖊𝖗𝖆𝖓𝖈𝖊, 𝕷𝖎𝖙𝖊𝖗𝖆𝖙𝖚𝖗𝖊, 𝕾𝖔𝖈𝖎𝖆𝖑 𝕽𝖊𝖋𝖔𝖗𝖒, 𝕹𝖊𝖜𝖘 𝖆𝖓𝖉 𝖙𝖍𝖊 𝕴𝖓𝖙𝖊𝖗𝖊𝖘𝖙𝖘 𝖔𝖋 𝕮𝖊𝖓𝖙𝖗𝖆𝖑 𝕴𝖑𝖑𝖎𝖓𝖔𝖎𝖘 — all in four pages published once a week. Editor of this versatile newspaper was an ambitious young writer named William Osborn Stoddard. On April 20, 1859, Stoddard published an editorial on

PARTY PRINCIPLES

When a public servant . . . does its duty well and fearlessly, every honest man must recognize the fact with sincere pleasure. No journal in the Northwest now holds a higher position or wields a greater influence than the Chicago Press and Tribune, and we note with pleasure the faithfulness with which it is vindicating the real sentiments of the Republican party. Especially have its managers displayed good and sound judgment in meeting with a decided condemnation the movement lately inaugurated by certain false conservatives at the north in connection with an important minority of half way liberal men in some of the northern slave states for the purpose of employing the Republican organization as a voting machine and to place men of very dubious political soundness in the position of leaders in the contest of 1860. Nothing will ever be made by sacrificing the least jot or tittle of the great principles for which we are contending in order to secure a shadowy and temporary success. . . . While we believe that the Republican party is strong enough single handed for the fight of 1860, we believe that so far as its purity, real strength and ultimate success is concerned we had far better be driven to the wall in that contest than to win a corrupting victory by departing a hair's breadth from the straight line of duty and sound principle. . . .

[1] Clipped in Chicago *Press & Tribune,* April 21, 1859.

One thing more — in connection with this movement. . . . We are sorry to see a disposition among too many men who really have the best interests of the party at heart to throw aside the old servants . . . and to look around among second rate men, "compromise men" and sapless political sticks, for those whom they consider "available" because their individuality, force of character, or unbending backbone, has never given offense to anyone. This is a radical error — there are men among our "old wheel-horses" whose deeds are associated in the minds of the millions with the very ideas of love of freedom and opposition to slavery; men whose names would ring in the ears of their fellow citizens as trumpet calls to the political battle field. Who these men are it is not hard to tell for they are already the objects of bitter assaults of the enemy. We need not specify — there is a long line of giants, from the man who for years stood *alone* on the floor of the United States Senate, the only champion of free labor against the encroachments of the slave oligarchy, to the gallant son of Illinois who won so proud a wreath of laurels in the last senatorial campaign. . . .

This rhetorical outburst was a protest against a recent drift of Western Republican opinion which suggested the nomination of Edward Bates. Bates, a distinguished Missouri jurist, was not even a Republican, but had strong Whig and Know-Nothing connections. Discussion brought up this point: might not the Republicans do well to nominate Bates and secure new support from the old Whig and Know-Nothing vote? Horace Greeley had been assiduously championing this notion by placing behind it the whole tremendous weight of his New York *Tribune* since shortly after the Lincoln-Douglas election.[1] In December Editor Greeley had said, replying to Billy Herndon's query about his position on 1860 candidates, that he favored Bates for President and John M. Read for Vice President, but was "willing to go for anything that looks strong. I don't wish to load the team heavier than it will pull through."[2] Some Republicans who did not wish the team loaded too heavily with radicalism wanted to create the "Opposition Party." Stoddard, like all enthusiastic Republicans, thought the idea monstrous.[3] But his editorial

[1] New York *Tribune*, late 1858 and early 1859; quoted in F. I. Herriott, "Iowa and the First Nomination of Abraham Lincoln," *Annals of Iowa*, Vol. IX, pp. 58–59.
[2] *Herndon's Lincoln*, p. 338.
[3] Chicago *Press & Tribune*, April 21, 27, 1859. Preston King to Gideon Welles, July 20, 1859; Welles MSS.

~~s obviously not a proposal that Lincoln be nominated, though it did recognize him as a possibility, even ranking him with Seward.

Two weeks later Stoddard published this "Personal" item [1] : —

We had the pleasure of introducing to the hospitalities of our sanctum a few days since the Hon. Abraham Lincoln. Few men can make an hour pass away more agreeably. We do not pretend to know whether Mr. Lincoln will ever condescend to occupy the White House or not, but if he should, it is a comfort to know that he has established for himself a character and reputation of sufficient strength and purity to withstand the disreputable and corrupting influences of even that locality.

No man in the west at the present time occupies a more enviable position before the people or stands a better chance of obtaining a high position among those to whose guidance our ship of state is to be entrusted.

These two items, which appeared in the *Central Illinois Gazette* as the flowers came out in that year which produced rumblings of a Lincoln boom that might develop to importance, became the basis of an interesting historical fraud. Young Stoddard in 1861 became private secretary to President Lincoln. Then he went on to acquire an ephemeral fame as an author, surviving until 1925, when he died at the ripe age of ninety. He published several books on Lincoln, and decided that posterity should know William Osborn Stoddard as the John the Baptist of the martyred President. Perhaps, as he grew old, Stoddard really believed he was the original Lincoln man, that he started Lincoln towards immortality back in that spring of 1859. Faulty memory is the best excuse that can be offered for him, and that is not very convincing. An Illinois editor of 1859 should have been familiar enough with the press of that day to know that a Lincoln-for-President suggestion of April or May, 1859, was not the first by over half a year. And Stoddard's "Party Principles" editorial and "personal" story admit, internally, that Lincoln was already being groomed for a place on the Republican ticket. At any rate, Stoddard in his highly unscholarly Lincoln books sought to prove his claim as President-maker. Looking back, a quarter-century later, at the things he published about Lincoln in the *Central Illinois Gazette*

[1] *Central Illinois Gazette*, May 4, 1859.

that spring of long ago, he found them too weak to bear his claim. But on December 7, 1859, he had published a lengthy, emphatic editorial with the title, "Who Shall Be President?" — arguing, with the same reasons Jesse Fell had urged, that in Lincoln Republicans must find their man of the hour.[1] He gave this to trusting Lincoln biographers as the editorial which launched the Lincoln boom, claiming that it appeared along with the Lincoln "personal" in the *Central Illinois Gazette* of May 4, 1859.[2] This evidence, furnished by a man so intimately associated with Lincoln, was unquestioned as authentic material, and early Lincoln biographers (and some late ones) presented Stoddard's editorial of December 1859 as the first, or at least one of the first, of the forces which led to Lincoln's nomination and election.[3] As Stoddard grew older he expanded his story of how he made Lincoln President until he had quite a lengthy yarn of it.[4] No clever deception this, but an insult to the methods of scientific history. For Stoddard did not have the originals in his control, and a careful examination of them quite destroys his claim.

Lincoln was busy with cases on the circuit as spring wore on, writing too an occasional letter on politics.[5] One went to Mark Delahay on May 14, giving advice on what the platform of Kansas Republicans should say.[6]

[1] *Cf.* p. 130.
[2] W. O. Stoddard, *Life of Abraham Lincoln,* pp. 174–176.
[3] Lamon, *Lincoln,* p. 422. Whitney, *Life on the Circuit,* p. 82.
Whitney, *Lincoln the Citizen,* pp. 262–265.
Ida Tarbell: *Life of Abraham Lincoln,* Vol. I, p. 337; *In the Footsteps of the Lincolns,* pp. 384–385.
Sandburg, Vol. II, p. 182. J. T. Morse, Jr., *Abraham Lincoln,* Vol. I, p. 161.
Barton, *President Lincoln,* Vol. I, p. 45.
J. F. Newton, *Lincoln and Herndon,* p. 235.
O. H. Oldroyd, *Lincoln's Campaign,* p. 5.
[4] W. O. Stoddard, *Lincoln At Work,* pp. 11–19, pp. 31–41.
W. O. Stoddard, Jr. (ed.), "A Journalist Sees Lincoln," *Atlantic Monthly,* Vol. CXXXV, pp. 171–177.
J. H. Brown (ed.), *Lamb's Biographical Dictionary of the U. S.,* Vol. VII, p. 226.
National Cyclopaedia of American Biography, Vol. VIII, p. 121.
Champaign *News-Gazette,* March 16, 1930, p. 10.
In 1896 Stoddard wrote to Ida Tarbell: "The 'Coming Out' leader was my own without suggestion from anybody. I sent copies to nearly every paper in the state and to a large number of journals all over the country. Hundreds of these reprinted the 'editorial' in whole or in part, and scores followed in the line of approval." (*In the Footsteps of the Lincolns,* p. 385.) This was wholly fictional, as will be found by an examination of the contemporary press.
[5] Lincoln to Salmon P. Chase, April 30, 1859; Tracy, p. 109.
[6] *Works,* Vol. V, pp. 128–129.

wrote in the rôle of Republican peacemaker. A prominent German
of Springfield was Dr. Theodore Canisius, publisher of the *Illinois
Staats-Anzeiger*. Canisius asked Lincoln to express his views on the
recent law passed by the Massachusetts Legislature, allegedly the
work of Republicans, which required of foreigners two years' residence after naturalization before they could vote. Germans feared
this restriction would become general.[2] The measure was a dangerous
rocking of the Republican boat, which might destroy the strong support of the German element in the North. Lincoln affirmed that "as
I understand the Massachusetts provision, I am against its adoption

[1] Cole, *Era of the Civil War*, p. 186.
[2] Schurz MSS., April, May, 1859, *passim*.

in Illinois, or in any other place where I have a right to oppose it." [1]
Canisius had also asked if Lincoln favored fusion of Republican with
other opposition elements for the 1860 struggle. The candidate replied cannily: —

I am for it, if it can be had on Republican grounds; and I am not for it on
any other terms. A fusion on any other terms . . . would lose the whole
North, while the common enemy would still carry the whole South. The
question of men is a different one. There are good patriotic men and able
statesmen in the South whom I would cheerfully support, if they would
now place themselves on Republican ground, but I am against letting down
the Republican standard a hair's-breadth.

This letter received wide publicity [2] as one of the series of public
letters from prominent Republicans declaring that they loved the
Germans and abhorred any discrimination against them. State Chairman Judd published a strong letter repudiating the Massachusetts
antiforeign measure as the official expression of the Illinois Republican Party. [3]

Dr. Canisius' German paper, the *Staats-Anzeiger*, was new, and
presently fell on evil days financially. Lincoln, acutely realizing the
value of press support, learned that Canisius was in debt and the
paper about to perish. Thanks to his recent success in the law, Lincoln was able to purchase title to the paper from Canisius' mortgage
holder, thus becoming, in late May, the secret owner of the sheet.
He drew up a contract which let Canisius run the paper, Lincoln's
property, so long as it supported the Republican Party. [4] The reasons
for Lincoln's unique conduct in making this deal become clear when
it is told that the Chicago *Staats-Zeitung*, Illinois' leading German
newspaper, was championing the claims of Seward for President. [5]
Lincoln was soon writing to Germans of his acquaintance, attempting
to drum up new subscribers. [6]

[1] *Works*, Vol. V, pp. 129–130.
[2] *Illinois State Journal*, May 18, 1859, and *Weekly Journal*, May 25. Chicago *Press &
Tribune*, May 21, 1859.
[3] Koerner, *Memoirs*, Vol. II, p. 75.
[4] Hertz, Vol. II, pp. 751–752.
[5] Barton, *Lincoln*, Vol. I, 421–422.
[6] Lincoln to Koehnle, July 11, 1859; in Angle, *New Letters and Papers of Lincoln*,
p. 207.

As often as he could Lincoln mingled with the leaders of his Party's machine. Does it not seem significant that, on the evening of June 9, the man who disdained social functions gave a party, his second of the year? A few days later he drank tea with Politicians Orville Browning, Jesse Dubois, Archibald Williams, Jackson Grimshaw, and others who could, if they chose, do him much good or harm in future political wars.[1]

Continually busy with law, Lincoln took time to wave the olive branch again in letters to Salmon P. Chase. The Ohio Republican convention of early June had adopted a plank calling for repeal of the Fugitive Slave Law, and Lincoln had on June 9 written to Chase complaining that the Ohio repeal plank "is already damaging us here. I have no doubt that if that plank is even *introduced* into the next Republican National Convention, it will explode it." [2] Chase had replied that the law was unconstitutional and needed repeal, so Lincoln wrote back (June 20) arguing the law's constitutionality, reiterating: "I believe . . . that the introduction of a proposition for repeal of the Fugitive Slave law, into the next Republican National Convention, will explode the Convention and the Party." [3]

Three days later he answered a letter from Nathan Sargent, once a Whig leader. Judge Sargent had suggested that all opposition elements unite on the platform, "Opposition to the opening of the Slave trade; and eternal hostility to the rotten Democracy." Lincoln forcefully, gracefully repelled this reactionary, Whiggish plan in a letter of considerable length.[4] Excerpts: —

Of course I would be pleased to see all the elements of opposition united for the approaching contest of 1860; but I confess I have not much hope of seeing it. . . . Such a platform, unanimously adopted by a National Convention, with two of the best men living placed upon it as candidates, would probably carry Maryland, and would certainly not carry a single other state. It would gain nothing in the South, and lose everything in the North. . . .

[1] Browning, *Diary*, Vol. I, p. 367.
[2] Angle, *New Letters*, p. 206.
[3] Ryan, "Lincoln and Ohio," *Ohio Arch. & Hist. Quart.*, Vol. XXXII, pp. 30–32. Angle, *New Letters*, pp. 206–207. Hertz, Vol. II, pp. 755–756.
[4] Tracy, pp. 111–113.

If the rotten Democracy shall be beaten in 1860, it has to be done by the North; no human invention can deprive them of the South. I do not deny that there are as good men in the South as in the North; and I guess we will elect one of them if he will allow us to do so on Republican ground. I think there can be no other ground of union. For my single self I would be willing to risk some Southern man without a platform; but I am satisfied that is not the case with the Republican Party generally.

Fourth of July celebrations furnished Lincoln with a chance to speak in public, so he journeyed forty miles north to Atlanta where "an immense multitude of people assembled" and paraded to a near-by grove. Lincoln, big man of the day, made a speech and was presented with a walking cane by the chairman.[1]

Two days later Peacemaker Lincoln sent a long letter to the Honorable Schuyler Colfax, powerful Indiana politician. Colfax had spoken at the July Fourth rally at Jacksonville, and Lincoln said he was sorry he was engaged elsewhere that day, for he wanted to meet Colfax and talk politics. But he would write what he wished to say.[2]

My main object in such conversation would be to hedge against divisions in the Republican ranks generally, and particularly for the contest of 1860. The point of danger is the temptation in different localities to "platform" for something which will be popular just there, but which, nevertheless, will be a firebrand elsewhere, and especially in a national convention. As instances, the movement against foreigners in Massachusetts; in New Hampshire, to make obedience to the fugitive-slave law punishable as a crime; in Ohio, to repeal the fugitive-slave law; and squatter sovereignty, in Kansas. In these things there is explosive enough to blow up half a dozen national conventions. . . . What is desirable, if possible, is that in every local convocation of Republicans a point should be made to avoid everything which will disturb Republicans elsewhere. . . .

In a word, in every locality we should look beyond our noses; and at least say nothing on points where it is probable we shall disagree. I write this for your eye only; hoping, however, if you see danger as I think I do, you will do what you can to avert it. Could not suggestions be made to leading men in the State and congressional conventions, and so avoid . . . these apples of discord?

[1] *Illinois State Journal,* July 9, 1859.
[2] *Works,* Vol. V, pp. 131–133.

Meantime, as Lincoln suavely argued and counseled, insisting on unity in Republican ranks, other dark-horse candidates were being groomed for the nomination which Lincoln was struggling to make worth while. Said the *Press & Tribune* [1]: —

The friends of Pitt Fessenden of Maine are urging him as a Republican candidate for the Presidency. With profound respect for that gentleman's talents, position and popularity, we must warn his friends that they are putting him into a press in which he will be squeezed to death long before the convention is called. Without any special candidate of our own, we see with pain the ill-directed zeal by which so many sterling Republicans will be killed off. Mr. Fessenden is too valuable a man to be slaughtered in the house of his friends.

Lincoln cannily avoided being slaughtered in the house of his friends by avoiding admission of his own candidacy and restraining his friends from such announcement, while utilizing every opportunity to augment his reputation and stature as a Republican leader.

When Lincoln was brought into contact with Samuel Galloway, an Ohio lawyer-politician, by a law case, he sent Galloway a long letter about the case. He had barely finished this when he received a very pleasing epistle from Galloway in which the Ohioan said that Lincoln deserved to win the next Republican presidential nomination. The honored individual hastened to scribble a reply.[2] Again he cautioned against the Ohio repudiation of the Fugitive Slave Law. It must be kept out of "our national convention. There is another thing our friends are doing which gives me some uneasiness. It is their leaning toward 'popular sovereignty.'" He presented three basic objections to this Greeleyan attitude. Then: —

As to Governor Chase, I have a kind side for him. He was one of the few distinguished men of the nation who gave us, in Illinois, their sympathy last year. I never saw him, but suppose him to be able and right-minded; but still he may not be the most suitable as a candidate for the Presidency.

I must say I do not think myself fit for the Presidency. As you propose a correspondence with me, I shall look for your letters anxiously.

[1] July 12, 1859.
[2] July 27, 28, 1859; *Works*, Vol. V, pp. 134–138.

These hot summer days, while Lincoln was busy preparing and arguing cases by the dozen before the courts, and seriously striving to forestall disunity in his Party, the engineers of the Illinois Republican machine were likewise hard at work. Jesse Fell was a brilliant corresponding secretary. He and Chairman Judd set about making the Illinois machine a powerful engine of political warfare. They sent to loyal Republican leaders in every county detailed instructions for creating strong local organizations and securing money to run the crucial campaign.[1] To organize a state-wide network of committees, Secretary Fell made unsentimental journeys up and down the state, contacting leaders and plain voters. Meeting the ordinary voter and discovering his reaction to the possible candidates for 1860 who were under discussion, Fell was strengthened in his conviction that "the people as a rule were eager to see 'Abe' Lincoln a presidential candidate."[2] Illinois politicians, however, had not yet with any unanimity succumbed to the attractions of that idea.

[1] W. E. Baringer, "Campaign Technique in Illinois — 1860," *Transactions*, Illinois State Hist. Soc., 1932, pp. 204–205.
[2] Morehouse, *Life of Fell*, p. 58.

☆   ☆   ☆

CHAPTER III

"Lincoln for President!"

UNTIL THIS August, the interstate speaking tours of Abraham Lincoln had been few and special. Since 1854 he had made but three political speeches outside Illinois.[1] For many months now the law business had been good to Lincoln; of late he had enjoyed eminent success in what the late John Galsworthy saw as the root of man's struggles, "the great battle of property." So he was able to spare the time for a remarkable series of political peregrinations. He made speeches west, north, east, and even went southward in December.

Business had prevented Lincoln's carrying out his plan to address the Kansas Republican Convention of May,[2] and the speech he wrote for that occasion remained undelivered.[3] But on August 9 he at last got away, at a time far less opportune. Accompanied by his bearded political comrade of Springfield officialdom, Secretary of State Hatch, Lincoln entrained for Kansas and Iowa and was away from home nine days. Iowa at this time was not far removed from a frontier condition. Iowa newspapers were few and feeble; practically all farmers who took a newspaper subscribed to that journalistic Bible, Greeley's *Weekly Tribune*.[4] What the Iowa press said about politics was of little importance to the press of the nation. Nevertheless Iowa editors kept

[1] Angle, *Lincoln, 1854–1861*, p. xxvi. E. W. Wiley, "Lincoln in the Campaign of 1856," *Journal*, Ill. State Hist. Soc., Vol. XXII, p. 587.
[2] Lincoln to Delahay, May 14, 1859; in Hertz, *Abraham Lincoln, a New Portrait*, Vol. II, p. 752.
[3] *Cf*. pp. 125–126n.
[4] F. I. Herriott, "Iowa and the First Nomination of Abraham Lincoln," *Annals of Iowa*, Vol. IX, pp. 46–48.

their readers informed on current presidential gossip.[1] When in late March the St. Louis Republican press announced Edward Bates as a presidential candidate and requested that the Party nominate him, the Burlington *Daily Hawk-Eye* reported the movement, uttered a familiar warning: "This is premature. It is too early yet to discuss the merits of candidates." Iowa was championing no special candidate for the Republican nomination,[2] so Lincoln knew he could lose nothing and might gain much by courting the favor of that neighbor state. Since July, Iowa had been more absorbed with its gubernatorial campaign than with national politics. The candidate for Governor, Samuel J. Kirkwood, had publicly declared his disapproval of the Ohio Republican resolution calling for repeal of the Fugitive Slave Law.[3] So the Iowa stage was well set for a display of the political views of Lincoln as a tentative presidential possibility. Last November, like most Republican papers, the Iowa Republican press had been loaded with tributes to Lincoln for his Douglas battle. But he had received considerably less publicity there as presidential timber than had Bates (the local hero) and Chase. Other long-shot candidates — Crittenden, McLean, John Bell, Ben Wade — who were being scrutinized by the ultra-conservative fusionists among the Republicans, had been talked about as much as Lincoln.[4] Iowa was definitely open-minded on the subject.

Lincoln's trip was not wholly political. He owned land in Iowa through his Black Hawk War service, and was considering a deal in Iowa land with Norman Judd. First he and Hatch journeyed to Kansas, probably conferring with Mark Delahay. On the return trip, stopping at St. Joseph, the pair went north on the Missouri River on Friday, August 12, to Council Bluffs, Iowa, Lincoln's primary reason being a desire to examine the land he might obtain from Judd. Leading citizens of Council Bluffs came to Lincoln at his hostelry with requests that he make a speech next evening.[5] Of course, said Lincoln, he would

[1] Herriott, pp. 49–64.
[2] Herriott, p. 46, pp. 53–54.
[3] Burlington *Daily Hawk-Eye*, Aug. 3, 1859; Herriott, p. 188.
[4] Herriott, pp. 49–64, pp. 201–217.
[5] Herriott, pp. 221–222, p. 227. Angle, *Lincoln, 1854–1861*, p. 293. G. M. Dodge, *Personal Recollections*, pp. 8–11.

be glad to help Iowa Republicans in their current hot campaign to turn
the normal Democratic majority. Next morning the Republican paper,
the *Nonpareil*, announced [1] : —

Hon. Abe Lincoln and the secretary of state for Illinois, Hon. O. M.
Hatch, arrived in our city last eve. . . . The distinguished "Sucker" has
yielded to the importunities of our citizens without distinction of parties,
and will speak on the political issues of the day at Concert Hall this evening. The celebrity of the speaker will most certainly insure him a full
house. Go and hear Old Abe.

The *Nonpareil's* editor next week told how Lincoln had "addressed
a very large audience of ladies and gentlemen" with a speech "masterly and unanswerable," which nobody could outline "in the brief
limits of a newspaper article. . . . The dexterity with which he applied the political scalpel to the Democratic carcass — beggars all
description at our hands. Suffice it that the speaker fully and fairly
sustained the great reputation he acquired in the memorable Illinois
campaign as a man of great intellectual power — a close and sound
reasoner."

The editor of the Democratic *Bugle* experienced no such difficulty
in analyzing Lincoln's speech. Contemptuously, he told how Lincoln
had apologized for appearing in a campaign in which he had no stake,
how the speaker [2]

with many excuses and a lengthy explanation, as if conscious of the nau-
seous nature of the black Republican nostrum, announced his intention to
speak about the "Eternal Negro," to use his own language, and entered
into a lengthy and ingenious analysis of the "nigger" question. . . . He
was decidedly opposed to the fusion or coalition of the Republican Party
with the opposition of the South, and clearly proved the correctness of his
ground in point of policy. They must retain their national organization
and sectional character, and continue to wage their sectional warfare
by slavery agitation; but if the opposition in the South would accede to
their views and adopt their doctrines, he was willing to run for President
in 1860, a Southern man with Northern principles. . . . His speech was
of the character of an exhortation to the Republican Party, but was in

[1] Council Bluffs *Nonpareil*, Aug. 13, 1859; in Herriott, pp. 222–223.
[2] Council Bluffs *Bugle*; in Hertz, Vol. II, p. 756.

reality as good a speech as could have been made for the interest of the Democracy. He was listened to with much attention, for his Waterloo defeat by Douglas has magnified him into quite a lion here.

As Lincoln and Hatch traveled homeward the Iowa press gave "some but not much" notice to his speech. But it was a gain. In September Lincoln received two invitations to speak in Iowa again, both of which he was forced to turn down because of political operations in other directions.[1]

Among the letters Lincoln found on his return home was one from Milwaukee, Wisconsin, inviting him to speak before the Wisconsin Agricultural Society. He replied that he should like to appear there, but was not sure he could spare the time from his law practice to make the trip and to write an address.[2] For the next two weeks Lincoln was less busy with law than he had anticipated, and he accepted the Wisconsin invitation. Meantime two requests for his oratorical assistance had come from Ohio. He replied, "I shall try to speak at Columbus and Cincinnati, but cannot do more."[3] The same day he wrote to an Iowan, saying that since he would not appear before the Federal Court at Keokuk, he could not, much as he would like to, address the citizens of that city.[4]

I am constantly receiving invitations which I am compelled to decline. I was pressingly urged to go to Minnesota; and I now have two invitations to go to Ohio. These last are prompted by Douglas going there; and I am really tempted to make a flying trip to Columbus and Cincinnati.

I do hope you will have no serious trouble in Iowa.

By mid-September Lincoln had received letters from Republican leaders inviting him to speak also in New Hampshire, New York, and Pennsylvania.[5]

Lincoln's Iowa trip received some little notice in the Illinois press,[6] and now and then something would appear about him in

[1] Herriott, pp. 225–227.
[2] Lincoln to D. J. Powers, Aug. 18, 1859; in Tracy, pp. 115–116.
[3] Lincoln to Peter Blow, Sept. 6, 1859; Tracy, p. 116.
[4] Lincoln to Hawkins Taylor, Sept. 6, 1859, Works, Vol. V, pp. 138–139.
[5] John G. Nicolay and John Hay, Abraham Lincoln, A History, Vol. II, p. 177, quoting letters to Lincoln.
[6] Chicago Press & Tribune, Aug. 20, 1859.

the public prints those hot, dull August days, as an 1860 possibility.
John Wentworth was not long in seeing that he had made a great
mistake in talking of Lincoln (however insincerely he had done it)
for President. When Wentworth saw other newspapers taking his
presidential remarks seriously and talking not at all about Lincoln
for Governor, the Machiavellian editor made haste to backtrack. In
March he was busily urging the nomination of Lincoln for Vice
President, with some Southern man heading the ticket.[1] Three
months later he was talking about Edward Bates as the man for
President, a proposal which met with solid opposition among the
vigorous Republicans of Illinois. In late August the famous Long
John announced that he had at last discovered the ideal man.

The success of GEN. SAMUEL HOUSTON, as the Opposition candidate for
Governor in Texas, places him in the front rank as a candidate for the
Presidency by the Opposition. He seems to be just the man for the crisis;
and so we have made up our mind that with him for President, and the
favorite son of Illinois (Abram Lincoln) for Vice President, we would
have an excellent ticket.

The *Press & Tribune* commented: "The favorite son of Illinois
will not feel flattered by the platform Long John would place him
on, nor complimented by making him play second fiddle to the
wearer of the tiger-skin jacket. Sam Houston . . . endorses the
Dred Scott decision, the Lecompton Constitution and Buchanan's
Administration. He condemns Popular Sovereignty but goes the
whole Democratic pro-slavery figure except the re-opening of the
African slave trade. From this we see where Wentworth stands. He
has bid good-bye to Republican principles and plunged his whole
length into the pro-slavery cess pool."[2]

In Springfield, the *Journal* reproduced the *Democrat's* editorial
on Houston, commenting in Lincolnian vein:

"He must define his position a little more distinctly before his

---

[1] Quoted in Herriott, *Annals of Iowa*, Vol. IX, p. 52.
[2] Chicago *Press & Tribune*, Aug. 24, 1859.

claims, so far as the Republican Party is concerned, can be canvassed."[1]

President-guessing had picked up considerably as summer days grew long and hot. On July 23 the *Press & Tribune* clipped an editorial from the Democratic New York *Herald* on "The Republican Party and Its Presidential Candidates," which mentioned only Seward, Banks, and Chase. Old James Gordon Bennett, staunch Buchanan supporter, had analyzed the situation quite accurately: "Seward expects the nomination — his friends demand it in his behalf as his, from every consideration of right, justice and expediency. They are also working systematically to gain the Convention which is to decide the question; and they may be able thus to extort his nomination. Let them do it, and the Republican Party will soon be reduced to a miserable minority in every state west of Vermont. . . . Let Seward be put forth as a Republican candidate for 1860, and that Party will come out of the battle frittered away to a mere abolition faction." As to Banks and Chase, the Massachusetts Governor would take well with the Know-Nothings but offend the foreigners. The Ohio Governor, a known opponent of "Native American restrictions," would reverse the difficulty. Prophetically Bennett concluded, "So in the way of a compromise between Seward, Banks and Chase, the Convention may be driven to that Democratic expedient of a candidate whose very obscurity will be his highest recommendation."

The Chicago *Press & Tribune* carried dozens of stories concerning Democratic possibilities, many of them ridiculing the movement behind Governor Wise of Virginia. A letter to the editor in late August, signed "A Republican," gave a sober mathematical argument. "The editor of the Chicago *Journal* has come out for W. H. Seward for President. . . . Permit me to ask the editor of the *Journal* a question or two. Suppose Mr. Seward nominated, how is he going to be elected?" The writer argued, with figures, that Seward could not get the 1856 Fillmore vote of Illinois, Pennsylvania,

<hr />

[1] *Illinois State Journal*, Aug. 25, 1859.

Indiana, New Jersey. Without the support of these Fillmore voters (assumed to be all Know-Nothings) "Seward could no more carry either of these four states than he can escape death. And how are the Republicans to elect a President unless they receive their electoral votes?"

Mr. Seward is a great orator, and a zealous anti-slavery advocate. . . . But the honor of having him for a candidate would hardly compensate the Republican Party for the moral certainty of defeat. No man can demonstrate that Mr. Seward would run better than the gallant Fremont. . . . His nomination would be the signal for a union of Americans with Democrats to beat him. Would it be *wise* to nominate a candidate however great his talents, or sincere his free soilism, who, instead of attracting to his support the conservative element would repel it, and drive its members into the ranks of the common enemy to ensure the defeat of our candidate?

While Lincoln as September began worked on his Ohio speeches, Chicago's *Press & Tribune* announced him: "Hon. Abraham Lincoln is announced in the Cincinnati papers to speak in Columbus, Ohio, on Friday the 16th inst., and in Cincinnati the 17th. In casting about for some proper person to reply to Mr. Douglas, the Republicans of Ohio have selected the right man. . . . Douglas' Popular Sovereignty will not be worth the cost of getting out the patent, after it has been ventilated by Lincoln." [1]

One day in mid-September Lincoln climbed on his train for Ohio. He was accompanied by Mrs. Lincoln, who went along to partake of the glory she had so long desired. The trip was tiresome, dangerous. Railroading was young, seats hard, ghastly accidents common. But "Old Abe" (he was often called this now, for he was fifty, and looked old, though in physical and mental vigor he was anything but aging) had plenty to think about as late summer landscapes handsome and sordid flashed by the windows. Senator Douglas had recently published a long, serious article in *Harper's Magazine*, designed to present to the nation his true position on popular sovereignty. The Douglas essay commanded all the publicity the press could give. Every paper reported and discussed it, went on to praise

[1] Chicago *Press & Tribune*, Sept. 10, 1859.

or condemn. Some even violated the copyright, so anxious were they to print Douglas' words. The *Press & Tribune* had printed, upon the essay's appearance, a long compendium and a very long editorial comment. Two days later the *Tribune* ran an editorial five feet long, pointing out the historical inaccuracies of the Douglas argument that popular sovereignty was a traditional American policy. Almost every day for two weeks the *Tribune* carried editorials or clippings from other journals on the Douglas article.[1] Contained in this tidal wave of publicity was much talk about Lincoln and his work in pointing out the iniquities of the Douglas doctrine. This was invaluable to Lincoln. Seeing his chance to use once more the Little Giant's fame to advertise Abraham Lincoln, he read the *Harper's* essay with great care and wrote his Ohio speeches as a refutation. The *Tribune* declared that the very fact of the Ohio invitation proved that the West saw Abraham Lincoln as the man to match against the great and powerful Douglas. But did it? Probably Ohio Republicans invited Lincoln simply because they wanted all the help they could get in a hot campaign. They asked Lyman Trumbull to come, and he, too, obliged. Lincoln himself, however, was intent on showing Ohio and the North that no man could oppose Douglas as effectively as his recent Illinois opponent.

And so "Old Abe" was happy as ambitious men are when musing on bright prospects of the future. Already, with the Fall campaign just begun, he had completed a successful interstate speaking tour, was on another, and was engaged for a third two weeks later. His stature as a Republican leader was steadily growing and he was on the way up, his oratory providing the dynamic force of elevation, regardless of how next year's nominations might turn out. He was not in the imminent presidential race so deeply that nomination of some other Republican leader would be a blow to his prestige. He had played the game cautiously, shrewdly, in a Lincolnian fashion. This astute politician was not placing all his political eggs in one basket, all his hopes on the 1860 nomination. A grand play for that might fail and reduce his strength as a possible nominee for some

[1] Chicago *Press & Tribune*, Aug. 27–Sept. 10, 1859.

later presidential battle. A cautious campaign for the impending nomination, if unsuccessful, would leave him in a position to make a stronger bid in a subsequent convention.

On Friday, September 16, Lincoln reached Columbus, and at two o'clock he stood on the State House terrace, an angular, stooping, melancholy giant, facing a small open-air audience. Six days before, Douglas had spoken at the same place, and Lincoln made answer with a long, serious speech. At once he began hammering Douglas. Lincoln read long extracts from what he called his "very 'memorable' debate with Judge Douglas last year" to prove that his own view favored neither Negro suffrage nor social equality of blacks and whites. He traced in detail the history of the Democracy's record on the Negro question since 1854, interpreting the Kansas-Nebraska Act and Dred Scott decision from the Republican point of view. "Looking at these things, the Republican party, as I understand its principles and policy, believe that there is great danger of the institution of slavery being spread out and extended, until it is ultimately made alike lawful in all the States of this Union; so believing, to prevent that . . . ultimate consummation is the original and chief purpose of the Republican organization. The chief and real purpose of the Republican party is eminently conservative. It proposes nothing save and except to restore this government to its original tone in regard to this element of slavery, and there to maintain it, looking for no further change in reference to it, than that which the original framers of the government themselves expected and looked forward to."

Douglas' popular sovereignty, urged Lincoln, was dangerous as the opening wedge in the South's fell efforts to nationalize slavery. "This is the miner and sapper. While it does not propose to revive the African slave trade, nor to pass a slave code, nor to make a second Dred Scott decision, it is preparing us for the onslaught and charge of these ultimate enemies when they shall be ready to come on." The speaker pointed out a difference between Douglasism and "genuine popular sovereignty." The latter meant, in the abstract, "that each man shall do precisely as he pleases with himself, and with all things which exclusively concern himself." This was the principle of the rights of man upon which the country's government was built. But the Douglas brand! "It is, as a principle, no other than that if one man chooses to make a slave of another man, neither that other man nor anybody else has a right to object." This was brilliant, forceful exposition of a conflict in abstract principle that was very bewildering to the plain voter. Democrats, Douglas included, thought that the principle of liberty, translated into action, bestowed the liberty to hold slaves, to destroy some other person's liberty. Lincoln saw the logical fallacy of this, and called his literary powers of presentation into play in a great effort to make everybody see clearly that huge sophism which is so palpable to any keenly logical mind.

Douglas, Lincoln went on, "has had a good deal of trouble with popular sovereignty. His explanations explanatory of explanations explained are interminable. The most lengthy, and, as I suppose, the most maturely considered of his long series of explanations, is his great essay in *Harper's Magazine*." Lincoln then shot holes in the historical precedents which Douglas offered in support of his popular sovereignty, in a lengthy passage (twenty pages in his *Works*) so sound in its history and so persuasive that it must be read in the original before such magnificent argumentation can be truly appreciated. To impartial, strictly logical minds (which unfortunately are so few as to be of no political force) Lincoln quite demolished Douglas' viewpoint.

One of his blasts is too good to omit. To smithereens went Douglas' contention that the Fathers founded the nation on the principle of non-intervention with slavery in the territories, when Lincoln gave a detailed, comprehensive history of the famous Ordinance of '87 which excluded slavery from the vast Northwest Territory. Summing up this argument he said: —

This period of history, which I have run over briefly, is, I presume, as familiar to most of this assembly as any other part of the history of our country. . . . And hence I ask how extraordinary a thing it is that a man who has occupied a position upon the floor of the Senate of the United States, who is now in his third term, and who looks to see the government of this whole country fall into his own hands, pretending to give a truthful and accurate history of the slavery question in this country, should so entirely ignore the whole of that portion of our history — the most important of all. Is it not a most extraordinary spectacle that a man should stand up and ask for any confidence in his statements, who sets out as he does with portions of history, calling upon the people to believe that it is a true and fair representation, when the leading part and controlling feature of the whole history is carefully suppressed?

But the mere leaving out is not the most remarkable feature of this most remarkable essay. His proposition is to establish that the leading men of the Revolution were for his great principle of non-intervention by the government in the question of slavery in the Territories; while history shows that they decided, in the cases actually brought before them, in exactly the contrary way, and he knows it. Not only did they so decide at that time, but they stuck to it during sixty years, through thick and thin, as long as there was one of the Revolutionary heroes upon the stage of political action. Through their whole course, from first to last, they clung to freedom. And now he asks the community to believe that the men of the Revolution were in favor of his great principle, when we have the naked history that they themselves dealt with this very subject-matter of his principle, and utterly repudiated his principle, acting upon a precisely contrary ground.

When Lincoln finished shooting holes in the Douglas version of history there was nothing left of it. Democrats of course were not moved; like the woman convinced against her will they held the same opinion still. Nor was much left of the speaker's time. Lincoln said that the second object of the *Harper's* essay "was to show that the Dred Scott decision had not entirely squelched out this popular sovereignty." And he spent several minutes presenting anew the proposition contained in the famous Freeport question.

The Dred Scott decision expressly gives every citizen of the United States a right to carry his slaves into the United States Territories. And now there was some inconsistency in saying that the decision was right, and saying, too, that the people of the Territory could lawfully drive slavery out again. When all the trash, the words, the collateral matter, was cleared away from it — all the chaff was fanned out of it, it was a bare absurdity — *no less than that a thing may be lawfully driven away from where it has a lawful right to be.*

Douglas, Lincoln went on, could not help seeing this absurdity, so "since his re-election to the Senate, he has never said, as he did at Freeport, that the people of the Territories can exclude slavery. He desires that you, who wish the Territories to remain free, should believe that he stands by that position, but he does not say it himself. He escapes to some extent the absurd position I have stated by changing his language entirely. What he says now is something different in language, and we will consider whether it is not different in sense too."

It is now that the Dred Scott decision, or rather the Constitution under that decision, does not carry slavery into the Territories beyond the power of the people of the Territories *to control it as other property*. He does not say the people can drive it out, but they can control it as other property. . . . Driving a horse out of this lot is too plain a proposition to be mistaken about; it is putting him on the other side of the fence. Or it might be a sort of exclusion of him from the lot if you were to kill him . . . ; but neither of these things is the same as "controlling him as other property." That would be to feed him, to pamper him, to ride him, to use or abuse him, to make the most money out of him "as other property"; but, please you, what do the men who are in favor of slavery want more than this? What do they really want, other than that slavery, being in the Territories, shall be controlled as other property?

This new point was only a beginning. He went on with aggressive attack based on constitutional factors, reiterating with withering force his arguments of last year.

Already Lincoln had exhausted the capacity of an audience to receive arguments which struck so deep, but he was speaking not merely to a single group. His aim was to show the entire Republican Party, every opponent of slavery, what a political thinker they had in Abraham Lincoln. So, as an illustration of his point that popular sovereignty offered the greatest current menace to the Republican Party's purpose of restricting slavery's spread, he made a long argument pointing out that Douglas' view would allow residents of territories to re-open the slave trade. Then, logically, Southern slaveholders could again import blacks from Africa.

I say if this principle is established, that there is no wrong in slavery, and whoever wants it has a right to have it; that it is a matter of dollars and cents; a sort of question as to how they shall deal with brutes . . . ; that it is a mere matter of policy; that there is a perfect right, according to interest, to do just as you please — when this is done, where this doctrine prevails, the miners and sappers will have formed public opinion for the slave-trade. They will be ready for Jeff Davis and Stephens, and other leaders of that company, to sound the bugle for the revival of the slave-trade, for the second Dred Scott decision, for the flood of slavery to be poured over the Free States, while we shall be here tied down and helpless, and run over like sheep.

His closing appeal in this staggering speech was a subtle stroke of practical politics. Following and re-emphasizing his previous argument, which showed the inefficacy of Douglasism as a preventive of slavery's spread, Lincoln in a superbly persuasive attack called upon Democrats who honestly opposed slavery to see the delusion of the Douglas teaching that "popular sovereignty is as good a way as any to oppose slavery," to desert Douglas and give their support to the only real instrument of opposition to slavery, the Republican Party.[1]

Lincoln had told the Ohio managers that he could speak no more than twice. But he found Ohioans begging to hear him. This was most encouraging and he was happy to oblige. That evening he spoke briefly in the City Hall to the Young Men's Republican Club of Columbus.

Next day Lincoln was on his way to Cincinnati. Columbus papers were full of his speech, the Republican organ printing the address in full, with enthusiastic comment, the Democratic sheet saying, "The speaker disappointed all who heard him. . . . He is not an orator. He can hardly be classed as a third rate debater. . . . Mr. Lincoln is not a great man — very, very far from it. . . . Indeed the Republicans feel that they have burned their fingers, by bringing him here." [2]

Changing trains that afternoon in Dayton, Lincoln had time for

---

[1] *Works*, Vol. V, pp. 140–189. Daniel J. Ryan, "Lincoln and Ohio," *Ohio Arch. & Hist. Quart.*, Vol. XXXII, pp. 35–61.
[2] *Ohio State Journal*, and *Ohio Statesman;* in Ryan, pp. 61–62.

a two-hour speech. To a crowd in the courthouse he addressed a variation of his Columbus remarks. Said the Republican paper [1]: —

> Mr. Lincoln is one of the "self-made" men — having, without the advantages of education, risen to the proud eminence which he now occupies in his own state and in the United States.
>
> He is remarkable for vigor of intellect, clearness of perception, and power of argumentation, and for fairness and honesty in the presentation of facts. Every man who listened to Mr. Lincoln on Saturday was impressed with the manner as well as the matter of his speech, abounding as it did in valuable historical information and great political truths.

The Dayton Democratic organ was moved to pay the speaker a half-compliment: "Mr. Lincoln is a very seductive reasoner, and his address although a network of fallacies and false assumptions throughout, was calculated to deceive almost any man, who would not pay very close attention to the subject, and keep continually on the guard." [2]

An hour's ride south of Dayton was Hamilton, where a crowd had gathered at the station to gape at the celebrity when the train rattled in. Lincoln came out and said a few words. Then the train chuffed on to Cincinnati, reigning Metropolis of the West. Pretentiously the orator was received by a company of Republicans and escorted between lines of cheering people to the Burnet House, his presence further celebrated by booming cannon. Lincoln snatched a bite to eat, then proceeded in grand style to a central square. Cannon roared and brass bands tootled; a mounted escort and squads of torchbearing marchers formed a guard of honor as Lincoln went by in an open carriage. From a balcony where he stood, ready to speak, Lincoln looked out through the glimmering darkness upon animated Market Square, seething with people and illuminated by crackling giant bonfires, brilliant with fireworks shooting gleaming streaks across the dark sky. Douglas had recently spoken in Cincinnati, as usual giving his interpretation that Lincoln's "house divided" and Seward's "irrepressible conflict" in-

[1] *Weekly Dayton Journal;* in Ryan, pp. 64–65.
[2] Dayton *Daily Empire;* in Ryan, pp. 65–66.

vited "continual war" between the free and slave states. 'Lincoln opened his speech by reviewing, for this new audience, the history of the conflict between himself and Douglas in interpreting the meaning and significance of the "house divided." The speaker was careful to deny (whatever Douglas said) "any purpose in any way interfering with the institution of slavery, where it exists."

This was an astute beginning. In pointing out the cleavage of party opposition on the leading issue of slavery, Lincoln sagaciously discussed Douglas as the expounder of the Democratic view, represented himself as the important Republican strategist. Then he addressed himself to Kentucky.

I say, then, in the first place, to the Kentuckians, that I am what they call, as I understand it, a "Black Republican." I think slavery is wrong, morally and politically. I desire that it should be no further spread in these United States, and I should not object if it should gradually terminate in the whole Union. While I say this for myself, I say to you Kentuckians, that I understand you differ radically from me upon this proposition; that you believe slavery is a good thing; that slavery is right; that it ought to be extended and perpetuated in this Union. Now, there being this broad difference between us, I do not pretend in addressing myself to you Kentuckians, to attempt proselyting you; that would be a vain effort. . . . I only propose to try to show you that you ought to nominate for the next Presidency, at Charleston, my distinguished friend, Judge Douglas.

He argued lengthily that Douglas stood as the South's best instrument for perpetuating slavery because Douglas alone could bring to their cause Northern support, without which believers in the right of slavery would be hopelessly in the minority. Lincoln used so many words demonstrating how (according to him) Douglas really favored slavery, that his audience became somewhat restive. A voice shouted up at him, "Speak to Ohio men, and not to Kentuckians." Several thousand words later the towering speaker did. Meantime he hammered with his Columbus arguments that popular sovereignty would reopen the slave trade, that popular sovereignty could not keep slavery out of the territories (even Douglas himself had not said specifically, since the debates, that it could, Lincoln again pointed out in detail).

Here he talked a long time about the Ordinance of '87, disputing Douglas' Columbus declaration that Federal legislation never made a free state, that popular sovereignty kept slavery out of Ohio, Indiana, Illinois. Lincoln cited much history to prove that the Ordinance really made Ohio free, as occurred, he said, in all states which grew from the Northwest Territory.

Realizing that his speech had been long, heavy, highly factual and humorless, not very entertaining to a crowd, Lincoln wondered aloud if he should stop, though he had another topic he wished to speak on. The crowd yelled "Go on." So Lincoln went on to elaborate his distinction between Douglas' popular sovereignty and genuine popular sovereignty. This led him into a discussion of the relations of capital and labor. By way of disproving the slaveholder's theory that capital should own labor, Lincoln celebrated the free laborer as one who can become an employer.

"Men are led only by force of the imagination." This speech needed something to touch the imagination and arouse enthusiasm if Lincoln's audience was to be sent home with a definite impression after the impact of long and involved argumentation. So Lincoln moved to a ringing conclusion: —

I have taken upon myself . . . to say that we expect upon these principles to ultimately beat [the proslavery forces]. In order to do so, I think we want and must have a national policy in regard to the institution of slavery, that acknowledges and deals with that institution as being wrong. Whoever desires the prevention of the spread of slavery and the nationalization of that institution, yields all, when he yields to any policy that either recognized slavery as being right, or as being an indifferent thing. Nothing will make you successful but setting up a policy which shall treat the thing as being wrong. . . . We believe that the spreading out and perpetuity of the institution of slavery impairs the general welfare. We believe — nay, we know, that that is the only thing that has ever threatened the perpetuity of the Union itself. . . . To repress this thing, we think, is providing for the general welfare. . . .

I say that we must not interfere with the institution of slavery in the states where it exists, because the Constitution forbids it, and the general welfare does not require us to do so. . . . But we must prevent the outspreading of the institution, because neither the Constitution nor general welfare requires us to extend it. We must prevent the revival of the African slave trade, and the enacting by Congress of a Territorial slave code. We must prevent each of these things being done by either Congress or courts. The people of these United States are the rightful masters of both Congresses and courts, not to overthrow the Constitution, but to overthrow the men who pervert the Constitution.

As an afterword he gave advice in practical politics. The Party which labors against slavery must not sacrifice principle to coalition, must nominate candidates and frame a platform in harmony with "our real purpose." Lincoln said he favored union of opposition elements only on these terms. Still, he was willing to support a Southerner as Republican nominee, provided the nomination should be firmly based on Republican principles of non-extension.[1]

Lincoln's speech and his extraordinary appearance were currently the main item of local political gossip. A brilliant Unitarian minister — who watched from the square as the stream of powerful words came from the man with sad eyes, hollow cheeks, prominent nose, and high and strong forehead, whose "face had a battered and bronzed look, without being hard" — fitted to him Browning's description of the German professor: "three parts sublime to one grotesque."[2] The Cincinnati press had much to say, the Republican paper publishing the speech in full.

Admitting that the crowd received the speech well, the Democratic sheet said: "We have glanced over the speech of Mr. Lincoln in the *Gazette*. We do not say we read it: it is not worth reading. . . . Among public addresses from the stump, the speech of Mr. Lincoln belongs to the lowest order. It is not the speech of a statesman; it is not the speech of a politician; it is not even the speech of a fair partisan. It is the speech of a pettifogging demagogue."[3]

[1] *Works*, Vol. V, pp. 190–235. Ryan, "Lincoln and Ohio," pp. 69–97.
[2] Reminiscence of M. D. Conway; in Ryan, p. 100.
[3] Cincinnati *Enquirer;* in Ryan, p. 98.

Another paper compared the two Illinois politicians who had recently addressed their city [1]: —

The republicans proposed that, as the democrats had made an immense lion of Mr. Douglas, they would cause Mr. Lincoln to play the lion on a scale equally extensive. But Mr. Douglas had a great advantage. He has become the most noted politician in the country. For some years he has been the central figure of American politics. There are thousands of persons who have an abiding faith that he is to be some day the president of the United States, and, animated by a lively sense of favors to come, they take every occasion to show their devotion to his person. Mr. Lincoln is not conspicuous as a presidential candidate.

Lincoln stayed in Cincinnati over Sunday, where he received an invitation to speak at Indianapolis on his way home. Monday afternoon he reached the Hoosier capital, and that evening spoke for two hours to an enthusiastic crowd in Masonic Hall. Such was his reputation as a speaker that the Governor came to listen. They laughed when Lincoln told how he "grew up to his present enormous height" in Indiana. He recalled what a wilderness the state then was. Getting down to business, he harangued them with a speech presenting the main arguments he used so effectively at Columbus and Cincinnati. The crowd devoured it.[2]

This triumphant tour made quite a splash in the press. Papers which especially favored Lincoln, like the *Illinois State Journal* and the Chicago *Press & Tribune,* printed in full both Columbus and Cincinnati speeches. Of Lincoln's Columbus address, significant as his first careful, serious oration since the campaign last autumn, the *Tribune* published an extended critique. The editors were sharp enough to see in this speech not mere crowd-delighting talk, but an ideological contribution to Republicanism. Readers' attention was directed to Lincoln's "new and fatal discovery among the maze of Douglasisms" that Douglas had, since the debates, "dropped the 'unfriendly legislation' dodge and commenced prating about the right to control slavery as other property. . . . It is patent as

[1] Cincinnati *Commercial;* in Ryan, p. 99.
[2] Angle, *New Letters,* pp. 210–219.

sunlight that Popular Sovereignty is abandoned by the great popular sovereign himself." [1] Stress was laid on the important difference that while "unfriendly legislation" implied exclusion of slaves, "control as property" looked toward admission, as Lincoln demonstrated in his horse illustration. Thus the penetrating Lincolnian reasoning of the Ohio speeches began to take root in other Republican minds as weeks went by.[2] And Buchanan's Washington organ, the *National Intelligencer,* was so pleased with Lincoln's Cincinnati attack on Douglas that they reprinted the speech, praising the orator for handling "the honorable Senator's doctrines without gloves." [3]

Eight days after Lincoln's return from the Ohio junket he was again aboard a train, heading north this time, bound for Milwaukee. He was to deliver, under auspices of the Wisconsin Agricultural Society, the annual address at the Wisconsin State Fair, a job rather out of his line. His talk was chiefly rustic. Newspapers called it "dignified and impressive." But after discussing the value of agricultural fairs in developing the country, he made what amounted to a political argument. He outlined the "mud-sill" theory of labor (which slaveholders espoused): that hired laborers are the mudsills of society, that the ideal labor system requires capital to own labor. The speaker then outlined the opposite view: "that labor is prior to, and independent of, capital; that, in fact, capital is the fruit of labor, and could never have existed if labor had not first existed; that labor can exist without capital, but that capital could never have existed without labor. Hence . . . labor is the superior — greatly the superior — of capital." He pointed out how the industrious laborer could by husbanding his resources become a hirer of labor, that "a large majority" of the country's labor is performed by persons who are neither capitalists nor laborers, but a combination of both. Lincoln was careful to avoid open politics. He made no mention of Southerners as exponents of the mud-sill theory, of the North as believers in free labor; leaning over back-

---

[1] Chicago *Press & Tribune,* Sept. 19, 1859.
[2] New York *Independent;* clipped in Chicago *Press & Tribune,* Oct. 14.
[3] Chicago *Press & Tribune,* Sept. 26, 1859.

wards to avoid partisanship, Lincoln said his purpose was only to outline the two theories. "I suppose, however, I shall not be mistaken in assuming as a fact that people of Wisconsin prefer free labor, with its natural companion, education." His hearers knew perfectly well that Lincoln was hammering at the proslavery ideology.[1]

Lincoln would probably not have taken the trouble to prepare and deliver this agricultural address had he not expected it to serve as a springboard from which he could make some political speeches that would create a bigger reputation for Abraham Lincoln in this northern region where he was not well known. And before he left Wisconsin he was three times asked to speak on "topics of the day." That very evening, after his bucolic remarks, he spoke impromptu at the Newhall House,[2] and received an invitation to appear in Beloit. Next day he reached Beloit at noon, and found a large crowd awaiting him at the depot. Before a throng which packed Hanchett's Hall he stood for a couple of hours, banging at popular sovereignty with the powerful arguments he had recently used in Ohio.

Lincoln, in beginning, was careful to say that the South detests Republicanism only because "Democratic leaders there sedulously strive, by misrepresentation and falsehood, to produce the impression that the Republicans desire to meddle with their existing institutions." The real Republican position, said the speaker, is to resist the spread of slavery "in every *legitimate, Constitutional* way." The Beloit *Journal* told its readers that "Mr. Lincoln makes no attempt at rhetorical display, but in his simple unpretentious manner, he brings out his arguments with great clearness and force. He was repeatedly applauded while speaking, and as he closed, the audience gave three rousing cheers for Abraham Lincoln."[3]

A few miles north of Beloit lies Janesville. Hearing that Lincoln was speaking so near, a committee of Republicans hurried down

[1] *Works*, Vol. V, pp. 236–256.
[2] Charles Caverno, in *Magazine of History*, Vol. XXXVI (Extra number 142), pp. 195–200.
[3] Angle, *New Letters*, pp. 220–223.

and invited him to speak in their town. So that evening Lincoln held forth for an hour and a half in the Janesville courthouse. Janesville's *Gazette* reported a speech substantially like the one he delivered in the afternoon, apologized because (in a long column of abstract) it could report "only a few of the ideas broached by Mr. Lincoln." The *Gazette* gave its readers a vivid picture of this striking politician at work.[1]

Many present saw Mr. Lincoln for the first time; and as his person is tall, lean and wiry, his complexion dark, his physiognomy homely, and his phrenological developments being peculiar, he attracted much attention. His style of oratory is plain and unpretending and his gesticulations sometimes awkward. . . . Whatever unfavorable opinion any person in the audience may at first have formed of Mr. Lincoln's ability as an orator soon vanishes, and the power of the high order of intellect which he undoubtedly possesses, makes itself felt, not only while the speech is being delivered, but afterwards. His speeches are not easily forgotten, and we doubt not that all his audience that heard him through, still remember his points and his hits, and will do so for many a day; and that they still have a vivid recollection of that tall, gaunt form, stooping over towards his hearers, his countenance full of humor or frowning with scorn, as he lays bare to the gaze of the audience the ridiculous positions of Douglas or withers with his pungent sarcasm the false positions of the believers in popular sovereignty.

On his way back home Lincoln stayed in Chicago a few days looking after his political fences, the *Press & Tribune* noting that he had spoken at Beloit and Janesville.[2] Three days earlier, for no good reason except that its editors were fond of Lincoln, the *Tribune* had published his agricultural address, recommending it "to the perusal of our readers of all classes — to the farmers particularly." The *Tribune* was the best press support a Western Republican could want, for its influence extended far beyond Chicago. As the chief Republican paper of the West it published long accounts of autumn campaign speeches and tactics in all Western states, even California, also saying much about politics East and South.[3]

[1] Angle, *New Letters*, pp. 223–226.
[2] Chicago *Press & Tribune*, Oct. 4, 1859.
[3] Sept., Oct., 1859, *passim*.

Soon after reaching home Lincoln went to Clinton as the autumn circuit court season opened. A friend who had become impressed with Lincoln's chances of landing on his Party's national ticket wrote to the candidate suggesting that Lincoln put himself on record concerning his tariff ideas. So Lincoln wrote to the inquirer a long letter, not for publication, in which he cautiously perched on the fence. "I was an old Henry Clay-Tariff Whig. . . . I have not since changed my views." He now favored a "moderate, carefully adjusted protective tariff," arranged to please everybody! But for the present, "the revival of that question will not advance the cause itself, or the man who revives it." [1]

October 13 brought the thrilling news that in October elections several Northern states had gone Republican, exposing heavy Democratic losses. Next evening Clinton Republicans held a rally to celebrate the victory news from Pennsylvania, Ohio, Iowa, Minnesota. "Hon. A. Lincoln, Leonard Swett, Esq., and L. Weldon, Esq., made eloquent and stirring speeches, and were greeted with immense applause and enthusiasm by the crowd which filled the court house." [2]

Next day Lincoln returned to Springfield, and that evening participated in another jollification. Learning that "the giant killer" was in town, several hundred Republicans made up a party and "headed by a band of music, called upon Mr. Lincoln to exchange congratulations upon the result of the elections." Lincoln responded to the serenade with a speech. [3]

He set out by alluding to the fact that Judge Douglas and himself fully agreed upon one point as set forth in Douglas' Columbus speech, viz: that the fathers of this Government understood its powers over . . . slavery better than we do now; and he proceeded to show that the Democratic party had departed from the old landmarks; had set up a new theory and a different policy, and at their present rate of progress, would speedily make slavery a national institution. . . . In this the Democracy were resisted, and must be resisted by the Republicans, that their position was

[1] Lincoln to Dr. Edward Wallace, Oct. 11, 1859; *Works*, Vol. V, pp. 256–257.
[2] Bloomington *Pantagraph;* clipped in *Illinois State Journal*, Oct. 26, 1859.
[3] *Illinois State Journal*, Oct. 17, 18, 1859. Chicago *Press & Tribune*, Oct. 20, 1859.

identical with that occupied by the founders of the Government . . . ; and referred to the recent glorious victories achieved by the Republicans in Ohio and other states, as clearly indicative, that the good old doctrines of the fathers of the Republic would yet again prevail. . . . He continued his remarks at considerable length, and made many strong points, which again and again brought down the crowd.

We have never observed such general joy and gratification as pervaded the Republican hosts of our city. They were wild with excitement, and kept up their shouts till a late hour.

October's elections moved the *Press & Tribune* to utter a triumphant requiem to Douglas' career. "The necessity of warring upon Douglas seems to be at an end. The October elections in Pennsylvania, Ohio, Iowa, Indiana and Minnesota, resulting in the overthrow of the Democracy, have, by destroying whatever remaining chances he may have had for the Charleston nomination, sealed his fate. There is not a shrewd politican or a live party that would touch him with a 'forty foot pole.' He is as dead as a mackerel." [1]

But elections were not the biggest news of these October days. While Lincoln was attending court at Clinton the national press broke out in a rash of tense stories relating the death in a duel of California's Senator Broderick. Broderick, once a Tammany politician and saloon-keeper, had gone West — where he became a rough, tough forty-niner, a grafter dealing in gold coins which contained less bullion than face-value required. When the California Legislature made him Senator on a political bargain he burst into national affairs as a kind of 1859 Huey Long. His violent attacks on the Administration got him a challenge from a pro-slavery politician, Justice David Terry. As the two men faced each other, pistol in hand, Broderick's gun, before he could take aim, accidentally went off in the air. Terry, no sportsman, took deliberate aim and sent a ball drilling into Broderick's burly chest. The wounded man lingered a few days and his dying words were carefully heroic. Instantly the North made a martyr of him, screaming at the South the charge "Murder!" [2]

[1] Oct. 19, 1859.
[2] *Illinois State Journal*, Oct. 11, 1859. Chicago *Press & Tribune,* Oct. 11–18, 1859. *Dictionary of American Biography*, Vol. III, pp. 61–62.

A week later, while Lincoln was busy with law at Urbana, the press blazed with even more sensational news — the first accounts of how old John Brown, the fanatical Kansas fighter, had with a handful of men seized the United States arsenal at Harpers Ferry as the first step of a planned Negro insurrection. The *Press & Tribune* was giving much space to election returns, the Broderick funeral and its repercussions, when on the morning of October 19 the first telegraphic news of "the Virginia Insurrection" was published — a long series of thrilling dispatches from the scene. The editors commented: —

The news from Harper's Ferry, in which the insurrectionary attempt of a handful of blacks, aided by two or three white men, is related, will produce a profound sensation in all the slave-holding states. Osawatomie Brown, who seems to have been the head and front of the movement, figures not unexpectedly to us in this purposeless and senseless riot. Since the death of his son Frederick, who was shot down at his own door by a Missouri mob tenfold more revengeful and bloody than that which now fills Virginia with terror, and since the old man witnessed, on the same occasion, the destruction of the property that he had been a life-time in accumulating, he has been a monomaniac. He has supposed himself divinely appointed to free all American slaves by some violent and decisive move. . . .

Partisan minds instantly clicked to place responsibility on the other side. Democrats pointed fingers; here was a case illustration, they insisted, of the violent effects of Republican sectional doctrine. Republicans replied by placing the blame squarely on the Democrats.[1]

Who supposes that such an outbreak would have been possible in 1853? Who supposes that in the whole country during that year before the introduction of the Kansas-Nebraska bill, the repeal of the Missouri Compromise and the renewal of a fierce and bitter sectional warfare, men could have been found to put themselves at the head of such a movement? The country was at peace then. The old policy of the Fathers of the Republic had not been openly attacked except by the faction of which Mr. Calhoun had been the leader. . . . What stirred up the bitter waters anew? What

[1] Chicago *Press & Tribune*, Oct. 21, 1859.

produced that aggression in the South that gives fanaticism like that of Brown a pretext for such deeds as have just been done in Virginia? Are the Republicans responsible? Did they break up the old compact between the North and the South? Did they disregard the policy and forget the traditions of the Fathers? . . . Did they carry bloodshed to Kansas in the attempt to plant Slavery there by fire and the sword? Did they awaken the passions of hate and revenge by which the country has been torn, and by which slave insurrections with the aid of white men are made possible? Let the Democrats reply! If the Republicans did none of these things, they have none of their consequences to answer for. Let the fear and trembling that have run through the Old Dominion and which will haunt the pillow of every slaveholder in the land, be charged to the account of those who have set the causes in motion. Let the Democracy of the North — particularly of the Northwest — who, under the lead of Douglas, have stopped at nothing to degrade Freedom and elevate Slavery, bear the burdens which their causeless criminality had imposed upon them. Republican skirts are clear. . . .

Such was the supercharged beginning of a rising tide of political criminations and recriminations which was to make the John Brown raid one of the most sensational events in American history. In a few days every issue of every paper was saying something about the affair, remarks colored according to each editor's political hue.

Meantime a party contest was going on in Lincoln's home congressional district. The Democratic incumbent, Thomas L. Harris, close friend of Douglas, had died some months before, and Democrat John A. McClernand and Republican John M. Palmer were fighting a hot battle for the seat. In the last two weeks of the canvass Lincoln worked hard to help Palmer win in this normally Democratic district. On the twenty-seventh Palmer and McClernand courted Springfield votes in a joint debate at the courthouse. Both parties were demonstrating relentlessly.[1] After the debate "the Springfield Republican Club, headed by a band of music, and joined by a large concourse of our citizens, paraded through the streets in torchlight procession, with fire rockets, flags and banners flying; after which they marched to the American House, where Judge Palmer was stopping.

[1] *Illinois State Journal*, Oct. 29, 1859.

"The Judge being called out, addressed the crowd in a neat and eloquent speech. The line then again formed and escorted Judge Palmer to the Republican Head Quarters, where a lively and enthusiastic meeting was held.

"The first speech was made by our eloquent townsman, J. E. Rosette, Esq., who portrayed in livid colors, the base purposes to which the Democracy have prostituted the constitution and the government. . . . His remarks were loudly cheered.

"Samuel Parks, Esq., of Logan county, followed and made a most able vindication of the principles of the Republican party, which he showed were those taught by Washington, Jefferson and the fathers of the constitution, and repelled with merited indignation the vile slanders which dough-faced demagogues are uttering against them.

"When Mr. Parks closed, Judge Palmer was again called up, and spoke for three quarters of an hour. . . . Every sentence was a hit and was greeted with round after round of applause. . . .

"As he sat down the crowd discovered Mr. Lincoln in the back part of the hall, and the hurrah after hurrah for 'old Abe' which went up, could have been heard all over town. In answer to their call, he went forward and addressed them in his well known eloquent and impressive manner, bringing down the house time and again by the pungency and power of his oratory."

Lincoln had received a letter from a Pennsylvania politician, one Frazer, suggesting a Cameron-Lincoln ticket for the Party. His reply was subtly worded, covering all possible contingencies: "It certainly is important to secure Pennsylvania for the Republicans in the next presidential contest, and not unimportant to also secure Illinois. As to the ticket you name, I shall be heartily for it after it shall have been fairly nominated by a Republican national convention; and I cannot be committed to it before. For my single self, I have enlisted for the permanent success of the Republican cause, and for this object I shall labor faithfully in the ranks, unless, as I think not probable, the judgment of the party shall assign me a different position. If the Republicans of the great State of Pennsylvania shall present Mr. Cameron as their candidate for the Presidency, such an indorsement for his fitness for the place could scarcely be deemed insufficient. Still, as I would not like the public to know, so I would not like myself to know, I had entered a combination with any man to the prejudice of all others whose friends respectively may consider them preferable." [1]

As Election Day neared Lincoln did his best to help Palmer win. Though hardly hopeful, he wrote several letters exhorting friends to bring out every possible vote for Palmer.[2] On the evening of November 4 he addressed to the people of the nearby hamlet of Mechanicsburg "a most able and eloquent speech." [3]

He arraigned the Democratic party for the agitation which now exists throughout the country showing that they and they alone, were responsible for it all, and urged that sectionalism and wrangling on the slavery question would never be brought to an end until the power of the so-called Democratic party was broken in the nation. Douglas, the prime mover in the conspiracy must be rebuked, and in his own home. The absorbed attention and earnest enthusiasm which greeted him showed that his remarks told with powerful effect.

Elections over, and the reconvening of Congress a month off, the interesting game of President-guessing became important again and occupied much space in the press. The *Press & Tribune* on October 25 had carried a tiny item: "PRESIDENTIAL. — The Aledo *Record* and the Rock Island *Register* favor the nomination of Hon. Abraham Lincoln for the Presidency." [4] Three days earlier: "The Greenville *Advocate* is out for Senator Trumbull for President, and Hickman, of Pennsylvania, for Vice President." [5] On Election Day Lincoln read in Springfield's *Journal* a story clipped from the faraway Boston *Traveler:* "A western paper starts a 'Chase and Bates' ticket for the Opposition. It is not a bad one . . . but wouldn't a 'Read and Lincoln' ticket do as well? Ohio we are sure of, and

[1] Lincoln to Frazer, Nov. 1, 1859; *Works,* Vol. V, pp. 257–258.
[2] *Works,* Vol. V, p. 258. Tracy, pp. 118–119.
[3] *Illinois State Journal,* Nov. 7, 1859.
[4] Chicago *Press & Tribune,* Oct. 25, 1859; also Canton *Register,* Nov. 1, and *Central Illinois Gazette,* Dec. 14.
[5] Chicago *Press & Tribune,* Oct. 22.

Missouri we can't get, do what we may; but Pennsylvania and Illinois are states worth fighting for, and cannot be had without hard fighting for." [1]

Next day the *Journal* carried a proud reminder clipped from one of the early Lincoln-for-President papers, the Olney *Times*.[2]

On the 12th of November, 1858,[3] we placed the name of this eminent Statesman at the head of our columns as our choice for the Presidency in 1860, and it is with no little pride and satisfaction that we see the name has been gaining favor not only in Illinois but throughout the whole Union. His triumphant defense of the principles of the Republican party during the canvass of '58 in this state, has engraved his name on the tablets of enduring memory. At the present time no man stands more prominent for the nomination at the Republican National Convention than he does, and no man is more eminently qualified to lead us to victory. . . . It is with pleasure that we see many of the leading journals of our country are hoisting his name to the breeze, and will rally under his standard all who are waiting for deliverance from the bondage of a corrupt Administration.

Two days after the election Lincoln was in Chicago on business; a few miles west of Chicago the Aurora *Beacon* headlined, "THEY SAY OLD ABE IS THE MAN," gave the usual Illinois Republican arguments to convince outsiders who had no personal interest in nominating the Illinois orator, those whose "lively sense of favors to come" was attached to some other Republican, that Lincoln could carry the doubtful states and "has every element of popularity and success." [4] In Lacon two days later the *Illinois Gazette*, less favorable to Lincoln than last year when Jeriah Bonham worked there, published a long discussion of "The Next Presidency." Approvingly quoting the letter of "A Republican" which the *Press & Tribune* ran late in August,[5] restating the argument that Seward could not be elected because he could not get the Fillmore support of 1856 in the doubtful states, this Lacon editor clipped from a

[1] *Illinois State Journal,* Nov. 8, 1859.
[2] *Illinois State Journal,* Nov. 9.
[3] Since the original of this paper has been lost, we cannot know for certain whether the Olney *Times* first came out for Lincoln on November 12 or on November 19, as a reliable secondary source dates it. Cf. above p. 62. But the difference is not important.
[4] Aurora *Beacon,* Nov. 10.
[5] Cf. p. 95.

Pennsylvania paper, the Harrisburg *Telegraph*, the alternative suggestion that the Republicans nominate Cameron for President, Lincoln for Vice President. "To this ticket there should not be a single dissenting voice in the Republican ranks. Pennsylvania and Illinois must be carried, and with Cameron and Lincoln they can be secured beyond a doubt." [1] The Harrisburg *Telegraph* was the personal organ of Boss Simon Cameron. In the same issue the *Illinois Gazette* corralled the Republican victory news and reaffirmed the opinion "that the opposition, as sure as fate, holds the next Presidential election in their hands." [2]

Since the elections the *Press & Tribune* had been busily and proudly pointing out the trend away from the Democracy. One day they listed in bold type the Republican majority in thirteen Northern states, concluding that "in every state north of Mason and Dixon's line in which elections have been held the present year, except California and Oregon, the Republicans have achieved a triumph. A more brilliant summer's campaign has never been witnessed. It is but the presage of what is to come in the great national contest of 1860." [3]

One day in mid-November while Lincoln was busy with law at Springfield, the *Press & Tribune* ran a penetrating, analytical editorial, two feet long, which soberly discussed the problem the Party faced in selecting their candidate. [4]

PRESIDENTIAL

The Buffalo *Express*, now that the Republican ticket is ascertained to have a majority in New York, makes a strong appeal, or more literally asserts a considerable *claim*, in behalf of Senator SEWARD for the Republican nomination. . . . The Pittsburgh papers in virtue of the larger majority given by Pennsylvania to the Republican or Opposition ticket . . . are equally strenuous in behalf of Judge READ or Senator CAMERON. The St. Louis *Democrat* and *Evening News* are quite solicitous for the nomination of EDWARD BATES. . . . The friends of Gov. CHASE and

---

[1] *Illinois Gazette*, Nov. 12, 1859.
[2] *Illinois Gazette*, Nov. 12, April 16.
[3] Chicago *Press & Tribune*, Nov. 11.
[4] Chicago *Press & Tribune*, Nov. 16.

Gov. BANKS have abstained, wisely as we think, from urging the claims and qualifications of their respective favorites at this time. So also have the adherents of Judge McLEAN and Col. FREMONT. Senator FESSEN-DEN, of Maine, Judge LANE, of Indiana, Senator TRUMBULL and Mr. LINCOLN, of Illinois, and Gov. RAMSEY, of Minnesota, are possible candidates for one or the other of the places on the Presidential ticket in 1860. . . . There are doubtless others who are fairly entitled to have their claims considered in this connection, but since we are here arguing the cause of no one individual, they need not deem themselves underestimated. . . .

We premise that no man has any *claims* on the Republican party for a Presidential nomination that are worth talking about. . . . The right of each in the premises is measured, *first*, by his ability to administer the government on Republican principles; and, *second*, by his strength in the matter of electoral votes. . . .

What man can carry the five Northern states which Fremont lost, or a sufficient number of them to make a majority of the electoral college? The states are New Jersey, Pennsylvania, Indiana, Illinois and California. . . . Does Senator Seward meet the requirement? Has Pennsylvania, or Indiana, or Illinois, indicated him as the man most likely to consolidate the elements of opposition to the Democracy in favor of the Republican party? If he is the man for those states, he is the man for us. If not, not — and there is an end of argument. Can Gov. Chase secure those doubtful but most necessary votes? If so, he is the man. If not, not. Can Judge Read? Can Judge McLean? Can Gov. Bissell? Can Gov. Banks? Can the Hon. Edward Bates? Can Mr. Lincoln, or Mr. Fessenden? Here is the question in a nut-shell. The representatives of the four doubtful states in the National Convention will throw some light upon it. They will exercise an influence on the result quite out of proportion to their numerical strength. . . . We have the utmost faith that the decision will commend itself fully to the judgment of all sections of the country.

A few days later the *Tribune* ran another interesting editorial.[1]

CAMERON AND LINCOLN

We observe that an article from the Lancaster (Pa.) *Examiner and Herald,* is being copied into certain Illinois papers, recommending Simon Cameron of Pennsylvania, for President, and Abraham Lincoln of Illinois, for Vice President, as the ticket which would *certainly* secure a majority

[1] Nov. 19, 1859.

of the electoral college next year. . . . We think these President-makers have commenced altogether too early. . . . But if the persons, who have commenced the agitation, insist upon having a ticket consisting of Cameron and Lincoln, we fancy the Republicans of the Northwest will insist upon turning it end for end, so that it may read LINCOLN FOR PRESIDENT, and Cameron for Vice President. We think they will prefer to put the strongest man at the *top* of the ticket, instead of the bottom. We are as fully warranted in demanding the nomination of Mr. Lincoln for the Presidency as the Lancaster people are in calling for that of Mr. Cameron. . . .

We make these suggestions not to insist that the Republican party . . . shall nominate Mr. Lincoln for the Presidency, but to state what sort of ticket we should prefer.

A few days more, and the *Tribune* had something to say about another dark horse: "A considerable movement seems to be on foot in New England in favor of the nomination of Judge John M. Read of Pennsylvania for the Presidency, as the most available man in the Republican ranks." [1] A sketch of Read's career, clipped from the Providence *Journal,* followed, after which came this: "The Norwich *Courier,* one of the ablest journals in Connecticut, speaks of a strong feeling in that section in favor of the Hon. Abraham Lincoln, of Illinois, for the Presidency or Vice Presidency." Editor Baker of Springfield spotted this encouragement from the East and ran it in the *Journal* two days later.[2] Then three days after that, the *Journal* ran an item clipped from a neutral sheet, the Kendall (Ill.) *Clarion* [3]: "ABRAHAM LINCOLN. — There are a great many influential journals, not only in the west, but also in the middle and eastern states, who have expressed themselves in favor of the man whose name heads this article, as a candidate for the Presidency. Although not a politician and having nothing to expect from him, elected or not, we would be glad to see that gentleman the candidate of the Republican party in 1860 for that office."

Far more important than newspaper gossip concerning Lincoln for President or Vice President was a new drift of opinion among

[1] Nov. 21, 1859.
[2] *Illinois State Journal,* Nov. 23.
[3] *Illinois State Journal,* Nov. 26.

certain Republican leaders. As the strongest Republican of the important doubtful state of Illinois, Lincoln was being seriously considered by several presidential hopefuls as a possible running mate. Joseph Medill of the Chicago *Press & Tribune,* an energetic Chase man, told Chase about the new development. "The Pennsylvanians are settling down on Cameron and Reed [*sic*]. . . . Both . . . are making overtures to Lincoln friends to have him run for Vice P. (Bank's friends have been throwing out feelers to the same end). This has set Lincoln's friends to talking of him for the first place on the ticket, on the ground that he is a . . . more available man than either Cameron or Reed — even in Pa. We have had several visitors from Pittsburg, Harrisburg, Lancaster & Phila. to negotiate for C. or R., with L." [1] Another Chase man reported from Michigan. "It is very strongly talked here that Hon. Abram Lincoln of Ill. will receive the nomination for Vice President." He advised against it, judging that Lincoln would not make the best running mate for Chase.[2]

We should like to know what Lincoln's reactions were to all these morsels of political gossip, but he gave no hint. He certainly saw and pondered them all, as it was his business to do. How much more we would know about Lincoln's hopes, as the presidential year drew nigh, if we could discover the nature of his psychology when he read in the *Press & Tribune* as November neared its end, this very significant presidential item. Clipped from the Philadelphia *Press* was a list of persons "who have been named in connection with the next Presidency." [3]

Illinois — Stephen A. Douglas.

Kentucky — John J. Crittenden, James Guthrie, John C. Breckenridge [*sic*].

Oregon — Joseph Lane.

Tennessee — John Bell, Andrew Johnson.

California — John C. Fremont.

New York — Daniel S. Dickinson, Horatio Seymour, Wm. H. Seward.

Michigan — Lewis Cass.

[1] Medill to Chase, Oct. 30, 1859; Chase MSS., Hist. Soc. of Pa.
[2] J. H. Maze to Chase, Dec. 28, 1859; Chase MSS.
[3] Nov. 28, 1859. *Central Illinois Gazette,* Dec. 14, 1859.

Mississippi — Jefferson Davis, Albert G. Brown, James Thompson.

Virginia — R. M. T. Hunter, Henry A. Wise, Wm. L. Goggin, John Minor Botts, A. H. H. Stuart, W. C. Rives.

Texas — Gen. Sam Houston.

Louisiana — John Slidell.

Georgia — A. H. Stephens, H. Cobb.

Massachusetts — N. P. Banks, Charles Sumner, Edward Everett, R. C. Winthrop.

Maine — Wm. Pitt Fessenden.

Ohio — Thomas Corwin, John McLean, Salmon P. Chase.

Pennsylvania — Simon Cameron, John M. Read, Geo. M. Dallas, James Buchanan.

Missouri — Edward Bates, Thurston Polk, J. S. Green.

Alabama — Wm. L. Yancy [sic].

New Hampshire — Frank Pierce, J. P. Hale.

South Carolina — James H. Hammond, James L. Orr.

What a sloshing of cold water on all political dreams of Abraham Lincoln this must have been! The Philadelphia *Press* was an influential sheet, published by the famous journalist and politician, John W. Forney. Forney had once been the journalistic shadow of James Buchanan, but since his split with the President over patronage, had turned Republican. Looking over the hazy panorama of presidential possibilities, Forney listed a crowd of forty-five politicians, some of them so obscure in history that even the historical specialist can say, "Who the deuce were W. C. Rives, James Thompson, Thurston Polk, J. S. Green?" Yet the name Abraham Lincoln was conspicuously absent.

Perhaps Lincoln did not see Forney's disheartening roster until several days after its appearance, for on a cold day at November's end he took a train west, setting out on his final political peregrination of the year. He went to Kansas at the behest of two Kansas editors, Daniel Wilder of the Elwood *Free Press*, and his old friend Mark Delahay of the Leavenworth *Times*. In July, two weeks before his first Western trip, Lincoln read in the *Journal* that Wilder's paper had declared its presidential preference: Seward for President, Lincoln for Vice President.[1] Lincoln reached St. Joseph,

---

[1] Elwood *Free Press*, clipped in *Illinois State Journal*, July 29, 1859.

Missouri, on December 1, where he was met by the two journalist-politicians. They took no chances of having the famous orator lose his way, for an election was coming on December 6, and Lincoln's job was ostensibly to create as many Republican votes as possible. Delahay and Wilder were certain that antislavery candidates would win, but sought to build up their personal prestige as associates and sponsors of the man now recognized as the ablest Republican orator of the West. In St. Joseph Lincoln was anxious to see all the late newspapers he could get. Wilder procured them and Lincoln perused the latest news about John Brown, whose execution was near. In the cold wind of evening the trio sat on a big log at the bank of the muddy Missouri River, waiting for the ferry to transport them to tiny Elwood, Kansas.[1]

Reaching Elwood, Lincoln as usual looked down at the heel sartorially, and in addition was feeling "under the weather" after his long two-day trip on comfortless trains. But politicians must make speeches, so that evening he addressed a crowd in the rambling frontier village's largest hall, the hotel dining room. Avoiding discussion of local issues, Lincoln pointed out the national significance of the impending election, in which Kansas would at last make secure its position as a free state. He used his familiar argument: when the Republic was young nobody said "that slavery is a good thing"; the slave trade was cut off to help slavery disappear and the word slavery kept out of the Constitution so that future generations might not be reminded that bondage once existed in America. The Kansas Territory, he said, "has had a marked history," with strife and bloodshed, with "both parties . . . guilty of outrages." Not the best way to settle disputes, that. "There is a peaceful way of settling these questions — the way adopted by government until a recent period. The bloody code has grown out of the new policy in regard to the government of territories."[2]

Mr Lincoln, in conclusion, adverted briefly to the Harper's Ferry affair He believed the attack of Brown wrong for two reasons. It was a violation

[1] Barton, *President Lincoln*, Vol. I, pp. 19–20. Angle, *Lincoln, 1854–1861*, p. 309.
[2] Angle, *New Letters*, p. 229.

of law; and it was, as all such attacks must be, futile as to any effect it might have on the extinction of a great evil.

"We have a means provided for the expression of our belief in regard to slavery — it is through the ballot box. . . . John Brown has shown great courage, rare unselfishness. . . . But no man, North or South, can approve of violence or crime."

Next day Lincoln went on a cold thirty-mile ride west to Troy, where he addressed a small group, then headed south across the windswept prairie to Doniphan. Another speech there; then by evening he reached Atchison, delivering speech number three. This was the Friday on which the State of Virginia sprung a trap under the feet of old John Brown and he slowly choked to death at the end of a rope specially made of cotton for the occasion.

Saturday morning found Lincoln voyaging down the river toward Leavenworth, current home port of his soldier-of-fortune friend, Mark Delahay, who had arranged that Lincoln should make the chief address of his Kansas junket there. A brilliant reception greeted him; several hundred lively Republicans formed a parade. "Along the sidewalks a dense crowd moved with the procession. All the doors, windows, balconies and porticos were filled with men and women, all anxious to get a sight of honest old Abe. On arriving at the Mansion House, the concourse halted, and three long and loud cheers were given for Lincoln." [1]

That evening he rose before a crowd which packed Stockton's Hall. He pointed out that Kansas would soon become a state, and as such would have to form "a policy in relation to domestic slavery. . . . It must deal with the institution as being *wrong* or as *not* being wrong." The speaker then gave in detail that unanswerable argument of his which showed how "the early action of the General Government upon the question" indicated plainly "that the early policy was based on the idea of slavery being wrong; and tolerating it so far, and only so far, as the necessity of its actual presence required." The Kansas-Nebraska Act had destroyed that tradition. He said, "You, the people of Kansas, furnish the example of the

[1] Leavenworth *Register*, in Angle, *New Letters*, p. 230.

first application of this new policy. At the end of about five years, after having almost continual struggles, fire and bloodshed, over this very question, and after having framed several State Constitutions, you have, at last, secured a free-State constitution under which you will probably be admitted into the Union. You have at last, at the end of all this difficulty, attained what we, in the old Northwestern Territory, attained without any difficulty at all." He argued at length to show how popular sovereignty had utterly failed in its promise to give territories greater control over their own affairs and end slavery troubles. This led him to loose his broadside against the Douglas principle: it had been almost killed by the Dred Scott decision; it would revive the African slave trade; it would have fastened slavery upon Kansas if a few thousand slaves had been living there before state organization had been put through; therefore it was useless as a device against slavery expansion.

On the side of practical politics, Lincoln argued that the Republican Party stood neither sectional nor radical. Republicanism did not endanger the Union; "our policy is exactly the policy of the men who made the Union. . . . Old John Brown has just been executed for treason against a state. We cannot object, even though he agreed with us in thinking slavery wrong. That cannot excuse violence, bloodshed, and treason. It could avail him nothing that he might think himself right. So, if constitutionally we elect a president, and therefore you undertake to destroy the Union, it will be our duty to deal with you as Old John Brown has been dealt with. We shall try to do our duty. We hope and believe that in no section will a majority so act as to render such extreme measures necessary." [1]

Delahay's paper reported that the "immense crowd" breathlessly hung on Lincoln's words, roared approval at the end. "Truly," said this cautious journalist, "never did a man win the affections of an audience so completely as did Mr. Lincoln." [2]

---

[1] Angle, *New Letters*, pp. 230–235.
[2] Barton, *President Lincoln*, Vol. I, p. 37.
In the interests of scientific history, I think it well to take time here to correct a mistake of Lincoln's editors, Nicolay and Hay. Nicolay and Hay discovered among Lin-

For three days more Lincoln stayed on at Leavenworth, discovering old friends who had gone West, making himself personally agreeable on all sides as a politician should. On Monday afternoon "he delivered another speech to an immense audience." Tuesday was Election Day; then next morning Lincoln started home, reaching Springfield Thursday evening after two weary days on jittery trains.[1]

The last three weeks of Lincoln's year were busy ones of law and politics. He wrote numerous letters skillfully manipulating the tenuous wires of politics. Norman Judd in particular required attention. The Wentworth clique of Chicago Republicans were trying hard to destroy Judd's leading position in the Party, and Judd had grown restive under the attack. He sued Wentworth's Chicago *Democrat* for libel, asking $100,000 damages.[2] Lincoln on his return from Kansas found a long letter from Judd awaiting him, the writer complaining because Lincoln had not publicly denied whispered stories that Judd had been guilty of treachery against him. Replying, Lincoln insisted that he *had* denied such stories on all hands every time he heard them, but since Judd wanted something more, he would send a formal vindication. "As to the charge of your intriguing for Trumbull against me, I believe as little of that as any other charge. . . . I do not understand Trumbull and myself to be rivals. You know I am pledged not to enter a struggle with him for the seat in the Senate now occupied by him; and yet

coln's papers, "a number of disconnected sheets of autograph manuscript," an undated speech the content of which indicated that Lincoln intended the words for a Kansas audience. So they published these pages as "Speeches In Kansas, December 1–5, 1859" (*Works,* Vol. V, pp. 260–281). The fact is that Lincoln never delivered this speech. Internal evidence, along with Lincoln's letters to Delahay (Tracy, pp. 99 and 103; *Works,* Vol. V, p. 128; Hertz, Vol. II, pp. 752–753) prove that Lincoln wrote most of this speech in March or April to deliver before the Kansas Republican Convention of May. Lincoln wrote the first seven pages (260–267) in late August or early September as his reaction to Douglas' *Harper's* essay, filing the pages away on top of the undelivered Kansas speech. So Nicolay found them. Unable to attend the Kansas convention, Lincoln wrote instead to Delahay a letter of advice on how the convention should declare itself. Then in September Lincoln used the main arguments of these first-draft pages, at times word for word, in his speeches at Columbus, Dayton, Cincinnati, Indianapolis. Then when he finally reached Kansas in December, his speeches were very different from that given in his *Works.*

[1] Angle, *New Letters,* p. 236. Angle, *Lincoln, 1854–1861,* p. 310.
[2] Chicago *Press & Tribune,* Dec. 3, 1859.

I would rather have a full term in the Senate than in the Presidency." [1]

A few days later Lincoln sent Judd the desired vindication, addressed to "our old Whig friends," those who were gunning for Judd the former Democrat. It was very carefully worded to avoid allowing the public to read between the lines and glimpse disharmony.[2]

While keeping Illinois Republican politics in as much order as possible, Lincoln never ceased to think about the election of 1860. In a personal note to Judd, sent along with the absolution, he wrote: "I find some of our friends here attach more consequence to getting the national convention into our state than I did, or do. Some of them made me promise to say so to you." Judd was the Illinois member of the Republican National Central Committee, which body would soon meet and fix the site of the important convention. Lincoln's words to Judd show clearly his hearty skepticism that his own "dark horse" race for leadership of his Party would come to anything in the way of a place on the national ticket. But Judd saw, as did those whom Lincoln called "some of our friends here," that their man would certainly lose nothing by an attempt to secure the Republican Convention for Illinois.

From Ohio came a letter which gave Lincoln's self-confidence a mighty boost. With the endorsement of practically every Republican bigwig of Ohio (Chase excepted) came a request that Lincoln send copies of his debates with Douglas, along with his Ohio speeches of 1859, for publication in permanent form. These speeches, wrote the Ohioans, as "luminous and triumphant expositions of the doctrines of the Republican party," would "make a document of great practical service to the Republican party in the approaching Presidential contest." [3]

Lincoln's first attempt to publish the debates in book form had failed. Unwise in publisher's ways, he had told Publisher Ross that

[1] Lincoln to Judd, Dec. 9, 1859; *Works*, Vol. V, pp. 281–282.
[2] Lincoln to Messrs. Dole, Hubbard, and Brown, Dec. 14, 1859; *Works*, Vol. V, pp. 283–284.
[3] Ryan, "Lincoln and Ohio," pp. 107–109.

he could use Lincoln's scrapbook copy of the debates only by printing the book in Springfield under Lincoln's supervision, so afraid
was he of losing the copy he had laboriously clipped and pasted.
This amazing request was tantamount to saying that the book must
be published without the author sending the manuscript! But by
December Lincoln knew better, and he sent the copy without any
fuss, glad to have the opportunity of using books along with politics
to make himself a national leader.[1]

The day after he wrote to his Ohio friends about debate publication was December 20, according to the calendar on the shabby
wall of the office of Lincoln and Herndon, Attorneys and Counsel-
lors At Law. Ambition running strong and hopes high, Lincoln sat
down and wrote a long letter to Jesse Fell. It contained the famous
autobiography. Recent developments had convinced Lincoln that
he ought to follow the advice Fell had given him in Bloomington
just a year earlier. He explained: "Herewith is a little sketch, as
you requested. There is not much of it, for the reason, I suppose,
that there is not much of me. If anything be made out of it, I
wish it to be modest, and not to go beyond the material. If it were
thought necessary to incorporate anything from any of my speeches,
I suppose there would be no objection. Of course it must not appear
to have been written by myself." [2]

Catching up with the newspaper gossip he had missed while away
in Kansas, Lincoln found many things which interested him profoundly. On the front page of the *Press & Tribune* of December
3, the day after John Brown's hanging, he read columns that presaged an apotheosizing of the man who, for the cause of freedom,
met his punishment so heroically — solemn harbingers for the
future of the Union: a long editorial eulogizing Brown as a warrior
for liberty; a requiem composed by a local poet for the melancholy
occasion; a long story which told how churches all over Chicago
had held "meetings in sympathy with John Brown" and piously

---

[1] Lincoln to G. M. Parsons and others, Dec. 19, 1859; *Works,* Vol. V, p. 285.
[2] *Works,* Vol. V, p. 286.

offered up prayers for his soul; a telegraphic story soberly giving details of the hanging.

Two days later the papers carried the first stories about the assembling of the new Congress. Everybody expected a session of bitter conflict and acrimony, a long fight over organization since no Party had a majority, Republicans commanding only a plurality.[1]

Lincoln also read and pondered, in the somber security of his dusty law office, press items of even greater interest because they concerned himself. The *Illinois State Journal* of the fifth clipped a story from the Reading (Pa.) *Journal*.[2] Approvingly quoting some of Lincoln's remarks to Kentuckians in his Cincinnati speech, this Pennsylvania sheet continued: —

Of unbounded personal popularity and irreproachable integrity, Mr. Lincoln has no superior as a statesman throughout the great West; and whilst he is a decided Republican his views are so moderate and conservative as to commend him to the consideration of all men embracing the great Opposition party of the country. . . . The West has never had a President except for the short month in which Gen. Harrison occupied that position, and she certainly has claims which it will be difficult to set aside, should she unite upon one of her leading men, more especially should she put forward *as her candidate,* the Hon. Abraham Lincoln; or as he is more familiarly termed at home, "Honest Old Abe, the Giant Killer." A Kentuckian by birth, the wild enthusiasm his name would excite throughout the great West, would make it a matter of perfect indifference who might be the nominee of the office-holders clique about to assemble at Charleston.

The Keystone State conceived a liking for Candidate Lincoln because, as an old Henry Clay Whig, he was right on the issue of their beloved tariff.

And Lincoln's confidence expanded as he saw what invaluable publicity accrued from his autumn oratorical labors. Next day the *Journal* ran a brief story on his Leavenworth speech of the third, claiming that "his audience comprised the largest political gathering

[1] Chicago *Press & Tribune,* Dec. 5, 1859.
[2] *Illinois State Journal,* Dec. 5.

which ever met in Kansas." Three days later the *Tribune* clipped on the front page the Leavenworth *Register's* story of Lincoln's rousing reception, and excerpts from its synopsis of the speech.[1] Three days more, and the *Journal* likewise clipped the Leavenworth *Register*, adding that "The Leavenworth papers speak of the speech as being the ablest ever delivered upon the soil of Kansas."

Stoddard's *Central Illinois Gazette* on December 7 printed extended remarks (a thousand words) on the subject, "Who Shall Be President?" Stoddard explained that owing "to the vastness of the interests depending on the political campaign now commencing . . . we do not consider it possible for the office of President . . . to become the personal property of any particular politician, how great a man soever he may be esteemed by himself and his partisans. . . . The truest wisdom for the Republican party in this campaign will be found in such a conservative and moderate course as shall secure the respect and consideration even of our enemies, and shall not forget National compacts within which we are acting and by which we are bound: and the proper recognition of this . . . should be allowed its due influence in the selection of our standard-bearer." Discussing the situation in Pennsylvania and Illinois, he concluded, "If these two states can be added to the number of those in which the party seems to possess an unassailable superiority, the day is ours. . . ."

As for Illinois it is the firm and fixed belief of our citizens that for one or the other of the offices in question, no man will be so sure to consolidate the party vote of this state, or will carry the great Mississippi Valley with a more irresistible rush of popular enthusiasm, than our distinguished fellow citizen,

ABRAHAM LINCOLN.

We, in Illinois, know him well, in the best sense of the word, *a true democrat*, a man of the people, whose strongest friends and supporters are the hard-handed and strong-limbed laboring men. . . . A true friend of freedom, having already done important service for the cause, and proved his abundant ability for still greater service; yet a staunch conservative,

---

[1] Chicago *Press & Tribune*, Dec. 9, 1859.

whose enlarged and liberal mind descends to no narrow view, but sees both sides of every great question, and of whom we need not fear that fanaticism on the one side, or servility on the other, will lead him to the betrayal of any trust. We appeal to our brethren of the Republican press for the correctness of our assertions.

A few days after Lincoln wrote out his autobiography and sent it off to Bloomington, the nation read that the Republican Party's national committeemen had met and located the Party's 1860 convention. For several months Western Republicans had been talking about the importance of the West to the Party, pointing out how the East and South had monopolized important Government positions, demanding that "the great West" be given its due by placing a Westerner at the head of the Republican ticket.[1] In 1856, the Democratic Party had bowed to the voting strength of the West by holding its convention at Cincinnati. This set an example for Republicans; for, considering Seward's position, it seemed highly unlikely that a Westerner would be made the presidential nominee. Late in December the national committee met in New York to make the decision and write a formal call. Committeeman Judd, abetted by other Westerners, was ready to manage unobtrusively a victory for Chicago and Lincoln. Friends of Seward argued that the convention should meet in some New York city; Chase men were sure Cleveland or Columbus would be the ideal location. Bates men told how the Party would actually carry Missouri if the convention would only meet in St. Louis. Quite a struggle was developing, when Judd secured consideration of Chicago as a compromise. Tongue in cheek, he pointed out that since Illinois had no prominent candidate of its own, Chicago, neutral ground, would satisfactorily break the deadlock. The committee swallowed hook, line, sinker.[2]

When the press reported that "The National Republican Committee in session at the Astor House, New York, yesterday, decided to hold the great Convention at CHICAGO on the 13th of June

[1] Chicago *Press & Tribune*, Aug. 13, 16, 1859. F. I. Herriott, "Republican Presidential Preliminaries in Iowa — 1859–1860," *Annals of Iowa*, Vol. IX, pp. 245–249. J. L. Sellers, "James R. Doolittle," *Wisconsin Magazine of History*, Vol. XVII, pp. 288–290.
[2] *Memoirs of Gustave Koerner*, Vol. II, p. 80.

next," the official explanation of course said nothing about the squab-
ble between champions of the three leading candidates. The public
was told that Indianapolis had been considered, passed over because
of lodging inadequacies. St. Louis and Chicago were left, and Chicago won because the Party could not carry Missouri and would
only waste its substance by meeting in St. Louis.[1] Said Gustave
Koerner in reminiscence: "I am pretty certain that, had the Convention been held at any other place, Lincoln would not have been
nominated."

The day after Lincoln composed his autobiography, Stoddard's
paper put at the head of his editorial columns, in huge black
letters [2]: —

FOR PRESIDENT IN 1860,
ABRAHAM LINCOLN,
OF ILLINOIS.

FOR GOVERNOR OF ILLINOIS,
LEONARD SWETT,
of Bloomington, M'Lean County.

A week later Springfield's *Journal* clipped from the Greensburg
(Indiana) *Republican* an editorial calling for a Lincoln and Cameron
ticket.[3]

. . . Who then is fit to be the standard bearer of the Republican party
in the great contest of 1860? Undoubtedly, the best man in the Union for
that position is Abraham Lincoln, of Illinois. He is the ablest, the most
reliable leader and exponent of Republican principles to be found in the
party. This every man is bound to acknowledge who is acquainted with
his recent contest with Stephen A. Douglas, in Illinois. . . . Mr. Lincoln
is a national man — a true and tried friend of the Union. . . . He is, in
our opinion, the most available man the Republicans have, and were he
and Simon Cameron, of Pennsylvania, nominated for the Presidency and
Vice Presidency, there could be no doubt of their success.

[1] Chicago *Press & Tribune*, Dec. 22, 1859.
[2] *Central Illinois Gazette*, Dec. 21.
[3] *Illinois State Journal*, Dec. 28.

It is utter foolishness for Republicans to talk about nominating some old, broken down Whig, or of uniting with the Americans on some Fillmore man, when they have such men, in their own ranks, as Lincoln and Cameron. If the Republican party wants to accomplish anything . . . let it nominate Republicans, and cease to clamor about men who have no sympathy with it. . . . Lincoln and Cameron is the ticket the Republican party wants.

And so it happened, Lincoln writing on Christmas Day a routine letter to Senator Trumbull concerning distribution of Government documents,[1] that the eventful year 1859 passed into history. It had been a valuable twelvemonth for Abraham Lincoln, who only a year before was depressed by defeat and pecuniary embarrassment. He had followed the good advice of another eminent literary American who likewise suffered from attacks of blackest melancholia; he had ridden boldly in search of political Eldorado, traveled four thousand miles to deliver twenty-three political speeches, not one of which was really necessary in the sense that his 1858 debates were a political duty. Partly the result of his own efforts, but mainly the fortuitous effect of events beyond his control, was the creation of a burgeoning presidential boom, the future of which was quite conjectural. And how did the man himself regard these "Lincoln for President" winds? On December 9 he had written to Trumbull, "I would rather have a full term in the Senate than in the Presidency." Looking ahead a bit, we can be certain that Lincoln did not flatter himself that the coming year would make him President-elect of his nation. But he encouraged the "Lincoln for President" men to the best of his ability, because their efforts in pushing him forward would materially aid him in his current plan to win Douglas' seat in the Senate when the Little Giant should next come up for re-election.

[1] Tracy, p. 122.

CHAPTER IV

Political Plumbing

> Double, double toil and trouble,
> Fire burn, and caldron bubble.

MORE LIKE a witch's caldron than the traditional political pot, which quadrennially boiled up furiously, importantly, but gave off nothing more dangerous than copious steam, was the aspect which the 1860 political pot assumed at the opening of the presidential year. As week followed week national affairs now and again added one ingredient after another —

> For a charm of powerful trouble,
> Like a hell-broth boil and bubble.

A *Tribune* editorial of mid-January sounds the swelling crescendo of danger [1]: —

No man who loves his country but is shocked and horrified by the daily proceedings at Washington. Threatened violence of action and gross intemperance of speech in the House, furious criminations and recriminations in the Senate, open declarations in favor of disunion, and excitement which is without parallel in the history of the republic — these have filled every patriot with well-founded alarm — alarm not for the perpetuity of the Union, but for the peace, good name and dignity of the country, all imperiled by the events of the hour. . . .

[1] Chicago *Press & Tribune*, Jan. 19, 1860.

"From the moment of John Brown's raid and the dramatic importance given in the House of Representatives to Hinton Rowan Helper's *Impending Crisis* to the day of the election, there was no moment when politics were not under popular domination. . . . The tide of the 'irrepressible conflict' had . . . already set in. . . . The resulting popular reaction against slavery far exceeded any ever before known." [1] Because in those days politics were the national sport, the vast political kettle was never without subtle stirrings somewhere in its depths. But the presidential season of 1860 found it becoming so agitated that a Republican cohort of Abraham Lincoln could look back on 1859 as "comparatively a quiet" year,[2] in spite of Broderick and Brown and Douglas' energetic public efforts to entrench himself as leader of the Democracy, efforts which created violent internecine strife between Northern and Southern wings of the Party in power.[3]

Lincoln himself, in January of the great year which would bring imperious influences to bear on his career, was too busy professionally to spend much time on anything but law.[4] Lincoln and Herndon appeared in dozens of cases as the Federal Court and Supreme Court held sessions in Springfield.[5] When a Chicago Republican leader wrote asking Lincoln for ammunition to aid the Lincoln boom (perhaps at the behest of Norman Judd), the busy lawyer replied, "our Republican friend, J. W. Fell, of Bloomington, Illinois, can furnish you the material for a brief sketch of my history." [6]

This January was the open season for local politicians to busy themselves organizing political clubs. And clubs sprang up spontaneously like beer taverns after Repeal. Politics being in that day the national sport, live citizens with social ambitions joined political clubs instead of bridge or country clubs. Most such clubs were leaves of the political season, but some were permanent. In Springfield, for

---

[1] E. D. Fite, *Presidential Campaign of 1860,* pp. ix–x.
[2] *Memoirs of Gustave Koerner,* Vol. II, p, 71,
[3] Milton, *Eve of Conflict,* pp. 356–369.
[4] Lincoln to Koerner, Jan. 20, 1860; Tracy, *Uncollected Letters of Lincoln,* pp. 129–130.
[5] Angle, *Lincoln, 1854–1861,* pp. 314–318.
[6] Lincoln to Fernando Jones, Jan. 15, 1860; Tracy, p. 123.

instance, was the Young Men's Republican Association, with a headquarters where the boys came to talk things over and read newspapers, holding regular meetings. In the clubroom's front window hung "a handsome transparency . . . on which," rhapsodized Springfield's *Journal*, "is emblazoned the names of the *sixteen States* that have this year enrolled themselves in the Republican ranks. It lights up handsomely at night, and warns the bogus Democracy that next year will put a quietus upon their political aspirations." [1]

One cold, snowy day in early January Lincoln's faithful *Journal* announced [2]: —

REPUBLICANS ATTENTION

A regular meeting of the Young Men's Republican Association will be held on Thursday, January 12th, at half past 7 o'clock, at the headquarters over the new Postoffice Building, for the purpose of making arrangements for the organization of a Lincoln Club. Let every Republican and friend of Abe. Lincoln turn out.

G. B. SIMONDS, Pres.
J. G. STEWART, Sec'y.

A good crowd answered the call, heard a resolution presented which they enthusiastically adopted [3]: —

WHEREAS the great Republican party of this nation will soon enter upon the Presidential canvass of 1860; and *whereas* the Republicans, not only of the State of Illinois but of the whole Union, regard the Hon. A. Lincoln, of this city, as the great expounder and defender of sound National Republican principles; and *whereas we,* as Republicans, desire to use all honorable means to secure his nomination for the President of the United States of America, therefore

Resolved, That the name of this association be and is hereby changed, and be hereafter called the "LINCOLN CLUB" of the city of Springfield.

This inspiring proclamation moved the *Journal* to bestow formally upon Lincoln its support for the presidential nomination.

[1] *Illinois State Journal,* Nov. 16, 1859.
[2] *Illinois State Journal,* Jan. 11 and 12, 1860.
[3] *Illinois State Journal,* Jan. 14.

We doubt not that as the favorite son of Illinois, the suggestion of "Old Abe's" name for the Presidency will meet with a loud and cordial response throughout the state and the entire Northwest. Already, in all directions, the public press are making him their first choice for the nomination. . . .

ABRAHAM LINCOLN has arrived at that period of life when man's mental and physical powers and faculties are in their prime. God gave him a mind of unusual strength, and time and labor and study have made him one of the great men of the land. The purity of his patriotism, his incorruptible integrity and his ability to sustain himself and the country in any position in which he may be placed, no one who knows him can for a moment doubt. The people of Illinois are justified in their determination to place the name of their distinguished citizen before the country for the highest honors in the nation's gift. They do it because they know him; because they have confidence in him as *a man for the times;* . . . because he is a conservative National Republican.

The Great West will give a telling vote at the next Presidential election, and the candidacy of ABRAHAM LINCOLN will secure that vote for the Republicans beyond controversy. . . . The Republicans of other states could not cast their votes for a worthier, or abler, or more available man. . . .

The Republicans of Illinois will sustain and support . . . the Presidential nominee of the Chicago Convention, whoever he may be; but they respectfully, yet earnestly, call upon the Republicans of the Union to weigh the claims, estimate the qualifications and availability, and consider the fitness and propriety of giving the nomination to Abraham Lincoln of Illinois.

Such editorializing was fulsome, exaggerated, expressing not fact but hope. "Old Abe's" stock, however, was undeniably rising in the West. Perhaps by convention time he would really be regarded as "one of the great men of the land" by Republicans living outside Illinois. Early in January the *Press & Tribune* had approvingly announced that Ohio Republicans were publishing the Lincoln-Douglas debates as a campaign document.[1] This story the *Journal* clipped (January 12), adding that the publication "is a most delicate and expressive compliment. . . . The name of 'Old Abe,' the leader of the great Republican army of the North West, has become a word

[1] Jan. 10, 1860.

of power and might, and will we believe, be their rallying cry in the great approaching contest."

Having come out so vigorously for Lincoln, the *Journal* editors, poring over newspapers which came in daily as exchanges, carefully clipped the press items favoring Lincoln while ignoring those which argued for other candidates.[1]

Chicago's aggressive *Tribune* intermittently ran a "vox pop" column labeled "PRESIDENTIAL." This column on January 12 carried three letters, one arguing the claims of Lincoln, one for Seward, one for Chase. Said "L. B. G., of New York City": —

My business takes me over the West for two or three months each winter, and during that time I am scarcely two nights in the same place; hence I hear much said for this and that candidate for the Presidency.

Our amiable and modest friends — called as for a joke *Democrats!* — uniformly nominate for the Republicans that great and good man of my own state, Mr. Seward. The Republicans I find do not all concur with their officious fellow citizens in this. Not that they disregard the claims of Mr. Seward, but think they can suggest a name, stronger in the West, where, after all, the tug of war must come. Names of various distinguished men are mentioned in place of Mr. Seward, but among them all I hear none which seems to bring out such a hearty and enthusiastic response as that of your own good citizen, Hon. Abraham Lincoln — or rather, in station house and hotel phrase, "OLD ABE." In conversation with a strong Douglas man at Springfield last week, I asked him what would be the result if "Old Abe" was the candidate of the Republicans. He replied, *"It would be devilish bad for us!!"*

A few days earlier three would-be prophets had spoken their preferences. From Wisconsin came an argument for Lincoln, from Iowa a plea for Chase, from Chicago one for Simon Cameron.[2]

Observers were awakening to the fact that the convention's location at Chicago improved the chances of the Illinois favorite son.[3]

The Chicago correspondent of the New York *Herald* writes:
"The friends of Lincoln are highly pleased with the selection of Chicago as the place for holding the Republican National Convention. Many of them

[1] *Illinois State Journal*, Jan. 17, 1860.
[2] Chicago *Press & Tribune*, Jan. 9.
[3] *Illinois State Journal*, Jan. 18.

now declare that his nomination is a foregone conclusion; they even go so far as to assert that Senator Seward will use all his influence for him."

A press story like that gave infinite encouragement to everybody who had a stake in nominating Lincoln. For if politicians could be persuaded that Lincoln had grown so strong that Seward had come to fear him, Lincoln would graduate from the potential dark horse class and become a leading presidential possibility.

Chicago newspapers in January carried an announcement almost every day, along with candidate gossip and alarming news of Congressional bickerings, that some political club would meet at a certain place on a certain date. By the end of January a Republican club had been organized in every ward, with officers, constitution, meeting place, ready to work hard at the great American game. Biggest was the "Young Men's Republican Club of Chicago," which drew up a model organization they hoped other clubs throughout the state would be inspired to emulate.[1] Too, there were special clubs: a Cameron-Lincoln club (working hard to make Lincoln Cameron's running mate whether he liked it or not), "Swedish Republican Club," "Mechanics and Working Men's Club," and the like.[2]

The *Tribune* pointed out the reason why Republicans were organizing so briskly [3]: —

The campaign of 1860 may be said to have commenced with the assembling of Congress in December last. The extraordinary course which the Democratic members of that body entered upon on the very first day of the session . . . has stirred up the masses of the people in the free states, as they were never stirred before. . . . The punic faith which broke down the Missouri Compromise — the outrage and bloodshed which followed upon the plains of Kansas — the new reading of the Federal Constitution by which slavery is made national and freedom sectional — the bold demand for a Congressional slave code and for the re-opening of the African slave trade — the attempt, in short, to administer the government for the sole benefit of three hundred-fifty thousand slave-holders — all these things have aroused the indignation of the masses of the free North

[1] *Illinois State Journal*, Jan. 24, 1860.
[2] Chicago *Press & Tribune*, Jan. and Feb., *passim*.
[3] *Press & Tribune*, Jan. 25.

These feelings find vent, to some extent, in the organization of political clubs. . . . In this city the movement towards organization is remarkable. Numerous clubs have been formed, and the number enrolled in each is constantly increasing. We . . . trust every Republican voter will enroll himself in some of these organizations. . . .

Stoddard's *Central Illinois Gazette,* having placed Lincoln's name at the head of its columns in big black type, gave further explanations why "Old Abe" was the man,[1] in one of those long, verbose editorials which young Stoddard dearly loved to compose. He began: —

When we placed the name of the Hon. Abraham Lincoln at the head of our columns . . . we did so not only as declaring our own individual choice, but believing that we spoke in accordance with the decided feeling of the people of Illinois and of the Northwest generally. We are still of that opinion. . . . We find that the mention of his name in this connection meets with an enthusiastic response in all the region of the country referred to, and that he possesses at the far East and in the middle States a much greater degree of popularity than we had been prepared to believe. All men who have the success of the great cause at heart, and who are able to divest themselves of local feelings and personal predilections, seem to see clearly the force of the elements of which his strength consists, and to recognize in him a man who possesses in an unsurpassed degree that *availability* which will be stronger than all other considerations in determining the Chicago nominations. . . .

Four questions will include most of the important inquiries that the Chicago Convention will make concerning every candidate whose name is brought before it in connection with the presidential nomination.

1st. Is he honest?
2d. Is he capable?
3d. What is his *geographical* position?
4th. What is his political record?

Thirteen hundred words later Stoddard had demonstrated that his man most impressively filled these four requirements. Edward L. Baker thought this worth reprinting, and a week later ran as much of it in the *Journal* as space permitted.[2]

[1] Jan. 18, 1860.
[2] *Illinois State Journal,* Jan. 25.

Springfield's *Journal* on January 17, getting down to cases, had discussed mathematically the Republican prospects, tabulating and discussing how many electoral votes the Republican Party must have to win. Fremont had won 114 votes, all counted safe for 1860. Fremont had failed to carry seven free states: Pennsylvania, Illinois, Indiana, New Jersey, Minnesota, California, Oregon. These were doubtful states of 1860, from which Republicans must secure 38 electoral votes to win.

It is evident therefore that the great battle ground will be Pennsylvania, Illinois, Indiana, and New Jersey. In the last state elections Pennsylvania and Illinois both gave popular majorities for the Republicans and it is next to certain that in the Presidential Campaign with available candidates they will do so again. Looking over the whole field, we regard it that *the success of the Republicans depends upon those two states,* and the Republican nominating Convention should select its candidates with direct reference to the exigency which exists. . . . It is with this view and with the further consideration that the Great West deserves the Presidency, that the Republicans of Illinois present the name of ABRAHAM LINCOLN as their first choice for the nomination. With him at the head of the ticket and the Vice-President from Pennsylvania, we believe that the success of the Republican party will be sure and certain. With any other arrangement the result of the contest cannot be foreseen.

Stoddard, thinking this argument of Baker a good one, returned the compliment.[1]

The Illinois dark horse was acquiring strength in Illinois press gossip as rapidly as could be, but such support, while long on noise, is short on potency. What a wonderful thing for a politician to have local newspapers doing their best to make him President! — a fine thing for his future and a marvelous yarn to relate to his grandchildren. But in the hard actualities of politics, in conventions and secret caucuses, such support means almost nothing. If Lincoln's young boom was really to boom, his candidacy would require that Illinois Republican leaders back him to the limit. In 1859 Lincoln did not receive that essential support. For instance, Orville Brown-

[1] *Central Illinois Gazette,* Jan. 25, 1860.

ing wrote in his diary on October 12: "N. B. Judd Esqr of Chicago here to night. Had long political talk with him. Assured him I would not . . . be a candidate for Governor — He wishes to be. . . . I urged Mr. Bates claims for the Presidency. He is willing to go for him, if he shall appear to be the strongest man, and will place himself on Republican ground." [1] So Browning was actively for Bates; and Judd, Browning reveals, was more interested in making himself Governor than anything else.

By late January conditions were much changed. Wide publicity had augmented Lincoln's personal strength, and Judd's work in bringing the convention to Chicago lent an air of reality to the prospects of any "possibility" from Illinois. In January's last week the lawyer-politicians of Illinois gravitated to Springfield to ply their trade before the Supreme Court and Federal Court in session there. One cold night,[2] a selected group of Republicans assembled in secret caucus in the office of Secretary of State Hatch. Jackson Grimshaw of the State Central Committee (long an Illinois leader, an old Whig like Lincoln, unsuccessful Republican candidate for Congress from the Quincy district in 1858) had on his own initiative urged Lincoln "very strongly" to approve a caucus of his "intimate friends" to arrange for launching a concerted movement in his behalf.[3] Browning was not invited. Besides Grimshaw, Lincoln, and Hatch, the conspirators were: Norman Judd (on hand after having been in Washington the past week looking things over),[4] Leonard Swett, Jesse Dubois, Ward Lamon, John Bunn, Ebenezer Peck, Nehemiah Bushnell, and a few other prominent Republicans.[5] Our most reliable source for what happened at this important gathering, destined to exert so powerful an influence on American history, is Jackson Grimshaw, who for several weeks had been actively identified with a burgeoning movement for organizing Cameron-Lincoln clubs all

---

[1] *Diary of Browning*, Vol. I, p. 382.
[2] Baringer, "Campaign Technique," p. 210.
[3] Lamon, *Lincoln*, p. 424.
[4] *Illinois State Journal*, Jan. 25, 1860, Washington Correspondence.
[5] Lamon, p. 424. Whitney, *Life on the Circuit*, pp. 82–84. Baringer, pp. 210–211. C. A. Church, *History of the Republican Party in Illinois*, pp. 73–74. *Herndon's Lincoln*, p. 366.

over the state.[1] Cameron and Lincoln, politicians were aware, made a natural combination, for if each man could carry his own state victory would be theirs.[2] Since Jackson Grimshaw, state committee-man from Quincy, was the prime mover in calling the conference, what he had in mind is perfectly clear. He wanted to make Lincoln himself and the other leaders of the Illinois Republican machine active members of the Cameron-Lincoln Club. But, by way of compliment, flattery, he planned first to ask Abraham if he desired to be a candidate for President. Grimshaw recalls [3]: —

We all expressed a personal preference for Mr. Lincoln as the Illinois candidate for the Presidency, and asked him if his name might be used at once in connection with the nomination and election. With his characteristic modesty he doubted whether he could get the nomination even if he wished it, and asked until the next morning to answer us whether his name might be announced. Late the next day he authorized us, if we thought proper, to place him in the field.

Ostensibly modest though he was, Lincoln acted the astute politician as he guided the strategy of this private and most important "Lincoln for President" club. Grimshaw, coming to the point, asked Lincoln (with the air of a practical politician making plans to fit every possible circumstance) if, missing the presidential nomination, the men pledged to Lincoln might push him for the Vice Presidency. "No!" was Lincoln's reply — a stroke of consummate strategy. With one declaration he defeated the Cameron-Lincoln plan, wiped out the possibility that, in the complex wire-pullings between late January and the Chicago convention, some of these political friends would be satisfied to acquire for him the second place on the ticket, which he did not want.[4] Doubtless many of these politicians, as they

[1] "Occasional," in *Central Illinois Gazette*, Jan. 4, 1860.
[2] A variation of the plan called for Read of Pennsylvania and Lincoln. (W. Bryce to Chase, Feb. 6, 1860; Chase MSS.)
[3] Grimshaw to Herndon, April 28, 1866; in Herndon and Weik, *Lincoln*, Vol. II, p. 163.
[4] A persistent Lincoln myth tells how Lincoln, after the fame he acquired in the debates, began to hope that he would be the first Republican Vice President, but was made President by the intervention of an omniscient Almighty, or something awesome and mystical. Edwin Markham in his famous poem on Lincoln etches a touching scene: —

converged upon Hatch's office that night, agreed with Grimshaw in thinking the Vice Presidency an office quite large enough for Abe Lincoln.[1] But when they walked back to their lodgings through the cold, dark streets of Springfield, minds clicking with political plans, Lincoln's able strategy caused them (whatever their private and previous opinions) to think of him *for President*. A politician with imagination could easily see that the most effective way to make Lincoln the running mate of Seward or Cameron would be to push Lincoln with all force for the leadership of the Party; then, in the furious welter of plot and counterplot at the convention, trade off Lincoln's presidential strength in return for Seward or Cameron support of Lincoln for Vice President. This, perhaps, explains why these men so readily assented to follow the gleam, to aim high, when Lincoln gave his consent next day. Lincoln did not seriously imagine that the press talk about him for President would actually send him very far along the difficult road to leadership of his Party, but he wanted Illinois to vote for him for President at Chicago to help him succeed Douglas in the Senate four years hence.

Editorial expressions that such and such a man should be President are tossed off easily. But experienced politicians move slowly, cautiously. Lincoln's future, therefore, seemed far less promising in private consultation than in printed opinion. Even his close political friends outside the group which met in secret in Hatch's office were not, at this date, taking the presidential talk seriously. Governor Bissell of Illinois wrote to Salmon P. Chase [2]: —

> When the Norn Mother saw the Whirlwind Hour
> Greatening and darkening as it hurried on,
> She left the Heaven of Heroes and came down
> To make a man to meet the mortal need. . . .

This vice-presidential error is a natural one, considering the position of Seward, and the Lincoln vice presidential vote in 1856. As 1859 closed an Iowa paper remarked that securing the Republican Convention for Chicago was "a stroke of policy . . . on the part of the friends of Lincoln which will doubtless place him upon the ticket for Vice-President." (Sioux City *Register*, Dec. 31, in *Annals of Iowa*, Vol. IX, pp. 249–250.) Henry J. Raymond in his *Life and Public Services of Abraham Lincoln* (p. 100) gives a preposterous story which has Lincoln saying he hopes he will be Vice President because of the salary he would get. One looks through Lincoln's many letters on presidential politics without finding a scrap of evidence that he wanted the Vice Presidency, in contrast to his numerous statements showing his senatorial, then presidential, ambitions.

[1] Nicolay and Hay, *Abraham Lincoln*, Vol. II, p. 258.
[2] W. H. Bissell to Chase, Feb. 4, 1860; Chase MSS.

You have not a few friends in this state, among whom I count myself, who would be very glad to have you nominated at Chicago; and we would ere this have had several papers wheeled into your support, but that our folks have recently taken a notion to talk up Lincoln. . . . Of course while that is so it would be ungracious . . . to start anybody as his seeming rival. Lincoln is everything that we can reasonably ask in a man, and a politician. Still, I do not suppose that many of our friends seriously expect to secure his nomination as candidate for the Presidency. In fact they would be very well satisfied, probably, if he could secure the second place on the ticket.

One tentative plan would have brought Lincoln forward as a Chase puppet. In the summer of 1859 an active Chase worker in the East, James Ashley, had heard it rumored that Edward Bates of Missouri was to be brought forward prominently by having him preside and speak at an Emancipation Republican State Convention to be held in Missouri. Could not this plan, the strategist suggested, be stopped "by letting our friends in Illinois put Lincoln on the track and have our friends in Kentucky — Delaware and Maryland — call similar conventions to this one in Missouri, *if it is to come off*, and put men forward that will go so much farther than Bates as to throw him into the shade?" [1]

Springfield's Lincoln Club was actively in the game, holding weekly meetings with speeches by important Republicans. Billy Herndon and James Conkling had been the orators of the week before, and on February 1 the boys heard Lincoln himself and Jackson Grimshaw, at which meeting the inevitable "large and enthusiastic" audience cheered the announcement that the Republicans of the House of Representatives had finally elected a Speaker, Pennington of New Jersey. This, Lincoln must have reflected, added another name to the long list of Republican "possibilities." In the same paper which announced Pennington's election Lincoln read of a new Republican paper starting in Danville, the *Republican*, and learned that "the Republican flies 'Chase and Lincoln' from its mast-head." [2] Hardly an encouragement.

[1] J. M. Ashley to Chase, Aug. 26, 1859; Chase MSS.
[2] *Illinois State Journal*, Feb. 2, 1860.

With the die cast, with leading Republicans of Illinois committed to a campaign to make Lincoln leader of their Party, Norman Judd wanted no stone left unturned. He had discussed with Lincoln the advisability of bringing to Illinois a man to manage the Lincoln-for-President campaign, having in mind an aggressive young lawyer-politician of New York named Emery A. Storrs.[1] Lincoln thought it over, wrote in reply [2]: —

Whether Mr. Storrs shall come to Illinois and assist in our approaching campaign, is a question of dollars and cents. Can we pay him? If we can, that is the sole question. I consider his services very valuable.

Apparently sly Mr. Judd, knowing Lincoln, had disguised the real work he expected this Mr. Storrs to do by proposing that he be used not for Lincoln personally, but for the Party. Lincoln's letter added some words about Party harmony. "Some folks are pretty bitter toward me about the Dole, Hubbard, and Brown letter." Lincoln valued the services of Judd, and chose to offend Judd's enemies before he would the State Chairman.

On the night of February 8 Lincoln paid a visit to Orville Browning at his hotel. That day the State Central Committee had met and selected Decatur as the site of the Republican State Convention. Lincoln wanted to find out, before Browning left for Quincy early next morning, how he stood on the candidate proposition since the happenings in Hatch's office. Browning chronicled [3]: —

We had a free talk about the Presidency. He thinks I may be right in supposing Mr Bates to be the strongest and best man we can run — that he can get votes even in this County that he [Lincoln] cannot get — and that there is a large class of voters in all the free states that would go for Mr Bates, and for no other man. He says it is not improbable that by the time the National convention meets in Chicago he may be of opinion that the very best thing that can be done will be to nominate Mr Bates.

[1] *Appleton's Cyclopaedia of American Biography*, Vol. V, p. 708.
[2] Feb. 5, 1860; *Works*, Vol. V, p. 290.
[3] *Diary*, Vol. I, p. 395.

Browning, therefore, knew about the meeting in the Secretary of State's office, but his views remained unchanged.

Next day Lincoln was writing to Judd again. "I am not in a position where it would hurt much for me to not be nominated on the national ticket; but I am where it would hurt some for me to not get the Illinois delegates. What I expected when I wrote the letter to Messrs. Dole and others is now happening. Your discomfited assailants are most bitter against me; and they will, for revenge upon me, lay to the Bates egg in the South, and to the Seward egg in the North, and go far toward squeezing me out in the middle with nothing. Can you not help me a little in this matter in your end of the vineyard? I mean this to be private." [1] We can in this letter, for once (reading between the lines) discover what Lincoln really thought about his presidential boom. He was, like most politicians, not yet taking it seriously. "His own characteristic language . . . plainly reveals that he believed this would be useful to him in his future Senatorial aspirations solely, and that he built no hopes whatever on national preferment." [2] Thus wrote two men who were closely associated with the Illinois candidate during this presidential year.[3]

Though Lincoln was no Plato,[4] his mental processes were finer, more powerful, than those of any other public man of his day. In his intellectual maturity as a thinker he ranks with the wisest Americans of his time, Emerson, Hawthorne, Thoreau. So Lincoln was easily

[1] Feb. 9, 1860; *Works*, Vol. V, pp. 290–291.
[2] Nicolay and Hay, Vol. II, p. 258.
[3] Tyler Dennett, *John Hay, From Poetry to Politics*, pp. 33–34.
[4] Fortunately, we have evidence in his own words that Lincoln was no master of the subtleties of metaphysics. Closing his Wisconsin agricultural address, he said: "An Eastern monarch once charged his wise men to invent him a sentence to be ever in view, and which should be true and appropriate in all times and situations. They presented him the words, 'And this, too, shall pass away.' How much it expresses! How chastening in the hour of pride! How consoling in the depths of affliction! 'And this, too, shall pass away.' And yet, let us hope, it is not quite true. Let us hope, rather, that by the best cultivation of the physical world around us, and the best intellectual and moral world within us, we shall secure an individual, social, and political prosperity and happiness, whose course shall be onward and upward, and which, while the earth endures, shall not pass away." Lincoln thought this an utterance of great profundity. But if he had been a really profound logician he would have seen that even the enduring things do pass away. Enduring ideals endure not because they do not pass away but because they are constantly reborn.

able to play the great game of politics to perfection, considering every angle and possibility in his resolute efforts to advance himself. Not hopeful of reaching the Presidency in 1860, he at the same time saw that it would be unwise not to leave the road open for the remote possibility of a nomination for President. Stranger things had happened in conventions of the last two decades. Soon, however, this skeptical attitude toward his presidential chances was to be transformed by a magnificent oratorical triumph.

During February Lincoln had several law cases on his hands, but his chief activity was literary. In the gloomy office of Lincoln and Herndon he worked hard on a speech to be delivered in Henry Ward Beecher's famous Brooklyn church on February 27, labored more carefully than he had in creating any previous oration. His object was the shrewd practical one of delivering a speech that would dazzle New York by its brilliance, demonstrating to the free states and the Party what sort of political thinker they possessed in the Illinois favorite son. He was obliged to turn down an invitation to speak in Wisconsin because he was engaged to appear in Brooklyn.[1]

While Lincoln worked at his speech, striving to advance himself on the wings of his forensic powers, the home Republican press was pushing him forward with all haste. Stoddard's sheet said in mid-February: "From every portion of the state we are daily receiving tokens of the strength of the current of public opinion now gathering in favor of Mr. Lincoln. . . . One-half of the papers of the state known as staunchly Republican have already come out strongly for honest Old Abe, and at least half of the remainder have published articles favoring his nomination." [2]

On the morning of February 16 Chicagoans read that the *Press & Tribune* had come out editorially for Lincoln for President.

We have no hesitation in saying that . . . Abraham Lincoln, of Illinois, is the peer of any man yet named in connection with the Republican nominations, while in regard to availability, we believe him to be more certain to carry Illinois and Indiana than any one else, and his political

---

[1] Lincoln to White, Feb. 13, 1860; *Works*, Vol. V, p. 292.
[2] *Central Illinois Gazette*, Feb. 15, 1860.

antecedents are such as to commend him heartily to the support of Pennsylvania and New Jersey. . . . We briefly sum up some of the elements
of his popularity and strength: —

1st. A gentleman of unimpeachable purity in private life. . . .

2d. A man of, at once, great breadth and great acuteness of intellect. . . .

3d. Right on the record. . . .

4th. A man of executive capacity. . . .

The editorial closed in a tone typical of pious political myth. "We
do not know, however, that he has any aspirations for the position.
While others are intriguing and trading, he is at his professional
work, content to be let alone. Should the Convention give him this
position, then the honor which he has not sought, but which his
admirers have hoped he might attain, will, like ripe fruit, fall into
his hands. Abraham Lincoln will never be President by virtue of
intrigue and bargain."

This emphatic endorsement was purely tentative, opportunistic.
When James Ashley wrote to Chase suggesting that "our friends in
Illinois" might "put Lincoln on the track" to help Chase against
Bates, he meant that Charles Ray and Joseph Medill of the *Tribune*
should do it. The Missouri Emancipation Convention scheme was
not carried out. But the clever politicians of the *Tribune* emerged
from an intuitive study of the signs of the times to abandon their
private negotiations in favor of Chase and come out publicly for
Lincoln. Lincoln's strength in the Illinois press, his recent endorsement by the Illinois machine, the strategic position of Illinois as a
doubtful state, and Chicago's success in securing the convention,
revealed to Ray and Medill a path of greater opportunity as supporters of their own state's rising favorite son.[1]

Without delay the *Press & Tribune* began to do everything possible to advance the cause of the man its proprietors had so recently
taken up. "Let us have Lincoln clubs in every ward of every city
and in every precinct and township in Illinois. We take it for granted
that LINCOLN is the first choice of every Republican in the state.

---

[1] Medill to Chase, April 26, June 8, July 29, Oct. 30, 1859; Nov. 25, 1861; Chase MSS.,
Hist. Soc. of Pa. J. H. Baker to Chase, Feb. 24, 1860; Chase MSS.

. . . If this is so, let us organize at once and in his behalf!"[1]

As March drew near the *Tribune* thumped loudly on the Lincoln drum by announcing the startling news that Lincoln was looming in the national field [2]: —

Our Washington letter, printed herewith, points out with great clearness the path in which both principle and expediency demand that the Republican party go. Avoiding, on the one hand, the radicalism which the popular belief, rightfully or wrongfully, attributes to Mr. Seward and the politicians of his school; and on the other hand the profound conservatism of Mr. Bates and gentlemen of his belief, it leads, through a fearfully fought field, straight to victory.

This letter was the work of Lincoln's new friend of the *Tribune,* young Joseph Medill. As the *Tribune's* propaganda agent for Lincoln, this rising journalist-politician had recently journeyed to Washington.[3] Having come so late to the belief that Lincoln might be the man to do what many an obscure politician had done in conventions since 1840, these opportunists were neglecting no opportunity to further the cause they had made their own. Medill's opening gun was a penetrating fifteen-hundred word analysis of the Republican situation, pointing out with an abundance of factual evidence and inexorable logic that nominating the radical Seward would chase off conservative Republicans, that the case with Bates stood *vice versa.* He hammered his point home: "Does not common sense whisper in every man's ear that the middle ground is the ground of safety?" — concluding vigorously: "I hear the name of Lincoln mentioned in Washington circles, ten times as often as it was one month ago.

---

[1] Feb. 24, 1860.

[2] Feb. 27.

[3] H. I. Cleveland, "Booming the First Republican President. A Talk with Abraham Lincoln's Friend, the Late Joseph Medill"; *Saturday Evening Post,* Vol. CLXXII (Aug. 5, 1899), pp. 84–85. According to Cleveland, Medill as an old man told how it was done. "The campaign which made it possible for Lincoln to be first nominated for President was planned in the office of the Chicago *Tribune* by Mr. Medill and the State Central Committee. It was arranged that Lincoln's name was to be 'mentioned' by the press, but the *Tribune* was not to take the initiative. Four or five county papers down in the old Whig belt were to broach the subject, then a paper in Springfield was to take it up; then another, say in Rock Island or Champaign, until in due time the 'boom' was to reach Chicago. This plan was carried out." This unreliable testimony was perhaps less a case of faulty memory than an attempt to conceal the fact that neither Medill nor the *Tribune* owners were Lincoln men until very late in the contest.

The more the politicians look over the field in search of an *available* candidate, the more they are convinced that 'Old Abe' is the man to win the race with. If the States of the Northwest shall unite upon him, and present his name to the Chicago Convention, there is a strong probability that he will receive the nomination, and as certain as he is nominated he will be President." Careful thought went into this argument. Medill, with the aid of Judd and his band of ambitious politicians, planned the persuasive editorial before he left Chicago and used its arguments in lobbying for Lincoln among the Republican leaders at Washington. When he showed the editorial to members who wanted Seward nominated, Medill says they "jumped on" him.[1]

So forceful were Medill's arguments that Senator Seward himself took notice of them. The distinguished Senator, recently returned from a long European vacation, planned to finish off his Senatorial career in a blaze of glory this session, then rest with quiet dignity while his Party made him President. He confidently expected the nomination, for did not all regard him as the great leader of his Party? He was personally so popular that when in May, 1859, he embarked for Europe, a cheering crowd, music, and salutes, bade him *bon voyage;* when he returned in late December a great demonstration welcomed him home.[2] He had for his campaign manager Thurlow Weed, New York Republican boss, a manipulator of long experience, and Seward's intimate friend. With every device known to the politician's craft Weed was laboring to line up behind Seward a great block of New England and Western delegations which, he was confident, would make Seward's nomination at Chicago a foregone conclusion.[3]

On the other hand, however, the eloquent little Senator was painfully aware of many voices saying that Seward's opinions contained too much radicalism to attract conservative, antiextension support

[1] Cleveland, p. 85.
[2] Frederic Bancroft, *Life of William H. Seward,* Vol. I, pp. 494–495, 518–519, 522.
[3] T. W. Barnes (ed.) *Memoir of Thurlow Weed,* pp. 260–262. E. B. Croker (California) to Chase, March 1, 1860; E. Hopkins (Massachusetts) to Chase, March 10, 1860; S. N. Wood (Kansas) to Chase, March 12, 1860; H. Smith (Indiana) to Chase, March 22, 1860: "It is said that the delegates . . . are nearly . . . unanimous for Seward." Chase MSS.

in the North's doubtful states.[1] That danger, he thought, could be avoided, to which end he had sent his law partner, Benjamin Hall, into the West as plenipotentiary. On January 27, Envoy Hall dropped in at Edward Bates's St. Louis law office. Introducing himself as a friend of Seward, Hall began to talk politics, assuring Bates that Seward (as Bates chronicled it for his journal) "is really a conservative man, and not an ultra." Seward was not really the author of the extra-constitutional "higher law" doctrine which had become so famous after Seward formulated it in his historic speech against the Compromise of 1850, Hall continued. Seward had got the doctrine from none other than President Taylor, whose agent Seward was in telling the Senate about the higher law.[2] In the same line of strategy Seward had written a serious speech for delivery in the Senate when a good opportunity should come, that would show how the irrepressible conflict could, after all, be repressed — provided statesmen such as only the Republican Party offered, should be put in charge of the Government.

The dangerous truth of Medill's arguments for Lincoln, therefore, so alarmed Seward that he determined to stop such publicity by squelching the whippersnapper responsible for them. Medill recalls that [3]

The article irritated Seward when he read it, and he took occasion to see me immediately thereafter, and "blew me up" tremendously for having disappointed him — "gone back on him" — and preferring that "prairie statesman," as he called Lincoln. . . . He gave me to understand that he was the chief teacher of the principles of the Republican Party before Lincoln was known other than as a country lawyer of Illinois. He considered himself as the logical candidate of the Party for the Presidency, and, if rejected for that position, he would give no more of his time and mind to its service. . . .

Springfield's Democratic *Illinois State Register* on February 23 sarcastically chronicled the departure of Abraham Lincoln to de-

---

[1] Bancroft, *Seward*, Vol. I, pp. 523–526.
[2] H. K. Beale (ed.), *Diary of Edward Bates*, pp. 93–94.
[3] Medill to Bancroft, Feb. 18, 1896, in Bancroft, *Seward*, Vol. I, p. 531. Also S. Colfax to S. Bowles, March 1860, in O. J. Hollister, *Life of Schuyler Colfax*, pp. 143–144.

liver a speech in New York: "SIGNIFICANT. — The Hon. Abraham Lincoln departs to day for Brooklyn, under an engagement to deliver a lecture before the Young Men's Assn. of that city, in Beecher's church. Subject, not known. Considerations, $200 and expenses. Object, presidential capital. Effect, disappointment." [1] One day last October Lincoln had rushed gleefully in upon Billy Herndon with a letter inviting the tall orator to lecture at Beecher's church. This fine compliment sent his spirits soaring. Remembering his unsuccess as a formal lecturer, Lincoln asked advice on a subject. His friends suggested a speech on national politics. He asked the committee if a political lecture would be acceptable (he did it so diplomatically they could hardly refuse),[2] and obtained consent. So he set to work developing an authoritative, historically accurate discussion of a theme he had touched many times during his many speeches of 1858 and 1859: the Republican Party, far from being radical or revolutionary, was merely seeking to perpetuate the principles upon which the Fathers founded the Republic. Douglas resolutely denied this, insisting that his popular sovereignty perpetuated the principles of the Fathers. To dislodge Douglas from the coat-tails of Washington, Madison, *et al.*, Lincoln adopted the brilliant technique of employing scientific research to discover what the Fathers really did think and do about slavery. He dug deep into his six-volume set of Elliot's *Debates on the Federal Constitution.* And he spent many weary hours at the State Library searching the *Annals of Congress,* the *Congressional Globe;* he grubbed like a careful historian bent over dusty, yellowed newspaper files. Despite all this effort, when late February came and the speech was ready, Lincoln and his friends "had many misgivings" concerning the possible fate of the orator from the West when he would face a cultured audience at the nation's metropolis.[3]

Lincoln reached New York on Saturday, February 25, after a tiring two-day journey, and registered at the Astor House. He soon discovered that he would speak at New York's Cooper Institute

---

[1] *Illinois State Register,* Feb. 23, 1860.
[2] Lincoln to James A. Briggs, Nov. 13, 1859; *Works,* Vol. V, pp. 258–259.
[3] *Herndon's Lincoln,* p. 367.

instead of in Beecher's church, the engagement having been taken over by "the Young Men's Central Republican Union" of New York, which was staging a series of "political lectures." So he made some changes in his address.[1]

All day Monday Lincoln held levee at the Astor House as a visiting celebrity. Partisans came to shake his huge hand. Invitations arrived pressing him to speak at Patterson and Orange, New Jersey, which he was obliged to refuse. He visited the photographic studio of Mathew Brady and sat for his portrait.[2] Brady captured an amazing image which made uncomely Abraham look like a handsome, mature Byron. Then after sundown came the big event. Outward purpose of the Young Men's Republican Union series of political lectures was to attract "our better but busier citizens who never attend political meetings." [3] But a secret *raison d'être* was a desire on the part of prominent New York Republicans like David Dudley Field, George Opdyke, James A. Briggs, William Cullen Bryant, — all of them opponents of the Weed machine, — to bring forward outstanding Republicans and subtly advertise them as presidential timber, thereby building up strength in opposition to Seward. Earlier in the series, Francis P. Blair, Jr. and Cassius Clay had been presented to the Eastern public.[4] On the positive side, Chase was the favored man,[5] but they desired a broad canvass of Seward's possible conquerors. Snow was falling that evening, and the huge pillared auditorium of Cooper Union was not full. Admission was twenty-five cents. Fifteen hundred people came to examine the man they knew as Douglas' doughty opponent, most of them probably expecting to hear something "wild and woolly." To New Yorkers, Illinois was provincial and backwoodsy. Still, Lincoln's reputation and a natural curiosity to set eyes on this frontier giant had assembled a

---

[1] *Works*, Vol. V, p. 293. Albert Shaw, *Abraham Lincoln, His Path to the Presidency,* pp. 251–252. Henry B. Rankin, *Intimate Character Sketches of Abraham Lincoln,* pp. 177–181. J. F. Newton, *Lincoln and Herndon,* pp. 266–267. F. F. Browne, *Every-Day Life of Lincoln,* pp. 214–215.

[2] Henry J. Raymond, *Life and Public Services of Abraham Lincoln,* p. 100.

[3] C. C. Nott to Lincoln, Feb. 9, 1860; in George H. Putnam, *Abraham Lincoln,* pp. 223–224.

[4] Donnal V. Smith, "Salmon P. Chase and the Election of 1860," *Ohio Arch. and Hist. Quarterly,* Vol. XXXIX, pp. 516, 521, 527.

[5] James A. Briggs to Chase, Nov. 11, 1858, March 17, 1860; Chase MSS.

notable audience. "Since the days of Clay and Webster no man has spoken to a larger assemblage of the intellect and mental culture of our city," Greeley's paper was to say. The famous editor himself sat on the platform, with a crowd of important Republicans, all exuding distinction.

Cheers rang out as Lincoln appeared, escorted by the celebrated New York lawyer, David Dudley Field, and that great literary idol and editor of the New York *Evening Post,* William Cullen Bryant. Just a look at this gaunt figure from the barbaric frontier was worth the two-bit admission. He looked like the speech they expected to hear, when he stalked across the platform clad in a brand-new suit of black broadcloth which fit badly and was lined with out-of-place creases, appearing woefully misplaced in such distinguished company. For once Lincoln felt ashamed of his ungainly attire, appeared to the audience conscious of his huge feet and hands. Byrant gave him a warm introduction, dwelling on Lincoln's works against Douglas. Lincoln stepped forward and diffidently began to speak as applause died down. Skeptical journalists listened intently in the press section as he spoke uncertainly in his high voice: —

"The facts with which I shall deal this evening are mainly old and familiar; nor is anything new in the general use I shall make of them. If there shall be any novelty, it will be in the mode of presenting the facts, and the inferences and observations following that presentation."

Surprised by this sober tone, the crowd listened closely as Lincoln recalled "old and familiar" facts about the founding of the Republic. He recalled that Douglas in his speech at Columbus the previous autumn, had said of slavery: "Our fathers, when they framed the government under which we live, understood this question just as well, and even better, than we do now." Riveting attention with a paradox, the speaker said, "I fully indorse this." He discussed the Constitution and the men who framed it, gaining confidence as he advanced, his voice acquiring a new dignity. Presenting the results of his original research, he demonstrated historically, with extended factual evidence, that the nation's early statesmen had legislated, on the slavery issue, to wipe out bondage in the land of freedom by controlling slavery in the territories. The audience was amazed by the speaker's scholarship, won by his subtle flattery when he had said that history they never before knew was old and familiar to them. He threw out a challenge: "I defy any man to show that any one of them [the Fathers] ever, in his whole life, declared that, in his understanding, any proper division of local from Federal authority, or any part of the Constitution, forbade the Federal Government to control as to slavery in the Federal Territories. I go a step further. I defy any one to show that any living man in the whole world ever did, prior to the beginning of the present century (and I might almost say prior to the beginning of the last half of the present century), declare that, in his understanding, any proper division of local from Federal authority, or any part of the Constitution, forbade the Federal Government to control as to slavery in the Federal Territories."

Now, and here, let me guard a little against being misunderstood. I do not mean to say we are bound to follow implicitly in whatever the fathers did. To do so would be to discard all the lights of current experience — to reject all progress, all improvement. What I do say is that if we would supplant the opinions and policy of our fathers in any case, we should do so upon evidence so conclusive, and argument so clear, that even their great authority, fairly considered and weighed, cannot stand. . . .

If any man at this day sincerely believes that a proper division of local from Federal authority, or any part of the Constitution, forbids the Federal Government to control as to slavery in the Federal Territories, he is right to say so, and to enforce his position by all truthful evidence and fair argument which he can. But he has no right to mislead others . . . into the false belief that "our fathers who framed the government under which we live" were of the same opinion — thus substituting falsehood and deception for truthful evidence and fair argument.

Swinging to the present, Lincoln addressed some words to the Southern people, not expecting them to listen. He argued that when Southerners regard Republicans "as reptiles, or, at the best, as no better than outlaws" because they conceived of the Republican Party as radical, sectional, vindictive against the South, they deceived themselves. Skillfully he used historical evidence to show that his Party stood neither radical nor sectional, because its principles were identical with those of George Washington and his compeers. "Could Washington himself speak, would he cast the blame of that sectionalism upon us, who sustain his policy, or upon you, who repudiate it? . . . Again, you say we have made the slavery question more prominent than it formerly was. We deny it. We admit that it is more prominent, but deny that we made it so. It was not we, but you, who discarded the old policy of the fathers." He argued like a brilliant lawyer to acquit his Party of the charge that John Brown's raid was a piece of Republican terrorism. "Slave insurrections are no more common now than they were before the Republican party was organized. What induced the Southampton insurrection, twenty-eight years ago, in which at least three times as many lives were lost as at Harper's Ferry?"

And how much would it avail you, if you could, by the use of John Brown, Helper's book, and the like, break up the Republican organization? Human action can be modified to some extent, but human nature cannot be changed. There is a judgment and a feeling against slavery in this nation, which cast at least a million and a half votes. You cannot destroy that judgment and feeling — that sentiment — by breaking up the political organization which rallies around it.

Then the orator dwelt impressively upon fine points of constitutionality concerning the issue of slavery extension, pointing to the Supreme Court's mistakes, to this conclusion: "Under all these circumstances, do you really feel yourselves justified to break up this government unless such a court decision as yours is shall be at once submitted to as a conclusive and final rule of political action? But you will not abide the election of a Republican President! In that supposed event, you say, you will destroy the Union; and then, you say, the great crime of having destroyed it will be upon us! That is cool. A highwayman holds a pistol to my ear, and mutters through his teeth, 'Stand and deliver, or I shall kill you, and then you will be a murderer!' "

Tapering off toward a conclusion, Lincoln advised Republicans to refrain from provoking the South further, to "calmly consider their demands, and yield to them, if, in our deliberate view of our duty, we possibly can." What are their demands? "This, and this only: cease to call slavery wrong, and join them in calling it right. And this must be done thoroughly — done in acts as well as in words." To that demand, can Republicans ever yield? And he swept to a smashing close. "Wrong as we think slavery is, we can yet afford to let it alone where it is, because that much is due to the necessity arising from its actual presence in the nation; but can we, while our votes will prevent it, allow it to spread into the national Territories, and to overrun us here in these free States? If our sense of duty forbids this, then let us stand by our duty fearlessly and effectively. Let us be diverted by none of those sophistical contrivances wherewith we are so industriously plied and belabored — contrivances such as groping for some middle ground between the right and the wrong: vain as the search for a man who should be neither a living nor a dead man; such as a policy of 'don't care' on a question about which all true men do care; such as Union appeals beseeching true Union men to yield to Disunionists, reversing the divine rule, and calling, not the sinners, but the righteous to repentance; such as invocations to Washington, imploring men to unsay what Washington said and undo what Washington did.

"Neither let us be slandered from our duty by false accusations against us, nor frightened from it by menaces of destruction to the government, nor of dungeons to ourselves. Let us have faith that right makes might, and in that faith let us to the end dare to do our duty as we understand it."

The crowd sprang up shouting, waving hats and handkerchiefs, so great was their surprise at the calm, closely reasoned, logical arguments of the oration this astonishing speaker from the West had delivered. While many swarmed up to congratulate Lincoln, reporters wondered how they could do justice to so profound a speech. Noah Brooks of the New York *Tribune* burst out, "He's the greatest man since St. Paul," rushed to the *Tribune* office where he wrote for next day's paper: "The tones, the gestures, the kindling eye, and the mirth-provoking look, defy the reporter's skill. The vast assemblage frequently rang with cheers and shouts of applause, which were prolonged and intensified at the close. No man ever before made such an impression on his first appeal to a New York audience." [1]

Next morning Lincoln saw that four New York papers had printed his speech in full. They praised it extravagantly. Plainly, he had captured New York.[2] Many historians have told how this great speech boosted Lincoln's reputation so vigorously that he became Seward's leading competitor for the presidential nomination.[3] This is a romantic sentiment, no more. Practical politics, not speeches, win nominations. For all the celebrity this brilliant speech won for Lincoln, it changed the vote of not one delegate to the Chicago convention.

Lincoln, lion of the hour, found himself showered with invitations to speak in New England towns and cities. He might have refused them all and returned to Illinois without delay had he not wanted to see his eldest son, Robert. When Robert Lincoln had tried the autumn before to enter Harvard, he had failed in fifteen out of sixteen subjects on the entrance examination. So he had gone up to an academy at Exeter, New Hampshire, for a year of solid preparatory schooling. His father was anxious to visit him there to see how he was getting on. This was one of the reasons for his coming to New York. So Lincoln decided to deliver a few speeches on his way to New Hampshire.[4]

The day after the Cooper Institute speech he started north, stopping at Providence for an evening speech. The Governor of Rhode Island attended; the hall overflowed. When Lincoln finished, a swarm of people came up to shake his hand. Next day he entrained for Exeter, reaching there in the evening and meeting Robert. The

[1] New York *Tribune,* clipped in *Illinois State Journal,* March 3, 1860. Chicago *Press & Tribune,* March 2. Brooks, *Lincoln,* pp. 186–187.
[2] *Herndon's Lincoln,* p. 368.
[3] L. E. Chittenden, *Personal Reminiscences,* p. 382. Browne, *Every-Day Life of Lincoln,* p. 220. Emil Ludwig, *Lincoln,* p. 222. R. H. Browne, *Abraham Lincoln,* Vol. II, p. 274. J. G. Holland, *Life of Abraham Lincoln,* p. 212. C. P. Bissett, *Abraham Lincoln,* p. 154.
[4] Barton, *Lincoln,* Vol. I, pp. 409–410.

news that Lincoln of Illinois would soon be in the vicinity had traveled fast, and at Exeter a committee met and engaged him for a speech at Dover. Next day Lincoln addressed a large audience at Concord in the afternoon, and that evening in Manchester he spoke to the inevitable "immense gathering." Here, local Republican Chairman Frederick Smyth was inspired by brief contact with the traveling orator's wisdom to present Lincoln as "The next President of the United States" — an unusual introduction.[1] On the following day, Friday, Lincoln filled his Dover engagement, then Saturday evening he made an hour-and-a-half-speech at Exeter.[2] He spent Sunday with Robert, who proudly showed off his father to classmates. While resting for the day he wrote to his wife, "I have been unable to escape this toil. If I had foreseen it, I think I would not have come East at all." Like all true literary spirits, Lincoln had a horror of repeating himself. "The speech at New York . . . gave me no trouble whatever. The difficulty was to make nine others, before reading audiences who had already seen all my ideas in print." [3]

Monday morning he started south again, addressing an audience at Hartford, Connecticut's capital, that evening. The Governor introduced him, and Lincoln presented an extremely able variation of his Cooper Union speech.[4] Lincoln's presence was an occasion in Hartford; after the speech he was escorted to his hotel by a group of young chaps shouldering flaming torches, cambric capes about their shoulders — paraphernalia which presently became the uniform for the multitude of Republican enthusiasts who took the name "Wide-Awakes" and made it famous in the presidential canvass.[5]

Tuesday evening he spoke to an enthusiastic crowd at New

---

[1] Barton, Vol. I, p. 410.

[2] E. L. Page, *Abraham Lincoln in New Hampshire*, pp. 5–114. Long after, when Frederick Smyth was furnishing material for his own biography, he conformed to a charming American custom by telling "how I made Lincoln President." He told of meeting Lincoln on the Concord-bound train, telling the orator that Seward would not make a good Republican candidate, then announced Lincoln to his audience as the next President, thereby putting ideas in Lincoln's head which made him the sixteenth President.

[3] In Putnam, *Lincoln*, p. 49. Hertz, Vol. II, p. 770.

[4] *Works*, Vol. V, pp. 329–338.

[5] Nicolay and Hay, Vol. II, pp. 284–286.

Haven,[1] and after the speech was escorted to his lodgings by a parade with a band. These processions had become a fad. Next evening Lincoln went from New Haven in a special train packed with partisans to Meriden, where a torchlight procession lighted his way to the hall. His speech was two hours long as usual. Then back to New Haven went the Republicans, escorting the great man from Illinois to his lodgings with a brass band and procession. Thursday evening, after a long trip east along Connecticut's seacoast and north into Rhode Island, he spoke with the power consistently his now, at Woonsocket. From Providence to Woonsocket and back the celebrity had an escort of a band and several hundred admiring Republicans. Friday evening the overworked orator held forth effectively in the crowded town hall of Norwich, Connecticut.[2] Then on Saturday evening he made the eleventh and final address of this strenuous fortnight in New England, speaking to a capacity crowd in Bridgeport's most capacious hall. When the tumult and the shouting died he boarded the night train for New York.[3]

Sunday Lincoln heard Beecher preach at his famous Brooklyn church and went sight-seeing in New York. Monday morning he stepped into a railroad car and sat down for the long ride back to Springfield. Of the departing hero Greeley's *Tribune* said: "Mr. Lincoln has done a good work and made many warm friends." Mr. Lincoln believed he had.[4] He remembered how he was introduced at Manchester as the next President. But at Norwich, the Honorable Daniel P. Tyler had presented him as a possible Vice President, running mate for Seward. This was the limit of the sober Eastern view of Lincoln's chances, for, political folkways being what they are, had he been recognized as a really strong candidate for the leadership of his Party he would have been pompously introduced

[1] *Works*, Vol. V, pp. 339–371.
[2] *Works*, Vol. VI, pp. 1–5.
[3] Angle, *Lincoln, 1854–1861*, pp. 322–323, Barton, *President Lincoln*, Vol. I, p. 75, P. C. Eggleston, *Lincoln in New England*, pp. 5–11.
[4] James A. Briggs wrote to Chase, March 17, "Mr. Lincoln of Ill. told me he had a very warm side toward you. . . . I urged him by all means to attend the Convention. I was pleased with him." Chase MSS.

to every audience he faced as "the next President of the United States!"

Robert Todd Lincoln used to say drolly that he made his father President by failing in fifteen of sixteen subjects as a Harvard candidate. If he had flunked less than fifteen, perhaps his father would not have been so solicitous about Robert's education, would not have made the Cooper Union speech and the eleven others which established Abraham Lincoln's oratorical reputation in the East where they knew him not.[1] There is some truth in this notion, truth relative not to the nominating votes of delegates but to a change in the psychology of the candidate himself.

Wednesday morning found Lincoln back in Springfield, dead tired but in fine humor, starting a rest of several days. Anxious to offend nobody, he wrote some letters apologizing for having been unable to do what had been requested, explaining that business demanded his return.[2] Perusing the back newspapers he had missed while away, Lincoln saw how the *Journal* had carefully followed him about New England for its readers, printing the Cooper Union speech in full and clipping from eastern papers the generous praise they gave.[3] In the *Press & Tribune* he also saw his great speech printed in full, with the comment, "We are by no means surprised that it called out the highest encomiums of the New York Republican press, or that it was at once determined to issue it in pamphlet form as a campaign document."[4] Presently this pamphlet appeared, price one cent. What satisfaction it was for the orator to observe his political stature growing because of the literary success his speeches were enjoying. Even before he went east he had read that a Pennsylvania paper, apropos the news from Ohio that the Lincoln-Douglas debates were in press, remarked[5]: "This is a most delicate, but very significant compliment to Mr. Lincoln, whose speeches are regarded as among the very best expositions of Republican doctrine, any-

[1] Barton, *Lincoln*, Vol. I, p. 409.
[2] *Works*, Vol. VI, p. 5. Tracy, p. 134. *Illinois State Journal*, March 15, 1860.
[3] *Illinois State Journal*, March 3–15, 1860.
[4] March 2.
[5] Berks and Schuylkill (Penn.) *Journal*, clipped in *Illinois State Journal*, Feb. 20, 1860.

where, on record. Well may Illinois be proud of her Mr. Lincoln; no wonder that the West claims his nomination at Chicago."

Press gossip concerning the Chicago nominations now ran at flood tide; almost every issue of every paper printed some speculation about it. Lincoln read an Ohioan's letter on the Presidency which the *Journal* clipped from the New York *Courier and Enquirer,* discussing the situation at length without even mentioning the name Lincoln. The writer was sure that "if they nominate Seward he will be elected, but I think almost any other man would be defeated. . . . If *any* milk-and-water candidate is put in nomination at Chicago, it will ruin the Republican party." [1] In his own state, on the other hand, Lincoln saw that he was steadily gaining strength. The Clinton *Transcript* said [2]: —

The Pike County *Journal* . . . has placed the name of Hon. Abraham Lincoln at the head of its columns as its choice for the Presidency. This makes twenty-nine newspapers that advocate the nomination of this distinguished statesman.

In an adjacent column of Lincoln's faithful *Journal* two more converts were spotted — the Bloomington *Pantagraph* and the Kansas *Daily Register.* Joseph Medill wrote prophetically from Washington [3]: "The Republicans are delighted with Lincoln's New York speech. There were 70,000 copies of it subscribed for today, by members of Congress, for distribution among their constituents. The speech has created a sensation through the eastern states such as few speeches have ever done.

"Bates' stock culminated last week, and is now fast falling. By the time the Convention is held it will be out of the market. The signs now are, that if Seward is not nominated, Lincoln will be. If the delegates of the four close and doubtful states shall say to the Convention that they can be carried for Seward, he will be our standard bearer. But if they shall declare that he can not carry them,

[1] *Illinois State Journal,* Feb. 25, 1860.
[2] Clipped in *Illinois State Journal,* Feb. 27.
[3] Clipped in *Illinois State Journal,* March 8.

then Lincoln, in all probability, will be chosen to head the ticket, and run the race set before him."

With all these things crowding in upon his consciousness, there came about in the heart of Abraham Lincoln a profound change. Billy Herndon, who knew so well the inside story of Lincolnian politics (but tells so little about the wire-pullings which boosted his partner to the top) for once vouchsafes us a look behind the scenes.[1]

Lincoln's return to Springfield after his dazzling success in the East was the signal for earnest congratulations on the part of his friends. Seward was the great man of the day, but Lincoln had demonstrated to the satisfaction of his friends that he was tall enough and strong enough to measure swords with the Auburn statesman. . . . It was apparent now to Lincoln that the presidential nomination was within his reach. He began gradually to lose his interest in the law and to trim his political sails at the same time. His recent success had stimulated his self-confidence to unwonted proportions. He wrote to influential party workers everywhere. I know the idea prevails that Lincoln sat still in his chair in Springfield, and that one of those unlooked-for tides in human affairs came along and cast the nomination into his lap; but any man who has had experience in such things knows that great political prizes are not obtained in that way. The truth is, Lincoln was as vigilant as he was ambitious, and there is no denying the fact that he understood the situation perfectly from the start. In the management of his own interests he was obliged to rely almost entirely on his own resources. He had no money, with which to maintain a political bureau, and he lacked any kind of personal organization whatever. Seward had all these things, and, behind them all, a brilliant record in the United States Senate with which to dazzle his followers. But with all his prestige and experience the latter was no more adroit and no more untiring in pursuit of his ambition than the man who had just delivered the Cooper Institute speech.

When the Illinois favorite son decided that his prospects were in fact better than those of an ordinary favorite son, and that as a "stop Seward" possibility he might actually be chosen to lead the ticket because what Medill had suggested as a possible result might

[1] *Herndon's Lincoln*, pp. 369–370.

really come about, he lost no time going into action to that end.[1]
Two days after his return he sent off a significant letter to his old
friend Mark Delahay, who was still asking Lincoln to use his influence toward creating Senator Delahay. Mr. Delahay had also
generously offered to manage a Lincoln-for-President campaign in
Kansas if Lincoln would finance him. Lincoln's reaction was surprisingly favorable.[2]

As to your kind wishes for myself, allow me to say I can not enter
the ring on the money basis — first, because, in the main, it is wrong; and
secondly, I have not, and can not get, the money. I say, in the main, the
use of money is wrong; but for certain objects, in a political contest, the
use of some, is both right and indispensable. With me as with yourself,
this long struggle has been one of great pecuniary loss. I now distinctly
say this: If you shall be appointed a delegate to Chicago, I will furnish
one hundred dollars to bear the expenses.

Next day Lincoln wrote to an Illinois Republican named E. Stafford, who had suggested that Lincoln's presidential ambitions could,
with the aid of a ten-thousand-dollar war chest, be made an actu-
ality. To him Lincoln said [3]: —

Thanking you very sincerely for your kind purposes toward me, I am
compelled to say the money part of the arrangement you propose is, with
me, an impossibility. I could not raise ten thousand dollars if it would
save me from the fate of John Brown. Nor have my friends, so far as I
know, yet reached the point of staking any money on my chances of
success. I wish I could tell you better things, but it is even so.

Not only in connection with his striking Eastern tour was Lincoln
commanding the attention of the North's press. Jesse Fell, his ambitious Bloomington friend, according to the plan unfolded to Lincoln in December, 1858, had sent Lincoln's recent autobiography
to Joseph J. Lewis, a lawyer of West Chester, Pennsylvania. Fell
had convinced his friend Lewis that the Republicans could best

[1] J. B. Bishop, *Presidential Nominations and Elections*, pp. 37–39. Horace White, *Life of Lyman Trumbull*, p. 102.
[2] Tracy, pp. 134–136.
[3] *Works*, Vol. VI, p. 7.

nominate Lincoln, and the two politicians, appraising the situation in Pennsylvania, thought that Lincoln propagandizing in the Keystone state might have important results. From the autobiographical letter in Lincoln's handwriting and information which Fell gave him on Lincoln's public career, Lewis had written a biographical article of nearly three thousand words which was careful to celebrate Lincoln's services to the Republican Party, his modesty, his humble beginnings, his oratorical powers, his long record of sustaining the protective tariff. Of the man whose portrait he drew, Lewis believed it "impossible to doubt that he will be vigorously pressed upon the Chicago Convention, by the representatives of a large and earnest constituency, as a proper standard-bearer of our great national party in the impending struggle for the Presidency." In case any reader should wonder why so great a man had been defeated for high office so many times, Lawyer Lewis smoothly explained: Lincoln left the House of Representatives after one term but "he would have been re-elected had he not declined to be a candidate"; he failed to become U. S. Senator in '55 because of "magnanimity," "generous self-sacrifice"; he failed again in '58 because of "grossly unequal apportionment of the districts." This biography appeared in the Chester County *Times* in February, Lewis sending marked copies to numerous Republican editors. And it was widely copied, for from no other source could most Northerners learn much about the history of the Republican hero of the West about whom so much political gossip was floating round.[1]

By late March the alert Stoddard could report: "It seems as if the whole West was about to rise *en masse* in favor of the nomination of Abraham Lincoln by the Chicago Convention. . . . Paper after paper throughout not only Illinois but the whole north-west, has put his name at the mast head, until the ones which have not done so are the marked exceptions." [2] Springfield's *Journal* had

---

[1] *Central Illinois Gazette*, March 7, 1860. Chicago *Press & Tribune*, Feb. 23, 1860. Barton, "The Lincoln of the Biographers," *Transactions*, Ill. State Hist. Soc., 1929, pp. 61–63, 80–86. Morehouse, *Life of Fell*, pp. 58–60. Barton, *President Lincoln*, Vol. I, pp. 63–64. J. W. Fell to W. H. Lamon, Feb. 19, 1872, in Dorothy Lamon (ed.), *Recollections of Lincoln*, pp. 11–12n.

[2] *Central Illinois Gazette*, March 28.

become so warm in support of its man that it objected when the *Press & Tribune* ventured a discussion of the candidate situation based on facts [1]: —

The Chicago *Press and Tribune* which a week or so ago came out in a pointed and well-timed leader in favor of ABRAHAM LINCOLN, as *its first choice* for the Presidency, in its last Saturday's issue appears to take a new tack, and, while uttering one word for Mr. Lincoln, indites an extended leader urging the claims of Mr. Seward. We do not object at all to our able and respected contemporary freely and frankly canvassing and avowing — even changing — its predilections in the important matter of the selection of the Republican standard-bearer for 1860; nor do we intend to say one word against Mr. Seward, whom we regard [etc., etc.] . . . but we do protest against the questionable manner in which our contemporary is now disposed to treat Mr. Lincoln . . . , stating that Mr. Seward deserves the nomination, but suggesting in case Mr. Seward is not thought to be the most available candidate, "that Mr. Lincoln shall not be passed over."

The Republican party was organized not to advance this or that man to official station, but to work for the triumph of great principles. It recognizes nobody's "claims," but, in bringing candidates out for office, is only concerned in the question, which man is the most available exponent of its doctrines — under whose leadership are its principles the most likely to triumph? "The cause and not men" should be the motto, and we trust the approaching National Convention will be guilty of no mere man-worship in making its choice.

As February passed into history (same day the Lincoln promoters read in the *Press & Tribune* that the Minnesota Republican convention had pledged its delegates, to the accompaniment of echoing cheers, "to use all honorable means" to achieve the nomination of Seward for President), the Republican National Committee announced that the date of the Chicago convention had been moved forward from June 13 to May 16.[2] Soon the Illinois State Central Committee issued an official call notifying "the Republican voters of the several counties of the State to appoint delegates to meet in Convention at Decatur, on Wednesday, the ninth day of May next,

[1] *Illinois State Journal*, March 13, 1860.
[2] Chicago *Press & Tribune*, Feb. 29.

at 10 o'clock, A. M. for the purpose of nominating candidates for the following State offices . . . also . . . to elect 22 delegates to represent the State of Illinois in the National Republican Convention . . ." [1] Twelve Republicans comprised this State Central Committee; at least four of them (Judd, Herndon, Grimshaw, Fell) were working hard for Lincoln. Perhaps some or all of those other eight politicians, men whose personalities have faded like the snows of yesteryear, followed these aggressive Lincoln men. The state organization was clearly for Lincoln, and would do all possible to secure for him the twenty-two Illinois delegates.

Many had been the resolutions adopted presenting Abraham Lincoln as first choice for the Presidency by small Illinois Republican units like township and city conventions and local Republican clubs,[2] but these resolutions were valuable to Lincoln only as straws in the wind, the organizations issuing them having no power over the votes of Chicago delegates. But early in March the counties began to hold their Republican convention, and the resolutions they passed had some direct political force. First to meet was the convention of Wayne County, on March 3. This southern county *"Resolved,* That Hon. Abe. Lincoln is the unanimous choice of the Republicans of Wayne County for the Presidential nomination. . . ." Adjacent to Wayne on the south was White County, where the Republicans met on the fifth. Their resolutions were lengthy, as usual, but ominously silent on presidential recommendations.[3]

Since early March the *Press & Tribune* had published column after column of stories about Lincoln's Eastern tour, clipped from the Eastern press.[4] And as glowing reports of speeches piled up they created, thought the *Tribune,* an impressive result [5]: —

Our late advices from the East, both through private and public channels, concur in saying that Mr. Lincoln's introduction to the people of New England has produced a very remarkable impression on the public

[1] Chicago *Press & Tribune,* March 12, 1860.
[2] *Illinois State Journal,* March 8, 9. Chicago *Press & Tribune,* March 9.
[3] Chicago *Press & Tribune,* March 14.
[4] March 2–March 21.
[5] March 17.

mind in that quarter. . . . We hazard nothing in saying that no man has ever before risen so rapidly to political eminence in the United States. . . .

It is certainly due to one whose services have been so eminent, and whose abilities are so unanimously conceded by the entire North, that his own state should present his name to the Chicago Convention without dissent or difference. This, we are assured by the indications which have come up from the County Conventions already held, will be done. It seems to be quite generally conceded that if Mr. Douglas is nominated at Charleston, Mr. Lincoln is *the* man to beat him before the people. . . .

Not until April did county conventions begin to be generally held; as they met, the *Tribune* faithfully reported them. Meantime Republican papers continued to suffer from a rash of President-guessing. Day after day pro-Lincoln sheets gave out the argument of availability until reasons why "the Chicago Convention *ought* to nominate Abraham Lincoln for President," [1] become very old indeed.[2] A few stories had something new to say. The Rock Island *Register's* Washington correspondent wrote from the capital [3]: —

Republicans here, from all sections of the Union, are loud in their praises of Lincoln's magnificent speech in New York. It has stamped him as one of the leaders of the progressive thought of the age, and has caused his claims as a presidential candidate to be fully discussed among many who had not previously given them much consideration. A Senator, a well-known Seward man, said to me a few days since, "I don't know but we shall have to nominate Lincoln at Chicago." This is merely a specimen of the compliments that glorious Old Abe is receiving on all hands. I renew the expression of my belief that if Seward is not nominated at Chicago, Lincoln will be. . . .

In its first April paper the *Tribune* ran a summary editorial which is a remarkably factual, sober, discussion of the Republican presidential aspect [4]: —

. . . It is grossly unjust to Gov. Seward to suppose that either he or his advisers will insist upon his nomination by the Chicago Convention against

[1] *Menard Index*, clipped in Chicago *Press & Tribune*, April 3, 1860.
[2] Chicago *Press & Tribune*, March 21, 22, 24, 28, 29, 30. *Illinois State Journal*, March 12, 23, 26, 28.
[3] Clipped in Chicago *Press & Tribune*, March 24.
[4] April 2.

the judgment of the delegates from New Jersey, Pennsylvania, Indiana and Illinois, or a majority of them. Col. Fremont was nominated against the advice and remonstrances of all these states; he lost them all, and was defeated in the election. Gov. Seward has no ambition to repeat that experiment — not the least in the world. . . . He has the sagacity to perceive that a defeat before the people would foreclose his presidential prospects, if not finish his political career, and that his nomination against the wishes of the representatives of those states would be nearly tantamount to a defeat. On the other hand, if the delegates from those states above named, shall say that Mr. Seward *can* secure their electoral votes, he will be nominated, and all those who are now of the opinion that Mr. Lincoln is the more available man, will be among the first to rejoice at the fortuitous circumstances which shall have made it possible to give to our greatest statesman our highest honors. What the delegates from New Jersey, Pennsylvania, Indiana and Illinois may say when the Convention meets, we have no means of knowing which are not equally open to the public, but we feel warranted in saying that [they] . . . will tell the exact truth when they take their seats in our Republican Wigwam. . . .

We hesitate not to say that we think Mr. Lincoln can poll more votes in this state than any other man who can be named. We say this with a full knowledge that the four northern districts are primarily for Seward and the five southern ones for Bates. We are gratified to notice that all the County Conventions which have yet expressed an opinion on the Presidency have declared for Mr. Lincoln. Until the nomination is made, *our* duty is to Illinois.

Almost every day during April and the first week of May the *Tribune* reported the results of some county convention.[1] In every case but one, when resolutions were adopted concerning the presidential nomination, Lincoln was enthusiastically endorsed. But in counties far north and far south Lincoln was not the Illinois favorite son, and a great many counties said nothing about their presidential preference, leaving that problem to the Decatur Convention.[2]

Late in March Lincoln went to Chicago to work on an important case in Federal Court there, and stayed a fortnight. Busy in court as he was, law was not permitted to interfere with politics. There were serious confidential conferences with Judd and others. On his

[1] Chicago *Press & Tribune,* April 2–May 8, 1860, *passim.*
[2] As the *Tribune* reported county resolutions, the score stood: for Lincoln, 32; noncommittal, 32; for Bates, 1.

second day in Chicago, Lincoln wrote to Samuel Galloway, Republican politician of Columbus, Ohio.[1]

Before leaving home I received your kind letter of the 15th. Of course I am gratified to know I have friends in Ohio who are disposed to give me the highest evidence of their friendship and confidence. Mr. Parrott, of the legislature, had written me to the same effect. If I have any chance, it consists mainly in the fact that the whole opposition would vote for me, if nominated. . . . My name is new in the field, and I suppose I am not the first choice of a very great many. Our policy, then, is to give no offense to others — leave them in a mood to come to us if they shall be compelled to give up their first love. This, too, is dealing justly with all, and leaving us in a mood to support heartily whoever shall be nominated. . . . Whatever you may do for me, consistently with these suggestions, will be appreciated and gratefully remembered. Please write me again.

Candidate Lincoln's managers, as they surveyed the situation, noted with gratification that their work would secure for their man the votes of Illinois' delegates, that Lincoln was steadily gaining weight as his Cooper Institute speech came off the presses by the ten thousand as a campaign document.[2] Since late February the Lincoln-Douglas Debates volume had been off the press; the *Tribune* urged, "Let our Republican clubs avail themelves of the cheap edition of the Debates now within reach and give them the widest possible circulation." [3] But, unfortunately for Lincoln, some who would come to the Chicago Convention as delegates perhaps could not read. Nor would many delegates take time to go through that wordy tome. But even if they did read the book, finding there proof of high political genius, delegates could not vote for Lincoln if their delegation should be instructed for somebody else. So Lincoln and his managers, knowing that the future of their cause depended on the success of quiet negotiations for the votes of delegates from other states, — not upon newspaper support, "sentiment among the rank and file," fame as an orator or exponent of Party principles, began to lay their pipe.

---

[1] *Works,* Vol. VI, pp. 7–8.
[2] N. Baugher to Washburne, March 25, 1860; Washburne MSS.
[3] Chicago *Press & Tribune,* April 10.

Among the numberless predictions as to what the Republicans would do at Chicago, there was one line of thought which forecast the result perfectly. This point of view was well stated by a prominent Iowa politician, Fitz Henry Warren, in a letter to James S. Pike, brilliant Washington correspondent of the New York *Tribune*. Said Warren, "I am for the man who can carry Pennsylvania, New Jersey, and Indiana, with this reservation, that I will not go into the cemetery or catacomb; the candidate must be alive and able to walk at least from parlor into the dining room. I am willing to take the opinions of the delegates from these states on this point." [1] Norman Judd and his Lincoln men saw in their candidate a man who was not ready for the catacomb and who could carry the doubtful states. Obvious strategy, then, was to persuade the other doubtful state leaders to see the thing in that pleasant light. Judd wrote privately to Senator Trumbull about it [2]: —

Cannot a quiet combination between the delegates from New Jersey Indiana and Illinois be brought about — including Pennsylvania — United action by those delegates will probably control the convention — Nothing but a positive position will prevent Seward's nomination — The movement for Lincoln has neutralized to some extent the Bates movement in our state. . . . State pride will carry a resolution of instruction through our convention — This suggestion has been made to Mr. L.

This letter, not telling too much, for Trumbull was not a member of the Lincoln-for-President group, throws light behind the scenes upon the political plumbers of the Lincoln clique; we can almost see them sitting together in some Chicago room talking it over. Judd wrote to Trumbull on April 2, the same day the *Tribune* ran that significant editorial which argued that Seward would be nominated if the doubtful state delegations declared that he could carry their state, would not if they said he could not. Perhaps Judd himself wrote the editorial. Medill had written a parallel argument from

[1] Warren to Pike, Feb. 2, 1860; in F. I. Herriott, "The Conference in the Deutsches Haus, Chicago, May 14–15, 1860," *Transactions*, Ill. State Hist. Soc., 1928, p. 125.
[2] Judd to Trumbull, April 2, 1860; Trumbull MSS.

Washington a month before. It is certain that Judd read the editorial (his business, and Lincoln's too, was to examine all press comments relative to the nomination) and was impressed by the argument.

How clear it is — Lincoln, Judd, and a few others meeting somewhere on Sunday, All Fool's Day, when they are free from court duties, and discussing whether or not something can be done to stop Seward. Judd thinks something can, and relates his plan. Lincoln has a natural distaste for such dealings, as he said to Galloway a week earlier, but it is All Fool's Day and he is reminded that he must not play the fool by disdaining to play ball. Judd explains that tomorrow's *Tribune* will carry an editorial outlining the basic situation which gives the Lincoln men their opportunity. He writes the plan to Trumbull on April 2. The word is passed along at the capital to influential leaders of the three other states in question. They prick up their ears. Judd's primary object was to stop Seward to make way for Lincoln. Pennsylvanians have another idea; they will push Cameron as the man who could do what Seward could not. New Jersey will do the same for Senator Dayton. But the basic idea that the doubtful states must co-operate by insisting that the fate of Nominee Seward would be identical with that of Fremont — there was something to remember.   .

This line of strategy was, by the nature of the situation, being well discussed by supporters of other Seward opponents.[1] In one month, March, Salmon P. Chase read several such discussions. Said a New Hampshire correspondent [2]: —

Only one thing will prevent Seward's nomination at Chicago — the conviction that he cannot carry Pennsylvania and New Jersey. Those states, together with Indiana and Illinois, will be in a position to veto any nomination, by a united and persistent declaration that *they* cannot be carried for him. I rather expect them to apply that veto to Mr. Seward. . . .

With the *thinking* men of the party no man stands as well as Salmon P. Chase. With the *masses*, Seward is the favorite.

[1] J. T. Sherman to G. Welles, March 23, 1860; Welles MSS.
[2] G. S. Fogg to Chase, March 26, 1860; Chase MSS.

From Kansas a seer wrote that unless he was "much mistaken in the lay of the *wires*, the Chase, Lincoln, & Bates men will make common cause against Seward." [1]

Chicago was treating Lincoln as a celebrity. He sat for his bust to a young sculptor, Leonard Volk, whose sponsor in setting him off on an art career was none other than Stephen Douglas. One evening Lincoln went to Waukegan "at the earnest solicitations of citizens of Lake County" to make a political speech. He had barely started when a great fire broke out near by and everyone rushed to see it.[2] Another evening, when he was making a social call in Evanston, a crowd of Republicans came round and serenaded him. Lincoln gave them a little speech in response. When his case closed with a victory Lincoln went home with a respectable fee and banked it.[3]

Though he and his compeers were having no success in doing it, Candidate Lincoln was thinking hard about what ought to be done to secure a respectable number of Chicago delegates pledged for Lincoln, as April moved along and spring arrived once more to stir the ambitions. Soon after his return from Chicago he wrote in a tone of judicious modesty to a McLean supporter, R. M. Corwine of Cincinnati, member of Ohio's delegation to Chicago.[4]

. . . Remembering that when a not very great man begins to be mentioned for a very great position, his head is very likely to be a little turned, I have concluded I am not the fittest person to answer the questions you ask. Making due allowance for this, I think Mr. Seward is the very best candidate we could have for the North of Illinois, and the very *worst* for the South of it. The estimate of Gov. Chase here is neither better nor worse than that of Seward, except that he is a newer man. . . . Mr. Bates, I think, would be the best man for the South of our state, and the worst for the North of it. If Judge McLean was . . . younger, I think he would be stronger than either, in our state. . . .

I really believe we can carry the state for either of them, or for any

[1] S. N. Wood to Chase, March 12, 1860; Chase MSS.
[2] Chicago *Press & Tribune*, April 2, 1860. J. T. Frazer to Washburne, April 3, 1860; Washburne MSS. Frazer added, "I think him [Lincoln] really a great man. I wish he could be made our nominee at Chicago."
[3] Angle, *Lincoln, 1854–1861*, p. 327.
[4] Lincoln to Corwine, April 6, 1860; Tracy, pp. 138–139. Corwine to John McLean, March 19, 1860; McLean MSS.

one who may be nominated; but doubtless it would be easier to do it with some than with others.

I feel myself disqualified to speak of myself in this matter. I feel this letter will be of little value to you; but I can make it no better, under the circumstances. Let this be strictly confidential. . . .

Next day he wrote an optimistic letter to Trumbull, telling how the Springfield Republicans had in a recent city election for the first time beaten a united Democracy. On presidential politics, Lincoln told Trumbull that McLean "would be our best candidate" were he ten years younger.[1] Lincoln also wrote to the Harrison Literary Institute of Chicago, declining an invitation to lecture. He explained that he is not a professional lecturer, having "got up but one lecture, and that I think rather a poor one. Besides, what time I can spare from my own business this season I shall be compelled to give to politics." [2]

The next week, when circuit court was holding at Bloomington, Lincoln attended, and one rainy, muddy evening, delivered a political speech. Despite the mucky weather, Phoenix Hall was packed. Jesse Fell's *Pantagraph,* reporting the speech, gave an illuminating critique on the secret of Lincoln's power when he mounted the stump and harangued in his best vein. "Mr. Lincoln is probably the fairest and most honest political speaker in the country. While he convinces the understanding by arriving at legitimate and unavoidable sequences, he wins the hearts of his hearers by the utmost fairness and good humor. Several of his thrusts . . . went through the sophisms and duplicities of the Shamocracy with a terribly damaging effect." [3]

Two precious weeks had gone by since they made their plans in Chicago, without any tangible success for the Lincoln men, among the delegates other states would send to Chicago. Far from discouraged, the candidate sent a note to Mark Delahay, whose influence in Kansas has proved very weak. He had disappointed Lincoln. Abraham wrote: "You know I was in New England. Some of

[1] Tracy, p. 140.
[2] Lincoln to John M. Carson, April 7, 1860; Tracy, p. 141.
[3] Bloomington *Pantagraph,* clipped in Chicago *Press & Tribune,* April 13, 1860.

the acquaintances I made while there, write me since the elections that the close vote in Conn. and the quasi defeat in R. I. are a drawback upon the prospects of Gov. Seward; and Trumbull writes Dubois to the same effect. Do not mention this as coming from me. Both those states are safe enough for us in the fall. I see by the dispatches that since you wrote, Kansas has appointed Delegates and instructed them for Seward. Don't stir them up to anger, but come along to the convention, and I will do as I said about expenses." [1]

Another week went fruitlessly by. Then another, leaving but two days of April remaining. Lincoln and his friends were sorry to note that Seward, in addition to his overpowering strength in the East, was gathering up whole delegations from states farthest west — Minnesota, Wisconsin, Kansas, California. But Lincoln was not discouraged. A maxim of horse racing has it that the only part of the race which really counts is the finish. Events were soon to demonstrate that this is not inapplicable also to a dark-horse race.

Senator Trumbull had asked Lincoln if he honestly expected to be nominated. Trumbull wanted to get at the real facts for two reasons. He was pulling wires to further the cause of Judge McLean, and he had himself been slightly stung by the presidential bee. For a long time he had been getting letters suggesting Trumbull for President,[2] the kind of letters every man in high public office receives from boot-licking, job-hungry constituents.[3] Candidate Lincoln replied (April 29) [4]: —

. . . As you request, I will be entirely frank. The taste *is* in my mouth a little; and this, no doubt, disqualifies me, to some extent, to form correct opinions. You may confidently rely, however, that by no advice or consent of mine, shall my pretensions be pressed to the point of endangering our common cause.

Now, as to my opinions about the chances of others in Illinois. I think neither Seward nor Bates can carry Illinois if Douglas shall be on the track; and that either of them can, if he shall not be. I rather think

---

[1] Tracy, pp. 141–142.
[2] Trumbull MSS., 1859–1860, *passim.*
[3] J. B. Young, Marion, Iowa, to Senator Harlan of Iowa, Dec. 27, 1859; in *Annals of Iowa,* Vol. IX, p. 281.
[4] Tracy, pp. 142–144.

McLean could carry it with D. on or off; in other words, I think McLean is stronger in Illinois, taking all sections of it, than either S. or B.; and I think S. the weakest of the three. I hear no objection to Mr. McLean, except his age; but that objection seems to occur to every one. . . .

Lincoln explained that he would have answered Trumbull sooner, but had waited to see what the Democrats would do in their convention at Charleston. Since they had reached no decision, Lincoln delayed no longer. Would Douglas be nominated or not? Nobody could say. Douglas and Jefferson Davis had been saying terrible things to each other in the Senate. What would happen to the Little Giant when the Northern and Southern factions of the Democracy met in convention had been the great puzzle of Democratic President-guessing that season,[1] a problem which had a direct bearing on the chances of Abraham Lincoln,[2] as Abraham himself well knew and hinted to Trumbull.

Carl Schurz, since meeting Lincoln in 1858, had been extremely active as a rising Republican. In January 1860, at Springfield, Massachusetts, he delivered one of the great speeches of the period, on "Douglas and Popular Sovereignty." [3] The arguments with which he blasted Douglas' position were similar to Lincoln's but not the same. He did not mention Lincoln, did not consider Lincoln Douglas' ablest opponent. Indeed, from a literary viewpoint, the sparkling oratory of Schurz exceeds the brilliance of Lincoln's famous attacks on the Little Giant. Schurz, like Lincoln a litterateur in politics, wrote many interesting letters to Republican leaders, none of them to Lincoln. He was close to Wisconsin Republican chieftains like Doolittle and Potter; and Wisconsin was for Seward. Schurz wrote from Indiana to his wife on March 9, telling her he had found his Massachusetts speech "in almost everybody's hands. Indiana is the only state in which strong sympathy for Bates has been perceptible; elsewhere he is not mentioned. Seward is evidently gaining. If Douglas is not nominated in Charleston, I consider it most probable

[1] *Illinois State Journal*, April 30, 1860. Preston King to Gideon Welles, April 9, 1860; Welles MSS.
[2] J. E. Harvey to John McLean, April 7, 1860; McLean MSS.
[3] Frederic Bancroft (ed.), *Speeches, Correspondence, and Political Papers of Carl Schurz*, Vol. I, pp. 79–107.

that Seward will get the nomination in Chicago. If Douglas is nominated, Lincoln will probably be the man for our side. I should be very well satisfied with either." [1] A month later he sent Congressman Potter a long letter, writing about presidential politics: "Seward stock is rising in the West. Bates may have gained a little . . . but he will not get the foreign vote. I think Seward stands the best chance, but, if he should fail to get the nomination, Lincoln's and Wade's prospects are the next best." [2] The same day he wrote to Senator Doolittle: —

As to Wade I agree with you perfectly. I have a kind of fondness for the brave old Roundhead, but I think Lincoln will be stronger in the Convention. If Pennsylvania and New Jersey should unite upon Wade, that would alter the case. But as things now are it looks as though Seward would go into the Convention with nearly a majority of the delegates.

Only one day of April remained when Lincoln received a most important communication from C. M. Allen of Indiana's delegation to Chicago. Delegate Allen gave the interesting information that the Indiana delegation would arrive at Chicago unpledged, ready to award their votes to the highest bidder. Indiana being naturally partial to Lincoln, the Illinois favorite son was given the first chance to do business, thanks to the fact that certain Indiana delegates did not like the growing Bates strength in their state. This information, the first genuine encouragement Lincoln had got that he might corral enough delegates to win, left him undecided. Should he accept or not? All day the question bothered him. Political deals of this sort were always distasteful to him. Lincoln took the problem to bed with him, thought it over and over, considering every angle of the situation, then next morning rose early, ready to play the game. He sat down and wrote [3]: —

Springfield, Ills., May 1, 1860

HON: C. M. ALLEN:

My dear Sir: Your very kind letter of the 27th, was received yesterday. This writing being early in the morning, Douglas is not yet nominated;

[1] Bancroft, *Papers of Carl Schurz*, Vol. I, p. 111.
[2] Schurz to Potter, April 12, 1860; Bancroft, Vol. I, p. 113.
[3] Tracy, p. 145.

but we suppose he certainly will be before sun-set today, a few of the smaller Southern states having seceded from the convention — just enough to permit his nomination, and not enough to hurt him much at the election. This puts the case in the hardest shape for us. But fight we must; and conquer we shall, in the end.

Our friend Dubois, and Judge David Davis, of Bloomington, one or both, will meet you at Chicago, on the 12th.

If you let Usher and Griswold of Terre Haute know, I think they will co-operate with you.

Yours very truly,
A. LINCOLN.

Though he was here pulling the wires most adroitly, he finished with that as quickly as he could, perferring to write about national issues and to wax oratorical — "But fight we must; and conquer we shall."

Next day he wrote again to Delegate Corwine of Ohio: —

"Yours of the 30th ult. is just received. After what you have said, it is perhaps proper I should post you, so far as I am able, as to the 'lay of the land.' First I think the Illinois delegation will be unanimous for me at the start; and no other delegation will. A few individuals in other delegations would like to go for me at the start, but may be restrained by their colleagues. It is represented to me by men who ought to know, that the whole of Indiana might not be difficult to get. You know how it is in Ohio. I am certainly not the first choice there; and yet I have not heard that anyone makes any positive objection to me. It is just so everywhere as far as I can perceive. Everywhere, except here in Illinois and possibly Indiana, one or another is preferred to me, but there is no positive objection. This is the ground as it now appears. I believe you personally know C. M. Allen of Vincennes, Indiana. He is a delegate and has notified me that the entire Indiana delegation will be in Chicago the same day you name, Saturday, the 12th. My friends, Jesse K. Dubois, our auditor, and Judge David Davis, will probably be there ready to confer with friends from other states. Let me hear from you again when anything occurs." [1]

Pipe-laying season was over when the first week of May had gone by and bracing spring weather arrived in all its expansive vegetable beauty. With spring the convention season had arrived; party conclaves would presently meet and adjudge all booms, either bestowing the official blessing or tossing them into discard. The Lincoln boom, thanks to the fact that his backers ran the Party's Illinois machine, would win in the Decatur Convention in spite of a Seward boom in northern counties. But the Lincoln for President movement lacked the important element of vigorous enthusiasm. Let three Illinois Republican leaders bear witness. On April 16 Trumbull received a personal letter from Joseph Medill (now back in Chicago) and one from Gustave Koerner.[1] Medill in his strictly private opinion believed "an impression is gaining ground that the Chicago Convention *dare* not nominate Seward, and will not nominate Bates or Lincoln." Koerner was of the opinion that "the delegates from Illinois will be probably instructed for Lincoln, but finally they may have to decide between Seward and somebody else." Two months earlier, David Davis had written confidentially, "Who should be nominated at Chicago [?] Of course I should like it if Lincoln could be nominated, but I am afraid that is foregone conclusion. It seems to me . . . now, as if it would either be Mr. Bates or Gov. Seward." [2]

The fact is that until the ardently and surprisingly pro-Lincoln events of the Decatur Convention Lincoln was, like all dark horses, a colorless compromise candidate. His backers were either personal friends or politicians who thought they could do better for themselves by supporting Lincoln than by doing service for any other candidate.

Under certain conditions of intense internal antagonism, any Party may be forced to nominate a compromise man who is not a strong leader in his own right, but for the Republican Party to choose a colorless makeshift candidate would have been unthinkable. For 'twas a young Party, vigorous, crusading, thriving on en-

---

[1] Trumbull MSS.
[2] David Davis to ——, Feb. 20, 1860; Chicago Historical Society.

thusiasm. Its *première* national canvass had been a "hullabaloo campaign" (in the political scientist's term) second only to the riotous "Log Cabin and Hard Cider" campaign which elected William Henry Harrison. And harbingers foreshadowed a campaign even more spectacular than that of 1856.

In the spirit of the day Chicago Republicans had been preparing to receive in the grand manner their first nationally important political convention. The committee in charge of a meeting place had gone to the extreme of erecting a special building, which after the nominations would serve as Chicago's Republican headquarters for the canvass. Five thousand dollars had been raised by subscription, and early in April carpenters were busily manipulating timbers on a vacant lot at Market and Lake Streets, southeast corner, once the site of early Chicago's famous hostelry, the Saugnash Tavern, but of late occupied by puddles of water, "sundry tin cans, hoop-skirts, dead cats, and other debris attendant upon civic progress," erecting a rambling two-story wooden shed which would be "the largest audience room in the United States." On the Market Street front was a wide space that would accommodate a large overflow crowd. It was named "The Great Wigwam" after the terminology of New York politics.[1]

Shrewd Republicans at once began to celebrate the Wigwam as a symbol of Republican vigor and strength. Said the *Press & Tribune:* "The Wigwam 'takes.' It is going to be the 'daddy' of a numerous progeny of big and little wigwams. Every Republican club in every considerable town will have its wigwam. The log cabin days are about being revived." [2]

At the Macon County Republican Convention an aggressive Decatur politician named Richard J. Oglesby had been named head of a committee for providing the State Republican Convention with a meeting place.[3] Richard Oglesby's handsome head was full of political sense; he saw the value of Wigwam symbolism and deter-

---

[1] P. O. Ray, *The Convention That Nominated Lincoln*, p. 5. H. C. Whitney, *Lincoln the Citizen*, p. 286. Chicago *Press & Tribune*, April, 1860, *passim.*
[2] April 12.
[3] Chicago *Press & Tribune* April 23

mined to produce a Decatur Wigwam to house the Convention. Like his friend Jesse Fell, Oglesby was a man of wide interests and experience. He had been a fighter in the Mexican War, a forty-niner, a world traveler, a Whig; and as a Republican lawyer-politician he knew Lincoln well. Oglesby saw that if Lincoln was to receive the Republican nomination not as a makeshift but as a strong candidate, he would need "running qualities" of dramatic appeal to the common people. Was there not, Oglesby asked himself, something romantic about Lincoln that would make the popular heart go out to him, invest him with a catchword nickname which would make every good Republican want to shout every time the inspiring title rose into his consciousness, arousing an explosive enthusiasm like that conjured up by the pet names "Old Hickory" in 1828, "Old Tippecanoe" in 1840, "the Pathfinder" in 1856? Oglesby's impression was that his friend Lincoln, with his humble beginnings and courageous rise, his struggles for the cause of freedom, possessed capital running qualities. Did not the sobriquet "Old Abe" recall both Old Hickory and Old Tippecanoe? But Lincoln's personal elements of popularity lay dormant, and Oglesby's job was to discover and advertise them.

Still living in Decatur was old John Hanks, with whom Lincoln had cleared land and navigated rivers back in the good old days when, a giant barely old enough to vote, the lank Hoosier had first come to Illinois. Oglesby looked up the old-timer and wanted to know "what kind of work 'Abe' used to be good at." Old John stroked his long bushy beard, replied, "Well, not much of any kind but dreaming, but he did help me split a lot of rails when we made the clearing twelve miles west of here." What a beautiful parallel, thought the delighted Oglesby, to William Henry Harrison and his hard cider. So next day he drove west with Hanks to where the rails were chopped out. Old John walked over to a rail fence, took his knife and chipped away at the rails, indistinguishable after rains and snows of thirty years. He cried triumphantly, "There they are. They are the identical rails we made"—exhibiting as proof a handful of black walnut and honey locust shavings. Then he pointed out several walnut stumps. Oglesby appropriated two weatherbeaten rails, drove back to town with them dragging beneath his buggy, stole into his barn where the trophies were carefully hidden until convention day. Meantime Oglesby told his plan to some of the boys, and a big show was planned for Lincoln, "the Rail Splitter." [1]

When May 9 came round Oglesby had managed a Wigwam by borrowing a huge canvas and renting lumber. His men worked these meager materials into a large, flimsy tent, anchored it precariously to a building — the result looking like a place where ranting revivalists exhorted people to sin no more.[2] Beneath that low tent gathered the Republican leaders of Illinois, bursting with enthusiasm. A *Tribune* reporter caught the pre-convention tone [3]: —

The town is overflowing with delegates. The citizens are receiving them very cordially. The Republican latch string is out. Ninety delegates have already arrived. It is believed that every county in the state will be represented.

Egypt is here in strong force. The day has been spent in friendly consultation. . . . Everything is working harmoniously, the best of feeling prevails in spite of the efforts of various individuals to sow discord among the delegates in order to beat Judd. The Convention will be nearly unanimous for Lincoln for President, and the delegates to the Chicago Convention will probably be instructed for him. The central and southern counties are opposed to Seward and are divided between McLean and Bates for second choice. The northern counties generally favor Seward, but the Convention will express no formal second choice for President. . . .

This speculation about second choice indicates clearly that the Illinois delegates did not expect to vote for Lincoln very long when the balloting began at Chicago. But to name formally a second presidential choice would seriously damage Lincoln by advertising that expectation.

[1] Reminiscence of Oglesby, in J. M. Davis, *How Abraham Lincoln Became President,* pp. 63–67. Statement of John Hanks, in Weik, *The Real Lincoln,* pp. 276–277. Jane Martin Johns: *Personal Recollections of Early Decatur,* pp. 79–81; "The Nomination of Abraham Lincoln," *Journal,* Ill. State Hist. Soc., Vol. X, pp. 563–564. Barton, *President Lincoln,* Vol. I, pp. 79–82.

[2] Johns, *Personal Recollections,* pp. 79–80.

[3] Chicago *Press & Tribune,* May 9, 1860.

Lincoln arrived on Tuesday, the eighth, ready for the big event. He was aware that something concerning rails he had once split was afoot,[1] but did not know exactly what. And many people came to town who had no business with the Convention but came just for the fun of it. Decatur was full up, lodging difficult to secure.[2] The Lincoln men held the conclave absolutely in their control as proceedings began at half-past ten o'clock Wednesday with Jackson Grimshaw calling the six hundred odd delegates to order. A host of three thousand jammed the Wigwam, and outside was another crowd which could not get in, all gabbling about who would be nominated for Governor.

After lunch the Convention met in session again and rapidly put through the permanent organization. Joe Gillespie made a speech accepting the Chair; then Oglesby jumped up and sang out, "I am informed that a distinguished citizen of Illinois, and one whom Illinois will ever delight to honor, is present, and I wish to move that this body invite him-to a seat on the stand."

He paused as suspense spread, then shouted: *"Abraham Lincoln!"*

Shouts of approval rang out so tumultuously the Wigwam shook. Oglesby's motion carried in this hurricane of applause, and Lincoln was discovered sitting unobtrusively near the back. Somebody seized him and tried to propel him toward the stand. But the crowd was too dense, and to his amazement Lincoln found himself lifted up bodily, balanced horizontally on heads and shoulders. Squirming and wriggling, the uncomfortable six feet four of politician was gradually pushed toward the speaker's stand, which he at last reached "in the arms of some half-dozen gentlemen." It was a great demonstration and the crowd loved it, roared approvingly as the disheveled candidate thanked them for the affectionate reception, appearing (says a witness) "the most diffident and worst-plagued men I ever saw." [3]

This was the psychological moment for Oglesby's rail stunt. He

---

[1] "Viator," in *Illinois State Journal,* May 7, 1860.

[2] *Illinois State Journal,* May 10.

[3] Lamon, pp. 444–445. Reminiscence of J. G. Cannon, in "Speech of Hon. Joseph G. Cannon, of Illinois, before the Chamber of Commerce, Pittsburg, Pa., Feb. 12, 1910," p. 8.

announced that an old Macon County Democrat, who had grown
gray in the service of his Party, wished to contribute something.
The crowd roared, "Receive it! Receive it!" So down through the
crowd came marching old John Hanks himself, and a friend, bearing
those two rails upright, flags and streamers hanging in decoration;
and between them like a billboard was a banner: —

ABRAHAM LINCOLN
THE RAIL CANDIDATE FOR PRESIDENT IN 1860

Two Rails From a Lot of 3,000 Made in 1830
by John [1] Hanks and Abe Lincoln — Whose
Father was the First Pioneer of Macon County.

Applause thundered again. "The roof was literally cheered off the
building, hats and canes and books and papers were tossed aloft, as
men jumped and screamed and howled, until part of the awning fell
on their heads. When the enthusiasm finally subsided the Wigwam
was almost a wreck." [2] The tumult went on for fifteen minutes; people for miles around heard the uproar and reflected on the enthusiasm
of the Republicans. The shouters clamored for a speech from Lincoln. He stood up and told how, when he first came to Illinois, he
had split rails and helped build a cabin and fence a farm on the
Sangamon River. These rails, he had been told, were from that fence.
But whether they really were or not, he had mauled many better
ones in his day. Cheers exploded as he sat down.[3]
Then the convention hurried to finish with their gubernatorial business. A ballot showed Judd in the lead, Leonard Swett second, Richard

[1] The sign painter made two mistakes. Thomas Lincoln was by no means the first
pioneer of Macon County. And his sign read "Thos. Hanks" for John Hanks; he had
confused the Thomas of Thomas Lincoln with the John of John Hanks.
[2] Johns, "The Nomination of Abraham Lincoln," p. 564.
[3] *Illinois State Journal*, May 11, 1860. Speech of Hon. E. B. Washburne, of Illinois.
Delivered in the U. S. House of Representatives, May 29, 1860, pp. 1–2. Republican
campaign document.

Yates third. Judd was far from having a majority, and in two more ballots he held steady while Swett lost and Yates gained. On the fourth Swett released his support to Yates, making him the nominee. A German, Hoffman, was chosen by acclamation as Yates's running mate. Yates took the stand and spoke at length with his usual brilliance, saying that while he would support the nominee of the Chicago Convention, he strongly preferred Abraham Lincoln.[1] The crowd then called for Judd, who elaborately explained that he was "highly satisfied with the action of the Convention." They howled for Swett, who told them he likewise was not angry. Then, after adopting motions that a committee to name Chicago delegates, and another to frame a platform, be selected, they adjourned at six o'clock until next day. Before dark that evening the delegate committee, having left the Wigwam, went to a grove hard by and made out their list of delegates. This list they submitted to Lincoln and revised according to his directions.[2]

Next morning the first business was filling out the state ticket. This done, John M. Palmer jumped up and offered a resolution [3]:

Resolved, That Abraham Lincoln is the choice of the Republican party of Illinois for the Presidency, and the delegates from this State are instructed to use all honorable means to secure his nomination by the Chicago Convention, and to vote as a unit for him.

A Freeport delegate, speaking for the Seward forces from the north, made some remarks against the resolution, to which Palmer replied in a powerful speech.[4] The Sewardites then yielded to pressure and the Lincoln instructions carried unanimously, and the Committee on Delegates reported their selections. Delegates-at-large were: Gustave Koerner, N. B. Judd, David Davis, O. H. Browning.[5] Even though his Chicago delegates had been approved by Lincoln, Leonard Swett

[1] *Illinois State Journal*, May 10, 1860.
[2] Arnold, *Life of Lincoln*, p. 163.
[3] O. H. Oldroyd, *Lincoln's Campaign*, p. 9.
[4] Johns, *Personal Recollections*, p. 82. Davis, *How Lincoln Became President*, p. 71.
[5] *Illinois State Journal*, May 11.

believed that eight of the twenty-two would gladly have supported
Seward.[1]

When the Convention adjourned *sine die* that afternoon after adopting their platform, Candidate Lincoln held a position very different
from that of two days before. He had definitely outgrown the "favorite
son" status and become a threatening dark horse. His support, not
in itself impressive, was potentially dangerous because it came from
one of the pivotal doubtful states. And as a dark horse he had a far
stronger position than that which such a candidate usually enjoys,
because the nominating convention would meet in Lincoln's state,
under the thumb of Lincoln men. Many dark horses never get started
in convention; Lincoln as the Illinois favorite son was sure of a good
send-off. The rail explosion, making him the beloved Rail Splitter,
symbolizing the rights of free labor, had suddenly given the Lincoln
boom an emotional strength which, in the West, no other candidate
could approach. The latent strength of this popular force which came
swiftly to the aid of the Lincoln boom was something which Seward
men, Chase men, Bates men, and the rest, knew nothing about until
they reached Chicago. And when they did awaken, they found it quite
beyond their control.

[1] Swett to J. H. Drummond, May 27, 1860, in Oldroyd, *Lincoln's Campaign*, p. 71.

CHAPTER V

Gathering of the Clan

LORD BACON has it in one of his most famous essays that "all rising to great place is by a winding stair." Not quite all. The American convention system makes it possible for a man to be seized and jerked abruptly aloft. Political vicissitudes shot upward into great place Presidents Polk, Pierce, and Harding, Lincoln and Hayes. Sometimes, as when a deep sea diver rises too rapidly from oceanic depths to the top, the rapid change is too much for the man's constitution, causing great injury. But, as happened with Lincoln and Hayes, the man may be strong enough to stand the swift elevation.

If, as Americans believe, the convention system has provided better rulers than monarchic methods would have done, that opinion ought to be taken as slanderous to royalty rather than complimentary to our indigenous political habits. Politics, in the last analysis, exists not to furnish the body politic with efficient democratic government, but for its own sake — a kind of worldly "art for art's sake." Lifeblood to both a political Party and a political career is control of offices; hence the aim of a politician is not to put in office the best man, but to place *his* man. This well established custom, an outrage to a political philosophy, is an idiosyncrasy which the electorate tolerates and pays for because Parties perform the indispensable function of furnishing a governing personnel within the forms of a democratic political system. A nominating National Convention therefore serves as a preliminary heat in the hard race for offices; a conclave like that for which Chicago was excitedly preparing in April and early May provides the setting for energetic struggles of fellow partisans over choice offices which will be theirs should they succeed in bringing their Party into power the subsequent November. The ultimate object of the massing Party leaders is to agree upon such plans and leaders as are necessary to bring the Government safely into their hands; but there is always that immediate object of making the Party accept one's own favored leaders and issues. In the long and fascinating history of National Conventions there have been instances in which the conflict over choosing the presidential candidate became so bitter that a Party was forced to nominate an impossible person, thereby committing political suicide. Delegates, therefore, who came swarming into Chicago as May 16 drew nigh, arrived with orders to act, not to reason, deliberate, weigh.

During the weeks preceding the Republican pilgrimage to Chicago, President-guessing in newspapers had rolled merrily along as usual,[1] though arguments for this or that candidate were no longer news after so many repetitions. A wag on the Ohio *Cultivator* solemnly announced, "New Candidate!" urging everybody to support "GENERAL PROSPERITY." [2] Greeley's *Tribune*, doing all possible for Bates, was having an argument with James Watson Webb of the New York *Courier and Enquirer*. Wrote Editor Webb, firing solid shot [3]: —

While we believe that justice, principle and expediency, all demand the nomination of William H. Seward, and to throw him overboard is to insure the triumph of the democracy, we have no hesitation in saying that we shall labor earnestly for the election of any other Republican of 1856, as we should for the election of Seward, if nominated. That is to say, if Fremont, Chase, Banks, Hale, Fessenden, Cameron, Wade, Lincoln, Trumbull, or any Republican who acted with us in 1856, should be nominated instead of William H. Seward, this Press . . . will be found battling for the cause with as much zeal as if the convention had given us the strongest

[1] *Illinois State Journal*, April 6, 9, 23, 30, May 9, 1860.
Central Illinois Gazette, April 11, 18, May 9.
Chicago *Press & Tribune*, April 3, 12, 16, 18, 21.
[2] Clipped in *Central Illinois Gazette*, April 11.
[3] New York *Courier and Enquirer*, Feb. 11.
F. D. Parish to John Sherman, May 1, 1860; John Sherman MSS

name for our support. But if on the contrary, the Republican convention should so far forget what is due to their constituents, as to place in nomination and proclaim as our standard-bearer for 1860 Mr. Bates, or any other person who labored successfully to defeat us in 1856 and thus secured the election of James Buchanan, we repeat what we have hitherto said, no earthly power will induce us to support such a nominee. . . .

Webb was sure that no non-Republican of 1856 among the Republican possibilities, such as Bates, Bell, Crittenden, could carry New York. Greeley scathingly argued that Bates or any Republican nominee could carry New York easily, inviting Webb to bolt to his heart's content. "No ticket that Webb bolted ever failed to succeed in this state, and none ever will." [1]

An Indianapolis sheet ran a long story declaring McLean the most available man in spite of his age. He could carry the doubtful states, Seward or Chase could not. "McLean is old, but he is vigorous, and his temperate, regular life is a better assurance that he will fill his term than the dissipated vigor of younger men. . . . In the same class, and next to Judge McLean, we believe that Abraham Lincoln of Illinois presents the best combination of qualities as a candidate and officer." [2] Lincoln's friend Baker of the *Journal* triumphantly reported, on the last day of April, that "the Baltimore *Turnzeitung*, the central organ of the German Turner Bund of the United States, which society consists of more than 20,000 members, came out last week in a long and emphatic editorial in favor of ABRAHAM LINCOLN for the Presidency." Said the *Turnzeitung:* —

. Will Douglas be nominated by the Democrats, it is then the imperative duty . . . for the Republicans to assemble around a man, for whom the better part of the people can be excited to enthusiasm. Will we on the score of expediency pass Mr. Seward by, then will Mr. LINCOLN be *the* man as a matter of course. . . . He has already once fought a battle for life and death with the "Little Giant," and come out of that titan-fight as victor. . . . *Under a standard-bearer like him, the Republican party would be certain of victory,* even against Mr. Douglas. . . .

[1] New York *Tribune,* clipped in *Central Illinois Gazette,* April 18, 1860.
[2] *Indiana State Journal,* clipped in *Illinois State Journal,* April 23.

Greeley's potent *Weekly Tribune* printed, in weeks prior to May, correspondence in favor of Bates, Read, McLean, Bell, Cameron, Fremont, Dayton, Chase, Wade, but no Lincoln letters. As May opened the New York *Herald* discussed Republican prospects, mentioning "four living, two dead, aspirants." The living — Seward, Banks, Chase, Cameron; the dead — Bates, McLean. Nine days later the New York *Independent* editorialized on the impending Chicago nomination: "Give us a man known to be true upon the only question that enters into the canvass — a Seward, a Chase, a Wade, a Sumner, a Fessenden, a Banks." A. Lincoln would not do.[1]

And there had been an important new development in President-guessing. Magazines were joining the game. *Harper's Weekly*, "a first-class illustrated paper, the best and cheapest family newspaper in the world," ran an editorial that spring on "Presidential Candidates," alongside new fiction by Charles Dickens and Wilkie Collins, new poetry by Alfred Tennyson and George Meredith, a commemoration of the late Lord Macaulay, and two thrilling sea serpents, absolutely authentic. Douglas was discussed as the leading Democratic candidate. On the Republican side, according to the world's best and cheapest family newspaper [2]: —

Senator William H. Seward stands forth in prominent relief as the legitimate chief of the anti-slavery faction. He is the father of the Republican party; and if no considerations of policy or availability were permitted to interfere with the nomination, he would get it as a matter of course. It appears doubtful, however, whether he could carry Pennsylvania, New Jersey, and Illinois; and hence many ardent Republicans are looking elsewhere for a more available man.

Bates was discussed next because the New York *Tribune* was backing him. Called "a Fillmore Whig," his Republicanism was questioned. Then came Chase, Banks, Cameron. Of Senator Cameron: —

Outside of his state . . . his strength is unknown; and never having done any thing to attract general notice, it seems doubtful whether his

[1] Ida Tarbell, *Lincoln*, Vol. I, pp. 341–342.
[2] *Harper's Weekly*, Vol. IV, p. 162. March 17, 1860.

nomination would help his party in Indiana, Illinois, or the border states of the South. So with Abraham Lincoln, of Illinois, who has his partisans; he might do well in the Far West, but in Pennsylvania and New Jersey his name would add no strength to the ticket.

Books, too, were doing it. Late in 1859 a book had appeared from the pen of Republican journalist David W. Bartlett. This volume of *Presidential Possibilities* presented Author Bartlett's preliminary material from which he planned to write a campaign biography of each and every nominee. Bartlett wrote brief biographies of twenty-one "possibilities." First on the roster was William H. Seward, followed by Stephen A. Douglas. Then came the apparent second and third choice of the Republicans, Chase and Bates. The roll call went on through the smaller fry, concluding with John C. Fremont. No word was said about Abraham Lincoln.[1]

In *Harper's Weekly,* issue of Saturday, May 12, appeared a giant double-page lithograph exhibiting the solemn features of eleven gentlemen, "prominent candidates for the Republican Presidential nomination at Chicago." [2] From the central position of distinction, overshadowing the other ten, peered the lugubrious lineaments of Senator Seward. In the third and bottom row, between a sad-looking Fremont and a panorama of Washington, was the handsome portrait of Lincoln which doubly memorialized the Cooper Institute speech.[3] Homely Abraham, thanks to the artistry of Photographer Brady, looked the handsomest, most intellectual, of the lot. Appended was a huge page carrying a biography of all the aspirants except Cassius Clay. Seward's was almost a thousand words long. Lincoln's, shortest of the lot, was placed last.

The shrewd, erratic brain of Horace Greeley, (which bore a great reputation as a political prognosticator),[4] stocked with what he considered all the facts in the case, labored and brought forth a Greeleyan prophecy in the May 12 issue of his *Tribune.* He had written, before he entrained for Chicago, "Mr. Seward will lead, Mr. Bates will come

[1] W. E. Barton, "The Lincoln of the Biographers," p. 60.
[2] *Harper's Weekly*, Vol. IV, pp. 296–297.
[3] Reproduced in Albert Shaw, *Abraham Lincoln: The Year of His Election*, p. 45.
[4] *Illinois State Register*, in *Illinois State Journal*, March 3, 1860.

next, Mr. Chase will be third . . . Mr. Cameron will come next, and then Mr. Lincoln. The latter is being pressed by the Illinois delegation as a compromise candidate and would be accepted by all the Northwest cheerfully." [1]

On crowded special trains which rattled towards the mecca of Chicago, jammed with ebullient delegates and visitors, enthusiastic sentiments found a partial outlet in taking straw votes, results of which were published by the Chicago press as the Convention drew nearer and nearer. Straw voters on a Michigan Central special gave Seward 210, all other candidates 30. A Northwestern train from the north gave Seward 127, all others 44. From the west came a Chicago & Rock Island train, ten loaded coaches of Republicans giving Seward 113, others 41. From Milwaukee came partisans who gave Seward 368, Lincoln 93, all others 46. But when a special from Indiana reported, Lincoln had 51, Seward 43, all others 131 — Lincoln's only straw victory, and not a very impressive one. [2]

On one of those Chicago-bound cars were four men who well knew what a fight they had before them if their friend Lincoln was to have any chance to win the grand prize. They were Judge David Davis, at Decatur created generalissimo of the Lincoln-for-President coterie, and his lieutenants, Judge Stephen Logan, Leonard Swett, Jesse Dubois, [3] all of them old associates of the Rail Splitter in law and politics. Davis, corpulent, rich, acquisitive and not overscrupulous, was presiding judge of the circuit courts in which Lincoln practised. Logan was the second law partner of the rising splitter of rails.

What a candidate, what a man to beat, Seward appeared to them! [4] They were so fearful Seward would be chosen that they were "ready to unite on any other man" if Lincoln should prove unable to succeed. [5] Their man was so little known to the nation at large that when

---

[1] In Davis, *How Lincoln Became President*, p. 74.
[2] P. O. Ray, *The Convention That Nominated Lincoln*, p. 15.
[3] H. C. Whitney, *Lincoln the Citizen*, p. 286.
[4] Norman B. Judd, in H. B. Rankin, *Intimate Character Sketches*, pp. 198–200.
Frank D. Carpenter, "How Lincoln Was Nominated," *Century*, Vol. XXIV, pp. 853–854. Preston King to John Bigelow, Jan. 16, 1860, in John Bigelow, *Retrospections of an Active Life*, Vol. I, pp. 250–251. Preston King to Gideon Welles, July 30, 1858; James Dixon to Welles, Feb. 27, 1860; Welles MSS.
[5] William Jayne to Trumbull, May 20, 1860; in White, *Life of Trumbull*, pp. 106–107.

Harper's Weekly chronicled his nomination in its issue of May 26 the editors featured, with a huge lithograph of the Brady Cooper Union portrait, a long story about "Hon. Abram Lincoln of Illinois." Worse, a hurried hack writer dashed off after the nomination a campaign biography of one Abram Lincoln. The biographer did not know his subject's name! [1] The nation was several weeks getting straight the first name of the Republican nominee. But with Seward — so interested was the nation in the Senator that as early as 1854 his *Works* were published in three large volumes and sold widely. The next year a demand was met for a one volume edition with an up-to-date memoir.[2]

On February 29, when Lincoln was riding north toward New Hampshire, Seward had delivered his carefully considered speech against radicalism. During this session of Congress he had been almost daily attacked by Southerners in Congress as a revolutionary who cared nothing for the Union. An alarming number of people were placing blame for the John Brown raid upon the orator of the higher law and the irrepressible conflict. Shrewd observers like James Pike of the New York *Tribune* were writing, "I have had a very strong belief in Mr. Seward's nomination till Mr. Brown visited Virginia." [3] Fright of Northern conservatives at Republican extremism had caused the Party to lose ground in spring elections in Connecticut and Rhode Island, a fact which Abraham Lincoln and Lyman Trumbull noted as "a drawback on the prospects of Gov. Seward." [4]

Republicans in high office were awake to the drawbacks of Seward's radical reputation.[5] Senator Dixon of Connecticut wrote to Gideon Welles, chairman of Connecticut's Chicago delegation, "A singular state of feeling exists relative to his [Seward's] prospect at Chicago. I do not know a single Senator, except his colleague, who desires his nomination. Still almost every Senator believes he will be the chosen

[1] Barton, "The Lincoln of the Biographers," p. 66, pp. 88–89.
[2] G. E. Baker (ed.), *The Life of William H. Seward, with Selections from His Works,* p. 3.
[3] Pike to Congressman Washburn of Maine, Jan. 29, 1860, in Herriott, "The Conference in the Deutches Haus," p. 116.
[4] Herriott, "Deutches Haus," p. 120.
[5] Amos Tuck to Chase, Sept. 3, 1859; Chase MSS.

man." [1] James Sherman, chairman of New Jersey's Chicago delegation, attempted to promote the cause of New Jersey's favorite son, Dayton, by shaking a finger at J. H. Tweedy, Wisconsin's Republican national committeeman, because Wisconsin was for Seward. Admonished Sherman [2]: —

It is conceded by all judicious and well advised men that Mr. Seward's Nomination will revive the divisions of 1856 in Pennsylvania and New Jersey, and will be fatal to us in those states. I have great opportunity for knowing the feeling in Philadelphia and information for the whole of Pennsylvania concentrates there. I am sure that the whole of their Congressional delegation (except perhaps Mr. Cameron) are united and earnest in this opinion, and their candidate for Governor, Mr. Curtin, is exceedingly anxious, fearing that Seward's nomination would render his own election hopeless. . . . His (Curtin's) election is necessary to our success in November. . . .

The Candidate must be a true Republican and a conservative. He must be able to carry Pennsylvania and New Jersey. Judge Dayton is the man.

This real danger to his candidacy Seward had sought to repel, since his return to the Senate in January, by open conciliatory conduct. His Washington house, social center of Republicans in the Capital, blossomed with lavish hospitality. Backers of other candidates were wined, dined, impressed with the charming personality of William Henry Seward. On April 29 he gave an affair in honor of Salmon P. Chase (recently returned to the Senate) and Governor Dennison of Ohio. Other significant guests were three Bates promoters: Henry Winter Davis, Montgomery Blair, Frank Blair. [3] Earlier, Seward had made direct attack on the Bates support by personally visiting Maryland leaders and persuasively promising a fat harvest of plums for Maryland when Seward should be President. A Chase worker, reporting his fears that Maryland was leaning to Seward, moaned, "He & his friends *work — work*. They not only work, but *he works*." [4]

---

[1] Dixon to Welles, Jan. 4, 1860, in J. L. Sellers, "The Make Up of the Early Republican Party," *Transactions*, Ill. State Hist. Soc., 1930, p. 49.
[2] Sherman to Tweedy; in Sellers, p. 49. *Cf.* also *The Gate City*, Keokuk, Iowa, Jan. 11, 1860; in *Annals of Iowa*, Vol. IX, pp. 272–273.
[3] F. W. Seward, *Seward at Washington*, Vol. I, pp. 441–448.
[4] J. M. Ashley to Chase, April 5, 1860; Chase MSS.

Seward and Weed were quite familiar with the doubtful state argument of the stop-Seward forces. Appreciating the strategic importance of Pennsylvania's delegation, Thurlow Weed and Seward had been in touch with Senator Cameron for a year. Cameron, tongue in cheek, spouted promises that Seward would have Pennsylvania's support.[1] Some observers believed the Cameron movement a piece of Seward strategy, that in the convention the Cameron vote would swing to Seward at the proper time.[2] Seward even boasted that Cameron's friends were his friends.[3] Others were less naïve. Seward will find Pennsylvania false, said one realist. "They have both endeavored to cheat each other." [4] The same observer wrote in April [5]: —

Seward is deluded, & almost crazed on this subject. His whole heart is directed & absorbed by the thought of entering the White House, about which he speaks with a fanatical certainty.

One day late in the President-guessing season brilliant Murat Halstead of the Cincinnati *Commercial* sat in the Senate press gallery etching sprightly caricatures of presidential candidates in action on the Senate floor. "Now an individual appears . . . who at first sight seems to be rather a comical person. He has the most singular head in all the assortment before you. It rises above the ears like a dome, and looks not unlike a straw stack in shape and color. His nose — a high, sharp beak — strikes out below the strawy hair that thatches the dome. . . . This tall and peaked and pallid head is perched upon a body that is active and restless. It moves about with school-boy elasticity. It walks with a slashing swagger. It strikes off with a rollicking gait from one point to another, and is in and out of the chamber by turns. There is an oddity in the dress in harmony with the general queerness of the thing. The pantaloons have a dingy oaken appearance. . . . There is certainly a grotesque amount of coat tail. Now after making the round of the Republican side of the chamber about twice

---

[1] Seward to Weed, April 29, 1859, March 15, 1860; in Barnes, *Memoir of Thurlow Weed*, pp. 256, 261.
[2] J. Hanna to Chase, Sept. 8, 1859; E. L. Pierce to Chase, Sept. 21, 1859; Chase MSS.
[3] J. Dixon to Welles, Feb. 27, 1860; Welles MSS.
[4] J. E. Harvey to McLean, Sept. 5, 1859; McLean MSS.
[5] Harvey to McLean, April 7, 1860; McLean MSS.

in ten minutes he offers . . . a petition, in a hoarse croaking voice; and when the Vice-President recognizes 'The Senator from New York,' there is a stir in the galleries and a general stare at the gentleman with the top-knot and beak and voice. He sits down, takes a pinch of snuff, and presently you hear a vociferous sneezing, and the high-headed, straw-thatched gentleman is engaged upon his beak with a yellow silk handkerchief. And you remember that Seward takes snuff, and has ruined his voice by the nasty habit. In the Republican corner of the Senate-chamber is a familiar face and form — you recognize the portly person and massive intellectual developments, the thin frizzly hair and oval brow of Salmon P. Chase. . . . Seward comes up . . . and seems to be guilty of some good thing, for they laugh violently but quietly, and Seward rubs his oaken breeches with his hands and then gives his nose a tremendous tweak with the yellow handkerchief. He is wonderfully affable. He acts as though he would kiss a strange baby. Ah, he is a candidate for the Presidency." [1]

Gustave Koerner characterized Seward as "radical in theory, conservative in action." Seward's task was to make clear to the public and politicians, if possible, the accuracy of that description. On Leap Day, then, Senate galleries and floor packed with expectant listeners, Seward delivered his important speech. His language treating the slave problem was more subdued than ever before. "Irrepressible conflict" and "higher law" were not mentioned. He did not use his fighting words of other days that slavery "can be and must be abolished, and you and I can and must do it." The Republican Party, he insisted, had but one policy, "namely, the saving of the territories of the United States, if possible, by constitutional and lawful means, from being homes for slavery and polygamy." The Party, therefore, "feels the necessity of being practical in its care of the national health and life, while it leaves metaphysical speculation to those whose duty it is to cultivate the ennobling science of political philosophy." He elaborately denied, with subtle arguments, any Republican hostility to the South, any sectionalism in his Party. Applause thundered from the galleries. Nor could there be any disunion after a Republican national victory,

Seward insisted. "These hasty threats of disunion are so unnatural that they will find no hand to execute them." [1]

The Republican press loudly praised Seward's oration, and it was an intellectual feat. The pro-Seward New York *Times* proudly pointed out that the speech emanated from Seward's "desire to allay and remove unfounded prejudice from the public mind." [2] Quite true, for every paragraph was written to fit Seward's candidacy. Douglas chided Seward for having forgotten his "higher law." Abraham Lincoln, back home from his New England trip, saw that both those strong Lincoln papers, the *Illinois State Journal* and Chicago *Press & Tribune,* called Seward's oration "a great speech" and printed it in full.[3] The speech, said the *Press & Tribune,* "cannot fail of making a profound impression upon the country." Praising its moderation, the *Journal* urged everyone to read it carefully, for Seward had there vindicated "his position from the slanders, which unscruplous demagogism has heaped upon him." Lincoln, reading the speech, must have calculated its effect as improving Seward's chances while decreasing Lincoln's own opportunities. The speech at once became a campaign document and went into circulation by tens of thousands.

Historians have often told how the retractions of his February twenty-ninth speech damaged Seward as the Republican leader.[4] With Republican extremists, this was true. That picturesque, pugnacious Kentucky abolitionist, Cassius Marcellus Clay, fighter of many a bloody duel,[5] Republican national committeeman from Kentucky, nationally famed as an orator for more than a decade, dropped Seward like a hot potato. That speech, Clay exploded, "killed Seward with me forever!" [6] Clay was an old friend of both Seward and Chase. He had political control as Republican boss over considerable territory in Kentucky and western Virginia. Seward and Chase therefore treated him to their best honors. Seward in Washington invited Clay to dine; over the goblets Seward suggested that he confer with Weed at Albany.

[1] Frederic Bancroft, *The Life of William H. Seward,* Vol. I, pp. 511–517.
[2] Bancroft, Vol. I, p. 517.
[3] *Illinois State Journal,* March 8. Chicago *Press & Tribune,* March 5, 1860.
[4] E. D. Fite, *Presidential Campaign of 1860,* pp. 119–121.
[5] *Dictionary of American Biography,* Vol. IV, pp. 169–170.
[6] C. M. Clay, *The Life of Cassius Marcellus Clay,* Vol. I, pp. 241–243.

Clay went; Thurlow Weed received him "in a gushing way" but got no satisfaction from the Kentuckian.[1]

Greeley did not like Seward's eloquent speech either,[2] but this reaction was exceptional.[3] The popular view was expressed by *Harper's Weekly*[4]: —

Senator Seward's speech of the 29th of February (the last which he will ever deliver in Congress, his friends say) dissipated at once the fears of his opponents and the doubts of his more conservative friends.

Samuel Bowles, editor of that powerful Massachusetts paper, the Springfield *Republican,* having formerly preferred Banks, wrote to Weed that the favorable Massachusetts reaction to Seward's speech had been "very marked." The Massachusetts delegation to Chicago "will be so strong for Seward as to be against anybody else. All the New England delegates, save Connecticut's, will be equally satisfactory," thought Editor Bowles. "I hear of ultra old Whigs in Boston who say they are ready to take up Mr. Seward upon his recent speech. Banks writes me he is greatly impressed with it, and that it must and should enhance Seward's prospects."[5] Even Chase admitted that Seward had gained.[6] Well might Seward, awaiting results in his Auburn home, be confident that nothing could stop him.[7] Thurlow Weed would manage, Seward was sure, and doubted not Weed's ability to win even if he had not had Seward's long lead for a powerful starter. "A giant in ability," Greeley rated Thurlow Weed.

Other candidates too were confident the lightning was destined to

[1] Clay, Vol. I, pp. 239–247.
[2] J. S. Pike, *First Blows of the Civil War*, p. 301.
[3] Herriott, "Deutches Haus," pp. 120–121. E. B. Croker to Chase, May 18, 1860; Chase MSS.
[4] May 12, 1860.
[5] Bowles to Weed, March 5, 1860; in *Memoir of Thurlow Weed*, pp. 260–261.
[6] Bancroft, *Seward*, Vol. I, p. 519.
[7] Schuyler Colfax to S. Bowles, March 1859, in O. J. Hollister, *Life of Colfax*, p. 143. Also Colfax to Bowles, March 1860, *Ibid.*, p. 144.
G. W. Julian, *Political Recollections*, p. 177.
James G. Blaine, *Twenty Years of Congress*, Vol. I, pp. 165–166.
F. I. Herriott, "Iowa and the First Nomination of Abraham Lincoln," *Annals of Iowa*, Vol. VIII, pp. 94–95.
Wm. Cullen Bryant to J. Bigelow, Feb. 20, 1860, in Bigelow, *Retrospections*, Vol. I, p. 252. Preston King to Bigelow, March 8, 1860, *Ibid.*, Vol. I, p. 286.
Henry Wilson, *Rise and Fall of the Slave Power*, Vol. II, pp. 694–695.

strike them. Beneath the lofty brow of Salmon P. Chase flourished a strong opinion that Chase would be the next President of the United States. Chase, famed as a champion of freedom in the rôle of "Attorney General for the Negro," had been, like Weed, using all known means to capture the nomination. Shrewd Gustave Koerner rated him, in contrast to Seward, "radical in action as well as in thought." A dynamo of energy, Chase's career had been long, varied, distinguished. He had wanted the Republican nomination in 1856, but did not even come close.[1] Immediately thereafter he began pulling wires to secure the 1860 nomination. He wrote many letters to Republican leaders in 1857, soliciting their support, and the response gave him confidence. As Governor of Ohio during '58 and '59 he did everything he could think of "to inspirit his friends and to impress the public." [2] Chase held a mystical belief that his candidacy was a public duty. He wrote to an abolitionist editor who had come out for Seward [3]: —

> I cannot change my position. . . . A very large body of the people . . . would hardly vote for any man other than myself as a Republican nominee. . . . No effort of mine has produced this feeling. It seems to be of spontaneous growth.

Secure in this idea that the people would demand him, Chase scorned the practical methods by which delegates are won. He had no campaign manager; he held aloof from Seward's device of personal consultation with machine leaders of other states. He merely wrote letters. Many of his ardent supporters traveled wide in strenuous efforts to create Chase delegates,[4] but they lacked the weight of the candidate himself.[5] One traveler, telling Chase about Seward's Maryland visit, complained

---

[1] *Dictionary of American Biography*, Vol. IV, pp. 27–29.

[2] A. B. Hart, *Salmon Portland Chase*, p. 179.

[3] Chase to Gamaliel Bailey, Jan. 24, 1859; Chase MSS., Hist. Soc. of Pa.

[4] J. M. Ashley, Feb. 17, 1858; J. M. Walden, Feb. 18, May 3, 1858; J. M. Ashley, July 29, 1859, to Chase; Chase MSS. Chase to R. C. Parsons, April 4, 1860; Chase MSS. J. Medill to Chase, April 26, June 8, July 29, 1859; Chase MSS., Hist. Soc. of Pa. Medill asked for copies of an article from the Columbus *Gazette* for salting the Western press. The article argued that a Western man be the Republican nominee. Medill told Chase his strategy was "to work underground for you and openly for a *Western* man." The *Press & Tribune*, he continued, will not announce Chase as its choice until late, for an early coming-out for Chase would concentrate Seward fire on him — "We must not fire the mine until the powder is properly laid."

[5] J. H. Baker to Chase, July 31, 1859; J. M. Ashley to Chase, July 29, 1859; R. G. Orwig to Chase, March 5, 1860; Chase MSS.

because Chase did not go there and do some promising in his own behalf.[1] Another wrote [2]: —

The impression seems to be gaining ground that the Republican nomination lies between you & Gov. Seward. . . . The great point . . . is to secure the voices of Penna., New Jersey & Illinois in the Convention — in my opinion the man who shall be the choice of these three states will be the nominee.

When his workers reported that Chase's cause was damaged by his reputation as a free-trader, Chase modified his position, declaring that he favored a tariff for revenue.[3]

Candidate Chase received numerous letters which assured him he would win, many which said he would not. A Vermont politician wrote, "No other candidate . . . will be likely to have so many . . . friends at the start." [4] One correspondent, sending an alarming formula for a hair restorative, hailed Chase "The next President of this nation!" [5] An Ohio politician said [6]: —

You may as well make up your mind now as next summer to vote for Judge Bates, or go into a third party. . . . The same clique that backed Fremont, — Wilson, Greeley, Banks, the Blairs, and your friend Judge Wade, are in the plot, and all the office seekers . . . are with them.

As convention time drew near, Chase heard more bad news than good. One of his closest supporters said, "I predict the convention will nominate Seward, Chase, or Lincoln." [7] So Chase had a letter arguing his cause sent to the leader of every delegation.[8] Not only outside Ohio were Chase men rebuffed. His own state was not solidly behind him.[9] Some Ohio delegates were for McLean, some for Lin-

[1] Ashley to Chase, April 5, 1860; Chase MSS.
[2] J. A. Bingham to Chase, Jan. 14, 1860; Chase MSS.
[3] J. Hanna, Oct. 23, 1858; W. Wilkeson, Feb. 13, 1859; R. Hosea, May 16, 1860, to Chase; Chase MSS.
[4] J. H. Barrett to Chase, Nov. 30, 1858. Also J. W. Taylor, June 22, 1857, J. R. Meredith, Aug. 11, 1857, J. B. Shurtleff, Sept. 4, 1857, F. Ball, Nov. 5, 1857, to Chase; Chase MSS.
[5] J. L. Robertson to Chase, Jan. 18, 1860; Chase MSS.
[6] George Hoadly to Chase, Dec. 13, 1859; Chase MSS.
[7] Thomas Spooner to Chase, March 20, 1860. Also J. Elliott to Chase, March 20, 1860; Chase MSS.
[8] Spooner to Chase, April 3, 1860; Chase MSS.
[9] J. Elliott to Chase, Feb. 23, 1860; Chase MSS. D. V. Smith, pp. 515–524. Hart, Chase, pp. 188–189, R. Cortissoz, *Life of Whitelaw Reid*, Vol. I, p. 53.

coln, and several wanted Ohio's senior Senator, Ben Wade. Nevertheless, Chase clung to his confident belief in his destiny.[1] Carl Schurz, lecturing in Ohio, was invited to put up with Chase, for the Ohio candidate had confidential information that Schurz controlled the German vote and could be won over from Seward with proper handling. The German was surprised and flattered when Chase dropped his usual haughty, great-man bearing, and conversed warmly. Chase asked Schurz about his own chances in Wisconsin, receiving a candid reply. "If the Republican Convention at Chicago have courage enough to nominate an advanced anti-slavery man, they will nominate Seward; if not, they will not nominate you." Surprised at this guileless statement and deeply disappointed, Chase told Schurz he could not see why Seward should be placed above himself.[2] Schurz diplomatically declined to argue the point, which made Chase imagine he had changed the German's mind.[3]

Bewhiskered Edward Bates, living quietly in St. Louis, was politically active only in writing public letters to demonstrate to the Republican Party the attractiveness of his opinions.[4] Bates was so old he had actually served in the War of 1812. Like his Illinois friend and supporter, Browning, Bates kept a diary but not a great one, though his pages display a brilliant, cultivated man. In this diary he had much to say on national affairs, told how the ground was laid and the Missouri delegation solidly pledged to him,[5] pasting therein important documents of his race for the nomination. His diary thus presents a close-up of the inner workings of a presidential boom. Bates recorded a conference of April 27, 1859 [6]: —

Dined with F. P. Blair Jr. . . . invited specially . . . to meet Mr. Schuyler Colfax, M. C. of Indiana.

The object of Messrs. Blair and Colfax, no doubt, was to have a confidential conference with me and a few of my known friends, so as to

[1] S. Galloway to John McLean, April 20, 1860; McLean MSS.
[2] *Reminiscences of Carl Schurz*, Vol. II, pp. 169–171.
[3] Chase to W. G. Hosea, March 18, 1860; in D. V. Smith, p. 524.
[4] *Diary of Edward Bates*, pp. 1–10, 15, 71.
[5] Bates, pp. 80, 108.
[6] Bates, p. 11.

approximate the terms upon which the Republican party might adopt me as its candidate for the Presidency. . . .

Both those gentlemen are influential leaders of their party, and both declare that I am their first choice. They both say that Mr. Seward cannot get the nomination of his party, perhaps not because he is not the acknowledged head of the party and entitled to the lead, but because the party is not quite strong enough to triumph alone; and his nomination therefore would ensure defeat. . . .

During the ensuing twelvemonth Bates's pages are full of letters from Colfax and other Bates men reporting on the Bates boom, his own political letters, and press notices and clippings which argued the propriety and wisdom of nominating him as the best man to beat the Democracy. And all the while this Missouri lawyer of sixty-six winters saw himself gaining ground, pleading modesty while he held his ear firmly to the ground.

In late November he wrote: "These all are very flattering to my vanity; and lead me to believe that (without some great change before next spring) my nomination for the Presidency, is more probable than that of any other man." [1]

One argument he brought up constantly: Republicans will not nominate Seward because he cannot win votes of moderate Republicans, Whigs, Americans, without which the Democracy cannot be beaten. Seward's staunch friends will, then, in retaliation, "take care that no other man within that party shall be nominated." The Chicago convention will then be forced to select an anti-slavery man from outside Republican ranks; specifically, they will take Edward Bates. [2]

Another firm notion in the Bates brain was the probability of a coalition of all opposition forces. Should the Republicans nominate a conservative opponent of slavery extension like himself, Bates actually believed that all political elements except the defenders of slavery would rally behind him in the North and border states and send him sweeping to overwhelming victory. [3]

[1] Nov. 21, 1859; Bates, p. 64.
[2] Bates, p. 66.
[3] Bates, pp. 29–30, 78–79, p. 89, pp. 94–95, pp. 106–107, pp. 117–119.

When state conventions began to appear he had new assurances. Bates's campaign manager, Charles Gibson of St. Louis, attended the Indiana Republican Convention, and returned with news that Indiana's delegation had a heavy majority in favor of Bates.[1] At the close of February Bates noted [2]: —

The signs indicating my nomination are growing, in number and strength every day. Several state conventions (as Indiana and Connecticut) have appointed "Bates" Delegates to the Chicago Convention. The People and the Press too, have taken the thing in hand. Many town and County meetings, in all the northern half of the Union, have declared for me; and a vast number of Newspapers, from Massachusetts to Oregon, have placed my name at the head of their columns.

But, knowing the fickleness of popular favor, and on what small things great events depend, I shall take care not so to set my heart upon the glittering bauble, as to be mortified or made at all unhappy by a failure.

A former student of law under Bates, who had gone to Pennsylvania, become a Republican leader there, and been chosen a Chicago delegate, slopped over with encouragement. Pennsylvania's delegation, he admitted, was pledged to Cameron. But that was purely complimentary, and Pennsylvania was sure to go for Bates unanimously on the second ballot. Add to that, Delegate Coffey calculated, Bates's increasing strength in other states, and you have a certain Bates victory.[3]

This notion was not as far-fetched as it sounds. Of all the Republican candidates, only Seward and Bates commanded full delegations from more than one state prior to the gathering of the Republican clan. The effective Bates support outside Missouri came directly from the Blairs.[4] The Blair family was a commanding political group. Francis Preston Blair, Sr., once a powerful member of Jackson's "Kitchen Cabinet," had quit the Democratic Party when, in the 'forties, Southerners gained control and deserted Jacksonian principles. Blair practised his thoroughgoing Jeffersonianism by becom-

---

[1] Bates, p. 102.
[2] Bates, pp. 105–106.
[3] Bates, p. 107.
[4] W. E. Smith, *The Francis Preston Blair Family in Politics*, Vol. I, pp. 457–469. Charles Gibson, "Edward Bates," *Missouri Hist. Soc. Collections*, Vol. II, p. 55.

ing one of the new Republican Party's organizers in 1856, engineering Fremont's nomination. Francis P. Blair, Sr. was ably assisted by two sons. Francis P. Blair, Jr., known as "Frank" Blair, was an aggressive Republican leader of Missouri. Montgomery Blair held the same position in Maryland, where he lived with his father, and was also powerful in Delaware.[1] Frank Blair was quite sure that only three Republican possibilities had any chance of election: most preferable, Bates; second, McLean; third, Ben Wade.[2] Schuyler Colfax, powerful Indiana politician, believed Bates could win, with Wade the best second choice. But he despaired of stopping Seward. Said he to Editor Bowles of the Springfield *Republican* [3]: —

If Seward's reliable friends are not awfully deceived, he is to be nominated, and on the first ballot . . . and we shall go forward to a defeat . . . even if the Democratic ranks are all shattered and disorganized at Charleston. . . . With a formidable third party in Pennsylvania, New Jersey, Indiana, and Illinois, we are beaten, even if we poll a million majority in the other free states. Seward's nomination will make just that third party, and with it certain defeat.

The three Blairs were in close co-operation to do for Bates what they did for Fremont. Montgomery Blair invited Cassius Clay to visit him in Maryland. When Clay came, Blair said in plain language that if Clay would go for Bates he would be made Secretary of War by President Bates. Clay refused; "for this," wrote Clay in his autobiography, "I lost favor with the Blairs." [4] Too, Bates had Greeley's support because the old Missouri lawyer was conservative while opposing slavery extension.[5] Greeley was sure that Bates, as a border state man, would widen Republican strength and wipe out the main objection to the Republican Party, sectionalism. He clung to this view even after Lincoln's nomination.[6] Greeley, who had learned all the political tricks from Thurlow Weed himself, had dispatched two

[1] *Dictionary of American Biography*, Vol. II, pp. 000-000, p. 000.
[2] F. P. Blair, Jr., to James Rollins, April 7, 1860, in W. D. Smith, *The Blair Family*, Vol. I, p. 468.
[3] In O. J. Hollister, *Colfax*, pp. 143–144.
[4] Clay, *Life*, Vol. I, pp. 244–246.
[5] Don C. Seitz, *Life of Horace Greeley*, p. 181.
[6] Statement of Greeley, in James Parton, *Life of Greeley*, p. 477.

plenipotentiaries, James Van Alen to the West, James Pike north, to spread the stop-Seward gospel. Snooping in various states, Van Alen and Pike sent back encouraging reports. Greeley credited them, and he too arrived in Chicago deluded as to the true state of the towering Seward strength.[1]

Candidate Bates wrote in his scrapbook diary thousands of words concerning the nominations of 1860. In all this, until the nomination became a *fait accompli*, he mentioned Lincoln once, in striking contrast to his numerous remarks about Seward, Chase, McLean, Cameron, Bell, Fremont. On April 26 Bates was visited by, among others, one Mr. Pettyjohn of Illinois, editor of a Centralia paper. Bates learned that "there is good feeling for me in *Egypt,* but first (on a point of state pride), they must support Lincoln." [2]

Associate Justice John McLean of the U. S. Supreme Court was the old man's candidate. Though some of his supporters were, like Lyman Trumbull, still in the front line, most of his strength came from men like the famous old orator, Tom Corwin of Ohio, who led in another day. McLean had been a prominent candidate for the Republican nomination in 1856, but his excessive age and personal coldness would have handicapped any Party. By 1860 he was seventy- five. Yet, some Republicans thought him the only candidate their Party could elect.[3] One McLean man reported, "Knavish politicians are industriously circulating reports that your health is infirm and giving way, otherwise you would be unobjectionable as a compromise man." [4] From another supporter, the aged jurist was directed to a familiar line of reasoning. "With you, Lincoln, or Bates as the standard bearer we can succeed. . . . The choice of Pennsylvania, New Jersey, and Indiana ought to be the choice of the Convention." [5] An Ohio McLean man wrote to several members of Congress arguing that McLean be chosen for auld lang syne, only to receive the "cold shoulder of silent contempt." [6] Senator Trumbull, embracing Norman Judd's "quiet

[1] *Diary of Edward Bates,* pp. 97, 108. J. S. Pike, *First Blows of the Civil War,* p. 519. D. V. Smith, p. 525.

[2] *Diary of Edward Bates,* p. 122.

[3] C. Morris to John McLean, Oct. 25, 1859; McLean MSS.

[4] J. E. Harvey to McLean, July 4, 1859; McLean MSS.

[5] S. Galloway to McLean, April 20, 1860; McLean MSS.

[6] D. Keller to John Sherman, April 24, 1860; John Sherman MSS.

combination" strategy but shuffling the cards, broached a more practical strategic plan [1] : —

> In my opinion you are the only person who can be nominated at Chicago in opposition to Gov. Seward. His friends are active & will go to the convention in great force, & no man stands any chance to receive the nomination against him, who cannot command the united support . . . from the great states of Pa. & Ohio. There, I take it, as against Seward you could obtain. I think we could also give you Illinois.

So it went. Chase and Bates received from well-wishers flattering reports which they ingenuously believed, until they imagined themselves practically nominated. Lincoln too was the recipient of glowing news from enthusiastic friends, and had he credited their information, his reactions would have been the same as those of Bates and Chase. But, with the penetrating perception of genius, Lincoln took this impetuous individual favoritism for what it was, never as political fact.

Nor were the Lincoln managers counting their gains prematurely. They knew that Seward was far ahead of everybody else, possessing upwards of 150 delegates, against Lincoln's 22, while Bates, Chase, Cameron were expected to have around 50 each on the first ballot. So great indeed was the New Yorker's lead that historians, reviewing the pre-Convention evidence, have found the Lincoln victory hard to believe, impossible to explain. The fashion has been to chronicle the indubitable fact of the Rail Splitter's nomination, leaving indefinite the subtle why of it. Pious souls, including some noted historians, have sought refuge in the notion that here was the Omnipotent at work in all his inscrutability.[2] Unsatisfactory attempts to explain this historic

---

[1] Trumbull to McLean, April 21, 1860; McLean MSS.

[2] *Cf.* above, Foreword. Whitney, *Life on the Circuit*, p. 78. Hertz, Vol. I, p. 4. Lloyd Lewis, *Myths After Lincoln*, p. 106, pp. 334–349, p. 368, pp. 378–382. A. G. Procter, *Lincoln and the Convention of 1860*, p. 14. James Schouler, *History of the U. S.*, Vol. V, p. 459 (1894 ed.). F. E. Chadwick, *Causes of the Civil War*, p. 123. Chauncey Depew, in *Addresses Delivered at the Lincoln Dinners of the Republican Club . . . of New York, 1887–1909*, p. 168. Henry Watterson, "Abraham Lincoln As a Man Inspired of God," in *Works of Lincoln*, Vol. III, pp. x, xlv. Bigelow, *Retrospections*, Vol. I, p. 290. W. E. Curtis *The True Abraham Lincoln*, p. 15. John Drinkwater, *Lincoln: the World Emancipator*, p. 43. I. H. Bromley, "The Nomination of Lincoln," *Scribner's*, Vol. XIV ((new ser.), p. 645. H. B. Rankin, *Personal Recollections*, p. 148. Browne, *Lincoln*, Vol. I, p. 33, pp. 37–42, pp. 101–102, Phebe A. Hanaford, *Abraham Lincoln,*

event have been so numerous that one careful scholar concludes that Lincoln's nomination, "despite the countless addresses, articles, brochures and books, biographies and histories by annalists, eulogists, and critical students — continues to be a mystery to the layman and a perplexity to the learned." [1] Such bewilderment proceeds from the naïve assumption that behavior at political conventions must have a reasonable basis. Lincoln's authorized biographers, the famous John Hay and John Nicolay, offer as their explanation that "Lincoln was chosen not by personal intrigue, but through political necessity." [2] They are exactly half right. Lincoln *was* the man who best suited the Party's current need of acquiring a majority in the nation despite its sectional character [3] — Seward and Chase being inexpediently radical, Cameron possessing no strength except as Republican boss of Pennsylvania as the G.O.P. Tammany began its long and distinguished career, [4] Bates no Republican, a onetime slaveholder and wanting color. In the words of an Iowa delegate, the Republican problem "was to nominate a man whose views on the slavery question were solid and clear-cut, who would represent and attract those in all the old parties who strongly opposed the extension of slavery and the aggressions of its leaders, and whose character and career would not suggest attacks upon the property rights of Southern slave owners." [5] Had the Convention, carefully weighing these men, seriously thought their problem through and made nominations in accordance with definite political facts, Lincoln would have been chosen with alacrity. But men do not often conduct themselves according to logic, never so in the ·struggle for political preferment. David Davis and his cohorts knew that their man, to win, need not be the best candidate; it was only necessary that the Convention be persuaded that he was best. But how

---

pp. 55–57. Charles C. Coffin, *Abraham Lincoln*, pp. 170–173. David Gregg, in W. H. Ward (ed.), *Abraham Lincoln, Tributes From His Associates*, p. 151. Henry M. Field, *Ibid.*, p. 209. A forgotten member of the St. Louis philosophers amusingly relates how Lincoln's leadership was "the decree of the World-Spirit," in Denton J. Snider, *Abraham Lincoln*, pp. 339, 346, 353, 359–360, 366. O. L. Barler, *Lincoln*, p. 27.

[1] Herriott, "Deutches Haus," pp. 101–104.
[2] Nicolay and Hay, *Lincoln*, Vol. II, p. 263.
[3] J. L. Sellers, "James R. Doolittle," *Wisconsin Mag. of History*, Vol. XVII, p. 288.
[4] Schurz, *Reminiscences*, Vol. II, p. 175.
[5] Reminiscences of C. C. Nourse, in *Annals of Iowa*, Vol. XII, pp. 454–457. Also Herriott, "Deutches Haus," p. 104.

to persuade, when the Party would gather already three-quarters convinced of Seward's complete fitness? The Lincoln strategists thought
they knew how, and had definite plans for leading the Convention,
willy-nilly, to select their man, who, as it happened, was also the best
man.[1]

On one thing they counted heavily: the setting, every feature of
which was favorable to Lincoln. Robust young Chicago, rapidly expanding and bragging of its importance,[2] was the West's most promising metropolis, and already had made itself the world's largest grain
center.[3] Visitors from the older East discovered in Chicago a cross
section of expanding American civilization, its denizens running the
gamut from suave society ladies to rough, tough frontiersmen. Said
that delightful traveler, Lillian Foster: "Such a motley set! You meet
there the nobleman and his suite; the backwoodsman in his coarse
clothes and fur cap (all the same, June or January); the illustrious
lady and party, over dressed; the German woman with her toys and
wares for sale," all in a hubbub of hurry and activity.

In railroads, manufactures and all internal improvements, Chicago is at
least a quarter of a century in advance of her sister cities. In gayety and
fashion she is entitled to rank A number one. Her wealth and luxury of
living are proverbial, whilst her belles and beaux seem the impersonation
of nature's noblemen and women. No city in the West can boast of more
sumptuous and luxurious accommodations for strangers.

Chicago streets were peculiar. Only a few blocks were paved with
flagstones; all other improved streets and sidewalks were temporarily
paved with oak planks.[4] Jerry-built buildings, tossed up in a hurry,
were built some high, some low, so the long plank avenues waved up
and down, according to the elevation of flanking buildings.[5] Board
sidewalks were interrupted by dozens of ascending and descending
steps. Beneath these planks lived millions of sleek rats. At night they
scampered about unafraid, feasting in swarms off the city's uncollected

[1] Gideon Welles, "Nomination and Election of Abraham Lincoln," Galaxy, Vol.
XXII, p. 300.
[2] C. Sandburg, Vol. II, p. 337.
[3] Harper's Weekly, May 12, 1860. Lillian Foster, Way-Side Glimpses, p. 202.
[4] Foster, passim. Clark E. Carr, The Illini, p. 40.
[5] Fenton, pp. 204, 205.

garbage. Thanks to this laxity in meeting the sewage problem, Chicago was reputedly not very sanitary. It might have been worse, however, for an obliging lake wind swept steadily, blowing away the redolent odors of decay, and rats were brilliant scavengers.[1]

Currently, politics was the chief interest of the thriving city on Lake Michigan. Fairly bursting with pride as host to its first political National Convention, — the body which was popularly expected to name the next President, since the Democracy had split asunder at Charleston, — Chicago was ready to receive the delegates in the grand manner. Streets and buildings were bedizened in gala holiday trappings. Chicago nourished well over a hundred thousand people, the majority Republicans and ready to do all they could to assist "Old Abe" Lincoln, the local boy who had made good. Republican clubs had during the past week held special meetings to prepare for the convention. Marching Wide-Awake clubs, recently formed, were called into action and new members welcomed. The active Cameron and Lincoln Club was likewise primed to labor for Cameron for President and Lincoln for Vice President.[2] In Springfield, the Lincoln Club held a special meeting and arranged a party to go to Chicago and do all possible for their distinguished favorite and townsman.

Symbolic of Chicago Republican zeal was the completed Wigwam, which stood ready to receive the delegates and a horde of spectators. Finished in the nick of time, the rambling barn of one hundred by one hundred and eighty feet had a capacity of ten thousand, was so well planned that a capacity crowd could be easily handled; acoustics were perfect. Carpenters left the interior rough, but on invitation of a decorating committee enthusiastic young Republicans came to decorate. On May 10, while a hundred and fifty miles south in a lesser Wigwam another pro-Lincoln force was being solidified, inside the Great Wigwam bustled "a bevy of ladies as busy as ants, decorating, sewing, and arranging wreaths and festoons." Patriotic props were plentifully strewn about — state coats of arms, bunting and miniature flags, busts of distinguished Americans. On the brick wall of the

[1] Foster, pp. 74–75, 205. Sandburg, Vol. II, p. 338.
[2] Chicago *Press & Tribune*, May 8, 9, 11, 1860.

THE REPUBLICAN WIGWAM
(From a Contemporary Photograph)

building to which the big barn was anchored, painters daubed what they hoped were impressive statues representing Liberty, Justice, and the like. Near by hung "the elegant and costly standard of the Young Men's Republican Club of New York. It bore its blazoned stars and legend all complete, save for two blanks following the lines, 'For President.................... For Vice-President...............' "
New Yorkers were ready to write "William H. Seward" in the top blank, and conceived that task as little more than a formality. An enthusiastic *Tribune* writer exclaimed: "These blanks were eloquent with a purpose, the purpose of the entire convention, all ready for the campaign but waiting for the names." When for the first time the lighting effects were added as the gas lights were turned up for the dedication ceremony, delighted Chicagoans thought they had seen a vision. "The effect was brilliant in the extreme," exploded a reporter. "Everybody, citizens and strangers, delegates and outsiders . . . fell in love with the Great Wigwam . . . and its praises were on more than half a score thousand tongues." [1]

This was on Saturday evening, May 12, at the Wigwam's formal opening. A seductive invitation had gone forth [2]: —

This evening the Republican Wigwam . . . will be dedicated to the cause of freedom with appropriate ceremonies, music, speaking, singing, and glorification generally will be the order of the night. . . . The council fires will be lighted in the hut. Come up and gather round for an old-fashioned talk. Come all and put a shoulder to the wheel, for to-night the ball begins to roll and the signal guns of the approaching contest between Freedom and Slavery will be fired. Let every man be at his post.

A capacity crowd paid its way in at twenty-five cents a head (defraying the remaining construction costs) to gaze raptly at "the intermingling draperies, flags, flowers and festoons; the busts of departed sages and heroes benignantly looking down upon a scene which they had dimly prophesied but never seen; the pealing music; all conspired to form a glorious omen of the future — a prophetic sign, large with golden promise of a glorious harvest of truth and right next

[1] Ray, pp. 7–8.
[2] Chicago *Journal*, May 12, 1860, in Ray, p. 5.

fall," according to one dithyrambic observer. Voices went hoarse roaring approbation of the speakers of the evening: homespun Delegate Johns from Iowa, weatherbeaten abolitionist preacher whose gray-whiskered countenance made him look like a talking grizzly bear,[1] and who had hiked one hundred and fifty miles to reach a Chicago-bound train; Henry S. Lane, Indiana's Republican candidate for Governor; Governor Morrill of Maine; Norman Judd; and handsome, white-haired Joshua Giddings of Ohio, hard-bitten veteran of many years' conflict for abolition. The old war-horse received "most deafening applause." Every evening, from dedication night to Wednesday, May 16, Convention opening day, crowds trooped into the Wigwam and a great political time was enjoyed by all.

Chicago boasted a dozen railways, hauling more than a hundred trains a day.[2] Already it had become a great railroad center.[3] Railroad Lawyer Judd had persuaded some roads to make excursion rates for the convention. Newspapers then demanded bargain prices from all roads.[4] Rates were so cheap that everybody who possibly could rode to Chicago for an exciting vacation — a capital chance to get away from it all and at the same time, excited Republicans felt, help "make history." The motley assemblage of merrymakers and history-makers swarming for the political extravaganza was so huge that Chicago's population was increased perhaps half. The Wigwam had been well advertised and the populace, in tourist spirit, was anxious to look at it.[5] Combined action of the numerous forces of popular attraction made this political conclave the "first of the great modern convention assemblages." Never before had such a meeting been held in a building specially built for its use; never before had the general public been admitted wholesale.[6] As Convention week opened hotels were "crowded with politicians, lobby men and delegates caucusing, comparing notes and arranging preliminaries," said a Chicago reporter.

[1] Herriott, in *Annals of Iowa*, Vol. VIII, opp. p. 186, p. 192; Vol. IX, pp. 403–404, 423.
[2] J. S. Currey, *Chicago: Its History and Its Builders*, Vol. II, p. 89.
[3] Foster, pp. 70–71.
[4] Whitney, *Lincoln the Citizen*, p. 285. Chicago *Press & Tribune*, May 3, 1860.
[5] L. D. Ingersoll, *Life of Greeley*, p. 338.
[6] Bishop, *Presidential Nominations and Elections*, p. 39.

"These are but a handful of the immense crowds yet to come who will tax our municipal accommodations to the utmost. But when the hotels fail, then without doubt our citizens will throw open their doors and extend their hospitalities cordially. The latch strings are all out and we can take care of all creation." [1]

Saturday, Wigwam dedication day, was the date of many other significant events. Convention key men began to arrive and to commence pulling wires in those quiet conferences behind the scenes from which the Convention was really controlled as a marionetteer manipulates his puppets. The huge bulk of David Davis was installed at the Tremont House, where with his three assistants he opened Lincoln headquarters. Rich Judge Davis was paying the bill out of his own pocket. [2] The Tremont was already uncomfortably full of Seward and Bates men. [3] Looking out the window, the Lincoln managers were spurred to their labors by sight of the Chicago *Journal* office across the street, brilliant with banners, flaunting with a huge sign their choice: "SEWARD." Governor Morgan of New York, National Chairman, came in Saturday. Another gentleman from the Empire State was Thurlow Weed, who established Seward headquarters at the sumptuous Richmond House. Also arriving was a third New York potentate, Horace Greeley. The round-faced editor, whose hair seemed to have grown in reverse, appearing beneath his chin while leaving his pate bald, was not a New York delegate, for Weed and Seward controlled the state machine and Lucifer himself could not have procured Greeley a New York seat. But the eccentric editor wanted a convention seat so he could operate efficaciously against Seward and repay Seward and Weed for failing to give their faithful Whig co-worker, Horace Greeley, a fat political job some years back. He had managed a seat on the floor and would sit with the Oregon delegation (pledged to Bates) as delegate by proxy. [4] He thought, with good reason, Bates would be the best man to beat Seward with, but so long

[1] Chicago *Journal*, in Ray, p. 11.
[2] Harry E. Pratt, "David Davis," p. 80.
[3] Whitney, *Lincoln the Citizen*, p. 286.
[4] Parton, *Life of Greeley*, pp. 476–477.

as the Senator went down, the philosophical editor did not much care who accomplished it.[1]

David Davis and his men had an engagement of prime importance with the Indiana delegation, the one which Lincoln himself had arranged. Indiana's 26 votes were for sale in exchange for two offices, Secretary of the Interior and Commissioner of Indian Affairs. Lincoln badly needed these votes, for if he had only Illinois' 22 votes on the first ballot he would be a mere "favorite son" and his delegates would go elsewhere on the second ballot. Quietly meeting the gentlemen from Indiana in a hotel room, the Lincoln men found (as Leonard Swett related it) the Hoosiers in individual preferences "about equally divided between Bates and McLean." [2] Davis readily promised that in President Lincoln's cabinet Caleb B. Smith of Indiana should run the Interior Department,[3] and William P. Dole manage the pesky redskins. Lincoln had, at least by inference, approved these deals by his letter to Delegate Allen of Indiana arranging the early conference. Success in the delegate market was no mere matter of promising offices, however. Before the Hoosiers would do business with Lincoln's managers they had to be convinced that Lincoln had a chance to win. So they shopped around for a few days.

The chances that Indiana might go for Bates instead of for Lincoln were more than good. Bates had far more delegates than Lincoln; confidential reports to Bates had told the old lawyer that Indiana's uninstructed delegation was inclined to him by about 20 to 6.[4] Schuyler Colfax, the Hoosier congressman, was one of the original Bates men. Discounting the usual exaggeration of partisan reports, Indiana at any rate did not seem a strong Lincoln force.[5] Frank Blair was quite

---

[1] Ray, pp. 11–12. Whitney, *Lincoln the Citizen*, p. 287. Greeley, *Recollections of a Busy Life*, pp. 311–322, pp. 389–390.

[2] In Oldroyd, p. 71.

[3] Caleb Smith to David Davis, Jan. 31, Feb. 5, 1861, in H. E. Pratt, "David Davis," *Transactions*, Ill. State Hist. Soc., 1930, p. 167. W. P. Fishback to T. Fishback, Jan. 19, 1861; Wm. P. Fishback MSS., Indiana State Library.

[4] *Diary of Bates*, p. 102.

[5] Charles Roll, "Indiana's Part in the Nomination of Lincoln," *Indiana Mag. of History*, Vol. XXV, pp. 3–4. Gibson, p. 55. G. R. Morton to S. P. Chase, April 19, 1860; Chase MSS. Morton, reporting a conversation with Caleb Smith of Indiana, said the Hoosiers could not be induced to vote for Seward or Chase because neither could carry the state. "The choice of Indiana would, therefore, be narrowed down to Bates, Lincoln, and McLean."

as good a promiser as David Davis. Leadership of the Indiana delegation was uncertain, but the Caleb Smith faction, wanting a cabinet
job for Smith, led by experienced, eloquent Caleb Smith himself (who
had been in Congress with Lincoln) stole a march on the pro-Bates
Colfax faction by acting with aggressive decision.[1] Securing the desired promise from Judge Davis, the Smith group worked to bring all
the Hoosiers to their way of thinking.[2] To aid these Indiana Lincoln
men, Illinoisans kept after the Hoosier delegation constantly. Need-
ing votes more than did Bates emissaries, with less prior commitments,
they could promise rather more convincingly. Too, the Lincoln cause
was aided by William P. Dole, Indian Commissioner-designate of the
hypothetical President Lincoln. Dole, onetime Indiana leader, had
moved to Paris, Illinois, was now a delegate from the Seventh Illinois
District along with Lincoln's friend Thomas Marshall of Charleston.
He made a perfect liaison agent. Still another cohesive force, perhaps the most important of all, was the fact that three Indiana leaders,
Caleb Smith, John P. Usher, Daniel Voorhees, were good friends of
Lincoln, had practised law with the Rail Splitter in county seats of
eastern central Illinois.[3] By late Monday, the Hoosier leaders having
satisfied themselves that nobody could offer a better bargain, the Indiana delegation, led by the Smith clique, came to Lincoln with 26
precious votes, and (wrote Swett) "from that time acted efficiently
with us." [4] But there was yet no certainty that the Hoosiers might not
discover a better bargain later and switch.[5]

Monday and Tuesday brought thousands streaming into town, causing railroad depots (in a perfervid journalist's eyes) to "beat like
great hearts with their living tide; Republicans from mountains Green,
Blue and White; Republicans from the woods of Maine, the green
valleys of all New England and 'the wild where rolls the Oregon';

[1] M. Gresham, *Life of Walter Q. Gresham*, Vol. I, pp. 110–111. J. D. Defrees to Colfax, May 18, 1860, in Hollister, *Colfax*, p. 148.

[2] Eight days after his nomination Lincoln wrote to "Hon. C. B. Smith. . . . I am,
induced, much indebted to Indiana; and, as my home friends tell me, much to you
personally." Hertz, Vol. II, p. 773.

[3] Clifton H. Moore, Clinton, Ill., in *Transactions of the McLean County Historical
Society*, Bloomington, Ill., Vol. II, p. 339. D. W. Voorhees, in Rice, p. 355.

[4] Oldroyd, p. 71. Whitney, *Lincoln the Citizen*, p. 288.

[5] C. E. Macartney, *Lincoln and His Cabinet*, pp. 49–54.

[5] Roll, pp. 6–7.

Republicans from the Golden Gate and the old plantation; Republicans from everywhere. What seems a brilliant festival, is but the rally for a battle; it is an army with banners." Several delegates who arrived early found lodgings in jail when the Chicago police made their regular Sunday night brothel raid.[1]

Pursuant to newspaper suggestions, immigrant Chicagoans organized as reception committees to receive in grand style the arriving delegation from their old home state. Monday evening a special was due, loaded with New England delegations.

"Michigan Avenue, Lake Street and all the avenues leading to the depot were thronged with an eager crowd of New Englanders and citizens, all expectant of the arrival of their friends and old neighbors. Michigan Avenue was finely illuminated, and as the train neared 12th Street, a brilliant rocket announced it to the crowd. Another rocket streamed from Jackson Street; a cannon boomed across the Basin; the bands struck up, and hearty cheers from the thousands of New England throats welcomed the train now nearing the depot. And the Wide-Awakes, with gleaming torches, as well as the crowd, took up their line of march for the depot. The immense interior of this terminal was soon packed with a vast throng. The train came to a standstill, and then the crowd with clapping hands and huzzas welcomed their old friends with a genuine New England warmth and zeal. Gilmore's band from Boston, which was aboard, stepped out upon the platform and played an air in splendid style, which was received with hearty cheers, after which the delegates were escorted to their various hotels."

Chicago had never before seen anything like the enthusiasm this Convention was conjuring up, never before been host to a gathering so important. It was as though the nation had saluted the expanding city (as Emerson did Walt) with the impressive words, "I greet you at the beginning of a great career." Bewildered Chicago reporters studied their dictionaries to find words to describe, even remotely, what they saw. When in the small hours of Tuesday morning the Pennsylvania delegation arrived with a mob of henchmen, six hundred strong, not forgetting two bands, fervid welcomers cheered and

---

[1] E. Hempstead to Washburne, May 14, 1860; Washburne MSS.

screeched as the Cameronites disembarked. Escorted by a Chicago band and "the sons of Pennsylvania" they marched off to the Briggs House, where they were "received by their countrymen with open arms." But "the spectacular event of the pre-convention days," in the eyes of Delegate Procter of Kansas, was the arrival of the Seward delegation from New York. Their train pulled in early Tuesday, "thirteen cars full of 'irrepressibles!' " On the same train from the East came the young journalist, Murat Halstead of the Cincinnati *Commercial,* stylistic idolator of Charles Dickens, whose graphic pen does credit to his master. Halstead sketched the New Yorkers en route to the battleground: —

I regret to say that most of the company were "unsound." . . . The number of private bottles on our train last night was something surprising. A portion of the Republicans are distressed by what they see and hear of the disposition to use ardent spirits which appears in members of their supposed to be painfully virtuous party. And our Western Reserve was thrown into prayers and perspiration last night by some New Yorkers, who were singing songs not found in hymn books. Others are glad to have the co-operation of Capt. Whiskey, and hail the fact of the enlistment of that distinguished partisan as an evidence that the Republicans are imbibing the spirit as well as the substance of the old Democratic party.

The Dickensian Halstead found that by Tuesday evening the crowd was "becoming prodigious. The Tremont House is so crammed that it is with much difficulty people get about in it from one room to another. Near fifteen hundred people will sleep in it tonight. The principal lions in this house are Horace Greeley and Frank P. Blair, Sen. The way Greeley is stared at as he shuffles about, looking as innocent as ever, is itself a sight. Whenever he appears there is a crowd gaping at him, and if he stops to talk a minute with some one who wishes to consult him as an oracle, the crowd becomes dense as possible, and there is the most eager desire to hear the words of wisdom that are supposed to fall on such occasions. . . . The city of Chicago is attending to this Convention in magnificent style. It is a great place for large hotels, and all have their capacity for accommodation tested. The great feature is the Wigwam, erected within the past month, expressly for the use of the Convention. . . . It is a small edition of the New York Crystal Palace, built of boards, and will hold ten thousand persons comfortably." [1]

As to the candidate situation at this early hour, "all seemed confusion and disintegration" to Delegate Procter of Kansas, except the towering Seward strength. Seward was expected on the first ballot to fall short of a nominating majority by some sixty votes only. It was therefore Seward against "the field." The field comprised Cameron, Chase, Bates, Lincoln, Senator Collamer of Vermont, Senator Dayton of New Jersey — all favorite sons (Bates a favorite son plus) who on the first ballot would have the votes of their own state.[2] Also represented in the race, lurking in the background, awaiting a deadlock, were several dark horses: Ben Wade of Ohio, Nathaniel Banks of Massachusetts, John Read of Pennsylvania. Their hopes were based mainly on the memory of Franklin Pierce in 1852. The numerous other "possibilities" had faded for the simple reason that they had acquired no delegates. Chief among these dark horses who had no votes as favorite sons was "Bluff Ben" Wade. Like Seward, Wade had been since the early fifties a Senator — first as antislavery Whig, then as Republican. A faction of the Ohio delegation had developed a pretentious undercover plan to start a swing to Senator Wade by displacing Chase as Ohio's real choice for the nomination. It was a clever scheme, one which might possibly have succeeded. As an absolutely new man in the contest, whose Republicanism could not be questioned, Wade might stampede the convention before his opponents could think up and advertise reasons for voting against him. The Wade men sought to swing Ohio to him as a unit after a complimentary vote for Chase, with as many delegates as possible from other states following suit. Norman Judd opened negotiations with the Wade group, exploring the possibility of swinging the Illinois vote to Wade after one ballot for Lincoln.[3]

[1] Halstead, p. 121.
[2] Procter, p. 5.
[3] H. Kreismann to Washburne, May 13, 1860; Washburne MSS.
    D. V. Smith, pp. 522–523. C. M. Clay, *Life,* Vol. I, p. 248.
    J. Giddings to G. W. Julian, May 25, 1860; in Sellers, "Make-Up of the Early Republican Party," p. 50.

THE REPUBLICAN NOMINATING CONVENTION

(*May, 1860*)

But if the Seward opposition did not speedily unite behind one man, it seemed, the New Yorker would win with ease. And how, considering all those antagonistic favorite sons, could a coalition be effected early enough to head off the genial, unpretentious Senator?

Naturally, in this madhouse which Chicago had temporarily become, Lincoln stood out as the best man of the Seward opposition because of the terrific outside pressure. Thousands of holiday-making Illinoisans overran the city, in the lusty spirit of the occasion yelling, talking, arguing, exhorting in behalf of their good friend Abe Lincoln. Norman Judd had planned this outside pressure when he labored to locate the Convention at Chicago; the Wigwam itself was part of the plot. The word had been quietly passed along that if plain Illinois Republicans wanted to see Lincoln nominated, they could help.[1] Judd asked his personal friends among Republicans if they would come to Chicago and work for Lincoln.[2] And the Lincoln managers carefully planned their wire-pulling tactics. Leonard Swett wrote, soon after the event: "Our programme was to give Lincoln 100 votes on the first ballot, with a certain increase afterwards, so that in the Convention our fortunes might seem to be rising, and thus catch the doubtful." [3]

Doubtless Thurlow Weed foresaw that Chicago Republican leaders were acting on motives not altogether pure when they troubled to erect the Wigwam. Quite naturally, he expected when he learned that the Wigwam would be far more commodious than was really necessary, that these chaps were trying to steal a march on Easterners by planning to pack the Convention hall with supporters of their favorite son. Hence the thirteen cars full of jolly wassailers from New York, who came led by Tom Hyer, famous prize fighter, to make sure that Chicago would hear plenty of Seward noise.[4] Pennsylvania too was ready, having brought a gang of roustabouts almost as large as New York's.[5] But even these elaborate preparations, Sewardites and Cam-

[1] Washburne MSS., April, May, 1860, *passim*. Browne, *Lincoln*, Vol. II, pp. 406-10?, p. 110.
[2] Reminiscences of G. M. Dodge of Iowa, in F. I. Herriott, "Memories of the Chicago Convention of 1860," *Annals of Iowa*, Vol. XII, pp. 447, 450.
[3] In Oldroyd, p 71
[4] Oldroyd, p. 72.
[5] Ray, p 11

eronites discovered to their chagrin, were none too good. Lincoln had
so many vociferous friends on the battleground there was no denying his strength. Even as early as Sunday the heavy pressure was apparent. An Illinoisan wrote on that day, "The sentiment against the
expediency and safety of nominating Seward [is] very strong. . . .
Our delegation will stick to Lincoln as long as there is a chance to prevent Seward getting any votes from us. . . . The town is nearly full
of people. . . . Ohio will make a push for Wade. Judd and Cook of
our delegation are inclined that way also. Wentworth is figuring with
the Cameron men. Caucusing is very brisk." [1]

Eastern journalists who reached Chicago unprepared for a popular
uprising in Lincoln's favor sent out dispatches which reveal the force
of outside pressure: Monday — "Abe Lincoln is looming up tonight
as a compromise candidate and his friends are in high spirits." [2] Tuesday — "Dudley Field, of New York, and his friends have joined the
party of Judge Bates, and efforts are making to concentrate the opposition to Mr. Seward upon him. Mr. Lincoln, however, seems to be
gaining ground, and his Illinois friends are greatly encouraged tonight
at the prospect of his uniting the doubtful states and the Northwest." [3]
And Wednesday morning prior to the Convention's assembling, Halstead found "the amount of idle talking that is done, is amazing."

Men gather in little groups, and with their arms about each other, and
chatter and whisper as if the fate of the country depended upon their
immediate delivery of the mighty political secrets with which their imag-
inations are big. There are a thousand rumors afloat, and things of incal-
culable moment are communicated to you confidentially, at intervals of
five minutes. There are now at least a thousand men packed together in
the halls of the Tremont House, crushing each other's ribs, tramping each
other's toes, and titillating each other with the gossip of the day, and the
probability is, not one is possessed of a single political fact not known to
the whole, which is of the slightest consequence. . . .
The current of the universal twaddle this morning is, that "Old Abe"
will be the nominee.
The Bates movement, the McLean movement, the Cameron movement,

[1] H. Kreismann to Washburne, May 13, 1860; Washburne MSS.
[2] Boston *Herald;* in J. M. Davis, *How Lincoln Became President*, p. 74.
[3] New York *Tribune;* in Davis, pp. 74–75.

the Banks movement, are all nowhere. They have gone down like lead in the mighty waters. "Old Abe" and "Old Ben" are in the field against Seward. Abe and Ben are representatives of the conservatism, the respectability, the availability, and all that sort of thing.

These press reports were however only opinion. Correspondents differed violently, even about so restricted a matter as the Indiana delegation's vacillations. An Indiana reporter's Tuesday dispatch pictured Bates on the down grade, Lincoln on the rise. "The opposition to Seward, which yesterday manifested some disposition to concentrate on Lincoln, has gathered closer and more compactly today, and now I think he is the strongest man next to Seward." [1] A New York writer cabled that Indiana was strong for Bates.[2] On Tuesday also, a Philadelphia correspondent telegraphed: "There is a strong outside pressure against Seward today. . . . Lincoln stock is on the rise but his chances are regarded as very poor. . . . The fight is generally regarded as between Seward and Bates." [3] But one reporter, of the Springfield *Republican*, merited a Pulitzer prize when he cabled to his paper the authentic keynote of the whole affair — "everything is doubtful." [4]

Mr. Seward's nomination is now claimed on the fourth ballot. His friends are firm, but New England is deserting him. Everything is doubtful. Abe Lincoln is gaining as a Western candidate.

There was still another important aspect to the journalistic side of convention wire-pulling. Seward's opponents fully appreciated the danger of the normal drift of convention voting, whereby the candidate who comes out far ahead on the first ballot ordinarily outgains all others on the next roll call. There was need, therefore, for subtle misrepresentation, intended to persuade as many as possible that Seward stood less strong than he really was. A pro-Bates reporter gave the cue in a Monday dispatch [5]: —

[1] Indianapolis *Journal*, May 17; in Roll, p. 7.
[2] New York *Times*, May 16; in Roll, p. 7.
[3] Philadelphia *Press*, May 15th dispatch, in Herriott, "Deutsches Haus," p. 128.
[4] Springfield *Republican*, May 14th dispatch, "Deutsches Haus," p. 157.
[5] St. Louis *Democrat*, in *Illinois State Journal*, May 16, 1860.

In the midst of such contrariety of opinion as exists here, it is hardly possible to make even an approximate estimate of the separate strength of any of the candidates. The most favorable count of Seward's strength is at this time eighty-six votes. . . . Lincoln, today, under the influence of an effort to unite the Northwestern delegates on him, has gained considerable strength. His friends claim that he will be the second choice of Indiana, Connecticut and part of Ohio and Iowa.

Bates's first ballot strength is placed by his friends today in the neighborhood of 65 votes. . . .

The New York *Tribune's* dispatch reported that "the highest calculation for Seward on the first ballot is eighty-five votes." [1] Taking the hint, the *Illinois State Journal's* correspondent declared, in a Tuesday dispatch [2]: —

Every train arriving brings large accessions to the already immense crowd in attendance. . . . The friends of the various candidates for the Presidency are all sanguine of the success of their particular candidate.

Mr. Seward's friends claim ninety votes on the first ballot. Uninterested parties think this is his entire strength. . . .

Gossip and noise and journalistic opinion in streets and hotel lobbies do not make votes on the Convention floor. They only help. The Convention's course was really being shaped behind the scenes, in innumerable caucuses in animated hotel rooms alive with politicians, money, smoke, liquor, gossip. At the Richmond House, Thurlow Weed invited arriving delegations to attend levee in his parlor. The great mogul himself, tall, white-haired, imposing, met the Kansas delegates most graciously at the door. He introduced them around, gave them seats, all with such expansive, unctuous good nature that Procter of Kansas was reminded of Byron's "Corsair," " 'the mildest mannered man that ever scuttled a ship or cut a throat,' politically, of course." Mr. Weed pleasantly surprised the Kansans by actually knowing their names and chatting with them like an old old friend. They were invited to lift their elbows copiously — champagne! Then Weed made a persuasive speech [3]: —

---

[1] *Illinois State Journal*, May 16, 1860.
[2] *Illinois State Journal*, May 16.
[3] Procter, pp. 6–7.

Four years ago we went to Philadelphia to name our candidate and we made one of the most inexcusable blunders any political party has ever made in this country. We nominated a man who had no qualification for the position of Chief Magistrate of this Republic. Why, that boy Fremont had not one single quality to commend him for the Presidency. The Country realized this. We were defeated as we probably deserved to be and we have that lesson of defeat before us today. We are facing a crisis; there are troublous times ahead for us. We all recognize that. What this country will demand as its chief executive for the next four years is a man of the highest order of executive ability, a man of real statesmanlike qualities, well known to the Country, and of large experience in national affairs. No other class of men ought to be considered at this time. We think we have in Mr. Seward just the qualities the Country will need. He is known by us all as a statesman. As Governor of New York he has shown splendid executive ability. As Senator he has shown himself to be a statesman, and a political philosopher. He is especially equipped in a knowledge of our foreign relations, and will make a candidate to whom our people can look with a feeling of security. We expect to nominate him on the first ballot, and to go before the Country full of courage and confidence.

Hardly were these Kansans back in their rooms at the Briggs House when in popped an exotic individual of "clear red and white complexion, blue eyes and flaxen hair," looking "like a well-to-do farmer fresh from his clover field." It was Horace Greeley, who had been busy Sunday and Monday interviewing early arrivals, discovering how things were going. To his consternation he found Seward much stronger than he expected.

Years later Greeley recalled: "I was somewhat surprised to meet there quite a number who, in conversations with me and others, had unhesitatingly pronounced his [Seward's] nomination unadvisable, and likely to prove disastrous, now on hand to urge it. I strongly felt that they had been right before, and were wrong now; and I did what I could to counteract their efforts; visiting, to this end, and briefly addressing, the delegations from several states." [1] Some of the politicians who had assured his agents Pike and Van Alen that Greeley was right in opposing Seward had had their ideas changed by Thurlow Weed's offers. Greeley, therefore, must try to argue them away from

[1] *Recollections of a Busy Life,* p. 390.

Seward, in which process he reached the Kansas group. Politician-like, he soon insinuated himself into their good graces with smiling manner and genial small talk, complimenting them on the thrilling news Kansas had provided for his *Tribune*. He came to the point.[1]

I suppose they are telling you that Seward is the be all and the end all of our existence as a party, our great statesman, our profound philosopher, our pillar of cloud by day, our pillar of fire by night, but I want to tell you boys that in spite of all this you couldn't elect Seward if you could nominate him. You must remember as things stand today we are a sectional party. We have no strength outside the North, practically we must have the entire North with us if we hope to win. Now, there are states of the North that cannot be induced to support Seward, and without these states we cannot secure electoral votes enough to elect. So, to name Seward, is to invite defeat. He cannot carry New Jersey, Pennsylvania, Indiana, or Iowa, and I will bring to you representative men from each of these states who will confirm what I say.

Presently Greeley came back with three men in tow, Andrew Curtin of Pennsylvania, Henry S. Lane of Indiana, gubernatorial candidates, and Governor Kirkwood of Iowa. All emphatically seconded Greeley's argument. Lane of Indiana was an extremely influential man who had great weight with the delegates because four years before he had been permanent chairman of the Party's first National Convention, in which capacity he had won national celebrity by delivering a fiery speech.[2] Procter, writing his recollections, related these Horatian arguments against Seward as though he and his fellow Kansans were profoundly impressed. But the Convention record shows that Kansas voted for Seward to the bitter end.

Greeley enjoyed a unique advantage as a stop-Seward operator. All politicians knew of the New York "political firm of Seward, Weed, and Greeley." In 1854 Greeley had withdrawn in a huff, but the break was kept secret, and Greeley had always been editorially friendly to Seward. Delegates, therefore, paid more attention to Greeley's arguments than they would had they known of the Greeley-Seward split.

[1] Procter, p. 8.
[2] *Dictionary of American Biography*, Vol. X, pp. 574–575. "Proceedings of the National Republican Convention . . . 1856," in C. W. Johnson (comp.), *Proceedings of the First Three Republican National Conventions*, pp. 25–27.

Henry J. Raymond, dapper editor of the pro-Seward New York *Times*, was shortly to accuse Greeley of lowest trickery in his successful Chicago fight against Seward. Immediately after the nomination Raymond wrote to the *Times* a bitter interpretation of the Seward defeat.[1] Excerpts: —

He [Greeley] labored personally with the delegates as they arrived, — commending himself always to their confidence by professions of regard and the most zealous friendship for Governor Seward, but presenting defeat, even in New York, as the inevitable result of his nomination. . . .

He was . . . allowed to represent to the delegates from Vermont, New Hampshire, Ohio, Indiana, and other states known to be in favor of Governor Seward's nomination, that, while he desired it upon the strongest grounds of personal and political friendship, he believed it would be fatal to the success of the cause. Being thus stimulated by a hatred he had secretly cherished for years, — protected by the forbearance of those whom he assailed, and strong in the confidence of those upon whom he sought to operate — it is not strange that Mr. Greeley's efforts should have been crowned with success. But it is perfectly safe to say that no other man — certainly no one occupying a position less favorable for such an assault — could possibly have accomplished that result.

We deem it only just to Mr. Greeley thus early to award him the full credit for the main result of the Chicago Convention, because his own modesty will prevent his claiming it. . . .

Thus began a hot press controversy. Greeley snapped back that personalities had been no motive. "If ever in my life I discharged a public duty in utter disregard of personal considerations, I did so at Chicago." [2]

As Mr. Greeley worked on one delegation after another in Chicago hotels, he was careful to say no unkind word about Seward. Some perspicacious opponent of Seward got the idea of dramatizing the fact that Greeley, whom everybody knew as Seward's friend, was certain that Seward could not be elected President. So, numerous placards were made carrying the legend, "Greeley at the Tremont, Weed at the Richmond House" and conspicuously posted in flood quantities.[3]

[1] Letter in Ingersoll, *Life of Greeley*, pp. 344–345.
[2] Ingersoll, *Greeley*, pp. 345–351. Seitz, *Greeley*, pp. 160–185. Parton, *Greeley*, 478–491. Barnes, *Weed*, pp. 268–290.
[3] Ingersoll, pp. 338–339. Ingersoll was an attending journalist. Barnes, *Weed*, p. 260.

When Carl Schurz, chairman of the Sewardite Wisconsin delegation, called at Seward headquarters, he had an unpleasant shock. Expecting to meet New Yorkers of learned distinction like William M.
Evarts, George William Curtis, Henry J. Raymond, Governor Morgan, he found only Weed, "and around him a crowd of men, some of
whom did not strike me as desirable companions," so Schurz related
his reaction to these henchmen Weed had brought along to help in
the work.[1] "What that work consisted in I could guess from the conversations I was permitted to hear, for they talked very freely about
the great services they had rendered or were going to render. They
had marched in street parades with brass bands and Seward banners
to produce the impression that the whole country was ablaze with
enthusiasm for Seward. They had treated members of other delegations with no end of champagne and cigars, to win them for Seward,
if not as their first, then at least as their second, choice, to be voted
for on the second or third ballot. They had hinted to this man and that
man supposed to wield some influence, that if he would throw that influence for Seward, he might, in case of success, count upon proper
'recognition.' They had spent money freely and let everybody understand that there was a great lot more to spend. Among these men
Thurlow Weed moved as a great captain, with ceaseless activity and
noiseless step, receiving their reports and giving new instructions."
Weed told Schurz he was quite confident Seward would win, but work
must be done. Seward men, said Weed, must advertise their confidence "in every possible way." He admonished the dark, influential
German to visit as many delegations as possible and assert that no
candidate could possibly attract as many German votes as Seward.
Schurz demurred; he was not sure that was true. This unprofessional
attitude left Weed thoroughly disgusted.[2]

Seriously participating in this bustling miniature canvass of hotel-
room caucuses, the Lincoln men worked at top speed. Lincoln himself
remained quietly at home, careful that no public statements should
come from him in the interval between the Decatur Convention and

[1] *Reminiscences of Carl Schurz*, Vol. II, pp. 176–177.
[2] Schurz, Vol. II, p. 179.

the Chicago nomination.[1] Leonard Swett asked Lincoln, after the Decatur Convention, if he expected to be in Chicago next week. Lincoln allowed that he was "too much of a candidate to go, and not quite enough to stay at home." [2] But all Lincoln backers went to Chicago as naturally as to bed. Their basic strategy was of necessity a stop-Seward stratagem. If this failed, Weed would stampede the convention. The Lincoln men therefore co-operated with the delegations for Cameron, Dayton, Bates, all maintaining in innumerable colloquies that Seward could not carry the state each represented.[3] Judd's suggestion that "a quiet combination" against Seward could stop him had therefore met with tacit agreement. Greeley used it to the limit, as Procter revealed. It was simple, effective.[4] That *Press & Tribune* editorial on that day in early April had said: —

It is grossly unjust to Gov. Seward to suppose that either he or his advisers will insist upon his nomination . . . against the judgment of the delegates from New Jersey, Pennsylvania, Indiana and Illinois, or a majority of them. . . . Gov. Seward . . . has the sagacity to perceive that a defeat before the people would foreclose his presidential prospects, if not finish his political career, and that his nomination against the wishes of the representatives of those states would be nearly tantamount to defeat. On the other hand, if the delegates from those states above named, shall say that Mr. Seward *can* secure their electoral votes, he will be nominated. . . .

Impressed with the perfect applicability of Judd's "quiet combination" idea when told about it by Judd's Washington agents, the doubtful state politicians were energetically using that stratagem as their only effective weapon for stopping Seward.[5] Seward men, getting wind of the plot, had sought to checkmate it by trying to make all anti-Sewardites believe that Seward's candidacy would not be aggressively pushed. By way of smoke screen, Raymond's New York *Times*

[1] Lincoln to Wallace, May 12, 1860; *Works*, Vol. VI, pp. 11–12.
[2] Swett in Oldroyd, pp. 70–71.
[3] James G. Blaine, *Twenty Years of Congress*, Vol. I, p. 167. Reminiscences of Leonard Swett, in Barnes, *Weed*, pp. 291–292.
[4] Schurz, *Reminiscences*, Vol. II, pp. 174–175.
[5] Thomas H. Dudley, "Inside Facts of Lincoln's Nomination," *Century*, Vol. XL, p. 477.

thus pusillanimously reported the overwhelming endorsement of Seward at the New York Republican Convention [1]: —

There was nothing like blind devotion to Seward, inside or outside the convention; no evidence of a purpose to resort to extraordinary means to procure his nomination; no such idea as demanding him or nobody; nor was there the least indication of an extreme sentiment on the subject of the nomination either way. While the feeling for Mr. Seward was unmistakable, there was at the same time a readiness to acknowledge that a state of things might arise requiring the nomination of some other man — in fact a state of feeling that seemed to have quite prepared itself for such a necessity. Devotion to the success of the Republican party and its principles was clearly stronger than personal attachments. Desire for success was paramount.

This camouflage fooled nobody and the stop-Seward forces relaxed not, as shown by numerous observers on the battle front. Edward L. Pierce, Massachusetts delegate and later biographer of Charles Sumner, wrote to his friend Salmon P. Chase a Sunday letter reporting the hard facts of the Chicago outlook [2]: —

A large number of delegates have arrived and are comparing notes. I have never deceived you and shall not begin now. I do not believe from present indications that Seward or yourself will be nominated. The pressure against him from Pennsylvania, Indiana and Illinois is as strong as it possibly can be. The delegates from Indiana — who are apparently very sincere — declare defeat with him to be certain. The delegates from Indiana say that for similar reasons they cannot carry the state for you. They say that they can carry Lincoln, McLean or Bates — Pennsylvania delegates insist on Cameron but he is out of the question. Curtin, who appears to be a sincere man and not under Cameron's control, says that they could carry Fessenden. . . .

Believe me in such things as these it is not the activity of friends who determine the result. It is the mere exigency of the moment — the current or drift of popular sentiment which cannot be controlled by friends. . . .

Senator Fessenden of Maine, like all Republican Senators save King of New York and Simmons of Rhode Island, remained in Wash-

[1] N. Y. *Times,* April 21, 1860.
[2] Pierce to Chase, May 13, 1860; in Herriott, "Deutsches Haus," pp. 127–128.

ington during the Convention. But he had reports from Chicago through his protégé, young James G. Blaine, rising Maine legislator. Soon after reaching Chicago Blaine wrote [1]: —

The Seward force is on the ground and assume an air of dictation which is at once unwarranted and offensive, and which I think will create a re-action before Wednesday. . . . I do not myself believe that he will be nominated, though a great many here think otherwise. If he is not, I will adhere to the opinion . . . that the game lies between Lincoln and your-self — Chase, McLean, Banks, and Bates stand no chance. Cameron is hotly urged by a majority of the Pennsylvanians, but the proposition is scouted on all hands outside of that state. . . . Wade cannot be made a compromise candidate. . . .

But Fessenden had sternly refused to be a candidate.[2] Blaine was merely kowtowing by mentioning him alongside Lincoln.

Maine's other Senator, Hamlin, likewise refused to run, saying he would rather be Senator than President. So Maine's delegation went uninstructed, leaning heavily toward Seward. But Hamlin's finger was in the pie. Though he was a close friend of the little hay-thatched New York Senator, Hamlin believed Seward could not be elected, tentatively selecting John M. Read of Pennsylvania, paired with Bates, as a ticket which could win.[3] Suiting the action to the thought, he pulled Maine wires not *for* anybody, but *against* Seward. Hamlin directed his Maine machine to avoid instructing the Maine delega-tion to Seward, and engineered a victory of Hamlin henchmen over several Seward men who sought election as delegates. To these, his Chicago representatives, Hamlin gave detailed orders: "Appoint one of your numbers to canvass the delegates from the three doubtful states of Pennsylvania, Indiana, and Illinois. Have him obtain from them in writing the names of three men who can carry these states." In Chicago, Hamlin's workers followed orders, found that while a minority of doubtful state delegates claimed Seward could win, a majority said he could not, but that Lincoln could. This decided

[1] Blaine to Fessenden, May 14 (?), 1860; in Francis Fessenden, *Life and Public Services of William Pitt Fessenden,* Vol. I, p. 112. (Misdated May 16.)
[2] Fessenden, Vol. I, pp. 109–113.
[3] Hamlin to J. H. Drummond, Dec. 16, 1859; in C. E. Hamlin, *Life and Times of Hannibal Hamlin,* p. 335, *Lincoln Lore,* No. 795

Hamlin's men for Lincoln and persuaded other Maine men to change from Seward to Lincoln, substantially reducing Seward's majority in the delegation.[1]

"So," wrote Swett, "the first point was gained, that is, the united assertion of the four doubtful states, Pennsylvania, New Jersey, Indiana and Illinois, that Seward would be defeated." This initial success told the Lincoln men that they had a fighting chance to win the grand prize, so for the time being they waived the possibility of making Lincoln Vice President.

The next step was to secure for Lincoln more votes on the first ballot than any other opponent of Seward would have — a consummation vastly more difficult. Bates, Cameron, and Chase were all ahead of him at the start. Lincoln headquarters at the crowded Tremont, unlike the turbulent Weed demesne, had no crowds of boisterous henchmen. It was a quiet, unobtrusive center with but few workers. Frank Blair's Bates headquarters was also at the Tremont, making great noise. Perhaps, when Weed saw the magnitude of the Lincoln camp, he felt more confident than ever. The Lincoln strategy on this point was of the gum-shoe type; they had noise, more than all the others, but it was seemingly unconnected with the quiet Lincoln headquarters. About the only Lincolnites working steadily from headquarters were Judges Davis and Logan, Dubois, Judd, Dick Yates, John M. Palmer, B. C. Cook, Browning, Koerner, — Browning and Koerner not arriving until Tuesday.[2]

Davis, aggressively taking charge, had "seated himself behind a big table in the rooms of the headquarters and organized committees of visitation to the various delegations. . . . For instance, he had Samuel C. Parks . . . who was born in Vermont, organize a delegation of about four also from Vermont, to visit the delegates from that state; and he had me," Leonard Swett recalls, "from the State of Maine, organize a delegation from the Pine Tree State, and every man was to come back and report to him."[3] The Lincoln men planned, to aid and abet their schemes in the delegate market, an

[1] Hamlin, pp. 339–344.
[2] Koerner, *Memoirs*, Vol. II, p. 85.
[3] Swett, in Wakefield, *How Lincoln Became President*, pp. 111–112.

unscrupulous stroke of gum-shoe strategy. No other group could have utilized this system, for the physical arrangements of the Convention were entirely in Illinois hands. Koerner tells how at Lincoln head-quarters the plan was developed. "We held communications with all our Illinois friends, and received regular and reliable information from all parts of the city. While the friends of the other candidates held processions and marched around with bands of music, we had made arrangements that the Wigwam should at the earliest opening every morning be filled with Illinoisans. We had them provided with tickets before tickets were distributed to others." Valuable as errand boys and pressure assistants were several enthusiastic young Republicans whom Judd had fired with Lincoln cause.[1]

Monday, as the Indiana delegation was about to give in, Delegate Knapp of the Springfield district sent off a letter to Lincoln who awaited news at his law office [2]: —

Things are working; keep a good nerve — be not surprised at any result — but I tell you that your chances are not the worst. We have got Seward in the attitude of the representative Republican of the East — you at the West. We are laboring to make you the second choice of all the delegations we can where we cannot make you first choice. We are dealing tenderly with delegates, taking them in detail, and making no fuss. Be not too expectant, but rely upon our discretion. Again I say brace your nerves for any result.

Tuesday morning at dawn Orville Browning reached Chicago in one of the brand-new sleeping cars, "long train of cars & all crowded," ready to go to work.[3] From the Lincoln workers at the Tremont he learned how things were going. Important business in hand was to gather fifty more first-ballot votes for Lincoln. Secondarily, the Lincolnites had to persuade as many additional delegates as possible to swing to Lincoln on the second ballot. "We let Greeley run his Bates machine, but got most of them for a second choice," Swett wrote. The New England delegations, though most of them came unin

[1] Reminiscences of G. M. Dodge, in *Annals of Iowa*, Vol. XII, pp. 450–451.
[2] C. L. Conkling, "How Mr. Lincoln Received the News of his First Nomination," *Transactions*, Ill. State Hist. Soc., 1909, p. 63. Weik, *The Real Lincoln*, p. 263.
[3] *Diary of Browning*, Vol. I, p. 406.

structed, were known to be mildly pro-Seward [1]; but good work for Lincoln might be done there. Davis and his workers could afford to let no opportunity slip. So on Tuesday Judge Davis, with Browning and Delegate Marshall of Charleston, went around to the Maine delegation for a conference. Browning had not forgotten his preference for Bates,[2] but, under Lincoln instructions, was loyally supporting the Rail Splitter. Greeley had sent his close friend Pike to Maine to pull wires in behalf of Bates, and from Pike's report thought Maine would go for Bates.[3] Davis therefore took Browning along and had him deliver a speech to the gentlemen from Maine as a specimen of a former Bates man who had acquired conviction that Lincoln had become the man of the hour. Davis, Browning, and Marshall next called on the New Hampshire delegation, and with surprising success.[4] They won promises of first-ballot votes from both Maine and New Hampshire.

The important Massachusetts delegation was known to be heavily pro-Seward, but the chairman, John Andrew, was warmly for Lincoln. This curly-haired Boston abolitionist thought either Seward, Chase, or Fessenden would make an admirable President, but when he reached Chicago he decided, despite his delegation's heavy Seward majority, that Lincoln would make the best candidate.[5] Andrew gathered about him a group of non-Seward-worshiping New England delegates and called on the four doubtful state delegations. A New Jersey delegate tells how they worked.[6]

Mr. Andrew was the spokesman. . . . He stated that it was the desire of all that the party should succeed; that he and others from New England were in favor of . . . Seward, but that they preferred the success of the party rather than the election of any particular individual; and when it was made apparent . . . that . . . Seward could not carry the doubtful states and that some other man could, they were willing to give up Mr. Seward and go for the man who could make victory certain. "You

---

[1] D. V. Smith, p. 520.
[2] *Diary of Browning*, Vol. I, p. 407.
[3] Greeley to Pike, May 21, 1860, in Pike, *First Blows*, p. 519.
[4] *Diary of Browning*, Vol. I, p. 406.
[5] H. G. Pearson, *Life of John A. Andrew*, Vol. I, pp. 112–113.
[6] T. H. Dudley, pp. 477–478. H. Kreismann to E. B. Washburne, May 16, 1860; Washburne MSS.

delegates all say . . . Seward cannot carry the doubtful states. When we ask you who can, you from New Jersey give us the name of William L. Dayton . . . ; but when we go to Pennsylvania they name Simon Cameron; and Indiana and Illinois, Abraham Lincoln. Now it is impossible to have all these candidates, and unless you delegates from the four doubtful states can agree upon some candidate, . . . we from New England will vote for our choice, William H. Seward. . . ." The talk of this committee made a profound impression upon the delegates from the four states, and the necessity of uniting upon some candidate was felt by all.

Tuesday evening Lincoln headquarters received a message from Massachusetts, and at once a group of Lincolnites went over to the Massachusetts rooms to fish for votes, Browning making the speech. They were not able to swing many Bay State votes to Lincoln, but next morning Andrew, having decided that Lincoln looked like the best man to lead a coalition, organized a band of New England Lincolnites and went from delegation to delegation showing off the unexpected Lincoln support from New England. Young Procter thought this "quite a group" when it appeared to the Kansas delegation.[1] Many other delegations were likewise astonished, causing a material improvement in Lincoln's prospects, making the Lincoln movement look like a going concern which still offered ground-floor openings. Virginia was another undecided delegation, and supporters of Lincoln, Bates, and Seward were scrambling for Virginia's twenty-three votes.[2] Most of the Bates first-ballot votes were to come from Connecticut, Maryland, and Delaware through the Blairs. Gideon Welles (of the Santa Claus beard), Connecticut's leader, headed a badly split delegation. Welles himself disfavored choosing Seward but was not sure whom he should support.[3] Into the Welles ear, therefore, the Lincoln men breathed whispers of a cabinet job should valuable services be rendered. The Lincoln managers likewise conferred with Montgomery and Frank Blair and confidentially assured them that if Lincoln should be made their second choice they might count on

[1] Procter, p. 9.
[2] Entitled to thirty, Virginia sent only twenty-three delegates.
[3] Preston King to John Bigelow, March 1, 1860, in Bigelow, *Retrospections,* Vol. I, pp. 285. King to Gideon Welles, Sept. 30, 1858; Welles to Senator James Dixon, Dec. 6, 1858, Welles MSS

substantial recognition for any aid they might give in nominating him.[1] So it was that the Lincolnites "let Greeley run his Bates machine, but got most of them for a second choice."

The surprising success of these preliminary Lincoln manoeuvers might seem to indicate that the sponsors of other candidates had abandoned the fight. But such was not the case. Every candidate still in the field had somebody working energetically. Most active of all were Weed and his men, equipped with a huge war chest with which to lubricate the ways. Greeley wrote, three days after the nomination, "If you had . . . seen how much money Weed had in hand, you would not have believed we could do so well as we did."[2]

Nobody knew, until the Convention had organized and the Credentials Committee made its report, just how many delegates would vote, but it was expected there would be between 450 and 475. Of these some 150 came unpledged, relatively free to vote for whomever they pleased. In addition, after the first ballot about 75 more would be released following the purely complimentary vote to favorite sons who had no serious chance of winning. These were the waters in which promoters of leading candidates must angle for enough votes to put their man over. When these floating and semi-floating delegations were approached by some ingratiating politician on behalf of Lincoln, Bates, or Seward, whom they would decide to support was primarily a matter of business, secondarily a matter of personal preference. The Seward organization offered a fairly safe investment, but low dividends, — preferred stock, so to speak, — while the Lincoln company offered a wildcat investment which, should it pan out, would pay colossal dividends.

[1] Gideon Welles, "Nomination and Election of Abraham Lincoln," Galaxy, Vol. XXII, pp. 300ff., p. 439. Welles does not here admit any deal. One must read between the lines, remember the methods of those few days, the shift of Welles's delegation in the three ballots, and note the future position of Welles under President Lincoln.
When the Cabinet was being built, Lincoln managed the Welles appointment with magnificent skill. He met Hamlin in Chicago and induced the Vice President-elect to choose Welles as his contribution to the cabinet. Macartney, Lincoln and His Cabinet, pp. 185–186. Diary of Gideon Welles, Vol. II, p. 388–392. Gideon Welles MSS., in American Historical Review, Vol. XXXI, pp. 486, 488–489. G. Welles to Edgar Welles, March 4, 1861; Welles MSS.
[2] Greeley to Pike; in Pike, First Blows, p. 520.

Boss Weed confidently hoped to pledge enough new votes for Seward from the delegate market to end all the confusion by nominating his man on the first ballot. A mere 50 votes would almost do it; to gather that many from the supply of 150 seemed no difficult matter when Seward was so far ahead of all others. Failing that, he seemingly could not lose on the second ballot. Victory was in sight, for him only. Weed thought he might, on ballot two, get some of Lincoln's Illinois delegates, having heard that 8 of Illinois' 22 were at heart pro-Seward. Many Lincoln delegates expected to vote their instructions on the first ballot only.[1] And the Lincolnites were highly embarrassed by Long John Wentworth, Chicago's Mayor. He had gone to the Decatur Convention, itching to be made an Illinois delegate; but Judd cut him out and now Wentworth was taking revenge. Towering in the smoky haze of hotel lobbies, high above everybody, was the Mayor's huge bald head, "talking openly and loudly for Seward." Judge Davis detailed a man to follow the Mayor about and provide neutralizing counterblasts.[2]

In this furious welter of bargaining conferences, managers of all candidates save Seward and Lincoln, seeking to snare as many of the floating votes as possible, found their efforts checkmated for the time being — held up by Seward because of his preponderant strength, by Lincoln because of the overwhelming outside pressure. As yet nobody could be sure how matters stood, because some delegations were promising everything, some nothing, with delivery of contracted votes always a question; but the contest seemed to have narrowed down to a fight between Seward and Lincoln. Congressman Elihu Washburne's Chicago informant wrote to Washington late Tuesday, somewhat overoptimistically [3]: —

The nomination at present lies between Seward and Lincoln. Wentworth has come out in his paper for Seward this morning, Weed having made a bargain with him. This will hurt Lincoln as he declares Seward can carry our state. . . . Indiana will go for Lincoln. New Hampshire and Con-

[1] H. Kreismann to Washburne, May 7; M. Smith to Washburne, May 8, 1860. Washburne himself had favored Senator Fessenden for the Presidency. J. M. Church to Washburne, Jan. 29, 1860. Washburne MSS.
[2] Davis, *How Lincoln Became President*, p. 75.
[3] H. Kreismann to Washburne, May 15, 1860; Washburne MSS.

necticut are the same way. Ohio after getting through with Chase is for Lincoln. . . . Pennsylvania also has many who are for Lincoln as their second choice. The Lincoln movement has become a serious thing. . . . Greeley is working hard against Seward. He is for Bates but if he can't get him will take Lincoln.

Gov. Morgan says it will not do to nominate Seward. We want the Presidency and he can't carry. Half of the Iowa delegation are for Lincoln.

Last night Lincoln stock was highest and bets were freely offered on his nomination.

Since an indispensable feature of the Davis force's strategy was the securing of many additional second-ballot votes for Lincoln, their candidate stood in pressing need of a vigorous build-up as the man who could not fail to win for the Party. Lincoln needed advertising as a man offering a great deal more than the somewhat negative virtue of availability in the doubtful states. So the Lincoln workers "impressed into service every man who knew Lincoln," one of their number recalls, "to go about and talk about him — to tell of his romantic life, his humble birth, his rail-splitting and flat-boating, his fine character and his great ability." [1] Mark Delahay was there, using the money Lincoln gave him for expenses.[2] But if he did anything of special value for Lincoln, nobody remembers it.[3] Billy Herndon too was on hand, of course.

In the delicate manipulations for second-ballot support, the "favorite son" states came in for close attention: New Jersey, Pennsylvania, Vermont, Ohio, and those pledged to Bates but not strongly for him — not beyond reason, according to Judge Davis' information

[1] Davis, pp. 75–77. Carr, *The Illini*, p. 272.
[2] Angle, *New Letters*, p. 243.
[3] Dr. Barton, (*Lincoln*, Vol. I, p. 431) on authority of Addison G. Procter, says that Delahay sent word to Lincoln on Thursday that he could not be nominated, asking if Lincoln would accept the position of Seward's running mate. Lincoln is alleged to have consented, according to Procter. I have found no evidence that anything of the kind occurred. And the story falls before the scientific method in history. Had Lincoln wanted the Vice Presidency, he would not have placed his case in hands as unreliable as Delahay's. Procter's testimony is to be accepted only when he is corroborated. For example, Procter in his published reminiscences tells of Cassius Clay making a stirring speech urging Lincoln's nomination. Clay was not at Chicago. Procter makes Henry S. Lane say, "I am Governor of Indiana. I know my people well. . . . These people want a man of the Lincoln type as their President. . . ." (pp. 12–13) Lane was not Governor of Indiana, only a candidate.

Press & Tribune.

SATURDAY, MAY 19, 1860.

"HONEST OLD ABE."

The People's Candidate for President.

"RAILS AND FLAT-BOATS."

Log Cabins and Hard Cider Come Again?

Biographical Sketch of Abraham Lincoln.

ABRAHAM LINCOLN is a native of Hardin county, Kentucky. He was born on the 12th day of February, 1809. His parents were both from Virginia, and were certainly not of the first families. His paternal grandfather, Abraham Lincoln, emigrated from Rockingham county, Virginia, to Kentucky, about 1781 or '2, where a year or two later he was killed by Indians, not in battle, but by stealth, while he was laboring to open a farm in the forest. His ancestors, who were respectable members of the Society of Friends, went to Virginia from Berks county, Pennsylvania. Descendants of the same much still reside in the eastern part of that State.

Mr. Lincoln's father, at the death of his father, was but six years of age, and he grew up literally without education. He removed from Kentucky to what is now Spencer county, Indiana, in 1816. The family reached their new home about the time the State was admitted into the Union. The region in which they settled was rude and wild, and they endured, for some years, the hard experience of a frontier life, in which the struggle with nature for existence and security is to be maintained only by constant vigilance. Bears, wolves and other wild animals still infested the woods, and young Lincoln acquired more skill in the use of the rifle than knowledge of books. There were institutions here and there known by the flattering denomination of "schools," but no qualification was required of a teacher beyond "readin', writin' and cypherin'," as the vernacular phrase ran, so far as the rule of three. If a straggler supposed to understand Latin happened to sojourn in the neighborhood, he was

of the prominence now given to the chief actor in that exciting event, it cannot fail to be interesting to all.

The affair came off on the fourth day of October, 1854. The State Fair had been in progress two days, and the capital was full of all manner of men. The Nebraska bill had been passed on the previous twenty-second of May. Mr. Douglas had returned to Illinois to meet an outraged constituency. He had made a fragmentary speech in Chicago, the people filling up each hiatus in a peculiar and good humored way. He called the people a mob—they called him a rowdy. The "mob" had the best of it, both then and at the election which succeeded. The notoriety of all these events had stirred up the politics of the State from bottom to top. Hundreds of politicians had met at Springfield expecting a tournament of an unusual character—Douglas, Breese, Koerner, Lincoln, Trumbull, Matteson, Yates, Codding, John Calhoun, (of the order of the Candle Box,) John M. Palmer, the whole house of the McConnells, Singleton, (known to fame in the Mormon War,) Thos. L. Harris, and a host of others. Several speeches were made before and several after, the passage between LINCOLN and DOUGLAS, but that was justly held to be *the* event of the season.

We do not remember whether a challenge to debate passed between the friends of the speaker or not, but there was a perfectly amicable understanding between Lincoln and Douglas, that the former should speak two or three hours and the latter reply in just as little or as much time as he chose. Mr. Lincoln took the stand at two o'clock—a large crowd in attendance, and Mr. Douglas seated on a small platform in front of the desk. The first half-hour of Mr. Lincoln's speech was taken up with compliments to his distinguished friend Judge Douglas, and dry allusions to the political events of the past few years. His distinguished friend Judge Douglas had taken his seat, as solemn as the Cock-Lane ghost, evidently with the design of not moving a muscle till it came his turn to speak. The laughter provoked by Lincoln's exordium, however, soon began to make him uneasy; and when Mr. L. arrived at his (Douglas') speech pronouncing the Missouri Compromise "a sacred thing which no ruthless hand would ever be reckless enough to disturb," he opened his lips far enough to remark, "A first-rate speech!" This was the beginning of an amusing colloquy.

"Yes," continued Lincoln, "so affectionate was my friend's regard for this compromise line,

---

THE FIRST NATIONALLY-READ BIOGRAPHY OF LINCOLN
(*In Chicago* Press & Tribune, *May 19, 1860*)

and analysis. Delaware was attacked; the usual argument won a promise to come to Lincoln after one ballot for Bates. They would keep the promise if, when the second ballot came to be taken, keeping it seemed the best thing they could do. Vermont promised the Davis negotiators to switch favorably after voting once for Collamer.[1] But (who could tell?) that promise might be an Indian gift. Weed worked so hard to get Vermont on the first ballot, made his cause apparently so agreeable to them, that most observers counted Vermont in the Seward list.[2] Little could be done with Ohio; Chase was too strong, just as Thurlow Weed could get little satisfaction from Illinois because of Lincoln, from Missouri because of Bates. When the Illinoisans reached the New Jersey delegation, however, they found that Weed had beaten them to the draw. Weed, laying his second ballot plans, must have wondered how he could miss them, even if he failed to nominate on ballot one. For he needed only one of the big "favorite son" delegations, like Pennsylvania, to put Seward over. And was it likely that he would lose *all* votes released by "favorite son" withdrawals? Not likely at all. But Weed's very real danger lay in the doubtful states' adamantine insistence that Seward could not carry them. Should the doubtful states retreat, he would win by default.

Obvious strategy for Weed to adopt when he found Lincoln so astonishingly strong in the Chicago setting was an attempt to knock Lincoln out of the race and start a doubtful-state retreat by putting the Illinois favorite son on the ticket as Seward's running mate. This stratagem had already been tried on the Bates forces. Old Francis Blair had been told that if he would swing the Bates support to Seward, Frank Blair might have the Vice Presidency. The Blairs had refused to sell out for a bid so low.[3] Weed then tried another tack. To attract Bates men to Seward as their second choice, he told a fairy tale to the Bates manager, Charles Gibson. The story was that if Seward were not nominated during the early presidential balloting,

[1] Swett, in Oldroyd, p. 71.
[2] Cf. p. 275.
[3] W. E. Smith, *The Blair Family*, Vol. I, p. 483.

Seward delegates would combine with Bates men and give Bates the nomination.[1]

The skillful Seward manager had meantime been dealing directly with the Illinois delegation, promising Lincoln the Vice Presidency in exchange for Lincoln's presidential votes (which would practically nominate Seward) but could make no sale. Time after time Weed and his workers went back. "They literally overwhelmed us with kindness," recalls one of the Lincoln men.[2] Weed then tried to achieve a similar result by an effort to persuade the convention to draft Lincoln for Vice President. Judge Davis found that New Jersey, after voting for Favorite Son Dayton, wanted to go for Seward with Lincoln as his running mate. To have New Jersey, a doubtful state, voting for Seward on Ballot Two, would probably upset the stop-Seward apple cart. So Davis, greatly worried, asked John Palmer to drop in at the New Jersey delegation's quarters and see if he could change their opinions.

On the way over to New Jersey headquarters with Davis, Palmer thought out his plan. As a former Democrat, Palmer addressed them with this argument: if Seward were candidate for President, with Lincoln for Vice President, hordes of Republicans who used to be Democrats would be frightfully offended because the Party had nominated two old Whigs and ignored old Democrats. This revolt would defeat the ticket, Palmer affirmed. Seward and Lincoln could never carry Illinois. The gentlemen from New Jersey were impressed, but did not want to believe what Palmer said, so attractive were Weed's bargains, so convincing his argument that Lincoln on the ticket with Seward would insure victory in Indiana and Illinois. They asked Judge Davis if those Democratic-Republicans would really shy off from an all-Whig ticket. The fat man (losing pound after pound in all this hubbub) hastily blurted, feigning distress: "Oh! Oh, my God, Judge, you can't account for the conduct of these old Locofocos. Will they do as Palmer says? Certainly. There are forty thousand of them [in Illinois], and, as Palmer says, not a damned one of them will vote

[1] Forty years later, Gibson still remembered this tricky promise as an arrangement which almost made Bates President. Gibson, p. 55.
[2] Reminiscence of John M. Palmer, in Davis, p. 77.

for two Whigs."[1] But Davis and Palmer were able to get little satisfaction from this delegation, for all their clever arguments and his-
trionics.

The fifty-four-vote Pennsylvania delegation was fertile ground.
Cameron was getting nowhere outside his own state, but his managers
still hoped their half-hundred-vote nest egg would burgeon into victory. Davis met this delegation very early and found that no business
could be done unless Cameron could be promised a cabinet post. To
make sure that Lincoln would tolerate a man like Cameron, Davis
telegraphed word to Lincoln that Pennsylvania looked good if Cameron could be promised the Treasury Department. Lincoln sent back
a cryptic message: "I authorize no bargains and will be bound by
none."[2]

There is no way of knowing for certain why Lincoln sent those
ten words which might well have scuttled all his chances of victory.
And it does require explanation. The best the historian can do, therefore, is to attempt a vizualization of Lincoln's psychology as it must
have been when he wrote that message, using clearly authenticated
facts as the foundation for recreative theory. First, Lincoln knew
quite well that without such deals he could get nowhere at Chicago.
And he had sanctioned Convention horse-trading, even to the extent
of helping to arrange that Indiana deal. The import of Delegate
Knapp's message, "We are dealing tenderly with delegates, taking
them in detail and making no fuss," was perfectly apparent to him.
Then why did he send to David Davis this message which, if taken
seriously, amounted to a complete about-face concerning his candidacy for President? The most plausible explanation seems to be
that Lincoln, consciously or unconsciously, was playing the political
game, as usual, with consummate astuteness. From a friendship of
years and close association in a wide variety of atmospheres, Lincoln
knew Judge Davis very well. He knew the corpulent jurist who looked
like a Franz Hals portrait for an honest man yet an astute realist,
who acted as the spirit moved him, with no trouble from his con-

---

[1] Davis, pp. 77–78. John M. Palmer, *Personal Recollections*, p. 81.
[2] Whitney, *Lincoln the Citizen*, p. 289. Hertz, Vol. II, p. 773.

science.[1] Therefore Lincoln must have reflected that he could rely on his manager to pay scant attention to any order from Springfield that interfered with the business in hand. Lincoln also relied on the discretion of Stephen Logan, had given him a letter authorizing withdrawal of his name should his managers find retreat necessary.[2] By giving out these two restraining orders to the right men, astute Candidate Lincoln, without sacrificing the advantages of bargaining, fortified himself against charges of corrupt bargaining.

Lincoln had executed a perfect hedge. If his Chicago managers chose to ignore his restraining instructions, well and good. He would have a fighting chance for the Presidency. Should they follow his orders, well and good too, for he would get Illinois' 22 votes on the first ballot and be in direct line for the coveted Senatorship of 1864.

Such in brief was the jumbled chaos of the presidential race Wednesday morning as the Convention was about to begin its work. As noon approached, Chicago's agitation, Halstead assures us, was "exceedingly great. Vast as the wigwam is, not one-fifth of those who would be glad to get inside can be accommodated." Seward men marched about displaying silk badges bearing their hero's portrait and name. Bates men adorned hats with a bearded woodcut of their pride and joy. But in the "universal twaddle," thanks to that Greek chorus of noisy Illinoisans, "Old Abe" was vociferously, insistently proclaimed the man of the hour.

Historians, following a broad current of contemporary political opinion, have often written the facile deduction that the Democratic Party's split at Charleston made a Republican victory inevitable. That notion is a world away from the truth. If Republican leaders had been convinced, when the torn Democracy disbanded at Charleston on May 3 with no nomination made, that their Party could coast downhill to victory, the presidential chances of Abraham Lincoln would have sunk like lead. Chicago delegates, released from the availability worry, would have nominated Seward by acclamation. Friends of Lincoln, reading the news that Douglas had failed of nomination,

---

[1] For a delightful account of Davis' land deals, cf. Sandburg, Vol. II, p. 40.
[2] *Herndon's Lincoln*, p. 373.

might on first thought fear that Lincoln's chances were weakened because the Little Giant, contrary to expectations, was not formally in the field as candidate for President. But on second thought, it was obvious that Douglas would be nominated when the Democrats reconvened at Baltimore on June 18; so in the North the situation was not, for Republicans, substantially changed.[1] Douglas might win the North and the Presidency, exactly as the Republicans planned to do, if the Republicans failed to nominate an available man. Or he might carry the North's doubtful states and enough border states to make him President. Still another possibility was that the Little Giant might be strong enough in the North to throw the election into the House of Representatives. A late April editorial of the Indianapolis *Journal* states the sober fact [2]: —

However eager-eyed speculators may see Seward's increasing strength before the probability of Douglas' defeat, . . . there is actually no change in the only place where a change can at all effect the result, the feelings of the people. Men who manipulate conventions, and are familiar with the tricks of nominations, no doubt see changes, but they all start in their own circle and end there. They never reach the popular sentiment below. And that sentiment is the foundation on which victory must be built, and it is to that and not to Charleston that the Chicago Convention must look. . . . We must nominate such a man as will be acceptable to the largest and broadest sentiment opposed to slavery. Who is that man? Not Mr. Seward, we are sorry to say, for he ought to be; not Mr. Chase; not any man who is regarded as the representative of an aggressive hostility to slavery; because such a man must be the centre of a narrower circle than the whole anti-slavery feeling. . . .

Indeed, since the spectacular Southern repudiation of Douglas at Charleston had at last caused the Little Giant to stand before the country in his true colors as a man of freedom, Republicans had good reason to fear that his strength in the North might increase.[3] Might not enough conservative, sectionalism-fearing Northerners regard a

[1] B. King to G. Welles, March 14, 1859. J. Dixon to Welles, May 4, 1860. Welles MSS. G. C. McRed to E. B. Washburne, April 15, H. Kreismann to Washburne, May 1, 1860; Washburne MSS.
[2] Clipped in Chicago *Press & Tribune*, May 1, 1860.
[3] Milton, *Eve of Conflict*, pp. 391–393, 399, 404–405. Herriott, "Deutsches Haus," p. 112. Blaine, *Twenty Years*, Vol. I, p. 151.

vote for Douglas as the safest, least sectional, way to oppose slavery, and deliver to Douglas some of the Fremont states of '56, completely upsetting Republican plans? [1]

Republican strategists knew there would be two Democratic tickets, a Northern and a Southern, in the field.[2] Further complicating the case was still another ticket, with candidates already chosen. In Baltimore, while Illinois Republicans at Decatur were making Abraham Lincoln "the Rail Candidate," a Party calling itself the "National Constitutional Union Party" had commenced organizing amid great enthusiasm. Avowedly conservative, like the Fillmore ticket of '56, this new Party was formed, as the only nonsectional ticket before the country, with the intention of capturing all voters who feared sectional parties. John T. Stuart, Lincoln's first law partner and early political tutor, went from Springfield as a delegate. The Party creed, compounded of Whig, Know-Nothing, and border-state Opposition elements, was mirrored in its candidate list: Botts of Virginia, Everett of Massachusetts, Bell of Tennessee, Crittenden of Kentucky, Houston of Texas, McLean of Ohio, several of whom were being favored by conservative Republicans for the Chicago nomination.[3] Edward Bates held out a faint hope that the Baltimore Constitutional Union Convention would nominate him on the strength of his chances of becoming the Republican presidential nominee, effecting thereby a powerful coalition of the North and border states.[4] Judge McLean had stronger hopes for the combination, with McLean the presidential candidate.[5] This was a rational scheme for beating the Democrats no matter what they should do in June, but it was not compatible with practical politics and did not work out, for the Constitutional Unionists nominated Bell and Everett on a platform which did nothing but view with alarm the dangerous phenomenon of sectional parties.

[1] E. S. Hamlin to S. P. Chase, Feb. 18, 1858; Chase MSS. David Davis to ——, Feb. 20, 1860; Chicago Hist. Soc.
[2] Nicolay and Hay, Vol. II, p. 259.
[3] Halstead, p. 105. J. B. Robinson to J. McLean, May 3, 1860; McLean MSS.
[4] *Diary of Bates*, pp. 118–119. G. D. Morgan to G. Welles, April 10, 1860; Welles MSS.
[5] R. W. Thompson, April 15, Thomas Corwin, April 21, G. W. Hill, April 27, 1860, to McLean; McLean MSS.

Nobody knew the real strength of the new Party, how it would affect the Party line-up; but its influence on Republican deliberations, though obscure, was to make leaders seek to nominate their strongest candidate. Bell might win enough electors from border states and upper South to throw the election into the House of Representatives.[1] Or, interpreting the recent Republican reverse in Connecticut and Rhode Island as a rising Northern fear of John Brown raids and all political sectionalism, an attractive conservative ticket might win enough Republican votes of 1856 to give some of the Fremont states to Douglas.[2] Shrewd Republicans, therefore, sought to discredit the new Party by impugning the sincerity of its Unionism. Said the Chicago *Press & Tribune* on Wigwam dedication day [3]: —

If there is any man green enough to believe that the National Union Constitutional movement at Baltimore is anything more than a repetition of the Fillmore swindle of 1856, for the benefit of the mulatto-making Democracy, he surely ought not to be permitted to go abroad when the cows are at large, else he might be mistaken for some other verdant thing and be swallowed up. . . . They have assumed the garb and set up the cries of Union men only that the Disunion Democracy might be served.

The Chicago Convention might cut the Gordian knot, when Republican strategists saw traditional political lines snarled by the new diversity of tickets and nominations, only by nominating a candidate who could carry the North.[4]

In press and in palaver, thousands of times in recent weeks, Republican wire-workers had felt the impact of two antagonistic claims: "Seward can sweep the North!" — "Seward cannot carry the doubtful states!" In Chicago's great convention the Party had to decide which to believe.[5] Delegates, jostled and shoved in packed hotels and

---

[1] Chadwick, *Causes of the Civil War*, p. 115.
[2] Ottawa *Free Trader*, May 19, 1860.
[3] Chicago *Press & Tribune*, May 12.
[4] Joseph H. Barrett, *Abraham Lincoln and His Presidency*, Vol. I, pp. 220–224.
[5] Henry Wilson, *Rise and Fall of the Slave Power*, Vol. II, p. 692. Senator Sumner wrote, "We can elect any man the convention at Chicago choose to nominate." Sumner to E. L. Pierce, May 4, 1860, in E. L. Pierce, *Memoir and Letters of Charles Sumner*, Vol. III, p. 604. Senator Wilson of Massachusetts told his colleagues that, since the Democratic split, Seward could not fail to sweep the North. J. Dixon to G. Welles, May 8, 1860; Welles MSS. Senator Dixon concluded, "There is danger that the Convention will be carried by storm, and the greatest firmness will be required, to break the torrent of artificial sentiment."

streets swarming like a great beehive, tired from travel and back-slaping and arm-pumping by jovial candidate-boosters, sleeping on billiard tables or three-in-a-bed, brains addled by frequent contact with John Barleycorn and effusive campaign managers who spouted assurances that their candidate would be the salvation of the country, were hard put to make a sober decision. But those who had a mind even a little open could not help noticing the prominence in the Chicago scene of the interpretation which looked distrustfully at Seward. All the doubtful state forces swelled the anti-Seward splatterdash. A Boston paper had said, "There are four free states which cannot be considered sure for the Republican candidate in 1860. They are New Jersey, Pennsylvania, Indiana, and Illinois. Now we would be almost willing to let the delegates from those four states nominate the candidate." [1] Should this view spread its influence as the Convention began work, the race would cease to be a Seward-dominated affair and become a fair fight between favorite sons. But the bulk of the outside pressure was more than negative; the steady insistence of Lincoln's legions that Seward could not win was but a preface to the vociferous declaration that Lincoln could win. The *Press & Tribune* of Tuesday, a paper almost completely filled with Convention reading, carried a capacity load of Lincoln boosts: a three-foot editorial, "THE WINNING MAN — ABRAHAM LINCOLN," which hammered the note "that MR. LINCOLN *can be elected*," emphasizing his honesty, his romantic background, his solid, non-radical Republicanism, his acceptability to all those diverse elements in the political group which Horace Greeley, in the rôle of historian of the Civil War, slyly called "the 'Republican'" Party,[2] his approval of a protective tariff, homestead legislation, internal improvements. For good measure, Ray and Medill reprinted "Mr. Lincoln's Apostrophe on the Declaration of Independence" which he delivered at Beardstown in the '58 canvass.

Next morning the Illinois favorite son, who was fast approaching dangerous "dark horse" stature, had additional valuable aid from

---

[1] Boston *Atlas*, clipped in Indianapolis *Atlas*, Sept. 2, 1859, in Roll, p. 2.
[2] Horace Greeley, *The American Conflict*, Vol. I, p. 319.

these influential Lincolnians of the fourth estate. Delegates, waiting for the Convention to open at noon, read in the *Press & Tribune* the editorial "THE WINNING MAN — ABRAHAM LINCOLN," reprinted, and several interesting letters. A New Yorker's long communication discussed the doubtful states and all prominent candidates; it concluded, "Give us Lincoln and victory is sure." An Ohioan's letter said the same thing in different words. A Pennsylvanian was even more emphatic: —

A nomination which will drive the Fillmore vote over to John Bell must necessarily prove fatal to the Republican ticket. Who has the hardihood to affirm that Mr. Seward is popular with the Fillmore men? . . .

Should not the delegates of these [doubtful] states be consulted; and if they declare that Mr. S. cannot carry them, should his friends by virtue of more numbers, force his nomination? From present appearances, Mr. Seward, if nominated, must be nominated over the heads and against the protest of the delegates from Pennsylvania, New Jersey, Indiana, Illinois, Connecticut, Rhode Island, and Oregon. These states cast *seventy-one* electoral votes. No Republican can be elected without their aid. Is the Convention going to nominate a candidate without their consent? If it is, who will elect him?

CHAPTER VI

How Presidents Are Chosen

L ONG before noon, scheduled convening hour, all streets near the Wigwam were jammed with people anxious to get inside to witness the great spectacle. At 11:30 the three big doors on Market Street were thrown open and ticket holders slowly filed in, pushing through the dense throng clogging all space roundabout the giant barn. Ticket holders inside, the doorkeepers escaped as the multitude surged forward in one grand rush that packed the Wigwam. Spectators, jostling for places as noon drew nigh, saw before them more than 450 delegates, some sitting, some milling about on a long platform, built against a brick wall elegantly painted in carnival mural motif, running the entire width of the building. Both ends of the huge platform on which the delegates sat were cut off for committee rooms, so that chairs for delegates were arranged in oblique rows, half-facing the audience, beneath a forest of placards labeling each delegation. Newspapermen, sixty or so, also sat up there. Directly in front of and below the platform began a series of wide landings, sweeping upward to the Market Street entrances. On these landings the ticketless mob was accommodated, actually standing, in close formation, delighted to be inside no matter how tired their feet became. This arrangement, however, gave them a good view of the platform. Why worry about seats for them? They were only the voters.

The select few holding tickets made a beeline for the balcony, built around three sides of the hall, up near the roof, pitched so that everybody clearly saw the platform where the action would take place. This balcony boasted chairs, seating two thousand or so, and was reserved for ladies and their gentlemen escorts. So when a ticket-holding gentleman found he could get a seat only with the aid of a lady friend, he swiftly hired the most likely-looking female he could find near by; then sent her about her business, with proper emolument, after he was safely installed upstairs. Ladies of doubtful character, present in force, did a rushing escort business. One Republican could find no better than an old squaw who was vending moccasins. "This was more than the doorkeepers could stand, and after a spirited argument, it was decided that she was no lady. The young Republican protested indignantly . . . , claiming equal rights for all womankind."

Full as the Wigwam was, a swarm of twenty thousand milled around outside, struggling and shoving to witness history in the making. "The scene," exclaimed one enraptured journalist, "is such as a man beholds but once in a lifetime." [1] The packed hall purred with loud conversational buzz and hum when, at 12:10, Governor Morgan of New York, Republican National Chairman, stepped forward. *Crack!* his gavel thwacked sharply. The buzz audibly died away; the Republican National Convention was in order. Morgan read in uninspired tones the call for the Convention, issued in December by the National Committee. This document lambasted the Administration, invited "the Republican electors of the several states, the members of the people's party of Pennsylvania and of the opposition party of New Jersey and all others who are willing to co-operate with them in support of the candidates which shall there be nominated," to send delegates to the Chicago Convention. [2] Then Morgan delivered a brief, eloquent speech, pointing out, amid much applause, the gravity of the work ahead: —

No body of men of equal number was ever clothed with greater responsibility than those now within the hearing of my voice. . . .

[1] Chicago *Journal,* in P. O. Ray, *The Convention That Nominated Lincoln,* p. 18.
[2] "Proceedings of the National Republican Convention Held at Chicago, May 16th, 17th, and 18th, 1860," in *Proceedings of the First Three Republican National Conventions,* pp. 83–84.

Let me then invoke you to act in a spirit of harmony, that by the dignity, the wisdom and the patriotism displayed here you may be enabled to enlist the hearts of the people, and to strengthen them in the faith that yours is the constitutional party of the country, and the only constitutional party; that you are actuated by principle, and that you will be guided by the light and by the example of the fathers of the Republic. [Renewed cheers.]

Morgan nominated, for Temporary Chairman, the Honorable David Wilmot, who was unanimously elected to the accompaniment of loud applause. Norman Judd had made efforts to secure the post for himself, but decided to avoid a contest.[1] Wilmot took the chair and delivered the keynote speech. For all his celebrity in connection with the famed Proviso, Wilmot was a simple, stupid-looking chap, and realistic observers thought him a dull dog and poor presiding officer.[2] He delivered a short, aggressive speech of indifferent merit, repeating several times the main arguments of Lincoln's Cooper Institute speech, the crowd applauding lustily at proper intervals. Temporary secretaries were appointed; then the great audience, quiet as a tomb, heard the Reverend Z. Humphrey intone a long, rolling prayer. Proceeding rapidly with the business of organization, the usual committees were appointed: Permanent Organization, Credentials, Rules. The crowd was treated to a dash of comedy by Greeley and David Cartter, chairman of the Ohio delegation (and leader of the Wade faction), in an argument on the problem of whether delegates should present their credentials to the Convention or to the Committee on Credentials.

Mr. Cartter: I move an amendment; I move to amend the proposition of the gentleman from Oregon or New York, Mr. Greeley, I am not sure which [laughter], that instead of each delegation presenting their credentials here, they present them to the Committee on Credentials.

Mr. Greeley: I accept the amendment of the gentleman from Maryland or Rhode Island, I am not particular which. [Laughter and applause.]

[1] H. Kreismann to Washburne, May 16, 1860; Washburne MSS.
[2] *Diary of Orville Hickman Browning*, Vol. I, p. 407. G. Koerner, *Memoirs*, Vol. II, p. 86.

Wilmot then tied up the proceedings by calling for a vote on Greeley's original resolution after Greeley had accepted Cartter's amendment. Finally the great problem of certifying delegates was ironed out, thanks to the intervention of the brilliant New York lawyer, William M. Evarts, floor leader of the Seward forces. Gossip said that Evarts would occupy Seward's Senate seat after the Auburn statesman had resigned to run for President.[1]

The Chair read a letter from the Chicago Board of Trade inviting delegates and visitors to take a boat ride on Lake Michigan at five o'clock. A resolution was adopted accepting the invitation; then the Convention fell to wrangling over whether or not a platform committee should be appointed prior to the Convention's permanent organization. Cartter, wanting the platform committee chosen at once, began a long-winded argument by pointing to the Lake excursion as evidence the delegates were more anxious to have a good time than attend to business. When the Convention voted, ten speeches later, to table the resolution calling for immediate appointment of a platform committee, and began to discuss at what hour the Convention should reassemble, the Lake issue became hot.

Cried an Ohio delegate, "I came here to work and am not going on the Lake; nor is any delegate who came here to work." They argued lengthily, discussing anew the platform question in an amusing parliamentary mix-up, frittering away much time, until at last they decided to sacrifice that tempting boat ride and meet again at five o'clock. A committee was appointed to explain diplomatically to the Board of Trade why the Convention could not accept that boat ride at once, but would be delighted to go later.

Delegates went out to lunch. But during the three-hour interval between sessions "an immense crowd of people" never left the Wigwam.

At 5:15 Wilmot called the Convention to order. First the Board of Trade Committee chairman gave a melancholy report. The Board of Trade, before his Committee could reach them, had assembled "a perfect fleet" of boats. "They say that if we are so pressed with business we can hold the Convention on the decks of their vessels if we desire it." A violent discussion ensued concerning the terrible insult the Party would perpetrate on the people of Chicago if the Convention did not take that ride. Confusion and noise became so great the chairman lost control and nobody could be heard.[1] Then a majority vote decided that business must take precedence over Chicago's feelings. Committee reports were called. The Committee of Permanent Organization reported, for permanent chairman, that they had agreed upon Mr. Ashmun, of Massachusetts.

A voice: George?
THE PRESIDENT: Hon. George Ashmun [a voice — "Good boy" — laughter], of Massachusetts, for President of the Convention. [Prolonged cheers.]

The report unanimously adopted, Ashmun was conducted to the Chair by tall, lank Carl Schurz and short, fat Preston King. The crowd roared at the contrast. Senator King, obscure in the Senate, was Seward's man Friday in political movements outside New York. An indefatigable letter writer and wire-puller, Seward's nomination had been uppermost in his mind for years.[2] Schurz too was an ardent Seward man. Seward men seemed to be running the Convention, now the real fight was approaching and partisanship beginning to appear. The President's speech, in order next, was short, powerful, "delivered with just warmth enough." [3] His closing note was a plea for harmony. "Not within the three days I have spent among you all have I heard one unkind word uttered by one man towards another. I hail it as an augury of success." Halstead dryly remarked that Ashmun "must have kept very close, or his hearing is deplorably impaired. He certainly could not stay long among the Seward men at the Richmond House, without hearing unkind and profane expressions used respecting brother delegates of conservative notions. He would very frequently hear brother Greeley, for example . . . called a 'damned old ass.' Indeed, that is a very mild specimen of the forms of expression

[1] Proceedings, p. 100.
[2] Preston King to Gideon Welles, 1858–1860; Welles MSS., passim.
[3] M. Halstead, Caucuses of 1860, p. 129.

used." But the President had to put up a window-dressing of harmony. Besides, Ashmun was a Seward man; his election was the first overt result of Seward's overshadowing strength.

Permanent organization was then completed, Ashmun proving himself "cool, clear-headed and executive . . . a treasure to the Convention." Norman Judd jumped up and presented to the President a beautiful oak gavel, embellished with silver and ivory. As Judd began a pompous presentation speech a California delegate interrupted and caused "great confusion." Ashmun quieted things in masterful fashion and Judd began again, explaining the history of the gavel, made by a Chicago Republican from "a piece of oak taken from Commodore Perry's flag ship — the *Lawrence*. [Applause.]"

It is not from its size that its power is to be estimated. It is, like the Republican rule, strong, but not noisy. [Great enthusiasm.] It is not that the Republicans require a noisy and violent government, or they require riotously to put down the sham Democracy; but they require, and intend to apply to them and to all those who seek disunion and keep up a cry about destroying our Government, the little force necessary to control and restrain them, like the little force which will be necessary for you, Mr. President, to use in presiding over the deliberations of this Convention. [Great cheers.]

There is a motto, too . . . which should be the motto for every Republican in this Convention — the motto borne upon the flag of the gallant Perry. "Don't Give Up the Ship." [Great applause.] Mr. President, in presenting this to you, in addition to the motto furnished by the mechanic who manufactured this, as an evidence of his warmth and zeal in the Republican Cause, I would recommend to this Convention to believe that the person who will be nominated here, can, when the election is over in November, send a despatch to Washington in the language of the gallant Perry, "We have met the enemy, and they are ours." [Terrific cheering. . . .]

Accepting the gavel, the President commented, "I have only to say today that all the auguries are that we shall meet the enemy and they shall be ours. [Cheers.]"

Then the important Committee on Resolutions was selected, and other Committee reports called for. But neither the Credentials nor

Rules Committees had reports ready, so the Convention adjourned till next morning at ten.

Gossiping, merrymaking, caucusing, imbibing, went on until the small hours. Seward men worked so hard to get enough additional delegates to nominate their man on the first ballot that the Lincolnites were obliged to labor furiously — with the availability argument (pointing grimly to the doubtful states), with blandishments and blarney and entertainment — to keep what they had gained. All the Lincoln conquests, even Indiana, might at any time turn a flip-flop and go over to Seward.[1] Davis' hold on those other first-ballot additions was even less firm. The New England converts looked fairly safe — unless the steady stream of insistent Sewardite declarations that Seward could easily carry the doubtful states became convincing. The uninstructed Kentucky and Virginia delegations received continued attention. Cassius Clay of Kentucky, controlling a portion of the Kentucky delegation, was not on the scene of action, but sent a trusty lieutenant, George Blakey. Clay had no favorite candidate,[2] had instructed his men to make the best deals they could and keep a sharp lookout for the bandwagon. The Lincolnites whispered in Blakey's ear that President Lincoln would be delighted to make Cassius Clay his Secretary of War or of the Navy.[3] So they counted on the Clay votes. Thurlow Weed was wooing Kentucky with hints that Clay would make Seward a good running mate, which (who could tell?) might endanger that Kentucky support. With the highly disorganized Virginia delegation[4] Judge Davis and his henchmen kept in constant touch, wheedling and arguing that the Party must nominate Lincoln.

The Virginians promised glibly to vote for Lincoln, but they could not resist the Seward blandishments either. They would deliver for the man most likely to win. The Lincolnites, therefore, if their negotiations to make Lincoln run strong from the start should be successful and impressive, could then confidently expect to gather most of

---

[1] Greeley to Pike, in J. S. Pike, *First Blows of the Civil War*, pp. 519–520.
[2] C. M. Clay, *Life*, Vol. I, p. 248.
[3] *Dictionary of American Biography*, Vol. IV, p. 170. Clay, *Life*, Vol. I, pp. 250–254.
[4] Nearly all the Virginia delegates came from the pro-Northern western counties which, during the war, broke away to form West Virginia.

Virginia's twenty-three votes. Also, Judge Davis could count on a total of twenty votes or so from Lincoln's strong friends of Massachusetts, Pennsylvania, Ohio, and Iowa. Adding up — lo! there were the hundred first ballot votes. Two big *ifs* remained, however. Davis had the necessary hundred, *if* Weed could not entice some of them away, and *if* the promisers chose to deliver when the proper time arrived. Victory still was by no means in sight.

In opposing Seward, however, the Lincoln cause had the indirect aid of Bates men, Chase men, Cameron men. The only course open to these other serious candidates was to co-operate with the Lincoln men to checkmate Seward, then try to deadlock the Convention and hope that in a battle of many ballots the Convention would finally choose their man.[1] So, Halstead reported: "The question on which everything turns is whether Seward can be nominated. . . . The Republicans have all divided into two classes, the 'irrepressibles' and the 'conservatives.' A new ticket is talked of here tonight, and an informal meeting held in this house since I have been writing this letter, has given it an impetus. It is 'Lincoln and Hickman.' This is now the ticket as against Seward and Cash. Clay.

"The Ohio delegation continues so divided as to be without influence. If united it would have a formidable influence, and might throw the casting votes between candidates, holding the balance of power between the East and the West."

Another letter writer, reporting the outlook after the first day, said, "Should Seward fortunately be disposed of then the fight will be between Lincoln & Wade." He had heard that Ohio, Wisconsin, many from Pennsylvania, and Frank Blair, Jr., had declared for Wade as their second choice.[2]

The Wade push, however, was destined never to start. Salmon P. Chase's staunch supporters were too smart for that. When the Wade faction tried to outvote the Chase group as Ohio met in caucus, the Chase men threatened to vote for Seward if Ohio votes belonging to Chase went to Ben Wade. Checkmated, the Wade men subsided, and

---

[1] *Diary of Browning*, Vol. I, pp. 407–408.
[2] H. Kreismann to Washburne, May 16, 1860; Washburne MSS.

the carefully planned second-ballot swing to Bluff Ben never took place. Several Wade men, still ambitious to back a winner, became interested in Lincoln.[1]

The Convention had adjourned early and some delegates hurried to the dock and went off on that famous boat-ride. In the Wigwam there was entertainment in the form of an exhibition drill by the U. S. Zouave Cadets. Some delegations marched around through crowded nocturnal streets, and "at two o'clock . . . part of the Missouri delegation were singing songs in their parlor. There was still a crowd of fellows caucusing — and the glasses were still clinking in the bar-rooms — and far down the street a brass band was making the night musical."

Somebody got some sleep Wednesday night, however, or else none was needed. For early Thursday morning Chicago was infested with the biggest crowd yet; the nomination was expected Thursday afternoon. Even Halstead admitted he could not adequately depict the swarming activity. "Masses of people poured into town last night and this morning. . . . All adjectives might be fairly exhausted in describing the crowd. It is mighty and overwhelming; it can only be numbered by tens of thousands. The press about the hotels this morning was crushing. Two thousand persons took breakfast at the Tremont House."

Important committee meetings were being held early, and outside there was exciting pageantry. The thousand Seward boosters formed in procession in front of the Richmond House, behind a "band in splendid uniform," all wearing the fluttering silk Seward badges. Band blaring loudly the popular strains of "Oh isn't he a darling?" this picturesque contingent, four abreast, flashing canes, marched jauntily off in a cloud of dust. "As they passed the Tremont House where the many masses of the opponents of 'Old Irrepressible' were congregated, they gave three throat-tearing cheers for Seward. It will be a clear case, if he is not nominated, that the failure cannot be

[1] D. Taylor, May 22, James Elliott, May 21, 1860, to S. P. Chase; Chase MSS. D. V. Smith, pp. 527–529. Halstead, p. 143. A. B. Hart, *Chase*, p. 193. Wade's biographer, A. G. Riddle, says nothing about the Convention.

charged to his friends. Few men have had friends who would cleave unto them as the Sewardites to their great man here.

"The Pennsylvanians declare, if Seward were nominated, they would be immediately ruined. They could do nothing. The majority against them would be counted by tens of thousands. New Jerseyites say the same thing. The Indianians are of the same opinion. They look heart-broken at the suggestion that Seward has the inside track, and throw up their hands in despair. They say Lane will be beaten, the Legislature pass utterly into the hands of the Democracy . . . Illinois agonizes at the mention of the name of Seward, and says he is to them the sting of political death. His nomination would kill off Trumbull, and give the Legislature into the hands of the Democrats. . . . Amid all these cries of distress, the Sewardites are true as steel to their champion, and they will cling to 'Old Irrepressible,' as they call him, until the last gun is fired and the big bell rings." [1]

As convening time drew nigh the Seward army marched impressively into the Wigwam. When the doors were thrown open the place was quickly packed more densely than ever and twice as many were left outside, shoving to get in. Gilmore's Boston Band played from the well of the theater directly in front of the platform. The packed galleries were a riot of color as great numbers of ladies came tricked out in their best, looking colorful and comic in the rococo fashion of the day which dictated sunbonnet headgear, great bright shawls, yards of skirt billowing out over innumerable petticoats.

When Ashmun rapped for order at ten, the first business was to get rid of individuals who had climbed on the platform and taken delegates' seats. "Amid great confusion" they were requested to leave.

Ashmun rushed preliminaries to get to those committee reports.

"The first business in order will be to hear the report of the Committee on the Order of Business. Is that Committee ready to report?"

Up rose R. M. Corwine of Ohio, to present the report, which instantly stirred things up violently. Reading the rules, he came to:

[1] Also R. Hosea to S. P. Chase, May 18, 1860; Chase MSS.

"RULE 4. Three hundred and four votes, being a majority of the whole number of votes when all the States of the Union are represented in this Convention . . . shall be required to nominate the candidate of this Convention for the offices of President and Vice President." Some applauded this while the Seward infantry howled "No! No!" The New York member of the rules committee jumped up and presented a minority report which proves conclusively that the Conservatives were acting together against the Irrepressibles. The New Yorker complained that the majority report on Rule 4 had been jammed through, by one majority, when only seventeen of the twenty-five committee members were present. Conservative collusion, then, hoped to stop Seward by causing the Convention to adopt what amounted to a two-thirds rule, since most states of the lower and middle South were not represented.[1] The minority report required only "a majority of the whole number of votes represented in this Convention" (233) to nominate. This time Seward men cheered and Conservatives roared "No! No!" To avoid a hot argument, Ohio's Cartter proposed, and the Convention approved, that the credentials committee should report before Rule 4 should "be litigated."

When the Credentials Committee reported, accepting the delegates from every represented state, war began. Conservatives sought to disqualify Virginia and Texas, especially Texas, fearing they would vote for Seward and put him over.[2] David Wilmot made an explosive speech asking that Maryland and Kentucky, too, be refused admittance, attacking those delegates who expected to vote while representing no constituency since they came from states in which there was, he insisted, no organized Republican Party. "I can see nothing better calculated to demoralize a party, and to break it up, than just such a proceeding. Why, sir, this nomination is to be the nomination of the Republican party in the Union, not the nomination of respectable gentlemen who may belong to the Republican party in Virginia, Maryland, or Kentucky." Then, dropping partisanship, he

---

[1] A strict two-thirds rule, such as Democratic Conventions used, would require 311 to nominate.
[2] Halstead, p. 133.

denounced Rule 4 of the majority rules report, drew "tremendous cheering," called for the "plain old Republican rule, that the majority — the real majority — shall control."

Several excited delegates jumped up to reply. Ewing of Pennsylvania cried, "It cannot be that a Convention of Republicans assembled here from these whole United States will ever adopt such an outrage as to disfranchise our friends that come from the Southern States. Why, sir, I was mortified at such a sentiment coming from my distinguished friend from Pennsylvania." A Maryland delegate, Armour, hit Wilmot hard in a moving, eloquent speech. When he told with deep sincerity how dangerous it was to be a Republican in a slave state, how he himself had been burned in effigy at home and menaced by mobs for daring to avow himself "the friend of freedom," while Pennsylvania Republicans, living in the safety of a free state, lacked courage to call their Party Republican, he won the Convention's heart and in sincere admiration thousands of voices cheered him time after time.

Three more speakers followed in the same popular vein, after which the argument went on and on, oratory giving way to catch-as-catch-can debate tactics. Much fur flew, presenting an interesting but hardly dignified show for the spectators. Time was getting on. A Minnesota delegate put a word in. "I am in favor of less talk and more work. ["Good, good," "no more speeches now."]" Resolutions referring back to committee the question of admitting the challenged delegates were presented, voted down. A motion was made to recommit the whole report. Roll was called and the motion carried. Sewardites instantly saw that in committee, each state having one vote, the Conservatives might muster a majority to exclude Texas and the others. So Goodrich of Minnesota jumped up and proposed to instruct the committee. A chorus of "No" silenced him.[1] Delegates were tired and hungry after the long debate, so adjournment was voted until afternoon.

At 3:15 Ashmun's thwacking gavel rang in the ears of reassembled delegates and the packed thousands of spectators who had not left

[1] Halstead, p. 133, Proceedings, p. 123.

their places since morning. The Chair: "The Chair begs leave to suggest that there are outside this building, vast as it is, twice as many
honest hearts and wise heads as there are here." So he dispatched two
orators, famed Tom Corwin and Gov. Randall of Wisconsin, to entertain the host outside. First business was to finish the credentials fight.
Chairman Benton (New Hampshire) of the Credentials Committee
brought in a report which settled the matter quickly by seating everybody. He said his committee had examined the credentials of disputed
delegates and been "almost unanimously" satisfied that they legally
represented a constituency. Even the Texas delegation, he said, had
been chosen by a mass convention of Texas Republicans. This report
was adopted unanimously with plenty of noise — a Seward victory.
The Conservative coalition had come to think it best not to contest
this issue for fear of wrecking Convention harmony; they commanded
a majority in committee, since each delegation had one vote, but
could not be sure that on the Convention floor the Seward forces
would not outvote them.[1]

Now came renewal of the rules argument. Chairman Corwine on
a carried motion took the majority report off the table, read it again.
Rules 1, 2, 3 were rapidly adopted, but on the mooted Rule 4, which
called for a practical two-thirds vote to nominate, debate burst. The
minority report on Rule 4 was read and speeches began. Debate was
limited to one speaker for each side. They had their say; then a
Pennsylvania Sewardite, William Mann, secured the floor and in a
short, direct speech told everybody, mentioning no names, that the
majority report was directed against Seward. He spoke his individual
preference (with an eye on patronage from President Seward) against
the collective will of the Pennsylvania delegation, but he cleverly
tried to make the Convention think he was speaking for the whole
delegation. The reading clerk sonorously called the roll as delegates
voted on the minority report; it carried easily, but amid considerable
confusion, 358½ to 94½.[2] Conservatives had again chosen to let

[1] In Southern states, wrote Reporter "Ike" Bromley, "there was notoriously no Republican organization. It was really a question of Seward and Anti-Seward, as indeed
all others were upon which there was any division." Bromley, p. 650.
[2] Proceedings, p. 129.

Seward win. The Illinois delegation was so flustered, not knowing how best to declare themselves, that only seven delegates voted, and they for the minority report. And the Pennsylvania delegation had to be called three times before they could get sufficiently organized to vote, 33½ to 20½, against the minority report.

Next business was the report of the Committee on Resolutions; everybody anxiously awaited it. Chairman Jessup of Pennsylvania announced that upon practically all planks of the platform the committee had been unanimous in approval. He read the platform "as amended and adopted" in committee. "Tremendous bursts of applause" interrupted Jessup as he read along. The Platform Committee had framed a document to appeal to conservative, practical opponents of slavery extension, avoiding radicalism and idealism. Votes of special groups in the North were courted by planks favoring a protective tariff (put in to please Greeley and Pennsylvania), denouncing the Massachusetts antiforeign naturalization law, and calling for a homestead law, internal improvements, and a Pacific railroad.[1] The Democratic Party and disunion sentiments were amply flayed; the Republican Party sternly denied "the authority of Congress, of a territorial legislature, or of any individuals, to give legal existence to slavery in any territory of the United States." But "the most enthusiastic and long continued" plaudits exploded as the homestead and tariff planks were read. At the tariff declaration "Pennsylvania went into spasms of joy, . . . her whole delegation rising and swinging hats and canes."

David Cartter jumped up and called for a vote on the whole platform without discussion. Up also was old Joshua Giddings, to offer an amendment. Amid "great confusion" they disputed the floor. The throng yelled for the popular Giddings to have his say. A long parliamentary argument was settled by a roll call on which the delegates voted, 301 to 155, to discuss the platform.

Giddings took the floor to present his amendment. He wanted to add —

[1] Koerner, *Memoirs*, Vol. II, pp. 86–87. Ray, p. 23. R. Hosea to Chase, May 16, 1860; Chase MSS.

That we solemnly reassert the self-evident truths that all men are endowed by their creator with certain inalienable rights, among which are those of life, liberty and the pursuit of happiness [cheers]; that governments are instituted among men to secure the enjoyment of those rights.

The practical platform-makers had merely pledged the Party to uphold the principles of the Declaration of Independence. Cartter, not knowing when he was beaten, tried to cut Giddings off. Giddings smote him with a smashing verbal blow, went on with a short, moving peroration supporting his amendment. "I offer this because our party was formed upon it. It has existed upon it — and when you leave out this truth you leave out the party. [Loud cheers.]" [1]

Cartter jumped up and called for a reading of the reported platform's words on the subject. He read them, with convincing effect. Abolitionist Eli Thayer of the Oregon delegation (like Greeley a delegate by proxy) secured the floor and remarked dryly: —

I agree with the venerable delegate from Ohio in all that he has affirmed to this Convention concerning the privileges of the Declaration of Independence. There are also many other truths than are enunciated in that Declaration of Independence. . . . But it is not the business, I think, of this Convention . . . to embrace in its platform all the truths that the world in all its past history has recognized. [Applause.] Mr. President, I believe in the ten commandments, but I do not want them in a political platform.

Then roll was called and Giddings' amendment voted down. The outraged old abolitionist rose from his seat and slowly started toward the door. Delegates implored him not to go. "But he considered everything lost, even honor." [2] As he went by the New York delegation they assured him that his Declaration amendment would be tried again. But he kept going.[3]

Now came some lengthy argument on the plank opposing discrimination against foreign-born in state naturalization laws, which came to nothing. Then the Declaration of Independence made its promised comeback. Delegate Hassaureck of Ohio, a German emigré, held

[1] Proceedings, pp. 135–136.
[2] Halstead, p. 136.
[3] Bromley, pp. 652–653.

forth sentimentally on the blessings of American liberty, told how in his native land, a victim of the ropes of tyranny, his soul had been fired by the example of Washington and Jefferson.

Gentlemen, I have seen the nations of Europe smarting under the arbitrary rule of despots, and I know what an inestimable treasure . . . freedom is to man. It is, therefore, one of the proudest moments of my life, to avail myself of this opportunity as one of the liberty loving Germans of the free West, before this vast assembly of so many of the best and true men of the nation, loudly to proclaim my undying and unfaltering love and adherence to the principles of true Americanism. [Great applause.] Gentlemen, if it is Americanism to believe, religiously to believe in those eternal truths announced in the Declaration of Independence, that all men are born equal and free, and endowed by their creator with certain inalienable rights, among which are life, liberty, and the pursuit of happiness, I am proud to be an American. [Applause.] . . . If it is Americanism, gentlemen, to believe that governments are instituted for the benefit of the governed, and not for the benefit of the privileged few — if it is Americanism to believe that this glorious Federation of sovereign States has a higher object and a nobler purpose than to be the mere means of fortifying, protecting and propagating the institution of human servitude — if it is Americanism to believe that these vast fertile Territories of the West are forever to remain sacred, to remain as free homes for free labor and free men, I shall live and die an American. [Tumultuous cheering.] . . .

Therefore he favored the Giddings amendment. This Americanized German talked so fervidly that cheers rang out fourteen times while he spoke. George William Curtis of New York, noted litterateur, secured the floor and offered the Giddings amendment in a variant form, proposing that the Declaration's words about inalienable rights be added to Clause 2 of the reported platform. Thayer and Cartter clamored about a point of order. Had not this amendment been voted down? Not exactly, Blair of Missouri pointed out. The floor was therefore given to Curtis and the handsome young essayist launched into a thriller.

I have to ask this Convention whether they are prepared to go upon the record and before the country as voting down the words of the Declaration of Independence? [Cries of "No, no," and applause.] . . . Bear in mind that in Philadelphia in 1856, the Convention of this same great party were not afraid to announce those by which alone the Republican party lives, and upon which alone the future of this country in the hands of the Republican party is passing. [Tremendous cheering.] . . .

I rise simply to ask gentlemen to think well before, upon the free prairies of the West, in the summer of 1860, they dare to wince and quail before the men who in Philadelphia in 1776 — in Philadelphia, in the Arch-Keystone State, so amply, so nobly represented upon this platform today — before they dare to shrink from repeating the words that these great men enunciated. [Terrific applause.]

A Hoosier declared: "I presume that all the Republicans here are in favor of the Declaration of Independence. Does it necessarily follow that we must publish it in our platform? [The crowd — "Yes."] . . . Well, then, it is there now." A wag chirped, "Put it in twice." The Conservatives seemed to be stalling for time, to prevent a vote at this session on the presidential nominee.

Disputed Clause 2 of the reported platform was read again, by Oyler of Indiana. "Does not that endorse it?" he shouted. "We believe in the Bible; shall we put it in from the first chapter of Genesis to the last chapter of Revelations?"

A New Yorker answered: —

I am only anxious, sir, that something should be done in this Convention to mark with great distinctness and in unmistakable terms, that we endorse the language of the Declaration of Independence that is moved as an amendment. [Cheers and voices, "You shall have it," "We will," "You shall have it if you say no more about it."] That, sir, is all I want. I am exceedingly glad that simply the fear of a speech from me should induce gentlemen to vote in that way. [Laughter and applause.]

A vote was taken and the amendment at last went into the platform. Giddings, who had lingered at the edge of the delegate group, quietly returned to his seat in the Ohio delegation, victor in the great teapot tempest.[1]

Now adoption of the platform as a whole was moved. Unanimously it carried amid thunderous noise. "All the thousands of men in that

[1] Humphrey H. Hood, Litchfield, Ill. to Editor of the Hillsboro *Free Press*, May 24, 1860, in *Transactions*, Ill. State Hist. Soc., 1904, pp. 370–371.
    G. W. Julian, *Life of Joshua R. Giddings*, pp. 371–375.

enormous wigwam commenced swinging their hats, and cheering with intense enthusiasm, and the other thousands of ladies waved their handkerchiefs and clapped their hands. The roar that went up from that mass of ten thousand human beings under one roof was indescribable. Such a spectacle as was presented for some minutes has never before been witnessed at a Convention. A herd of buffaloes or lions could not have made a more tremendous roaring." The Chicago *Journal* reporter was swept away. "That immense concourse of people, delegates and spectators . . . sprang to their feet, and cheers upon cheers, deafening, tumultuous, and rapturous, went up from every throat. Men waved their hats, ladies their handkerchiefs, reporters their written pages and all screamed with very joy. This wild excitement was kept up for some ten or fifteen minutes. It was a scene that can never be forgotten by those present, a spectacle that was worth a man's lifetime to witness. It made one feel good all over."

Quiet finally restored, Goodrich of Minnesota said, "I move that we adjourn. [Cries of "No," "No," "Ballot," "Ballot."] I withdraw the motion, and move that we now proceed to ballot for a candidate for the Presidency. [Applause.]" Eggleston of Ohio renewed the motion to adjourn. It was voted down. The motion to ballot was renewed. But the opponents of Seward were violently opposed to an early vote, and they raised such a howl that the Convention was again thrown into "great confusion." Cartter, astute Seward opponent, seized the floor and shouted, "I call for a division of ayes and nays, to see if gentlemen want to go without their supper. [Derisive laughter, and cries of "Call the roll."]" The Chair announced at the Secretary's request that presidential tally sheets "are prepared, but are not yet at hand, but will be in a few minutes." So discouraging was the prospect of hungry delay that when an anonymous voice called out, "I move that this Convention adjourn until ten o'clock to-morrow morning," roll call began. Voting was desultory, "very little voting being done either way." [1] But the Chair pronounced the motion carried and delegates streamed off the platform.

[1] Halstead, p. 141.

"As the great assemblage poured through the streets after adjournment, it seemed to electrify the city. The agitation of the masses that pack the hotels and throng the streets, and are certainly forty thousand strong, was such as made the little excitement at Charleston seem insignificant," Halstead observed.

Fortunate indeed for Abraham Lincoln that some Sewardites just then cared more for supper than for Seward. Thurlow Weed's men that day were hot on the trail of the nomination. Halstead recapitulated for his paper in Cincinnati: —

"The tactics of the Seward men in convention today were admirable. . . . They made a beautiful fight against Wilmot's proposition to examine into the constituencies of slave state delegations, putting forward men to strike the necessary blows who were not suspected of Sewardism. There was also a splendid fight on the subject of the two-thirds rule (as it was in effect), which was sought to be used to slaughter Seward. So perfect were the Seward tactics, that this rule, which his opponents-had hoped to carry, was made odious, and defeated by a two-thirds vote. Then Giddings was anxious, beyond all description, to have the initial words of the Declaration of Independence in the platform. In attempting to get them in, he was snubbed by Seward's opponents most cruelly. He had been working against Seward, and was not without influence. Now a New York man took up and carried through his precious amendment. So confident were the Seward men, when the platform was adopted, of their ability to nominate their great leader, that they urged an immediate ballot, and would have had it if the clerks had not reported that they were unprovided with tally-sheets. The cheering of the thousands of spectators during the day, indicated that a very large share of the outside pressure was for Seward. There is something almost irresistible here in the prestige of his fame."

As supper was gulped down, the mind of every manager was great with strategy in preparation for to-morrow morning's session. Thurlow Weed thought he knew how to hold his ranks firm, perhaps even to augment them. On the job was that thousand-strong battalion of worthies who could, Halstead reports, "drink as much whisky, swear as loud and long, sing as bad songs, and 'get up and howl' as ferociously as any crowd of Democrats you ever heard, or heard of. They are opposed, as they say, 'to being too damned virtuous.' They hoot at the idea that Seward could not sweep all the Northern states, and swear that he would have a party in every slave state, in less than a year, that would clean out the disunionists, from shore to shore. They slap each other on the back with the emphasis of delight when they meet, and rip out 'How *are* you?' with a 'How are you hoss?' style, that would do honor to Old Kaintuck on a bust. At night those of them who are not engaged at caucusing, are doing that which illtutored youths call 'raising hell generally.' "

The Conservatives, by and large, were considerably cast down. No wonder, for in every trial of strength the Seward forces had been victorious. Halstead's accurate observation was that "the Seward men have been in high feather. They entertain no particle of doubt of his nomination in the morning. . . . The delegation here is a queer compound. There is a party of tolerably rough fellows, of whom Tom Hyer is the leader, and there is Thurlow Weed (called Lord Thurlow by his friends), Moses H. Grinnell, James Watson Webb, Gov. Morgan, Gen. Nye, George W. Curtis, and others of the strong men of the state, in commerce, political jobbing, and in literature — first class men in their respective positions, and each with his work to do according to his ability. In the face of such 'irrepressibles,' the conservative expediency men — Greeley, the Blairs, the Republican candidates for Governor in Pennsylvania, Indiana, and Illinois — are hard pressed, sorely perplexed, and despondent."

Hopeless as the case looked, though observers thought the Conservatives appeared "thoroughly disheartened" as they went out of the Wigwam to supper, they lost no time. They must move heaven, earth, and the nether regions, to hold their forces against the Seward charms, or all their labors would go for naught. The Lincoln workers even hoped to acquire new strength. Lincoln himself, impatiently waiting in Springfield and devouring every scrap of information coming from the scene of battle, had sent another message, reaching Davis on Thursday,

Some Sewardite, arriving in Chicago early and swiftly noting the dangerous Lincoln strength, had a brilliant idea for slowing down the Chicago favorite. He telegraphed to Bates men in St. Louis, magnanimously informing them that Lincoln, far from being a conservative Republican and therefore an available man, stood as radical as Seward. Expecting a favor returned for a favor given, this subtle Seward worker urged the Bates men to swing to Seward in case Bates should fail. Elated, the Bates workers immediately published the telegram in the Missouri *Democrat*. When Editor Baker of the *Illinois State Journal* spotted this on Wednesday, he rushed to Lincoln's office with a copy of the *Democrat*. It was a tight spot for Lincoln if, as Baker feared, Lincoln's alleged radicalism was being talked in Chicago. Reading the telegram, Lincoln knew that he should do something to show that he was not as radical as Seward, yet was not a thoroughgoing conservative like Bates. The Missouri *Democrat* had sought to bolster the Chicago telegram by outlining Seward's slavery position, advertising it as dangerous radicalism which could be avoided by nominating Bates. On the margin of the paper, beside Seward's opinions, Abraham penciled, "I agree with Seward in his 'Irrepressible Conflict,' but I do not endorse his 'Higher Law' doctrine." As an afterthought, to refurbish his defense against possible charges of corrupt bargaining, he added, "Make no contracts that will bind me," and drew a line under those ominous words. He gave the paper to Baker asking if he would take it to the battleground as soon as possible. Baker boarded the next train and rolled up to Chicago. He reached Lincoln headquarters at the Tremont and read the message to Davis, Judd, Herndon, and Logan.[1] Probably (though there is no way of being certain) Lincoln knew what would happen when Davis and his men heard that embarrassing order. Whitney recalls the scene.

"Everybody was mad, of course. Here were men working night and day to place him on the highest mountain peak of fame, and he pulling back all he knew how. What was to be done? The bluff Dubois said: 'Damn Lincoln!' The polished Swett said, in mellifluous

[1] *Herndon's Lincoln*, pp. 373–374. Lamon, *Lincoln*, p. 449. Weik, *The Real Lincoln*, pp. 261–262, 264–265.

ORIGINAL LINCOLN MEN

(O. H. Browning, Judge David Davis; R. J. Oglesby, Leon
Jesse K. Dubois, Norman B. Judd)

accents: 'I am very sure if Lincoln was aware of the necessities — '
The critical Logan expectorated viciously, and said: 'The main difficulty with Lincoln is — ' Herndon ventured: 'Now, friend, I'll answer
that.' But David Davis cut the Gordian knot by brushing all aside
with: 'Lincoln ain't here, and don't know what we have to meet, so
we will go ahead, as if we hadn't heard from him, and he must
ratify it!" [1]

They were not interested in the other part of Lincoln's message.
In their campaign for delegates they had anticipated Lincoln's advice
and depicted him in glowing colors as the absolutely available candidate because he stood both conservative and Republican.

So Davis and his assistants, seeing their man far ahead of all other
Conservative candidates, labored and manipulated without scruple.
If they but could, with Conservative aid, stop Seward on the first
ballot to-morrow morning, Lincoln would inevitably appear as the
Conservative favorite for a few ballots at least, actually bringing
victory in sight. But great odds must first be overcome. Seeking ways
and means, the brains at Lincoln headquarters were active in an
unscrupulous atmosphere.

Somebody brought forth the notable idea that 'twould be well if
the thousand Seward shouters could be induced to stay out of the
Wigwam next day. Counterfeit tickets would do the job. Ward Lamon
and Jesse Fell therefore had a large supply of extra tickets printed
Thursday evening, and several Lincoln men spent the night forging
official signatures on the pasteboards. [2]

To replace the plotted lost battalion of Seward vocalists, Davis
assigned some assistants the job of recruiting a thousand rooters for
Abraham Lincoln. The whole night was spent in preparation. [3] Gen-
erals at the head of the noisy army were two men of great distinction
in such matters, past masters of the stentorian art. Dr. Ames of
Chicago had a larynx reputedly so powerful that on a calm day he
could shout clear across Lake Michigan! Delegate Burton Cook knew

[1] Whitney, *Lincoln the Citizen*, p. 289. Otto Gresham, *The Greenbacks*, pp. 37–38.
[2] W. E. Barton, *Life of Lincoln*, Vol. I, pp. 432–433. Morehouse, *Life of Fell*, pp. 61–
62n. Wakefield, p. 180.
[3] W. H. Lamon, p. 448.

a man near Ottawa who had never met his equal in long distance bel-
lowing. These two titans were called to the Tremont headquarters
and put to work.[1]

In the Weed rooms at the Richmond House delegates were thoroughly enjoying themselves. Reaching the very height of generosity,
"Lord Thurlow" was entertaining in lavish style with a champagne
supper. Three hundred bottles of the *liqueur élite* were poured down
grateful throats. Sewardite bands marched about in the warm evening, stopping at various delegation quarters and honoring them with
a serenade. The whole crowd of Sewardites, expansively confident,
were making a night of it, already seeming to be celebrating their
victory. "They did not fear the results of caucusing that night,
though they knew every hour would be employed against them." [2]
One exultant Seward leader told Greeley in great good humor that
the Conservatives ought to be deciding whom they wanted for
Seward's running mate. Greeley replied disarmingly, "Oh, never
mind; fix up the whole ticket to suit yourselves." [3]

Seward's opponents, amid the jollification, were highly uncomfortable. Current gossip said that Greeley was quite "terrified." The
Conservatives were united only in opposing Seward. Internal Conservative disagreement over favorite sons was so deep-seated that
Weed feared no united front to checkmate Seward on the first ballot.

After supper the Pennsylvania and Indiana delegation met for
consultation in the Cook County Court House. Pennsylvania might
go for Bates as their second choice, because the People's Party there,
which, like the Opposition Party of New Jersey, espoused "a super-
ficial and only half-developed Republicanism," [4] and contained many
old line Whigs and Know-Nothings, seemingly could carry the state
most easily with "a prominent Whig who had been more or less
affiliated with the American Party." [5] Bates promoters were there
in force to point out the perfect qualifications of their candidate.

[1] I. N. Arnold, p. 167.
[2] Halstead, p. 141.
[3] L. D. Ingersoll, *Greeley*, p. 341.
[4] G. W. Julian, *Political Recollections*, p. 177.
[5] Koerner, *Memoirs*, Vol. II, p. 88. W. E. Smith, *The Blair Family*, Vol. I, p. 477. R.
Errett to G. Welles, April 17, 1860; Welles MSS.

ORIGINAL LINCOLN MEN

(*William H. Herndon, General John M. Palmer; Ozias M. Hatch,*
Stephen T. Logan, Gustavus Koerner; Ward Lamon, Jesse Fell)

HOW PRESIDENTS ARE CHOSEN   269

Frank Blair, able orator, commenced speaking. One of Lincoln's Indiana friends ran out and over to Lincoln headquarters at the Tremont to tell them what was up. Judge Davis sent Gustave Koerner
and Browning hurrying to the court house to uphold the claims of
"honest Old Abe." They arrived as Blair was finishing his speech.
Despite the Know-Nothingism of Bates, several prominent Missouri
Germans were for him, to prove which Blair had two of them, Muench
and Krekel, speak in favor of Bates. Koerner rose to reply. By this
time many other delegates and Chicago citizens (at the behest of
Lincoln's men) had crowded into the courtroom. When Koerner mentioned Lincoln's name "the cheers almost shook the court house." He
argued that Bates could never carry Missouri, for Douglas would
certainly win that state. Subtly he confessed his astonishment that
any German should support Bates, pointing out how the Missouri
lawyer had been connected with the Native American organization.
Closing, Koerner said that if Bates were nominated, "the German Republicans in the other states would never vote for him." Koerner
cried that he for one would not, and would advise his countrymen to
do the same. Blair jumped up and made a short speech in reply, but
much of the wind had been taken out of his sails. Koerner had spoken
as a former Democrat. Browning secured the floor and argued from
the Whig standpoint, pointing out that Lincoln, a Whig, would sat-
isfy the old line Whigs of Pennsylvania and Indiana. Lincoln had
steadily opposed Native Americanism, which would secure to him
the whole foreign Republican vote. He swept to a close in an eloquent peroration on Lincoln as a great man, "which electrified the
meeting."

The two caucusing delegations then held an executive session to
talk over what they had heard. Lincoln headquarters soon had a confidential report that Indiana had voted to go for Lincoln at the start,
while a majority of the Keystone staters wanted to vote for Lincoln
as their second choice.[1] This meant, the Lincoln men knew, that these
delegations were favorable toward Lincoln — not that they were sure
to vote for him when balloting time should arrive.

[1] Koerner, *Memoirs*, Vol. II, p. 89.

So busy were the backers of Lincoln, Chase, Bates, Cameron, each in pushing their man, that they never got together in a general anti-Seward caucus. Closest to that was a caucus of the New Jersey, Pennsylvania, Indiana, and Illinois delegations, who met to consider seriously what John Andrew had said about the necessity of the doubtful states uniting on one man if they expected to beat Seward. Chase and Bates forces were absent. Iowa was not a pivotal state and therefore did not belong in this caucus. But Judd shrewdly invited all the Lincoln men of Iowa's divided delegation, to add the force of numbers and swell the "Lincoln Is Available" chorus.[1] New Jersey was anxious, after honoring Favorite Son Dayton, to back the winner and gather rich spoils,[2] but Pennsylvania's situation was more complex. Between the morning and afternoon sessions the four pivotal delegations had met at Cameron headquarters and talked business, but had had to adjourn without agreement for the afternoon session. Then, after a hasty supper, a committee of three from each of the four states met in David Wilmot's rooms. David Davis headed the Illinois three; Caleb Smith was chairman of Indiana's trio. The plotters stayed until eleven o'clock, discussing the situation fore and aft. About ten o'clock Greeley came in to learn what had happened. Learning that nothing had been done, he continued on his rounds. Visiting delegation after delegation and finding that Seward remained far ahead, he reluctantly telegraphed to his *Tribune* at 11:40: —

My conclusion, from all that I can gather tonight, is, that the opposition to Gov. Seward cannot concentrate on any candidate, and that he will be nominated.

Halstead wired similarly to the Cincinnati *Commercial*, affirming that "every one of the forty thousand men in attendance upon the Chicago Convention will testify that at midnight of Thursday-Friday night, the universal impression was that Seward's success was cer-

---

[1] Reminiscences of G. M. Dodge, in *Annals of Iowa*, Vol. XII, p. 451. Though several Iowa delegates were, like Gov. Kirkwood, active Lincoln workers, this did not mean several Lincoln votes, for Iowa sent so many delegates that each man had only one fourth of a vote.
[2] *Diary of Browning*, Vol. II, p. 110.

tain." [1] Likewise James Watson Webb telegraphed to the New York *Courier and Enquirer*, Henry Raymond to the New York *Times*.[2]

In Wilmot's rooms, after Greeley left, the delegates from the four doubtful states began to figure like scientists plotting an experiment. As accurately as possible they calculated the reasonable voting strength of each Seward opponent. Lincoln, thanks to Indiana, New England, Virginia, and Kentucky bargains, came out ahead. A New Jersey delegate then suggested that New Jersey drop Dayton and go for Lincoln, provided Pennsylvania would do the same with Cameron. New Jersey and Pennsylvania representatives agreed to recommend the plan to the two delegations in caucus, but could not be sure they would agree. The deliberators adjourned, New Jersey and Pennsylvania diplomats hurried off to lay the plan before their own delegation. In the small hours a New Jersey caucus considered the plan. Out of the smoke and talk came a decision to give Dayton a complimentary vote on the first ballot, then swing to Lincoln.[3] Dayton's manager, Thomas Dudley, had been quietly assured that, in the case of Lincoln's success, his assistance would be rewarded with a good job in the diplomatic service for both Dayton and Dudley.[4] But, to the chagrin of the Illinois men, Pennsylvania could not meet in caucus until next morning.

The suspense was uncomfortable, but they had plenty to do to pass the time. Every delegation which had promised to vote for Lincoln as first choice or as second had to be reminded of their promise in whatever fashion would be most convincing. The Lincoln workers were much encouraged by the caucus result. Kirkwood and Saunders of Iowa returned jubilant to Iowa headquarters to snatch a little sleep before to-morrow.[5] When Judd left the conference he found young Dodge of Iowa waiting for orders. They discussed the agreement and the possibilities of New Jersey and Pennsylvania delivering according to plan. "Judd was especially anxious to get our Iowa delegates to go

[1] Halstead, p. 142.
[2] Ingersoll, *Greeley*, p. 340.
[3] T. H. Dudley, "Inside Facts of Lincoln's Nomination," *Century*, Vol. XL, pp. 477–479. Bromley, p. 649. Wilson, *Rise and Fall of the Slave Power*, Vol. II, pp. 692–693.
[4] *Diary of Browning*, Vol. II, p. 110.
[5] Reminiscences of C. C. Nourse, in *Annals of Iowa*, Vol. XII, p. 459.

solid for Lincoln after the first ballot. Our being neighbors was a fact
that he urged very strongly." But this was impossible; too many
Iowans were staunchly for Seward.[1] Soon this valuable encouragement of the caucus result was being passed along to all Lincoln men
as ammunition in a final drive for the Rail Splitter. Indiana's Henry
Lane, Halstead tells us, "in connection with others . . . had been
operating to bring the Vermonters and Virginians to the point of deserting Seward. . . . The object was to bring the delegates of those
states to consider success rather than Seward, and join with the
battle-ground states — as Pennsylvania, New Jersey, Indiana, and
Illinois insisted upon calling themselves. This was finally done, the
fatal break in Seward's strength having been made in Vermont and
Virginia, destroying at once, when it appeared, his power in the New
England and the slave state delegations. But the work was not yet
done. The Pennsylvanians had been fed upon meat, such that they
presented themselves at Chicago with the presumption that they had
only to say what they wished, and receive the indorsement of the
Convention. And they were for Cameron. He was the only man, they
a thousand times said, who would certainly carry Pennsylvania. They
were astonished, alarmed, and maddened to find public opinion settling down upon Seward and Lincoln, and the idea spreading that
one or the other must be nominated. They saw that Lincoln was understood to be the only man to defeat Seward, and thinking themselves capable of holding that balance of power, so much depended
upon, and so deceptive on those occasions, stood out against the
Lincoln combination. Upon some of the delegations, Seward operations had been performed with perceptible effect. The Seward men
had stated that the talk of not carrying Pennsylvania was all non-
sense. Seward had a good tariff record, and his friends would spend
money enough to carry it against any Democratic candidate who was
a possibility. The flood of Seward money promised for Pennsylvania
was not without efficacy. The phrase used was, that Seward's friends
'would *spend oceans of money.*' "[2]

---

[1] G. M. Dodge, in *Annals of Iowa*, Vol. XII, p. 451.
[2] Halstead, pp. 142–143.

Thurlow Weed was utilizing to the limit the persuasive power of his slush fund. One evening he had called on Henry Lane and taken him out for a private, confidential talk. Weed pleaded and wheedled, oleaginously assuring Lane that if he would lead the Indiana delegation over to Seward, Lane would have enough money from New York to carry Indiana for Seward and elect Lane Governor. But Lane considered the Lincoln offers more attractive, and Weed could not sway him.[1] Weed used the same tactic on Andrew Curtin, with identical unsuccess.[2]

Weed's men constantly bragged about how much money they would throw behind Seward in the campaign and make victory inevitable. This gave the Lincoln men an opening, and they played up the Weed money offers as proof that Seward was the candidate of "commercialism" and "corrupt political rule," firmly denying that all the gold of Midas would help Seward carry the doubtful states. Said a Seward henchman to a Lincoln worker: "It is absurd for you westerners to want to nominate an Illinois man or any other man than Seward. No man can carry Pennsylvania or Indiana unless he and his backers have plenty of the sinews of war. . . . I mean money, of course." Nourse of Iowa: "That is one of the reasons why we from Iowa and the West are afraid of you and are fighting you. You and your kind think you can purchase the election as you buy stocks. . . . With such methods as you pursue at Albany endorsed at the polls and you will drain the national treasury dry. No, Sir! Mr. Seward must not be nominated."[3]

As Lane worked for Lincoln from a prominent place in the Indiana delegation, Andrew Curtin, Pennsylvania's candidate for Governor, labored for the Rail Splitter inside the crucial Keystone delegation. Both Curtin and Lane would be voted up or down as Governor in October state elections. Neither Indiana nor Pennsylvania had ever gone Republican in a national election, or elected a Republican Governor. "It was an accepted necessity that both Pennsylvania and In-

[1] Mrs. Henry S. Lane to A. K. McClure, Sept. 16, 1891; in A. K. McClure, *Abraham Lincoln and Men of War-Times*, pp. 30–31n.
[2] F. Curtis, *The Republican Party*, Vol. I, p. 361.
[3] C. C. Nourse, in *Annals of Iowa*, Vol. XII, p. 463. A. B. Hart, *Chase*, pp. 184–185. J. H. Barrett, *Lincoln*, Vol. I, p. 221.

diana should elect Republican Governors in October to secure the election of the Republican candidate for President in November." [1] So Lane and Curtin were determined to nominate an available man who could help each carry his doubtful, October, state. They believed Seward could not do it, that Lincoln could. Curtin was sure he required Native American aid, fused with Republicans in the People's Party, to beat the Democrats; and the Know-Nothings detested Seward because, as Governor of New York, he had not been sufficiently intolerant toward Catholics. [2] It would seem that Bates, who had worked with the Native Americans in 1856, would have been the logical choice. But the Germans, save those working with the Blairs, were violently opposed to Bates. The German element had gone to the extreme of meeting in conference in Chicago on Monday as a German lobby, resolutely determined to force the Party to do right by the Germans in its platform and nominations. According to the silence of dozens of Convention witnesses concerning the German convention, which met at Chicago's Deutsches Haus, it would seem they had no influence on the Convention's deliberations. But their pressure can be seen in the platform and in the rapid decline of Bates as Seward's leading opponent. [3] Lincoln, therefore, fulfilled Pennsylvania requirements much better than Bates. His opposition to Nativism had been quiet, unobtrusive; indeed few knew that he had opposed Nativism. Therefore, while attracting the Americans, he would avoid alienating the foreigners. A similar state of things existed in Indiana, and, to a lesser extent, in New Jersey. [4] So Curtin and Lane, with their campaign managers, McClure (Pennsylvania) and Defrees (Indiana), [5] and a few faithful henchmen, talked and argued energetically as wire-pulling continued, asserting positively

[1] McClure, *War-Times*, p. 31.
[2] A. K. McClure, *Colonel McClure's Recollections of Half a Century*, pp. 212–220. C. E. Hamlin, *Life of Hamlin*, pp. 331–332. Barrett, *Lincoln*, Vol. I, p. 221. W. Wilkeson to Chase, Feb. 13, 1859; Chase MSS.
[3] Herriott, "Deutches Haus," pp. 109–110, 117–120, 144, 185ff. Professor Herriott goes to the erroneous extreme of claiming that the German element was responsible for not only the defeat of Bates, but the victory of Lincoln.
[4] C. Roll, p. 3. Herriott, "Deutsches Haus," pp. 108–109. Sellers, "Make-Up of the Early Republican Party," p. 48.
[5] Defrees, a Colfax follower, wanted Bates, but the Indiana Bates men found "that the only way to beat Seward was to go for Lincoln as a unit." O. J. Hollister, *Colfax*, pp. 147–148.

that if Seward were nominated they would be defeated in October and the Republican Party tumbled in the dust again in November as it was in 1856.[1] Curtin, McClure, and their assistants stated dogmatically and often that if Seward were nominated, the press of Philadelphia, thoroughly opportunistic, would almost unanimously support the Bell-Everett ticket, leading Pennsylvania in that direction.[2]

None of Lincoln's enthusiastic backers went to bed Thursday night. Halstead noticed Henry Lane "at one o'clock, pale and haggard, with cane under his arm, walking as if for a wager, from one caucus-room to another, at the Tremont House. He had been toiling with desperation to bring the Indiana delegation to go as a unit for Lincoln." So the Hoosiers were not absolutely safe even yet. Lane was sure that Seward's nomination would bring defeat, but others of the Hoosier delegation thought either Seward or Bates could carry Indiana and the North. Even in the Illinois delegation some votes would have been lost to Seward and Bates had not their Lincoln instructions been ironclad.[3] Vermont, leading naturally toward Seward because Weed had almost captured custody of the bandwagon, required "desperate exertions," talks on availability, and no one knew how Vermont would vote on Ballot 2, until her vote should be spoken out in the Wigwam.[4] Virginia was worse. They had sold out so many times there was no telling who would get their votes. Greeley wrote later, "we had to rain red-hot bolts on them . . . to keep the majority from going for Seward."[5] And Pennsylvania, dazzled by that bright prospect of "oceans of money" might decide against Lincoln, vote for Seward on the second ballot and send him sweeping into the nomination. As was the case with Lane in Indiana, a great many Pennsylvania delegates were not wholly convinced by Curtin's insistent declaration that to select anybody but Lincoln would be ruin.

---

[1] McClure, *War-Times*, pp. 32–35. Julian, *Political Recollections*, p. 177. J. E. Harvey to J. McLean, Sept. 5, 1859; McLean MSS. V. Armour to E. B, Washburne, March 29, 1860; Washburne MSS.
[2] Carpenter, "How Lincoln Was Nominated," *Century*, Vol. XXIV, p. 854.
[3] Browning, *Diary*, Vol. I, pp. 407–408. Swett, in Oldroyd, p. 71.
[4] Greeley to Pike, *First Blows*, p. 519.
[5] In Pike, p. 520.

Part of Lincoln strategy that night was launching a whispering campaign, calculated to give new potency to the argument that the Party must carry Indiana and Pennsylvania, the October states, which could be accomplished only by avoiding Seward. "The cry of a want of availability which was from the start raised against Seward," Halstead observed "now took a more definite form than heretofore. It was reported, and with a well-understood purpose, that the Republican candidates for Governor in Indiana, Illinois, and Pennsylvania would resign, if Seward were nominated. Whether they really meant it or not, the rumor was well circulated, and the effect produced was as if they had been earnest. Henry S. Lane, candidate in Indiana, did say something of the kind. He asserted hundreds of times that the nomination of Seward would be the death of him, and that he might in that case just as well give up the canvass."[1] Lane and Curtin no doubt concocted this strategy, to cause their delegations to act as they wished; Yates fell in line with the good idea; and they all began to whisper energetically as dawn of the fateful day drew nearer and nearer.

Not long after early sunrise a crowd began to congregate about the Wigwam entrance; soon the streets were packed with people fighting for the great gift of witnessing the climax of the extravaganza, almost sure to come sometime Friday. The morning issue of the *Press & Tribune* carried a final appeal to the Convention to avoid Seward. "It simply begged that Seward should not be nominated," scoffed Halstead. This thousand word "Last Entreaty" gave once more the doubtful-state point of view — their number, by the addition of Connecticut and Rhode Island to the uncertain list, having been strategically raised to six states to add conviction. It spoke in grave, sober tones, in sonorous, involved sentences like sage pronouncements of Holy Writ. It called "incomprehensible" the position of Seward delegates who refused to heed the doubtful states' cries of anguish. "We ask, we entreat, we implore, that a candidate inside of the Republican party, radical up to the extreme limit of the platform, but not obnoxious to the charges which will be urged by the so-called Democracy against one prominent gentleman now in the field and in high favor,

[1] Halstead, p. 143.

may be selected, to the end that a triumph may not be a thing of infinite labor, and prolonged and painful doubt, but a certainty from the moment that the choice of the Convention is declared, let us, . . . who have labored so long and, we hope, so acceptably, for the Republican cause, warn the Convention that the voice of the united doubtful states cannot, must not be disregarded. They are six, if not seven, in number. . . . They are potent, and their approbation of the nominee, not only here at Chicago, but at the polls in November, must be secured, else an inglorious and fatal defeat stares us in the face. . . ."

At nine o'clock when the Pennsylvania delegation met for that important last-minute caucus, Judge Davis was on hand, glibly promising again that Cameron could have the Treasury Department if Lincoln should become President. It was no easy matter to secure Pennsylvania, even with the rosiest of promises. Wilmot, member of the Cameron machine, had been from the start for Lincoln, after a complimentary vote for Cameron. Curtin was for Lincoln, though on reaching Chicago he had preferred Bates. But other Pennsylvania leaders were for various other candidates. The delegation was highly disharmonious. At the close of Wednesday's sessions a caucus had been held to determine tentatively Pennsylvania's first, second, and third choice for President. Boss Cameron of course was the unanimous first choice. Irascible old Thad Stevens and his followers demanded that McLean be declared second choice. This was done, all except Stevens understanding the action as purely perfunctory. Third-choice declaration was important; the fight was between Bates and Lincoln, and Lincoln finally won over Bates by four votes, thanks to Indiana's declared support of Lincoln and the labors of Curtin and Lane.[1] Since Wednesday night Lincoln had been gaining favor, as shown in the vote at the Thursday evening courthouse caucus of Indiana and Pennsylvania, after the Blair, Koerner, and Browning speeches. By Friday morning, therefore, it was comparatively easy for the Key-

---

[1] McClure, *War-Times*, pp. 35–36. Bromley, pp. 653–654. C. B. Going, *David Wilmot*, pp. 540–541. A. J. Dittenhoefer, *How We Elected Lincoln*, p. 22. Carpenter, "How Lincoln Was Nominated," *Century*, XXIV, pp. 855–856. Carpenter says that Lincoln won by three votes, a victory possible only because, rather than see Bates chosen, several western Pennsylvania delegates who really favored Seward and Wade voted for Lincoln.

stoners to promise to swing to Lincoln on the second ballot. Secretly
they reserved the right to vote for Seward on Ballot 2 if Lincoln
could not muster an impressive vote and thereby prove he had a fighting chance to win.[1] At best, the delegation was highly disunited and
tricky and Davis could only hope for the best.

The Seward Irrepressibles Friday morning were expansively confident. Rumors of last night's caucusing floated about, "but the opposition of the doubtful states to Seward was an old story." In front
of the Richmond House early that morning stood the Seward band,
resplendent in brilliant uniforms with gleaming epaulets and caps
blossoming with white and scarlet feathers. Behind, in military formation, gathered the thousand pressure men. The long column went off
noisily, wound its way loudly through Chicago's main streets, arrived at the Wigwam. To their horror they could not get in. The places
from which, yesterday and the day before, they had shouted for
Seward, were occupied by a thousand limber-lunged Chicagoans,
ready to roar for "Old Abe." [2] These had packed in with the help of
those counterfeit tickets — a trick (in Whitney's phrase) "known
only to wicked Chicago." Weed's thousand had to stay outside with
the milling throng, cursing their luck at being shifted off the scene
of action when they were needed most.

Delegates ambled in and took places on the stage in front of the
standing thousands. Norman Judd had made it his business to have
himself put in charge of placing the delegations. Aided by Medill, he
mapped a clever arrangement. New York was placed on the remotest
edge, as far as possible from the wavering delegations. Pennsylvania
and New Jersey were located strategically between Indiana and Illinois.[3] Delegate Cook of Illinois had arrived early with the band of
Illinois interlopers. From his seat on the stage he looked out and
located the stentorian Dr. Ames and that other great voice. They had
been placed on opposite sides of the floor, instructed to sound off when

---

[1] Halstead, p. 143. Sandburg, Vol. II, p. 342. Carpenter, p. 857. Macartney, pp. 28–29.
[2] Carr, *The Illini*, p. 283.
[3] Cleveland, "Booming the First Republican President," p. 85. Edward Judd, in
Wakefield, pp. 176–177.

Cook took out his handkerchief and to keep going until he put it back.[1] Another important vocal plan had been perfected. Lincoln men in other delegations than Illinois had been instructed to offer a second to Lincoln's nomination at the proper time, to the end that when candidate presentation should begin, every ear in the Wigwam would hear, recurring like the theme of a Beethoven symphony, *"Abraham Lincoln, of Illinois."* The idea was to secure so many seconding speeches for Lincoln, from so many different states, that wavering delegates would judge him as stronger than he really was. In the Ohio delegation Joe Medill innocently took a seat. Giddings peremptorily ordered him out, but the Ohio Lincolnites demanded that he be let alone, so he stayed.[2]

Presently the three great doors were thrown wide and in surged three human torrents, until every inch of space was occupied. Weed's men shoved mightily but few could struggle inside, so great was the throng stationed at the doors ahead of them. Outside they had plenty of company in a vociferous, milling throng of between twenty and thirty thousand.

At ten the gavel thumped loudly for order, and the Reverend Green of Chicago spoke an impressive opening prayer. One of his sonorous flights was prophetic: "We entreat thee, that at some future but not distant day the evils which now invest the body politic shall not only have been arrested in their progress, but wholly eradicated from the system. And may the pen of the historian trace an intimate connection between that glorious consummation and the transactions of this Convention."

President Ashmun now spoke suspicious words: —

"The Chair feels it his first duty this morning to appeal, not merely to the gentlemen of the Convention, but to every individual of this vast audience, to remember the utmost importance of keeping and preserving order during the entire session — as much silence as possible; and he asks gentlemen who are not members of this Convention

---

[1] Arnold, p. 167.
[2] Cleveland, p. 85.

in the name of this Convention, that they will, to their utmost ability, refrain from any demonstrations that may disturb the proceedings of the Convention."

These words sounded very like an attempt, in the interests of Seward, to prevent the heavy Lincoln pressure in the audience from influencing the delegates on the platform. The thousand new claqueurs for "Old Abe" chuckled in their sleeves and the Illinois delegates furtively smiled.

Minor business was put aside, and the Chair was about to start the balloting for President when Montgomery Blair of Maryland secured the floor, seeking to fill up the Maryland delegation by asking the Convention to accredit five new delegates. The Bates men had not been idle last night; they had rounded up five men and hoped to get them seated to vote for Bates. An argument began over acceptance of the five. After several speeches one of the few Maryland Sewardites, the eloquent Armour, jumped up and denounced the five as outsiders. "We ain't outsiders." Cried Armour, "God almighty only knows where they live." A vote was taken and the five Bates men did not get in.

Everybody was anxious for nominating to start. Evarts of New York was about to nominate Seward when the Pennsylvania delegation hurried in through a side door at the last minute and found their seats taken by aggressive spectators. Interlopers were cleared out and Evarts tried again: —

"In the order of business before the Convention, Sir, I take the liberty to name as a candidate to be nominated by this Convention for the office of President of the United States, William H. Seward. [Prolonged applause.]" [1]

Judd was on his feet. Recognized, he said: "I desire, on behalf of the delegation from Illinois, to put in nomination, as a candidate for President of the United States, Abraham Lincoln, of Illinois. [Immense applause, long continued.]" In similar rapid fashion, without the modern long-winded eulogies which bestow praise so lavishly that they sound like caricatures, Dudley of New Jersey nominated Dayton, Reeder of Pennsylvania presented Cameron; Cartter of Ohio nominated, in unenthusiastic tones, Salmon P. Chase. Caleb Smith of Indiana sprang up and surprised the Convention with, "I desire, on behalf of the delegation from Indiana, to second the nomination of Abraham Lincoln, of Illinois. [Tremendous applause.]" This was a blow to Seward and a stroke of great value to Lincoln, for it showed him running strong at the start. It had been carefully planned at Lincoln headquarters; and the Lincoln men had arranged with one of the Ohio Lincolnites, Columbus Delano, to have another unexpected second for Lincoln come from the Ohio delegation.

Frank Blair nominated Bates; Blair of Michigan seconded Seward's nomination. Old Tom Corwin presented Judge McLean. With the lines thus drawn in battle array, Murat Halstead accurately saw how the contest lay: —

"The only names that produced 'tremendous applause' were those of Seward and Lincoln.

"Every body felt that the fight was between them, and yelled accordingly.

"The applause, when Mr. Evarts named Seward, was enthusiastic. When Mr. Judd named Lincoln, the response was prodigious, rising and raging far beyond the Seward shriek. Presently, upon Caleb Smith seconding the nomination of Lincoln, the response was absolutely terrific. It now became the Seward men to make another effort, and when Blair of Michigan seconded his nomination,

> At once there rose so wild a yell,
> Within that dark and narrow dell;
> As all the fiends from heaven that fell
> Had pealed the banner cry of hell.

"The effect was startling. Hundreds of persons stopped their ears in pain. The shouting was absolutely frantic, shrill and wild. No Comanches, no panthers ever struck a higher note, or gave screams with more infernal intensity. Looking from the stage over the vast amphitheatre, nothing was to be seen below but thousands of hats — a black, mighty swarm of hats — flying with the velocity of hornets over a mass of human heads, most of the mouths of which were open. Above, all around the galleries, hats and handkerchiefs were flying in the tempest together. The wonder of the thing was, that the Seward outside pressure should, so far from New York, be so powerful.

"Now the Lincoln men had to try it again, and as Mr. Delano of Ohio, on behalf 'of a portion of the delegation of that state,' seconded the nomination of Lincoln, the uproar was beyond description. Imagine all the hogs ever slaughtered in Cincinnati giving their death squeals together, a score of big steam whistles going . . . and you conceive something of the same nature. I thought the Seward yell could not be surpassed; but the Lincoln boys were clearly ahead, and feeling their victory, as there was a lull in the storm, took deep breaths all round, and gave a concentrated shriek that was positively awful, and accompanied it with stamping that made every plank and pillar in the building quiver.

"Henry S. Lane of Indiana leaped upon a table, and swinging hat and cane, performed like an acrobat. The presumption is, he shrieked with the rest, as his mouth was desperately wide open . . . but his individual voice was lost in the aggregate hurricane.

"The New York, Michigan and Wisconsin delegations sat together, and were in this tempest very quiet. Many of their faces whitened as the Lincoln *yawp* swelled into a wild hozanna of victory." [1]

Unexpected support came from Iowa. An Iowa delegate, Stone, who had in Iowa's voting caucus given his quarter vote to Chase, was so carried away by the stupendous Lincoln enthusiasm that he astonished his cohorts by shouting untruthfully: "I rise in the name of two-thirds of the delegation of Iowa, to second the nomination of Abraham Lincoln. [Great applause.]" [2]

Said Andrew of Massachusetts, "I move you that we proceed to vote." The brazen-voiced reading clerk shouted, "MAINE." Maine gave Seward 10, Lincoln 6 — an important figure, indicating to the David Davis group of schemers that their plan was working. The thunderous Lincoln support inside the Wigwam was seductive to

---

[1] Halstead, pp. 144–145.
[2] Proceedings, p. 149. C. C. Nourse, in *Annals of Iowa*, Vol. XII, p. 460.

wavering delegates.[1] "NEW HAMPSHIRE." Seward got 1, Chase 1, Fremont 1, Lincoln 7 — another smashing blow for Lincoln. Vermont gave 10 to Collamer — a stroke against Seward, for all delegates knew that Weed had tried to get Vermont on this ballot. Seward had been expected to sweep New England; but even Massachusetts gave Lincoln 4 of its 25. Next came Rhode Island and Connecticut. These 20 votes were very scattered, Bates getting more than anyone else (8), but Seward got none while Lincoln picked up 2. "NEW YORK." The rafters echoed as Evarts stood up and spoke calmly, proudly: "The State of *New York* casts her *seventy votes* for *William H. Seward.*" The crowd shook at this and some applause rose. It put Seward far ahead. As roll call went on, Dayton got New Jersey's 14; Pennsylvania went heavily for Cameron, but Lincoln picked up 4; Maryland and Delaware were for Bates, but Seward got 3 from Maryland after a tussle.

Cochrane, Maryland chairman, said: "The Republican State Convention of Maryland having requested that the delegation should vote as a unit, I therefore, in accordance with the wishes of a majority of the delegation, cast 11 votes for Edward Bates. [Applause.]"

Up spoke Coale of Maryland: "I object to that. I am a freeman in Maryland, although surrounded by slavery. If I were going to look for a place to be immolated upon the altar of slavery I should not come to Chicago — [great confusion and cries of "order."] Well, hear my point then. We are not instructed to vote for Edward Bates. Such a resolution was presented there and was instantly voted down. [A voice — "You are not in order."] Well, my point is that we were not instructed."

Armour leaped into the thick of things. "I will present the point of protestation a little clearer than my aged friend has done. [Cries of "Call the roll."]"

THE PRESIDENT — It is not a subject of debate. The question is, shall the Convention receive the eleven votes from the State of Maryland for Mr. Bates? and this must be decided without debate. [Voices — "Call the roll," "hear him," and great confusion.]

[1] Blaine, *Twenty Years of Congress*, Vol. I, p. 169. H. J. Raymond to N. Y. *Times*, in J. Parton, *Greeley*, p. 480.

MR. ARMOUR — I do not wish to debate the point. I wish to state succinctly and clearly the point of our protest. Have I leave? [Cries of "Yes" and "No."] At the Convention which assembled at Maryland, a resolution was offered instructing the delegates of the State of Maryland to vote as a unit. There was a general feeling against that resolution, and a number of gentlemen spoke against it, and I had risen to protest against it when some gentleman in my rear moved that we be simply "recommended." Not one man in that Convention considered that "recommend" and "instruct" were synonymous terms. . . . Therefore, we let it pass, believing then and now that we were free to cast our votes for the man of our choice, and we now claim that right on the floor of the Convention. [Cries of "Good," and applause.]

MR. R. M. CORWINE, of Ohio — One of the rules adopted yesterday declares that the Chairman of each delegation shall cast the vote of his delegation.

A VOICE — No, no! it says he shall "announce" it.

MR. COALE — We will vote as we please and we will not vote any other way.

The Chair then stated the question.

MR. FRANK P. BLAIR, of Missouri — I rise to a point of order. I desire to know whether this Convention is to be governed by its rules or not? I call the attention of the President to the rule which we have adopted, and under which we must act, unless it is intended now to violate it.

THE CHAIR — The Chair is aware of the rule. The rule adopted was that the vote of each state should be announced by its chairman.

A VOICE — He must but announce it and announce it truly.

They were getting nowhere in this argument in which the battle line for and against Seward can be traced in every utterance, so Ashmun called for a vote of the Convention on whether or not Maryland's vote as announced by the Maryland chairman should be received. The division turned it down; so Armour, Coale, and another Marylander voted for Seward.

Roll call proceeded. Fickle Virginia, "expected solid for Seward," [1] gave Seward 8, Lincoln 14. Anxious looks were exchanged in the New York delegation. Kentucky was in chaos: Seward 5, Lincoln 6, Wade 2, Chase 8. Ohio was for Chase of course, but Lincoln's Ohio friends won 8 for him. "INDIANA." Eyes shining, Henry Lane

[1] Halstead, p. 145.

proudly cast the whole 26 for Lincoln. Missouri gave 18 to Bates;
Michigan gave Seward all 12; then Illinois emphatically gave Lincoln their 22. Not many votes remained out, but Seward got most of
them — all of Wisconsin, California, Minnesota, Kansas. Oregon
gave 5 for Bates, while Lincoln picked up only 3 — 2 from Iowa and
1 from Nebraska.

The Secretary announced the result: Seward 173½, Lincoln 102,
Bates 48, Cameron 50½, Chase 49, McLean 12, Dayton 14, Collamer 10, scattering 6. The Illinois men were elated; their plan had
so far worked better than they had dared hope.[1] Thank Chicago for
that. And their man was running so strong that those second ballot
contracts would surely be carried out. Impartial observers saw that
the opening ballot "caused a fall in Seward stock. It was seen that
Lincoln, Cameron, and Bates had the strength to defeat Seward,
and it was known that the greater part of the Chase vote would go
for Lincoln." [2]

The ballot had been long, and partisans clamored for the second
to begin. Delegates were keyed to a pitch of excitement so great
they were rendered incapable of patience, "and cries of 'Call the
roll' were fairly hissed through their teeth." As the reading clerk
again commenced to roar the name of each state there appeared no
change in Maine's vote; New Hampshire gave Lincoln 9, Seward 1,
a gain of two for the Rail Splitter. Then Vermont came through according to plan with 10 for Lincoln — "a blighting blow upon the
Seward interest," reckoned Halstead. "The New Yorkers started as
if an Orsini bomb had exploded." Lincoln gained 5 more from Rhode
Island and Connecticut. New Jersey gave Seward 4, Dayton 10 —
not at all according to contract. Seward gained instead of Lincoln.

"PENNSYLVANIA," shouted the clerk. The delegation was in
confusion. Presently they were ready to vote, giving Lincoln 48, according to contract — a thumping gain of 44. This was the sensation
of the day; Pennsylvania had come in so late nobody but the Lincoln
men knew much about what they would do, and even Davis could not

[1] Swett, in Oldroyd, p. 71.
[2] Halstead, p. 146.

be sure. Unlike New Jersey, Pennsylvania had been convinced by Lincoln's astonishing strength, by his gains so far on the second ballot. New York was stunned. Halstead saw that "the fate of the day was now determined."

On down the roll call. Maryland held firm, but Delaware, seeing how the wind was blowing, switched her 6 from Bates to Lincoln. Three more Lincoln votes were gained from Kentucky and 6 from Ohio. Then, near the tail end of the roll call, Seward and Lincoln both gained 3, Lincoln's additions coming from Iowa.

During the balloting the crowd had been excited and noisy, keyed up to a state of extreme nervousness by the intensity and drama of the battle. The Secretary announced the result through the confusion: Seward 184½ — Sewardites screeched; Lincoln 181 — a thunderclap of applause burst and raged until the Secretary appealed for silence so the Convention's business could go on. Bates was announced with 35, Chase had 42½, Dayton 10, 12 scattering. Strategists saw that Lincoln had gained 79 votes while Seward was picking up 11. Halstead believed that "even persons unused to making the calculations and considering the combinations attendant upon such scenes, could not fail to observe that while the strength of Seward and Lincoln was almost even at the moment, the reserved votes, by which the contest must be decided, were inclined to the latter." But Seward was not yet beaten, would not be until he should begin to lose votes.

Ballot Three began "amid excitement that tested the nerves." No change in the first three states called. Then Massachusetts switched 4 votes from Seward to Lincoln. There it was! But the race was still on, for Rhode Island and Connecticut gave both Lincoln and Seward a gain of 2. At this crucial point cautious New Jersey delivered in part, Lincoln getting 8, Seward 5, one dull delegate clinging to Dayton. Now, to politicians of any imagination at all, 'twas apparent that not Seward but Lincoln had the best chance of commanding that opulent galleon on wheels, the bandwagon, carrier of a supremely attractive cargo of loaves and fishes. After Lincoln gained 4 more from Pennsylvania, Maryland left Bates and came to Lincoln, giving him a gain of 9 while Seward lost 1. For delivering these 9 when they did most good Montgomery Blair was to be richly rewarded as Lincoln's Postmaster General. No change in Delaware and Virginia; then Kentucky gave Lincoln an increase of 4 while depriving Seward of 1.

Ohio now gave Lincoln 29, a gain of 15 precious votes. This was seen as the final turning point away from Seward. Whispers rustled through the crowd — "Lincoln's the coming man — will be nominated this ballot." As Indiana and Illinois were passed the vocal clamor died down; the throng was intently watching while the tail end of the ballot reported. Calculating pencils scratched rapidly, to discover if Lincoln would go over with this ballot. Would Seward's strength in the West hold? — the breathless, silent crowd wondered. Pencils could be heard scratching and telegraph instruments clicking. As states west of Illinois reported one by one, Seward's strength held firm to the end. But Lincoln gained 4 more as Greeley's "Oregon boys" left Bates and, save one, went to Lincoln. As the District of Columbia cast 2 for Seward a hundred rapid mathematicians found in a trice that Lincoln had 231½ — only 1½ short of nomination. As this was whispered about the atmosphere was tensely silent. Something dramatic was expected to happen in the next few seconds.

Two rapid calculators were David Cartter and Joseph Medill — Medill sitting there in the Ohio delegation to assist the few original Ohio Lincolnites. Medill knew that another ballot would doubtless see Lincoln safely nominated; but why take a chance? Impulsively he whispered to Cartter, "If you can throw the Ohio delegation to Lincoln, Chase can have anything he wants." Cartter hesitated momentarily, doubting that Medill spoke with authority. Then, his mind clicking to the fact that now was the time to distinguish himself and secure a grip on the bandwagon by casting the deciding votes, he jumped on his chair.

Every eye was on the tall man with bushy black hair and glowing eyes as he gesticulated for recognition. His stuttering voice was the only sound in the Wigwam: "I-I a-a-rise, Mr. Chairman, to a-anounce the c-c-change of f-four votes, from Mr. Chase to Abraham Lincoln." [1]

For a moment the crowd was silent. Out once more came Cook's handkerchief. Then "the nerves of thousands, which through hours of suspense had been subjected to terrible tension, relaxed, and as deep breaths of relief were taken, there was a noise in the Wigwam like the rush of a great wind, in the van of a storm — and in another breath, the storm was there. There were thousands cheering with the energy of insanity.

"A man who had been on the roof . . . engaged in communicating the results of the ballotings to the mighty mass of outsiders, now demanded by gestures at the sky-light over the stage, to know what had happened. One of the Secretaries, with a tally sheet in his hands, shouted — 'Fire the Salute! Abe Lincoln is nominated!' As the cheering inside the Wigwam subsided, we could hear that outside, where the news of the nomination had just been announced. And the roar, like the breaking up of the fountains of the great deep that was heard, gave a new impulse to the enthusiasm inside. Then the thunder of the salute rose above the din, and the shouting was repeated with such tremendous fury that some discharges of the cannon were absolutely not heard by those on the stage." [2]

Emotions of the Lincoln workers exploded in a frenzy of exultation. Delegate Nourse of Iowa, jumping up and down and shouting his best, felt a restraining hand on his shoulder. A delegate from the phlegmatic New Jersey group soberly inquired, "Why are you so excited?" Emitting another shout, Nourse roared back, "Why, we have nominated the best man in the country for President and beaten that New York crowd of wire pullers. Why shouldn't we shout? We came from Iowa where we were suckled by prairie wolves! *Whoop!*" Nourse immediately went into "a series of ear-splitting performances." As an old man he joyfully remembered, "I never was so happy in my life before or since." [3] One reporter, speechless amid the ter-

[1] Reminiscence of Medill, in *Ohio Arch. & Hist. Quart.*, Vol. XXXIV, pp. 519–520. Cleveland, p. 85. Bromley, p. 655. D. Taylor to S. P. Chase, May 22, 1860; Chase MSS.
[2] Halstead, pp. 149–150.
[3] C. C. Nourse, in *Annals of Iowa*, Vol. XII, pp. 461–462.

rific din, saw that "the Indiana men generally were smashing hats and hugging each other; the Illinois men did everything except stand on their heads." [1]

In Springfield, while this surprising series of history-making events was taking place, the man in whose interest the astounding political upset was being achieved, fidgeted about the public square awaiting news of a Seward victory. Early Friday morning Lawyer James C. Conkling returned to Springfield from Chicago. Lincoln, downtown early, heard somebody on the street remark that Conkling had just returned from the Wigwam sector. Lincoln hurried to Conkling's office upstairs over Chatterton's jewelry store and asked for Conkling. A law student looked up from a legal tome to inform the tall candidate that his man would not be down for an hour. Lincoln went down to the square. Conkling arrived and Lincoln went up, flopped down on an old settee, two huge feet hanging over the end, and began to cross-examine his friend on the state of things at Chicago. The two Republicans talked long; Lincoln wanted all the details. As Lincoln stared at the ceiling Conkling told him he expected Lincoln's nomination before sundown, relating how the Seward opposition had been lining up to vote for Lincoln, and would if only Seward did not win on the first ballot.

Lincoln was less optimistic. He guessed that if Seward missed on the first ballot the Convention would finally nominate either Chase or Bates. Conkling reiterated his opinion that Lincoln would be chosen. About noon, after more than two hours of conversation, Lincoln stood up; he said, "Well, Conkling, I believe I will go back to my office and practise law."

While the two politicians talked, balloting had started in the Wigwam. Lincoln climbed the stairs to his back-room law office. Two students were trying to study. They paused to ask the news; their colloquy with the candidate was presently interrupted by Edward Baker of the *Journal*, who bolted in with the first ballot result. His astonishingly good vote keyed up Lincoln even more. Unable to sit still, he started for the *Journal* office. Passing the telegraph office, he

[1] Bromley, p. 656.

went up to see if news of the second ballot had arrived. Nothing there, so he went on to the *Journal* office. A crowd of men gave excited encouragement. Soon a telegram came telling of Lincoln's gain on the second ballot. Astonished, the candidate relaxed in a chair. Nervously he waited, chatting.

Presently a telegram was rushed in which told of victory on the third ballot. Lincoln, hardly surprised this time, shook hands calmly, hurriedly, and left the office to carry the great news to Mary Lincoln. A boy dashed up — whooped, "Mr. Lincoln, you're nominated!" It was Clinton Conkling, who had heard Lincoln talking in his father's office that morning. The leathery face brightened and the high voice exclaimed, "Well, Clinton, then we've got it" — seizing the boy's hand outstretched in congratulation.

Soon Lincoln read a scrawled telegram thrust in his hand: —

To LINCOLN
YOU ARE NOMINATED
J J S WILSON

An excited crowd gathered round and showered congratulations. A telegram came from Delegate Knapp: "WE DID IT — GLORY TO GOD." Then three more telegrams gave additional details.[1]

While the tempest raged in the Wigwam numerous politicians sat cursing their luck at not having changed to Lincoln before. Better late than never, however; better a hand-hold on the bandwagon than nothing. Besides, the Convention's prime purpose was to nominate a man who could be elected, and the campaign would be set off with a rush if the Convention should go on record as overwhelmingly in support of its presidential nominee. Half a dozen delegates stood on chairs clamoring for recognition as the audience howled, waved handkerchiefs, tossed hats in the air. Before the third ballot result could be officially declared, eleven delegations shifted their unanimous vote

[1] Clinton L. Conkling, "How Mr. Lincoln Received the News of His First Nomination," *Transactions*, Ill. State Hist. Soc., 1909, pp. 64–66. *Herndon's Lincoln*, p. 374. Weik, pp. 262–269. Angle, *"Here I Have Lived,"* p. 236. H. B. Rankin, *Personal Recollections*, pp. 187–191. Chicago *Journal*, in D. W. Bartlett, *Life and Public Services of Hon. Abraham Lincoln*, p. 145. Octavia Roberts, *Lincoln in Illinois*, pp. 94–96. The Lincoln Foundation, MS. no. 2, [J. C. Thompson], pp. 5–13.

to Lincoln and three more increased his vote but could not secure unanimity. Only the staunchest Sewardites refrained. While these changes were going on the crowd was clamorous. A huge, horrible charcoal portrait of Lincoln was brought in and enthusiasm mounted [1]; jubilant Lincoln partisans seized state placards and brandished them aloft deliriously. They made a rush for the New York standard but were angrily repulsed. Lincoln's managers sat weeping for joy, while Thurlow Weed shed great salt tears, so sorry was he for himself and so mortified.

Presently the plaudits quieted following exhaustion; and the Secretary, so excited he read out the wrong figures, announced: "Whole number of votes cast, 466; necessary to a choice, 234. For Abraham Lincoln, of Illinois, 364 votes." [2] The Chair shouted, "Abraham Lincoln, of Illinois, is selected as your candidate for President of the United States." Applause thundered. Chairman Evarts of New York, as soon as he could, "mounted the Secretaries' table and handsomely and impressively expressed his grief at the failure of the Convention to nominate Seward — and in melancholy tones, moved that the nomination be made unanimous." Each time Evarts mentioned Seward ("Gentlemen, it was from Governor Seward that most of us learned to love Republican principles and the Republican Party") loud cheers rang out. John Andrew seconded the motion with a lengthy speech in the July Fourth manner, throwing a sop to injured feelings by calling Seward "the brightest and most shining light of this political generation [applause and cheers]." He made the usual promise that his state would vote overwhelmingly for the nominee; "under Abraham Lincoln, of Illinois, we are bound to march with you to victory. [Tremendous cheers.]"

Carl Schurz, speaking for Wisconsin, made a short speech seconding Evarts' motion. "I know I am speaking in the spirit of Mr. Seward, when I say that . . . his ambition will be satisfied with the success of the cause which was the dream of his youth, and to which he has devoted all the days of his manhood, even if the name of

[1] Franklin Johnson, "Nominating Lincoln," *Youth's Companion*, Feb. 8, 1917, p. 72.
[2] The number of votes cast was 465, requiring only 233 for nomination. Since the mistake made no difference nobody noticed it.

Wm. H. Seward should remain in history . . . uncrowned with the highest honor. [Loud cheers.]" For another last-ditch Seward delegation, — Michigan, — Austin Blair, candidate for Governor, poured oil on waters which ambitious, office-hungry Republicans hoped would remain untroubled: "The State of Michigan . . . lays down her first, best loved candidate to take up yours, with some beating of the heart, with some quivering in the veins [much applause]; but she does not fear that the fame of Seward will suffer, for she knows that his name is a portion of the history of the American Union; it will be written, and read, and beloved long after the temporary excitement of this day has passed away, and when Presidents themselves are forgotten in the oblivion which comes over all temporal things. We stand by him still. We have followed him with a single eye and unwavering faith in times past. We marshal now behind him in the grand column which shall go out to battle for Abraham Lincoln, of Illinois.

"Mark you, what has obtained today will obtain in November next. Lincoln will be elected by the people. We say of our candidate, God bless his magnanimous soul. [Tremendous applause.]"

These affectionate speeches were all very well, Evarts remarked, but the Convention had yet to nominate a vice presidential candidate, so had better get down to business. He suggested that the chairmen of the delegations meet, after adjournment, at New York headquarters at the Richmond House, to arrange a vice presidential choice. This was agreed to; then his motion of adjournment until five o'clock carried.

Browning took the floor to reply, on behalf of Illinois, to the unanimity orations. Wrought up to a high emotional pitch, his voice quavered. Pulling himself together, he cried: "We are so much elated at present that we are scarcely in a condition to collect our own thoughts, or to express them intelligently."

I desire to say . . . that in the contest through which we have just passed, we have been actuated by no feeling of hostility to the illustrious statesman from New York, who was in competition with our own loved and gallant son. We were actuated solely by a desire for the certain advancement of

Republicanism. The Republicans of Illinois, believing that the principles of the Republican party are the same principles which embalmed the hearts and nerved the arms of our patriot sires of the revolution . . . were actuated solely by the conviction that the triumph of these principles was necessary not only to the salvation of our party, but to the perpetuation of the free institutions whose blessings we now enjoy, and we have struggled against the nomination of the illustrious statesman from New York solely because we believed here that we could go into battle on the prairies of Illinois with more hope and more prospect of success under the leadership of our own noble son. No Republican who has a love of freedom in his heart, and who has marked the course of Governor Seward, of New York, in the councils of our nation, who has witnessed the many occasions upon which he has risen to the very height of moral sublimity in his conflicts with the enemies of free institutions, no heart that has the love of freedom in it and has witnessed these great conflicts of his, can do otherwise than venerate his name on this occasion. I desire to say only, that the hearts of Illinois are today filled with emotions of gratification, for which they have no utterance. We are not more overcome by the triumph of our noble Lincoln, loving him as we do, knowing the purity of his past life, the integrity of his character, and devotion to the principles of our party, and the gallantry with which we will be conducted through this contest, than we are by the magnanimity of our friends of the great and glorious State of New York in moving to make this nomination unanimous. On behalf of the delegation from Illinois, for the Republican party of this great and growing prairie state, I return to all our friends, New York included, our heartfelt thanks and gratitude for the nomination of this Convention. [Applause.]

When a round of plaudits subsided the epochal session adjourned, after nearly four hours of breathless excitement. Delegates who voted for Lincoln, wearily exulting, trudged off the stage. Sewardites, "terribly cast down," gloomily departed. "They were mortified beyond all expression, and walked thoughtfully and silently away from the slaughterhouse, more ashamed than embittered. They acquiesced in the nomination, but did not pretend to be pleased with it; and the tone of their conversations, as to the prospect of electing the candidate, was not hopeful. It was their funeral and they would not make merry." [1]

1 Halstead, p. 151.

When the weary delegates came out their tortured ears were smote again by a terrific din. The throng outside, its enthusiasm previously restrained by ignorance of the exact state of affairs inside, had exploded upon learning of Abe Lincoln's success. Pent-up enthusiasm ran wild and conjured up in a trice a veritable maelstrom of exultation. Murat Halstead's vivid pen captures the terrific jubilation: —

"The town was full of the news of Lincoln's nomination, and could hardly contain itself. There were bands of music playing, and processions marching, and joyous cries heard on every hand, from the army of trumpeters for Lincoln of Illinois, and the thousands who are always enthusiastic on the winning side. But hundreds of men who had been in the Wigwam were so prostrated by the excitement they had endured, and their exertions in shrieking for Seward or Lincoln, that they were hardly able to walk to their hotels. There were men who had not tasted liquor, who staggered about like drunkards, unable to manage themselves."

Men with business yet unsettled rushed for dinner. One rough and ready Lincoln shouter from the stentorian shock-troops, "who could hardly believe that the 'Old Abe' of his adoration was really the Republican nominee for the Presidency, took a chair at the dinner-table at the Tremont House, and began talking to those around him . . . of the greatness of the events of the day. One of his expressions was: 'Talk of your money and bring on your bullies with you! — the immortal principles of the everlasting people are with Abe Lincoln, of the people, by ——.' 'Abe Lincoln has no money and no bullies, but he has the people by ——.' A servant approached the eloquent patriot and asked what he would have to eat. Being thus recalled to temporal things he glared scornfully at the servant and roared out, 'Go to the devil — what do I want to eat for? Abe Lincoln is nominated, G—d d—— it; and I'm going to live on air — the air of liberty by ——.' But in a moment he inquired for the bill of fare, and then ordered 'a great deal of every thing' — saying if he must eat he might as well eat 'the whole bill.' He swore he felt as if he could 'devour and digest an Illinois prairie.' And this was one of thousands."

In Auburn, New York, Friday morning, most of Cayuga County swarmed to the home of its popular Senator Seward, primed to do him homage, help him celebrate. His house and grounds were alive with admirers; a cannon stood ready to boom out the news of nomination. When a messenger galloped up with the first ballot result, the throng whooped confidently. The second ballot report arrived; Seward said, "I shall be nominated on the next ballot." Cheers rang out. Presently a messenger sped up and handed Seward a telegram; he read, "LINCOLN NOMINATED. T. W." He turned "pale as ashes." Rapidly the tidings spread and the crowd melted away; the cannon was rolled to downtown Auburn and puzzled partisans fired salutes to the Republican nominee.[1]

Congress that morning was more interested in the news from Chicago than in debate. Republican members were highly excited. "Every fresh telegraph served to increase the commotion," related a calm Washington dispatch in the press next day. "The Presidential nomination occasioned much surprise, and was not at once credited." [2]

[1] H. B. Stanton, *Random Recollections*, pp. 215–216.
[2] Chicago *Press & Tribune*, May 19, 1860.

CHAPTER VII

"Who Is James K. Polk?"

AT five o'clock the Wigwam was full again and the Convention called to order. Without delay they proceeded to the business of nominating a running mate for Lincoln. At New York headquarters that afternoon delegation leaders had expected Evarts to demand the privilege of naming the other nominee. Conservatives were ready to acquiesce, glad that Sewardite disappointments seemed so easily placable. Is not that mainly what vice presidential nominations are for? In the reception hall of the Tremont House that afternoon, Horace Greeley, beaming in triumph, had been surrounded by a group of admirers who asked, as though consulting an oracle, who would be chosen as Lincoln's running mate. Said Greeley, "The friends of Mr. Seward are very sore, and they must have their own way as to the Vice-President." [1] In the afternoon caucus Evarts had been asked to name his man, but the New Yorker refused. This looked dangerous, so the Conservatives conspired to stroke Irrepressible fur the right way by nominating a man of their own selection who would please Seward, and additionally, balance the ticket. After Evarts' refusal, Pennsylvania was asked to suggest a man. Cameron was offered, then Reeder of Pennsylvania, late Territorial Governor of Kansas. Neither was fully satisfactory. Preston King, Seward's New York colleague in the Senate, satisfied many; but King did not want it, so he suggested his close friend and colleague, Hannibal Ham-

---

[1] G. H. Stewart, in *Century*, Vol. XLI, p. 157. R. Hosea to S. P. Chase, May 18, 1860; Chase MSS.

lin.[1] Nominating sentences presented five Republicans: John Hickman of Pennsylvania, Senator Hamlin of Maine, Banks of Massachusetts, Cassius Clay of Kentucky, Reeder of Pennsylvania. As the first ballot proceeded, without much interest and with nearly all delegations split on their preference, the race was seen to lie between Clay and Hamlin. The crowd was for romantic Cassius Clay, shouting his name lustily and trying to force the delegates to nominate him by acclamation.[2] Clay, however, sober strategists knew, was not the best balance for Lincoln, because he too had old Whig affiliations and was a Westerner. Hamlin, a New Englander and old Democrat, fitted much better. And Senator Hamlin was a rumored good friend of Senator Seward. First ballot totals: Hamlin 194, Clay 101½, Hickman 58, Reeder 51, Banks 38½; 18 scattered among four others — Henry Winter Davis, Sam Houston, John M. Read (insulted by having his name spelled "Reed"), Dayton.

No one having a majority, a second ballot began. All dropped out save the three leaders; votes released thereby, following the normal drift to the leader, gravitated to Hamlin. Clay lost strength rapidly as the practical wisdom of choosing Hamlin became apparent. The only excitement came when Ashmun read a dispatch from Detroit, the throng whooping loudly at the intelligence that "One hundred guns are now being fired in honor of the nomination of Lincoln." Hamlin had almost enough to nominate before Clay got his first vote, and the ballot ended: Hamlin 367, Clay 86, Hickman 13.[3] The Chair announced Hamlin "as the candidate of the Republican Party for Vice President." Up jumped Chairman Blakey of Kentucky to move "in behalf of the friends of that gallant son of freedom, Cassius M. Clay" that Hamlin's nomination be made unanimous. Bald, eloquent Caleb Smith of Indiana, who had presented Clay, seconded the motion and continued with a prolix speech fulsomely praising both Clay and Hamlin. The crowd cheered loudly when he mentioned Seward by way of apology for Indiana's part in beating him, but yelled louder when he cried:

[1] *Diary of Bates,* p. 130.
[2] Halstead, p. 151.
[3] Proceedings, pp. 161 162.

Thirty years ago on the Southern frontier of Indiana might have been seen a humble, ragged boy, bare footed, driving his oxen through the hills, and he has elevated himself to the pinnacle which has now presented him as the candidate of this convention. It is an illustration of that spirit of enterprise which characterizes the West, and every western heart will throb with joy when the name of Lincoln shall be presented to them as the candidate of the Republican party.

As to the strength of the ticket and platform — "We stand upon a rock, and the gates of hell shall not prevail against it."

Now McCrillis of Maine took the floor to thank the Convention for nominating Hamlin. His speech too glowed with encomiums, and he went out of his way to praise Seward. In flowery language he told how all Republicans would stand "together as a band of brethren, as a united phalanx" behind the nominees. "Tumultuous applause" cheered his closing flourish, and the motion for unanimity was put to a vote and carried with great noise.

Its main business over, the Convention went on with details incident to a rousing conclusion. Two resolutions were quickly moved and adopted; then Henry Lane of Indiana secured the floor. The crowd gave him a cheer. He delivered himself of a spread-eagle harangue, not forgetting to eulogize Seward. He exploded, "I ask you by your action to sternly rebuke the disunion spirit which now disgraces the politics of the United States, and to burn hissing hot into the brazen front of Southern Democracy the brand of disunion, as God marked Cain, the first murderer. [Great applause.]"

The new National Committee was named, Judd staying on as the Illinois committeeman. Then Goodrich of Minnesota secured the floor and announced that at eight o'clock a "triumphal procession" would form at Washington Street and Michigan Avenue, march about, then migrate "to this Wigwam, or Tabernacle, where delegations, citizens and strangers are invited to join in one grand ratification of the nominations made here today. [Applause.]" He offered a resolution commending Chicago citizens on their "hospitality, taste, zeal, munificence," which was noisily adopted. Goodrich then started to make a stump speech, the audience becoming loud and impatient. Voices shouted: "No speech." "Read your resolution and sit down." Holding firm to his purpose, Goodrich got out several sentences. "One word more," he pleaded. Somebody yelled, "Dry up." The would-be speaker retorted, "I am not in the habit of being halloed down, even by opponents, and certainly not by friends." A voice shouted, "If you are our friend let us adjourn." While the crowd was laughing over this, Goodrich got started again: —

"The representatives from Minnesota feel that a seat in the Presidential chair would not add one jot to the stature of William H. Seward. Of all earthly fame he has seen the vanity. Lasting, exalted is his fame. Whenever lofty deeds — "

The audience had heard these maudlin maunderings so many times they wanted no more of them. Loud were calls to proceed with business, and poor Goodrich had to keep his platitudes to himself.

A few routine matters were dispatched; then a California delegate moved that the Convention "do now adjourn *sine die*, with nine cheers for the platform and the ticket." Nine terrific cheers echoed and re-echoed. The Chair began his valedictory address. He told how he had known Lincoln in Congress —

"There was never elected to the House of Representatives a purer, nor a more intelligent and loyal representative than Abraham Lincoln. [Great applause.] . . . There is not one man in this country that will be compelled to hang his head for anything in the life of Abraham Lincoln." This had a distinctly apologetic ring. "You have a candidate worthy of the cause; you are pledged to his success; humanity is pledged to his success; the cause of free government is pledged to his success. The decree has gone forth that he shall succeed. [Tremendous applause.]"

Now, gentlemen, that we have completed so well, so thoroughly the great work which the people sent us here to do, let us adjourn to our several constituencies; and, thanks be to God who giveth the victory, we will triumph. [Applause.]

A delegate suggested they "adjourn to meet at the White House on the 4th of March next." Out of order, said Ashmun. "As many as are

in favor of the motion that this Convention do now adjourn *sine die*
say aye." A rumble of ayes; then the Chair formally declared the
Convention adjourned *sine die*.[1]

In Washington, Senator Hamlin was totally unprepared for the
news of his nomination. He had even pledged his lieutenants to keep
his name entirely out of the Convention. Friday evening Hamlin
was playing cards, glad that a better candidate than Seward had
been chosen, when he was surprised by a group of his Republican
colleagues — Wade, Colfax, Zachariah Chandler, and several others.
They saluted him as "Mr. Vice President." After explanations, Hamlin said he did not want the place, but would run if that would help
the Party to win. Congratulators swarmed about him. Then he made
a speech to serenaders outside.[2]

While the delegates met for the last time, plans were going forward
for a gigantic Lincoln demonstration. The jubilation which had burst
when his nomination became known was spontaneous, but all afternoon and evening vigorous Chicago Republicans, fonder of Lincoln
than ever of course, were busily arranging a demonstration aimed to
reach the zenith of enthusiasm. They were bent on showing an alertly
observing nation that once again the spirit of Old Tippecanoe was
abroad in the land. Only the groundwork had been laid for populariza-
tion of Lincoln as the Rail Splitter; now ardent Lincoln backers of
the Oglesby type co-operated like modern advertising men in a swift,
high-pressure build-up to make the Lincoln rail the equivalent of
Harrisonian hard cider as a vote-winning symbol.

The army of Lincoln shouters, their main work done, were set to
work Friday afternoon gathering materials for a Mardi Gras of
celebration. They scurried about collecting fence rails, daubing signs,
gathering candles and lamps for an illumination, fireworks for a
pyrotechnical exhibition. At dusk Chicago's erratic streets and sidewalks were jammed by the seething, jubilating host of caterwauling
Republicans. Wide-Awakes turned out with great gusto, marching
and countermarching in full uniform, shouldering weather-beaten

[1] Proceedings, p. 169.
[2] *Hamlin,* pp. 345–347.

fence rails. This inspiring spectacle moved other hundreds of Lincoln votaries to form in impromptu parades, the lucky ones armed with rails, those not so lucky carrying rakes, brooms, cordwood. These processions trooped about in march cadence as a score of bands sent up a brassy cacophony. Halstead thought the city had gone "wild with delight. . . . Torrents of liquor were poured down the hoarse throats of the multitude." Lincoln's willing workers had brought out several cannon. One, hoisted to the roof of the Tremont House, roared out a hundred guns, the echoes of each blast "caught up and answered from other parts of the city almost as soon as their flashes were seen across the night sky."

In the Wigwam a giant rally was staged. The place was packed, while an overflow crowd of three thousand was entertained outside by the spirited oratory of Dick Yates. Inside, the enthusiasm of the packed thousands was (as usual) "beyond description." [1] Giddings held forth with his usual power, followed by Editor Pangborn of the Boston *Atlas*, who kept the house in an uproar of laughter and applause. Telegraphic dispatches were read from important cities "stating that ratification meetings were assembling, guns firing, processions upon parade, etc., throughout the whole country." [2] Indianapolis reported a hundred-gun salute shortly after noon; bonfires and speeches, "great enthusiasm" in the evening, announced "a grand ratification meeting" for Saturday night. Detroit reported "bonfires and illuminations." From Philadelphia: "Several thousand people had assembled in Independence Square, to await the news, and when it was announced that Lincoln was nominated, the air was rent with shouts; processions were formed and marched through the principal streets, cheering and hurrahing for honest old Abe." Dayton, Ohio, reported cannon salutes and "a large circular rail-fence . . . erected at the junction of Main and Third streets, enclosing a huge bonfire. A large and enthusiastic ratification meeting was held at the Court House. . . . Old rails in demand." News from Albany, New York, reported an initial incredulity at Lincoln's nomination,

[1] Chicago *Press & Tribune*, May 19, 1860.
[2] *Press & Tribune*, May 19.

but a hundred salutes were fired anyway, and at night ignited tar-barrels made a great red spectacle.

When darkness slow-sifted down upon the merry maelstrom the city twinkled exotically with myriad light effects. Marching Wide-Awakes replaced rails with their flaring kerosene torches which set their oilcloth capes aflash. Skyrockets, tracing scintillating streaks across the dark, "clove through the air like fiery telegrams to the stars." On numberless corners giant bonfires were kindled, each coloring the sky with a red glow and attracting its knot of noisy celebrants. For their "illumination," Republicans placed candles and lamps on window sills, lighting panes with dull glow. A large warehouse "made a very effective show of variegated lights in every window, while a banner was hung across the street, upon the folds of which was painted: —

'For President, Abraham Lincoln.' "

The *Press & Tribune*, with a great personal triumph to celebrate, arrayed its building most elaborately of all: —

"Illuminated from 'turret to foundation' by the brilliant glare of a thousand lights which blazed from windows and doors. . . . On each side of the counting-room door stood a rail — out of the three thousand split by 'honest Old Abe' thirty years ago on the Sangamon River bottoms. On the inside were two more, brilliantly hung with tapers whose numberless individual lights glistened like so many stars in contrast with the dark walnut color of the wood. On the front of the office and over the main door . . . was suspended an immense transparency with this inscription upon it: —

FOR PRESIDENT,
"HONEST OLD ABE."

FOR VICE PRESIDENT,
HANNIBAL HAMLIN.

"At dark several of the triumphal processions united, paraded through Clark street, and stopping before our office," the *Press & Tribune* proudly continued its chronicle, "rent the air with soul inspiring cheers and exclamations of victory." [1]

One superheated observer thought "Babel had come again, and the Democratic Jericho shook at the shouts and blowing of trumpets and holding of torches in the left hands of the Republican Gideons."

Enthusiasm was universal, demonstrated by music, cheering, speaking, parading, and also by a liberal display of fence rails, and other characteristic emblems of the people's choice.

In fact, everybody was happy, every heart filled with joy — except the Douglasites. They refused to be comforted.

Pausing glass in hand, "Republicans shouted that Lincoln and Hamlin were good men and true, abetted by steamboat whistles, steam whistles of factories and trains, and even church bells in their payment of bacchanalian homage to Abraham Lincoln, the Republican Party, and John Barleycorn." [2]

An encouraging harbinger of November's result was the conduct of the Pennsylvania delegation. "Crazy with delight," they went "almost beyond bounds" in expressing their pleasure at the chosen ticket. Several hundred Pennsylvanians met at the Briggs House, where Curtin harangued them. All affirmed that Lincoln would carry Pennsylvania by "at least 25,000 majority." They paraded with a vast number of rails and said they wanted the whole Lincoln fence from Decatur for campaign purposes.

In every Northern community where a respectable number of Republicans lived, a series of celebrations began. As a matter of campaign tactics, even in towns where Seward had been the local favorite Lincoln's nomination was zealously greeted. The outburst at Pontiac, Illinois, was typical. When the glorious news came over the wire Republicans began to congregate in the courthouse square. Having no cannon, they fired a hundred salutes with powder and anvils. The shouting ratifiers arranged a formal town ratification meeting

[1] *Press & Tribune*, May 19, 1860.
[2] Baringer, "Campaign Technique in Illinois — 1860," p. 312.

for the evening. Darkness fell and the courthouse was subjected to an illumination; the building "presented the appearance of a solid blaze, illuminated in every nook and corner, many people living away from the square supposing the building to be on fire, rushed to the scene. . . . The court house was full of enthusiastic Republicans, whose greatest difficulty was to suppress the outbursting of over-flowing feelings." Four speeches "worthy of the occasion" were de-livered, and resolutions adopted endorsing the ticket and platform. The meeting adjourned after three resounding cheers for "Honest Old Abe." Near by a large bonfire had been kindled, round which partisans lingered until late, disturbing the peace of the night.[1] Towns not on a telegraph line seldom heard the news until long after dark. Nevertheless, Republicans were ready to fire salutes and wake the town at any hour. Artillery that night "disturbed the quiet slum-bers of many a drowsy Democrat." [2]

In Springfield, even the Democratic *Register* admitted that upon receiving the astounding news of their townsman's elevation, "there was a general firing of guns, shaking of hands, ringing of bells, hurras and shouts that set the whole town in an uproar." [3] Looking ahead, the *Register* continued: —

The news of the nomination of Mr. Lincoln was received with enthusiastic joy by his party townsmen. Their gladness was, probably, increased by the fact that for a dozen hours previous to the receipt of the news they had nearly given up all hope of his success, and when the news came their de-light scarcely knew bounds. . . . Well, we, too, were pleased — that our neighbors were so happy — that a candidate for the Presidency should be taken from our town, but we shall be under the disagreeable (?) necessity of assisting in bringing all this joy to dolor on one of the early days of Novem-ber, when we hope our Republican friends will pardon us if we burn heaps of powder, ring numerous bells, (we shall not enlist church bells, however), and let them know, in many noisy ways, that Stephen A. Douglas is chosen President of the United States.

[1] C. C. Strawn, F. B. Johnson, G. H. Franzen (eds.), "History of Livingston Co.," in Newton Bateman and Paul Selby, *Historical Encyc. of Illinois and History of Liv-ingston Co.*, Vol. II, p. 659.
[2] Belleville *Advocate*, May 25, 1860. Canton *Weekly Register*, May 22.
[3] *Illinois State Register*, May 19.

Shortly after noon a hundred-gun salute began to reverberate in the Illinois capital, continuing most of the afternoon. Then bell ropes were pulled continuously until sundown. A stream of Republicans brought congratulations to the Lincoln home during the afternoon, and after dark a ratification rally was held in the State House, with speeches by James Conkling and others; "deafening cheers" burst at each mention of Lincoln. Upon adjournment "the vast crowd, preceded by the Young America Band, immediately started for Mr. Lincoln's residence."

Arriving in front of the house the crowd made loud calls for Mr. Lincoln, and they were soon gratified by seeing the tall form of the next President in front of them. Mr. Lincoln's appearance was a signal for renewed applause. When the cheering subsided, Mr. Lincoln commenced a speech, which, for appropriateness, was never surpassed.

The nominee said he did not interpret this honor as meant for himself as a man, but rather for the representative of a great Party. He foreshadowed his own conduct in making the canvass by saying that voters might discover "his position on the political questions of the day" by reading "his previous public letters and speeches."

Just previous to the conclusion of his speech, Mr. Lincoln said he would invite the whole crowd into his house if it was large enough to hold them, (A voice, "We will give you a larger house on the fourth of next March") but as it could not contain more than a fraction of those who were in front of it, he would merely invite as many as could find room.

Deafening cheers greeted the invitation, and in less than a minute Mr. Lincoln's house was invaded by as many as could "squeeze in!" The invaders were warmly received and many . . . had the pleasure of shaking the right hand of their hospitable host. When the crowd had partially dispersed, a number of ladies called upon Mr. Lincoln and wished him success in the coming campaign.

Many of the Republicans were so well pleased with the day's work that they could not make up their minds to go home till after midnight.[1]

Murat Halstead, leaving Chicago late Friday on a crowded night train, found the exodus a kaleidoscope of impressive scenes. "I never

[1] *Illinois State Journal*, May 19, 1860.

before saw a company of persons so prostrated by continued excitement. The Lincoln men were not able to respond to the cheers which went up along the road for 'old Abe.' They had not only done their duty in that respect, but exhausted their capacity. At every station where there was a village, until after two o'clock, there were tar barrels burning, drums beating, boys carrying rails; and guns, great and small, banging away. The weary passengers were allowed no rest, but plagued by the thundering jar of cannon, the clamor of drums, the glare of bonfires, and the whooping of the boys, who were delighted with the idea of a candidate for the Presidency, who thirty years ago split rails on the Sangamon River — classic stream now and for evermore — and whose neighbors named him 'honest.' " [1]

So began the crucial campaign destined to be the prologue to war, one of the three and last of the three most exciting presidential campaigns in American history. Saturday night Republicans in numberless communities staged their local ratification rally. Then sometime in June each county had its county ratification with a pretentious rally including bannered processions, succulent barbecues, campaign ballads loud and gay. In late July or early August the task of ratifying the nominations was finished by a gigantic state ratification meeting at some central point like the state capital, comprising close to a hundred thousand people, some of whom traveled for days to take part, dozens of speakers, an official parade several miles long.[2] Then the canvass rushed on to its peak and the nation swarmed with political speakers. There were rallies almost every day. No locality, however remote, where votes were lurking, was neglected by the locust swarm of orators.[3] "For the last two months business was almost suspended, the people hastening to and fro to hear stirring speeches and to march in mile-long processions." [4] Carl Schurz said "it looked as if people . . . had little else to do

[1] Halstead, p. 154.
[2] Baringer, "Campaign Technique," pp. 252–256.
[3] C. B. Johnson, "The Presidential Campaign of 1860," *Transactions*, Ill. State Hist. Soc., 1927, p. 117.
[4] Koerner, *Memoirs*, Vol. II, p. 101.

than to attend meetings, listen to speeches, march in processions, and carry torches after nightfall." [1]

The Saturday morning issue of the Chicago *Press & Tribune* was dedicated to the task of giving Lincoln's campaign a rousing start. Announced as "In press, to be issued at once," was a biography of Lincoln, published by Follett, Foster & Co. of Columbus, publishers of the Lincoln-Douglas Debates volume. Much space was occupied by a four-thousand-word biographical sketch. This, the first nationally read biography of Lincoln, followed very closely his autobiographical letter to Fell, emphasized Lincoln's rail-splitting and flat-boating, his labors for a protective tariff, his Republican service as the man who could handle Douglas. The lead editorial affirmed: —

The age of purity returns. After a succession of Presidents, who have not only been subservient to the interests of the Propagandists of Human Slavery, but corrupt to a degree alarming to the truest friends of Republican institutions, the nomination of ABRAHAM LINCOLN — Honest old Abe . . . is a guaranty that the country, wearied and outraged by the malfeasance of those invested with the Federal power, desires a return to the sterling honesty and Democratic simplicity which marked the Administrations of Jefferson, Madison, Adams, and Jackson. The party has not mistaken the man selected for a standard bearer.

MR. LINCOLN'S record on the slavery question is so well known and so clear that it needs no explanation. He is a conservative Anti-Slavery man, against whom no allegations of fanaticism will hold good. . . . Guided by the Constitution and the laws, in the interpretation of his obligations to party he will command the respect of the North and the South; and the country may be assured that if during such time as he may be invested with authority, there is an attempt from any quarter whatever to dissolve the bonds which tie the States of this Union together, it will be met by more than a Roman firmness which never yet yielded to threats or frowns. That beautiful evenness and integrity of his life, which have made him a man of mark, will not desert him in his promised official career. . . .

MR. LINCOLN is untried in a merely executive capacity. But we have not the smallest fear that he will be unequal to any emergency in which he may be placed. . . .

We refer to one matter with pride and congratulation. MR. LINCOLN

[1] C. Schurz, *Reminiscences*, Vol. II, p. 193.

has, by his own motion, never been a candidate for President of the United States; hence he has no pledges to redeem, no promises to make good. The uprising in his favor has been spontaneous — the outgrowth of a widespread conviction of his fitness and availability. . . . That during the past week, in which there have been such temptations to lead him into the practices which are unfortunately so common with politicians of less rectitude, he has in terms of just indignation refused all offers of votes which are based upon promises of future rewards, we have reason to know. With the spirit becoming an honest man, he rejected them all. . . .

The needs of the country are such, and the convictions of the people that a change is necessary are so profound, that MR. LINCOLN, were he but an ordinary man, in whose history there was no flow, would be elected. But being all that the exigencies of the times demand, whether estimated as to ability, tact, integrity or faithfulness to principle, his nomination will be taken up with the zeal and enthusiasm which foreshadow not only success, but majorities unequalled in the political history of the free States.

This ambitious attempt to build up a complete confidence in the prospect of Lincoln's success as President sounds like the effort of a pro-Lincoln Republican editor to convince himself, especially so in that paragraph where the writer coquetted with fact by insisting that Lincoln was chosen without benefit of bargain; and in an adjoining editorial he offered mystical explanation of Lincoln's nomination.

"Ever and anon there springs from the bosom of the people, a man qualified to meet the people's highest wants in great emergencies — a man who by reason of his many virtues, his moral heroism and his commanding qualities, is recognized by all classes as one endowed and anointed for a great work. His credentials bear the impress of a power whose fiat is irresistible, and his progress toward the appointed goal is as sure as the march of destiny." Such a conviction was badly needed as campaign material, for Lincoln as a practising statesman was an unknown quantity. He had never held a public office higher than the rather mediocre positions of Illinois representative (four terms), and his one-term membership in the national House of Representatives. Intelligent political observers could easily see the superiority of Lincoln to Seward as a candidate, but after election there would be other things than availability to think about. Conscientious Republicans, convinced of Seward's abilities in high office, deplored Seward's defeat even when they saw it as a political necessity.[1] And vast numbers of rabid Sewardites were not convinced of the necessity. As Murat Halstead summed it up, "The fact of the Convention was the defeat of Seward rather than the nomination of Lincoln. It was the triumph of a presumption of availability over preëminence in intellect and unrivaled fame — a success of the ruder qualities of manhood and the more homely attributes of popularity, over the arts of a consummate politician, and the splendor of accomplished statesmanship."

In a free political system like the American, as open and untrammeled as is consistent with order, the level of political understanding both of voters and candidates is necessarily low. Therefore, when an individual who has not conclusively proved his competence to manage large affairs is chosen as a candidate for high office, the opposition Party feels justified in jumping to the conclusion that since the man it wishes to defeat has not made famous his ability, he has none. Democrats lost no time attacking Lincoln with a barrage of obscurity and lack-wit charges. A few days after the nomination, Springfield's *Register* said [2]: —

The Republicans of Illinois, who, in urging the nomination of Mr. Lincoln as a candidate for the Presidency previous to the meeting of the Chicago Convention, intended only a little harmless pleasantry, now find that they were perpetrating a joke upon their party, that in its effect, is not likely to be proven "all a joke." As a matter of course, the usual demonstrations . . . will follow the nomination, but they are not accompanied with that sincere earnestness of approbation that characterizes the ratifications of a presidential nomination when the candidate is manifestly the first or even the second choice of his party. Here, at Mr. Lincoln's own home, in Springfield, the exhibition of feeling in his behalf, though attended with a considerable degree of noise and confusion, was evidently deficient in that heart-felt enthusiasm that springs from a positive regard for one who is considered, *par excellence*, the representative man of his party. In other places, beginning with Chicago, the news of his nomination has not been received with that unanimous cordial greeting that indicates a strong hold upon the popu-

[1] *Illinois State Register*, May 24, 1860.
[2] *Illinois State Register*, May 24

lar heart. Neither the Chicago *Journal* nor Wentworth's paper gave it that hearty and unqualified endorsement that his friends had a right to expect, or that either of the other prominent candidates would have received.

The Democratic sheet at Gustave Koerner's home town minced no words.

What has Mr. Lincoln ever done for his country that he should ask the people of the United States to make him President? . . . In fact, his nomination, if it had not been done by the forms of a numerous and powerful party, would be considered a farce. "He is honest!" Yes, we concede that. Who is not! "He is old!" So are thousands. "He has mauled rails!" What backwoods farmer has not? But what has he ever done for his country? Is he a statesman? . . . His nomination is an outrage on an intelligent people.[1]

From Cairo, at the southernmost tip of Illinois [2]: —

The nomination of Lincoln . . . was by no means expected here at home, and must, in those New England states where he is comparatively unknown, strike everybody with surprise. That Wm. H. Seward, the very father of Republicanism, and the great representative man of the party, should be thrust aside for such a man as Abe Lincoln, of Springfield, the people were not prepared to believe. . . .

Upon the whole, as compared with Seward, Sumner, or Chase, we regard Lincoln as a man of decidedly ordinary parts, and this no doubt is the opinion of his party.

The Douglas organ of Ottawa, Burton Cook's home town, exhibited contempt for the nomination that Cook had helped to achieve [3]: —

The nomination was a surprise to most of the people. That the Convention should pass over all the great Republican lights — over such men as Seward, Bates, McLean, Wade, etc., etc., and take up a man whom few out of Illinois had heard of until he was cruelly set up by the Republicans of Illinois in 1858, to be unmercifully pummelled through a whole summer's campaign by the Little Giant, seemed most curious, to say the least. . . .

The Convention was divided into two parties — one consisted of the "irrepressibles," who wanted Seward . . . and the other of the "moderates,"

[1] Belleville *Democrat*, June 2, 1860.
[2] Cairo City *Gazette*, May 24.
[3] Ottawa *Free Trader*, May 19.

the anti-John Brown-ites, such as the Cameron and Bates men. . . . The former party was largely in the majority, and would have nominated Seward, only here was the sticking point — can he beat Douglas? . . . As the nomination of Douglas appeared inevitable, the Seward men considered their favorite too valuable timber to be killed off just now, and so they looked around for a smaller man of the same stripe whom a drubbing by the Giant couldn't seriously damage. . . .

A week later: —

The news of the nomination of Abe Lincoln . . . flew from mouth to mouth with electric rapidity. By the Democrats it was hailed with marks of undisguised satisfaction. Their countenances looked unmistakably pleased and jolly. The Republicans, on the contrary, looked anxious and dubious. It was so unexpected — so fairly stunning.

Attacking from another angle, the *Illinois State Register* paid court to the conservative majority sentiment of southern central Illinois by asserting that Republicans, in choosing Lincoln, "cover their most ultra ground." Lincoln, said Douglas' friend Lanphier, is as radical as Seward; the "irrepressible conflict" and the "house divided" he interpreted as twins. He cautioned voters against the Republican representation that Lincoln is a conservative, calling such talk "simple vaporing to catch those who have been halting between Democratic and Republican ranks." [1]

When the opposition raised derisive cries of the "Who Is James K. Polk?" variety, supporters of the impugned candidate retaliated by subtly requesting the great unintelligentsia of the electorate to practise pleasant self-flattery by elevating one of their own kind to rulership of the nation.[2] Indeed, so small has been that group of voters who exercise the ballot on the basis of serious study of the fitness of the various candidates for national authority, that they are of slight importance in elections. Intellectuals ridiculed the idea of that unlettered backwoods soldier, Andrew Jackson, occupying the White House, but Jackson's popularity with the masses effected a political revolution. The Van Buren machine pointed scornful

[1] *Illinois State Register,* May 19, 1860.
[2] Alton *Courier,* in *Illinois State Journal,* May 21.

fingers at the Harrison "circus" campaign, but that circus put them out of business. Whigs maliciously inquired after the identity of James K. Polk, but Polk won more electoral votes than Henry Clay, idol of millions.[1] Electorally speaking, the Republicans had nominated their strongest candidate, but they had gambled on the ability of their man to successfully perform his duties should he get the Presidency. Republicans campaign arguments of course ignored that gamble. "Our ticket is now fairly before the people," said a Republican sheet, "and, to use the language of a prominent Democrat in this city, 'it is the strongest ticket that could possibly have been nominated,' and, our contemporary to the contrary notwithstanding, we think 'honest Old Abe' *will be the next President of the United States*. We are informed by them that the Democracy brought all the outside pressure they could to bear upon the Convention, for the purpose of securing Seward's nomination, well knowing that if the friends of Lincoln succeeded, their hopes of success would be forever extinguished." [2]

In fine, the ideal candidate for President, from the dual aspect of successful election and successful service to the nation, is the individual who is, externally, in habits and appearance, a "man of the people," but whose inner character and abilities tower far above those characteristic of the people. Voters were not long discovering that Abraham Lincoln's attractive homely personality amply carried out the first qualification. But nobody knew (though his intimate friends suspected) that he fulfilled the second desideratum eminently well also.[3] Not until Booth's bullet had let out life was there anything like unanimity in affirming that in the person of Abraham Lincoln a great man had done a great work.

During the canvass, according to expressions, the thought that Lincoln might be a great man did not occur in many minds. When Illinois citizens of Democratic persuasion, who had at least been exposed to those profound political treatises to which Lincoln had

---

[1] E. P. Oberholtzer, *Abraham Lincoln*, pp. 151–152.
[2] Quincy *Whig*, May 19, 1860.
[3] Roy P. Basler, *The Lincoln Legend*, pp. 52–82. J. G. Holland, *Life of Abraham Lincoln*, pp. 198–199. Stevens, pp. 299–301.

given utterance in the past two years, swiftly called his nomination a farce, an outrage, a joke, it was only natural that people who knew Lincoln less should be even more contemptuous. Professional abolitionists were most displeased; Wendell Phillips growled, "Who is this huckster in politics?" Stiffly intellectual New England Brahmins, outraged at Seward's defeat, conceived a distaste for Lincoln which they never outgrew.[1] Intolerant Southerners, hating all things Republican, slopped over with partisan spleen and amused themselves by discussing the Republican candidate's hereditary connections with "an African gorilla."[2] The Southern version of Honest Abe Lincoln was "that ape Lincoln." Twisting the rail and flatboat symbol quite out of shape, opponents characterized Lincoln as a tough riverman, a specimen of "the rough, half-horse, half-alligator character," whose chief virtue was that he had once mauled rails.[3] The Michigan delegation, leaving Chicago, plastered their special train with portraits of Lincoln and catchword mottoes designed to start the campaign with a bang. But the crowds along the Chicago-Detroit route which gathered as railroad-station rallies, sent up louder cheers for Austin Blair, Michigan's Republican candidate for Governor, than for Lincoln. One who was aboard that train recollected, a half-century later, "that the nomination of Lincoln . . . created at first over a large portion of the North more anxiety than enthusiasm."

The same witness tells about the conduct of an elderly political pundit of a Massachusetts town who was asked to preside at the organization of a Lincoln Club. The elder statesman exploded, "You fellows at Chicago . . . knew that above everything else these times demanded a statesman, and you have gone and given us a *rail splitter*."[4] Many Eastern delegates, Thurlow Weed and other New Yorkers among them, took a free Western excursion into Iowa, upon invitation of two railroads, after adjournment. At train stops cheering crowds called for speeches, and "some of the big guns from New

---

[1] C. F. Adams, *Memorial Address on William H. Seward*, pp. 22–23, p. 27.

[2] Sandburg, Vol. II, p. 355. Norman Hapgood, *Abraham Lincoln*, pp. 164–165. John S. Wise, *The End of An Era*, pp. 144–145.

[3] *Political Debates Between Hon. Abraham Lincoln and Hon. Stephen A. Douglas*, flyleaf advertising the Howells campaign Biography.

[4] Proctor, pp. 15–16, Oliver to O. Sumner, June 9, 1860, Oliver MSS.

York" soothed their own hurt feelings when they "referred deprecatingly to the nominee, apologizing for having a 'rail splitter' for the Party's standard bearer — a man without the culture or experience and trained ability of the great statesman of Auburn." [1]

So little did the public at large know about the real character of the Republican nominee that many serious students of public affairs, like Edward Bates, did not know what principles they would be voting for should they mark their ballot for Abraham Lincoln. The scholarly, bearded St. Louis lawyer confided to his *Diary* [2]: —

May 19. The Chicago Republican Convention is over. That party, will henceforth, subside into weakness and then break into pieces. . . .

By mere accident, I think, certainly unexpected by me, my name was made to loom up before the country, until my nomination by that Convention was thought probable. A large portion of the most moderate and prudent men of that party was anxious for my nomination, wishing to strengthen their party by giving to it more of a national character, and thus secure the alliance of the remnants of the Whig and American parties. This they thought they could do by selecting me. . . . But their views were not acceptable to the Convention. . . .

At the beginning it was generally thought that the contest would be between Mr. Seward and me, and that the Convention would take the one or the other, as it might determine the question whether the party should act independently upon its own internal strength . . . or modify its platform and mollify its tone, in order to win a broader foundation and gather new strength, both numerical and moral, from outside. . . . The show in favor of other candidates was understood to be complimentary only, to the respective local favorites. But all calculations based upon these views were, as the event proves, signally erroneous. . . .

Mr. Lincoln personally, is unexceptionable, but politically, is as fully committed as Mr. Seward is, to the extremest doctrines of the Republican party. He is quite as *far north* as Mr. Seward is. And as to the V. P. — Mr. Hamlin is not the right person: He has no general popularity, hardly a general reputation; and his geography is wrong. His nomination can add no strength to the ticket. . . .

In his Auburn home, a grievously disappointed Seward wrote a short note to Weed in which the Senator half-accused his manager

[1] C. C. Nourse, in *Annals of Iowa*, Vol. XII, p. 464.
[2] Bates, *Diary*, pp. 128–130.

of selling him out. Seward was convinced he could have been beaten only by treachery.[1] Weed wrote from Davenport, Iowa, telling how the thing happened, vindicating himself. Seward, satisfied, replied in a totally different tone. He had foreseen the defeat, he said, sparing Weed's feelings, and now feared for the Party's future. Seward said he hoped to retire next March 4, when his Senate term would run out; and he guessed that Greeley might become the Republican leader for the campaign. He suggested that Weed might go to Europe for six months while the Party drifted to disaster under Greeley, then Weed could return and assume control.[2] Publicly, however, Seward acted the faithful Party worker. To a curious crowd which gathered at his home Friday afternoon, he spoke magnanimously that he was deeply disappointed, but that Lincoln's nomination would prove best for the country, for Lincoln would unite the North. He asked his friends and supporters to suppress all personal grief and to support Lincoln heartily.[3]

Republicans of Abraham Lincoln's home town, not at all exhausted by their exertions of Friday afternoon and evening, touched an even higher pitch of excitement Saturday evening. Springfield had become the current political center of the nation. The town's entire population was astir. Even the Democrats came out for a rally in the courthouse, not to ratify any nomination but to show Republicans that Douglas was a greater man than the new hero, Lincoln. According to Springfield's *Journal*, the purpose of this Democratic meeting was to explain "how it happened that Mr. Douglas did not get the Charleston nomination."[4] Republicans planned a vociferous greeting for the committee scheduled to arrive from Chicago, bringing to the tall politician who resided in the unpretentious frame house at Eighth and Jackson Streets, official notification of his nomination for President. So the two Parties vied and all Springfield turned out.

Numberless bonfires blazed, fireworks made the night additionally

---

[1] Seward to Weed, May 18, 1860; in Barnes, *Memoir*, p. 270.
[2] Seward to Weed, May 24, 1860; Barnes, p. 270.
[3] Bancroft, *Seward*, Vol. I, p. 542.
[4] *Illinois State Journal*, May 21, 1860.

colorful, and periodic cannon detonations reverberated through the air. The Committee of Notification arrived from Chicago on a special train loaded with excited partisans. When the little locomotive with the turnip stack creaked to a stop at the depot, passengers saw people swarming over track, yards, all streets near by. In charge was the Springfield Lincoln Club. The Notification Committee comprised George Ashmun and delegation chairmen. To impress this distinguished and decidedly critical group of politicians with the greatness of Abraham Lincoln, the Springfield Lincoln Club had marshaled "a very large concourse of citizens, who escorted them through the principal streets to the Chenery House, the Young America Silver and the German Saxe Horn Bands discoursing music by the way, while the cannons fired, bonfires blazed, and rockets and other fireworks were sent up from various parts of the city, many houses upon the square being brilliantly illuminated. The streets meanwhile were crowded and the greatest enthusiasm prevailed. Upon the arrival of the Committee at the Chenery, cheers were given by the crowd to Gov. Morgan of New York, Francis P. Blair . . . , Gov. Boutwell of Massachusetts, and three cheers and a tiger for the Pennsylvania delegation. From the hotel the procession deployed off to the State House." [1]

The Committee itself, branching off, proceeded quietly to Lincoln's residence. The new standard bearer, hardly over his surprise at getting the nomination,[2] knew that the notification would be a personal crisis for him, appreciated the absurdity of his position. In the delegation were many leading men whose approval was important to him, men obliged to perform a congratulatory duty they mortally hated. So Lincoln pondered how he could best conduct himself. Mary Lincoln, proud as a queen with her new importance, had prepared to receive the Committee in the grand manner, was ready to serve champagne in the best glass she could find. But that afternoon Gustave Koerner and Ebenezer Peck had hurried in to see the candidate. Mrs. Lincoln asked what they thought of the

---

[1] *Illinois State Journal,* May 21, 1860.
[2] W. Jayne to Trumbull, in White, *Trumbull,* p. 106.

champagne and sandwiches. The two politicians said the alcoholics would never do and had better be sent back without delay. What if some of the Committee were strict temperance people? Mrs. Lincoln launched into a lively defense of her plans, but her husband, coming in, said that perhaps Koerner and Peck were right. So the liquor was replaced by inoffensive ice water.[1] This incident typifies Lincoln's conduct during the imminent campaign. His deepest concern was to avoid stubbing his toe.

Abraham Lincoln awaited the Committee in his north parlor, a double room reserved for special occasions, furnished rococo with plush chairs, littered whatnots, marble-top table, gaudy curtains and mournful wallpaper. Embarrassed, beset with that towering feeling which tall people feel in formal company, he leaned awkwardly on a chair. The Committee, every man alert, wondering, came into the hall. They filed into the parlor. Grouping there, the members gazed at their candidate, marveling at his ill-fitting clothes, ungainly form, melancholy expression. George Ashmun addressed to Lincoln, who stood before the group with folded hands and immobile face, a short, very formal speech which told Lincoln he had been nominated. He placed in Lincoln's hands a letter saying the same thing, and a copy of the platform. By this time there was no doubt that Lincoln had been nominated. The nominee and host, in grave tones, responded. He gave Ashmun his profoundest thanks for the high honor. He said he felt the great responsibility, said he could almost wish that responsibility "had fallen upon some of the far more eminent and experienced statesmen whose distinguished names were before the Convention." Every listener was struck by the appropriateness of his words.

In his last sentence Lincoln relaxed; his cadaverous expression disappeared as his face beamed like a lantern suddenly lit. He said he wanted to shake each man by the hand. The candidate greeted each member cordially and talked in his best jovial vein. Refreshments were served and several minutes passed in informal conversation. Then the Committee went quietly out. Some returned to the

[1] Koerner, *Memoirs,* Vol. II, pp. 93–94.

Chenery House where they held reception; some went to the big rally in the State House.[1]

So Lincoln could feel confident he had safely passed the crisis and made a favorable impression. Discussing the candidate as they departed, nobody of the Committee seemed offended, as some Easterners might easily have been, but some said the candidate was too simple-minded and inexperienced to deal with the problems he would have to face as President. No doubt these men were already thinking that Seward might after all be the Party's *de facto* leader. But Carl Schurz heard Kelley of Pennsylvania say, "Well, we might have done a more brilliant thing, but we could hardly have done a better thing." [2]

Along with the committee on the special from Chicago had come many Illinois delegates to congratulate Lincoln personally, and many politicians who ardently desired at earliest opportunity to secure the ear of Lincoln and tell what fine work they had done in achieving his nomination. Practical politicians, opportunists, reckoned that Lincoln had far more than an even chance to win the next Presidency, so they swiftly went into action to help him win and to let him know they were helping. Recognizing the popular value of the Rail Splitter symbol, two or three hundred of the crowd from Chicago came armed with rails. Shouldering them, they paraded to the State House. When they arrived for the evening rally in the Hall of Representatives, they stacked the rails like muskets. While Lincoln was being notified, the Republican mob listened to Hassaureck, the eloquent émigré. For an hour he harangued them with a speech which "electrified his audience" and "repeatedly brought down the house with volleys of deafening cheers." Notification over, several committee members arrived. Cartter of Ohio took the floor and eulogized "the railsplitter and Douglas mauler." Similar encomiums came from Amos Tuck of New Hampshire, Governor Boutwell of Massachusetts, Judge Kelley of Pennsylvania, all telling how Lincoln's success was assured in

[1] *Illinois State Journal,* May 21, 1860. C. C. Coffin, in Rice, pp. 168–171. *Lincoln Lore,* No. 374.
[2] Schurz, *Reminiscences,* Vol. II, p. 188. Gideon Welles to Mrs. Gideon Welles, May 20, 1860; Welles MSS.

their home state. Carl Schurz praised Seward elaborately, but said Lincoln "was the man of the times" and "that his nomination was tantamount to his election."[1]

These professions as to the inevitability of a Lincoln victory were wholly for popular consumption. Politicians, of course, publicly insist they are going to win even when they know they are in for a drubbing. Privately, smart politicians search the soul and hold serious conferences behind the scenes in order to view their situation in its worst weaknesses. They want to know the worst as soon as possible, to the end that before election day the weak may be made strong, the crooked straight and the rough places plane. Active Republican politicians, committed beyond retreat to Lincoln, rapidly went into energetic action to sweep the North and assure a Republican victory in November. The Party in power, though split, might reunite long before Election Day and defeat Lincoln if Republicans did not consolidate their position in the North by winning new strength in those free states which voted against Fremont. So, with nearly a month's lead on the Democracy, a great political machine swung into action.[2]

This machine, which in 1856 had risen to power in the free states and had been gaining in every subsequent election, acquired important new strength as opportunists of the North flocked to the Lincoln standard. These local political leaders, interested in loaves and fishes rather than government philosophy and policy, had been ardent Democrats for many years. Many of these "crossroads politicians in every county — the real depositories of political strength"[3] had already turned Republican. But the Lincoln nomination really turned the tide. Job-hungry ward heelers saw that Lincoln was a far better bet than Bell or any Democrats who might be nominated by the disorganized remnant of the Jackson steam-roller.[4]

[1] *Illinois State Journal*, May 21, 1860.
[2] Chase immediately found himself deluged by office-seeking letters; Chase MSS., late May, 1860. C. M. Clay, May 26; K. Jarvis, May 28; R. Hosea, May 18, 1860, to Chase; Chase MSS. S. P. Chase to R. C. Parsons, May 30, 1860; Chase MSS. Hist. Soc. of Pa. Washburne MSS., late May, 1860, *passim*. J. Youngs, May 20, I. Klady, May 26, J. A. Briggs, May 28, 1860, to John Sherman; John Sherman MSS. J. Dixon to G. Welles, May 25, 1860; Welles MSS.
[3] J. O. Cunningham (ed.), "History of Champaign County," in N. Bateman and P. Selby, *Historical Encyc. of Illinois and Hist. of Champaign County*, Vol. II, p. 788.
[4] Baringer, pp. 746-748.

The successful Lincoln managers, amid their exultation over a dream come true, were sufficiently aware of mundane realities to see that their wonderful work would be of little use, after all, if the Rail Splitter were not elected. And, considering the frayed state of Sewardite feelings, was there not danger that the Republican machine would creak badly in the New York area? Wasting no time, David Davis and Leonard Swett went, as peacemakers, to see Thurlow Weed as soon as they could after the Convention adjourned. They found Weed very sad but not angry at anyone. As Weed told them he was suffering the great disappointment of his life, the two Lincoln men conceived an admiration which surprised them. Practical always, they warmly urged Weed to visit Lincoln in Springfield en route to New York from his Iowa visit. The pleasing result was a definite arrangement for Swett and Davis to introduce the defeated manager to the successful candidate. On May 24 the two tall angular politicians met and had a general talk on the prospects of the campaign, a conference that was to prove productive of results advantageous to both.[1]

This was smart politics and a propitious start for the Lincoln campaign. Lincoln's managers, having done all in their power to place behind their man the progressive Seward element, applied the same tactics to the conservative Bates group. Orville Browning, in spite of his grandiose words to the Convention concerning the absolute fitness of Lincoln, still believed in his heart that his friend Bates would have made the best candidate, that nominating Lincoln had been a mistake. Four days after the nomination, Browning received a letter signed by David Davis, Norman Judd, Thomas A. Marshall, Ebenezer Peck, and O. M. Hatch (who had met in Springfield and laid plans for the canvass) earnestly requesting him to visit Bates at once in St. Louis and secure his assistance for the Lincoln ticket. These Lincoln men wanted Bates to make several speeches in Illinois as soon as possible, figuring that Illinois would be certain for Lincoln if Bates could bring in the Fillmore Whig element. Browning went

---

[1] Reminiscences of Leonard Swett; in Barnes, *Memoir of Thurlow Weed*, pp. 292–293.

to see Bates as fast as river steamers would carry him. Judge Bates had written lengthily in his journal to show how the Chicago Convention went wrong. "But after all," he concluded, "what better can be done than support Lincoln?" [1] When Browning asked Bates to take the stump for Lincoln the old lawyer declined, but said he would write a public letter urging election of Lincoln. Three weeks later Browning read the Bates letter in the St. Louis *Democrat* — a long, eloquent, convincing epistle which delighted Republicans.[2]

Starting thus cannily, Republican managers sent their campaign of great opportunity off to a fortunate opening. In addition, Lincoln's horde of workers commanded the advantage of a month's start on the riven ranks of the Party in power. Pursuers of the loaves and fishes, the opportunist crossroads politicians, having forecast that victory would attend the Republican standards, exerted their well-known talents in vote-gathering, contributing thereby to the accomplishment of their own prediction. In the Republican area north of the Mason-Dixon line, especially in the doubtful states, Republican workers began to organize the electorate on a plan so broad that Republican clubs were built farther south than ever before, so deep that the machine reached individual voters in every precinct. Membership expanded in the numberless Republican clubs organized before the nominations; new clubs were formed in areas previously neglected. The Wide-Awake idea, a brand new notion in political technique in March, speedily became famous and membership soared.

James W. Sheahan, editor of the Douglas-worshiping Chicago *Times*, had in February published the first biography of Stephen A. Douglas, statesman, ever to appear. It was an admirable work, surprisingly accurate for a campaign biography. All campaign biographers assume they are writing the history of a man soon to be President, but Sheahan went to the extreme of saying of his hero, on the last page of his book: "At this day he occupies the most extraordinary position of being the only man in his party whose nomination for the Presidency is deemed equivalent to an election." [3] Biogra-

[1] *Diary of Bates*, p. 131.
[2] *Diary of Browning*, Vol. I, pp. 408–412, 416–417. *Diary of Bates*, pp. 132, 136
[3] James W. Sheahan, *Life of Stephen A. Douglas*, p. 528.

pher Sheahan, whose book came from the press in time to appear
in great piles at Douglas headquarters at Charleston, based his confidence on the assumption that Douglas would make the race as
leader of a united, confident, national Party. How wrong he was!
The Charleston Convention had turned into a long-drawn-out brawl
between a majority of Douglas delegates and a fierce minority of pro-
slavery members, Jefferson Davis' followers. When the Davis-Yancey
faction failed to pledge the Party to a proslavery declaration and the
Douglas members clung to popular sovereignty, the Southern Ultras
bolted. Under the traditional Democratic two-thirds rule, then, the
Convention could nominate no candidate in fifty-seven ballots. The
Convention adjourned, to reconvene at Baltimore on June 18. Seceders, having met in another Charleston hall as a "Southern Rights"
Convention, adjourned with provision to meet again at Richmond in
early June.[1]

When June arrived, Democrats found two Parties already vigorously seeking to capture the Government. Upon hearing of Lincoln's
nomination, Democrats rejoiced, saying the Republicans would be
easy to beat because the Seward group would bolt their Party.[2]
That had not happened. Realistic Democratic leaders knew that,
to defeat Lincoln, they faced a Brobdingnagian task. The Ultra
Southerners were not disturbed about what they were doing to Party
unity. What if a Black Republican should win the Presidency? said
they. "Southern Rights" could in that event be protected by the
simple device of secession. Douglas was clearly the only Democratic
possibility who could prevent the Republicans from sweeping the
North and winning the Presidency even though not a single Republican vote might be cast in any slave state. But the bolters held
aloof from serious efforts to repair the Democratic breach. The
Ultras, meeting at Richmond, adjourned to await action of their
erstwhile compatriots at Baltimore. There, June 18, politicians of
the Democracy resumed their interrupted work. Charleston seceders
were on hand, seeking admission, but only to do further damage to

[1] Milton, *Eve of Conflict*, pp. 425–449.
[2] Milton, p. 458. J. S. Sheldon to E. B. Washburne, May 21, 1860; Washburne MSS.

the Little Giant or to wrest leadership of the Party from the unionist majority. When the Douglas forces refused to kowtow, a second bolt occurred. Those who remained speedily nominated, as candidate for President, Stephen A. Douglas, and the great horde of Douglas admirers burst out in spouting jubilation, beginning the rigmarole of ratification.

To complete the long series of conventions which opened the great campaign of 1860, the Ultra bolters met in Baltimore and nominated John C. Breckinridge. The Richmond conclave, gathering once more, ratified the Breckinridge choice. So, in striking contrast to the Republican Party, which selected its candidate in three days and at once swung its war machinery into action, the Democracy had over a period of six weeks held five "conventions," been quite unable to agree on candidate or platform. The invincible Party of Jackson, thanks to this fearful wasting of its substance, approached the lean years.[1]

Faithful Democrats organized clubs in an effort to catch the Republicans, even imitating the Wide-Awakes with marching companies of "Little Giants," and "Douglas Invincibles."[2] But the Lincoln men, far ahead, bent all energy to remain in the lead until the race had been run and won. Matching the swift popularity of the Rail Splitter symbol was the Wigwam idea. In every principal city of the North, Republicans contrived a flimsy structure which they called their "wigwam," where shouting partisans assembled for day and night meetings. Out from the national capital, through the hands of workers of high and low estate, from Senator to precinct canvasser, went a flood of campaign fliterature. Party newspapers swelled the deluge with documents from their own presses. Partisan sheets offered special low subscription rates for the duration of the war.[3]

Among the individuals not pleased with the nomination of Lincoln were those hack writers who planned to cash in on the nation's political frenzy by rushing into print with campaign biographies of

[1] Milton, pp. 450–479.
[2] Baringer, pp. 251–252.
[3] Baringer, pp. 250–251.

the nominees. The trick of success in such histories was to sketch each candidate as one of the greatest men of all time. His admirers would then copiously buy the book, to the profit of author and publisher. These hack works, though sold in vast numbers, had no discoverable effect on the balance of voting power. David Bartlett, the Republican journalist who had lately published *Presidential Possibilities*, found his preliminary research of no use when Lincoln was named. With true journalistic speed, several campaign biographers hastily padded the Jesse Fell-Joseph Lewis sketch of Lincoln's life; and before May was past, Lincoln biography had begun its long trek.[1] These earliest journalistic items, — slim, cheap, ground out in greatest haste,— purporting to present "a complete account of the Life, Services and Speeches of Hon. A. Lincoln of Illinois," actually did much less than that. Before Douglas was formally nominated, four biographies of the Illinois Republican favorite son were on the market.[2]

John Locke Scripps of the Chicago *Press & Tribune* was at work on a biography intended not primarily as a publishing venture but as a campaign document. He was dissatisfied with the paucity of fact, so he journeyed to Springfield and interviewed Lincoln himself. The nominee gave Scripps new material (some of it so intimate he swore Scripps to secrecy) and prepared a new autobiography of four thousand words.[3] This autobiography was made available to other writers also, through John G. Nicolay, the secretary Lincoln secured to handle the large correspondence which followed the nomination. One writer who used it was a young Ohio journalist named William Dean Howells, whose book was notable for its brilliant style and literary savor, which has hardly been equaled in the thousands of Lincoln books published since. Best book of the crop, however, was that by John Locke Scripps, who alone of these earliest Lincoln historians knew much about his subject. The Scripps *Life* was advertised by aggressive Republican sheets as a history written by "an Illinois politician" who knew Lincoln personally. Appearing in mid-July,

---

[1] Barton, "The Lincoln of the Biographers," pp. 63–65.
[2] Barton, pp. 65–68.
[3] *Works*, Vol. VI, pp. 24–38.

this thirty-two page pamphlet biography was published simultaneously by the Chicago *Press & Tribune*, New York *Tribune*, and Denver *Tribune*, and the Republican machine moved to flood the North with it. The *Press & Tribune*, announcing the book as "Campaign Document No. 1," was persuasive: —

We have issued a campaign biography of the Republican standard bearer, in a style so compact, and cheap, that with suitable effort on the part of clubs, canvassers, and local committees, it may reach every voter in the Northwest before the campaign is on. . . . It has been prepared with great care, and may be considered a reliable and authentic narrative of the life of Abraham Lincoln, embracing also the substance of the debates with Mr. Douglas in 1858, and a complete history of that remarkable campaign. It has been the purpose of the writer to make it *the* document of the times. A copy should be placed in the hands of every man in the Northwest who can read the English language.

This was a large order. But the document cost only five cents a copy, forty cents a dozen, three dollars and fifty cents a hundred, twenty dollars a thousand; and Republican workers blanketed their section with several hundred thousand copies.[1]

Readers accustomed to modern campaign expenditures may well be astounded at the small amount of money absorbed by the impetuous campaign of 1860. Though there were "batteries and flotillas of orators," who had to be paid while they "argued, threatened, promised, appealed to statistics, passions, history," though "bills for printing, cash vouchers for speakers and their railroad fares and hotel bills, outlays for thousands of torches, oilcloth uniforms and caps for Wide-Awake clubs, had to be met at campaign headquarters,"[2] central committees even in the important doubtful states of Pennsylvania, Indiana, and Illinois talked only in terms of thousands of dollars. The vast campaign hurrah was conjured up not by dollars but by hopes. The Douglas machine, lacking both strong hope and

[1] *Chicago Press & Tribune*, July 14, 1860. Barton, "The Lincoln of the Biographers," pp. 69–70, 91. M. L. Houser (annotator), *John Locke Scripps' 1860 Campaign Life of Abraham Lincoln*, p. 6.
[2] Sandburg, Vol. II, pp. 352–354.

money, bogged down, and the fight had to be carried by the Little Giant himself. Supporters of Breckinridge and Bell likewise lacked the confident, hard-working *esprit de corps* of the Lincoln men.

Since the time of Washington it had been a political form that no candidate for President should participate actively in his own campaign. Douglas, realist that he was, spurned tradition and launched a man-killing speaking tour. His chance of victory was slim indeed. He must carry the border states, the North's doubtful states, and even several of the Fremont states to win. On the Republican side, every Party chief save Lincoln himself was haranguing the people.

The Republican candidate, as he had promised, chose to follow tradition, and confined his campaign activities to strategy and control behind the scenes. Putting aside his law practice, Lincoln kept a firm yet unseen hand on the reins of the Party machine from a special campaign office he opened on the second floor of the State House. There he received, with the politician's best campaign hospitality, curious observers, reporters, portrait painters, photographers, political and personal friends. There he directed a large correspondence. Each day hundreds of letters came, and on busiest days his visitors likewise reached a toilsome total of hundreds. Some of his visitors he enjoyed, but most of it was routine which bored Lincoln and wore him down. It was part of the game, however, and the candidate carried on uncomplainingly.

Not only did Lincoln refuse to make any speeches, but he would make no new statement of policy. Since Southern Rights politicians never tired of saying that election of a Republican President would be ample reason for secession, many Republicans tried to induce Lincoln to pledge that as Chief Executive he would do nothing to menace Southern institutions. Lincoln had already said, time after time in his speeches of the preceding two years, that he favored such a policy. So he told all inquirers that his position was fully defined in his published speeches. He explained his silence by saying that any new statement from him would elicit new misrepresentation from his opponents.[1] His letter of acceptance was studiously general,

[1] Form letter, *Works*, Vol. VI, pp. 22–23.

permeated by a seductive pious tone. His program was, in his own words, that he "must not now embarrass the canvass."

Campaign orators work on the theory that votes are influenced by speeches and arguments. The host of Republican speakers had one big idea to impress upon their acres of listeners — that the Republican Party was not controlled by sectional policy. They ridiculed the secession threats as an old wives' tale. James Russell Lowell said, for New England intellectuals, that the Breckinridge forces were trying to scare people with a worn-out "Mumbo-Jumbo." Attacking Pennsylvania, a very important sector as an October state and because of its large electoral vote, Republican strategy soft-pedaled slavery and concentrated on rosy tariff promises. Seward, whose September speeches over a wide area to stupendous crowds were the Republican forensic feature, sought to shift attention from the dangerous issue, which had destroyed the traditionally simple lines of political cleavage and somewhat Europeanized American politics, by painting a glowing picture of empire. America would eventually absorb Canada, Mexico, he said, and federate Latin-American republics under the United States flag. Where did the Republican Party fit into this halcyon picture? The dream could only be realized by free labor; therefore the current Republican task was to restrict slavery's spread. Replying to Douglas and Bell arguments that votes for Lincoln were votes for disunion, Seward eloquently denounced the cowardice of voters who believed tall tales of secession.

Lincoln himself sincerely believed that secession threats were mere politics. As he kept a sharp eye on the progress of the campaign, he consistently expected to win. But he did not expect, as President, to be forced to deal with armed rebellion. In mid-August he wrote, "in no probable event will there be any very formidable effort to break up the Union." [1] This was the point of view of all Republican leaders. To believe thus was to their political advantage of course, but it was more than that. The Republican Party could not possibly win control of the Senate in 1860. How then could a Republican

[1] Lincoln to J. B. Fry, Aug. 15, 1860; *Works*, Vol. VI, p. 50. Don Piatt, *Memories of the Men Who Saved the Union*, pp. 30, 33–34,

President, even if he wished, enact legislation destructive to those famous "Southern Rights?" [1] Logical thinkers underestimated the mortal fear in which Southern fire-eaters stood of even an opening wedge against their "peculiar institution." [2] And if campaign speeches were to be believed, the Union was the object of a great love in the heart of every candidate for President. Even Breckinridge said so.

As the campaign rushed along the Republican leaders shrewdly appealed to conservative Northerners by painting the economic necessity of slavery restriction, and gained in the West by railroad and homestead law promises, Lincoln's three opponents saw that, without some drastic strategy, the work of the Chicago Convention in nominating Lincoln as the available candidate would be crowned with success. Maine, in its August state election, voted decisively Republican. Belated efforts went forward to repair the split begun at Charleston. One plan called for joint withdrawal of Douglas, Bell, and Breckinridge in favor of a new Democratic candidate.[3] But the Little Giant knew that he alone could compete with Lincoln in the free states with any chance of success, and all fusion efforts stopped short of successful consummation.

When in early October Pennsylvania and Indiana counted their gubernatorial votes, telegraphic flashes told of a smashing Republican victory. Douglas, stumping the West, heard the news in Iowa. He remarked to his secretary, "Mr. Lincoln is the next President. We must try to save the Union. I will go South." [4]

Election Day was November 6. Springfield made Election Night a festive occasion, Republicans swarming in thousands to hear the anticipated victory news. Before midnight, surrounded by lieutenants in his campaign office in the State House, Lincoln had a message from New York which told of Republican victory. With this, he knew he had won.

So Lincoln was safely elected, and this history arrives at its con-

[1] *Reminiscences of Carl Schurz*, Vol. II, pp. 202–203.
[2] Fite, *Presidential Campaign of 1860*, pp. 163–189.
[3] Milton, p. 487.
[4] Allen Johnson, *Stephen A. Douglas*, p. 437.

clusion. How on Election Night the statesmen of Southern Rights made detailed plans for electing state conventions to consider the serious matter of secession, how the cotton South did secede, how it became a moot question whether Lincoln would ever be inaugurated sixteenth President of the United States, how armed conflict broke out and President Lincoln through his innate genius won the ability to lead his nation safely through the storm and stress of the war which formed the prelude to modern America and gave the triumphant Republican Party a new base and a new purpose — all that is another Lincoln story, an oft-told history more important, more dramatic even, than the fascinating events of Abraham Lincoln's rise to power.

Afterword

I HAVE read many romances about how, why and by whom Abraham Lincoln was nominated for President at Chicago," wrote Alexander McClure of Pennsylvania, Andrew Curtin's 1860 campaign manager. So has the writer. "But the explanation is very simple," McClure continues.[1] To speak in broad generalization, the epochal event of Lincoln's nomination was the direct result of simple political expediency. It sprang from the same formula of availability which elevated Harrison, Polk, Taylor, Pierce, Buchanan, to the Presidency. Between 1840 and 1864, not one of the successful nominees for President received his nomination as a reward of distinguished Party service. This period, when Expediency was king, a unique era in our history, was no mere series of accidentally similar events. The period was one of extreme turmoil and political flux; old Party lines melted and new ones formed with such rapidity that old Party leaders were regularly abandoned in favor of less prominent politicians who fitted the exigency of the moment.

The Republican nominations of 1860, and two of the three unsuccessful tickets as well, were made in accordance with the political success formula which sets off this middle period of American politics from the earlier and later periods of more orderly political leadership. Had Seward been chosen, his success would have presaged a return to the older Party tradition, to selection of leaders not by the

[1] A. K. McClure, *Our Presidents and How We Make Them*, p. 155.

capricious demands of the moment but as the natural result of prominence in the Party hierarchy.

Generalizations concerning the era of political chaos, which gave
Abraham Lincoln his great opportunity to impress his genius upon
his time, are effective in dispelling the aura of mysticism with which
the hero-tradition has enwrapped the Emancipator's swift rise to
power, and, indeed, his whole career.[1] But they do not explain it.
The preceding pages have been mainly concerned with the How of
the nomination, leaving something to be said here to more adequately
elucidate the Why — important aspects of which have been passed
over in narrating the rapid flow of political event.

Henry C. Whitney, as a young lawyer of Urbana, was rather intimately associated with Lincoln as he traveled the Eighth Judicial
Circuit in the 'fifties. Decades later, Whitney wrote many pages of
reminiscence. Among them are several concerning the nomination.
According to Whitney, "the real effective work" in winning the prize
for the Illinois favorite son "was thus, viz" [2]: —

First — The State Convention which met at Decatur . . . enthusiastically nominated Lincoln, and also injected into the canvass the novelty and
glamour of the "rail-splitting" episode: which took like wild-fire.

Second — Norman B. Judd, one of the shrewdest and most effective of
politicians, . . . secured Chicago as the seat of the Convention.

Third — Reduced railway fares and other inducements were secured to
guarantee a large attendance of Illinoisans; and in other ways the machinery
of enthusiasm was set in motion for Lincoln.

Fourth — Whereas the Indiana delegation had been selected with the
primary object of securing general control of the Interior Department, and
special control of the Indian bureau; and the Pennsylvania delegation, in
part, had been organized with the intent of controlling the Treasury Department, therefore it was essential to pander to those wishes, in order to
secure the delegations . . . of those states.

Fifth — And to have a good "send off" it was needful that Indiana and
Illinois should be solid for Lincoln on the first ballot.

Many another writer, lured by mystery, has compiled lists of "influences" which made Lincoln President. Most of them are far less

---

[1] Basler, *The Lincoln Legend, passim.*
[2] H. C. Whitney, *Life on the Circuit,* pp. 84–85.

suggestive than Whitney's analysis. Others, impelled less by the Sherlock Holmes spirit than by favoritism, have named the Rail Splitter's Warwick. We may find the honor conferred upon Frederick Smyth, John Hanks,[1] Norman Judd, David Davis, Jesse Fell, Leonard Swett,[2] W. O. Stoddard, David Dudley Field, Horace Greeley,[3] Andrew Curtin, Henry S. Lane, God, the devil.[4] But, laying aside both special pleading and naïveté, it must be conceded that the political situation of 1860 was the result of a complex of forces that could not be controlled by any individual or group. Success in the turbulent cross-currents of 1860 politics meant that one political group would excell others by exercising superior skill in adaptation. This the Lincoln clique was able to do, using the disordered flow of public polity to their own ends so cleverly that the Weed group paid tribute to Illinois guile by asking if they might have some lessons in the Illinois technique.[5]

Soberly analyzed, Lincoln's chances in the Convention depended on two controlling factors: (a) Could the Party be persuaded that Seward could not be elected; (b) could the Party be led to believe that Lincoln could be elected? We have seen, in narrative, how against great odds the Illinois delegation, using every effective weapon which came to hand, was able to sweep the Convention. Why was the Party convinced that Illinois pointed the correct way? The answer, suggested many times in the above pages, will stand out more clearly if the causes are set down, as a final word, in more compact form.

Some weeks before the Convention Senator Dixon of Connecticut wrote out for his friend Gideon Welles his objections to Seward [6]:

1. He cannot be elected. . . .
2d. I do . . . believe his election would prove a misfortune for the country. He is . . . surrounded by a corrupt set of rascals. . . . His adminis-

---

[1] *Magazine of History*, Vol. XLII (Extra number 165), p. 21.
[2] S. D. Wakefield, *How Lincoln Became President*, p. 115.
[3] Leslie M. Scott, "Oregon's Nomination of Lincoln," *Quarterly of the Oregon Hist. Soc.*, Vol. XVII, pp. 201–214. Breckinridge and Lane Campaign Documents, No. 19, p. 3.
[4] *Abraham Africanus I*, in Basler, p. 123.
[5] I. N. Arnold, *Lincoln*, p. 168.
[6] Dixon to Welles, April 26, 1860; Welles MSS.

tration would be the most corrupt the country has ever witnessed. I regret
to be driven to this belief for personally I like Seward.

Many Republicans who sought reasons for disliking Seward were
much worried about his connections with the extravagant New York
machine.[1] This, however, was definitely secondary to the other objection offered by Senator Dixon, and it held comparatively little weight
in the discussion at Chicago.

The rock upon which Seward foundered was a magnified doubt,
spread in trumpet blasts at Chicago, that he could be elected. A Chase
correspondent had written prophetically: "The fight is in Pennsylvania, Indiana & Illinois. Tell me how to carry those states, & I will
make the President." [2] The doubtful states destroyed Seward not
by their inherent strength but by their vociferous predictions of
calamity on the Convention ground. Because their misgivings were
genuine, the doubtful state leaders so forcefully insisted Seward
could not win that they prevented the stampede to Seward which
would otherwise have occurred because of his great original strength.
The bogey of Seward's radicalism was exaggerated until, with a
majority of the delegates, it carried conviction.[3]

There is something to be said for the point of view that these
history-making fears as to Seward's availability would not have ma-

---

[1] J. Allison to J. McLean, Dec. 12, 1857; McLean MSS. C. Robinson to S. P. Chase,
Aug. 10, 1858; H. Dawes to Chase, Jan. 7, 1860; Chase MSS. James Ford Rhodes,
History of the United States, Vol. II, pp. 417–418. Gideon Welles, *Lincoln and Seward,*
pp. 27–29.

[2] G. Hoadly to Chase, April 3, 1858; Chase MSS.

[3] Autobiographical MS. of Senator Harlan of Iowa, in *Annals of Iowa,* Vol. IX, p.
248. A. K. McClure, *Our Presidents,* pp. 156–157. F. P. Stearns, *Life of George Luther
Stearns,* pp. 227–228. G. S. Merriam, *Life of Samuel Bowles,* Vol. I, p. 262. Leonard
Swett, in Oldroyd, p. 73. H. E. Pratt, "David Davis," p. 77.

R. Hosea wrote to Chase on May 18: "Indiana, Illinois and Pa. have been here in
force determined to accomplish the defeat of Seward . . . and by combining together
have at last succeeded." Chase MSS.

While the Convention was nominating its candidate for Vice President, Defrees of
Indiana, an original Bates man, interpreted the nomination for Congressman Colfax.
"The hardest-fought battle of the age has just closed in victory. I did not expect it last
night, but Providence smiled on us this morning. Greeley slaughtered Seward and
saved the Party. He deserves the thanks of all men, and gets them now. . . . We
worked hard [for Bates] but could not make it. We Bates men of Indiana concluded
that the only way to beat Seward was to go for Lincoln as a unit. We made the nomination. The city is wild with enthusiasm." O. J. Hollister, *Colfax,* pp. 147–148.

terialized in the campaign.[1] Had he been nominated, his Chicago opponents would have swallowed their words and worked manfully in
the doubtful regions to accomplish what they had insisted was impossible. Cameron, last of the Republican leaders to give his active
support in the canvass, said publicly that Seward could have carried
Pennsylvania. But no such opinion had come from him prior to the
nomination.[2] As Charles Beard has pointed out, the agrarian South
was destined to lose its dominant position in the national Government as "the sweep of economic forces" brought together the new
industrial East and the rapidly developing West. The successful
Party would be that which served the new monarch, Commerce,
rather than King Cotton.[3] The Republican Party, thus, stood on
firm ground. The Democracy did not. It was, indeed, this conflict
between sections, inside the Party, which caused the 1860 split.

Simultaneously with their work of stopping Seward, the Lincoln
men labored without stint to make their candidate the beneficiary of
the Party's lack of faith in its leader. Their success was the direct
result of two forces: outside pressure, inside deals.

Most writers have been wont to slide over the fact that Lincoln's
managers heavily mortgaged the presidential plum tree, or have found
reasons for disbelieving that such deals were made. The history of
these bargains seriously damages the Lincoln hero-myth. The great
tribe of Lincoln sentimentalists, therefore, have avoided the subject.
Scholars, insufficiently familiar with the evidence, have not given
this somewhat less savory phase of Lincoln history the prominence
it merits.[4] The fact remains that, without these Convention bargains,
Lincoln's political advance in 1860 would have been no more than he
originally planned — the gathering of new prestige toward securing
the Senatorial seat of Douglas in 1864.[5]

Though Convention horse-trading on a large scale had not been
definitely endorsed by Lincoln, the nominee was not seriously embarrassed because trades were made. In fact, he was not required to

[1] Carl Schurz, *Reminiscences*, Vol. II, p. 183.
[2] M. Halstead, p. 142. Milton, *Eve of Conflict*, p. 243.
[3] C. Beard, *Rise of American Civilization*, Vol. I, pp. 628–662.
[4] W. E. Smith, *The Blair Family*, Vol. I, p. 477.
[5] Whitney, *Life of the Circuit*, pp. 85–87.

keep the promises so lavishly made in the heat of battle.[1] But to ignore political promises is to wreck Party harmony. Lincoln chose to unite his Party behind him by repaying every political debt in the traditional legal tender of politics.[2] In framing his Cabinet, Judge Davis' promises caused Lincoln no little annoyance. He complained, "They have gambled me all around, bought and sold me a hundred times. I cannot begin to fill the pledges made in my name." [3] When Cabinet posts were exhausted, however, the pie counter was by no means barren. Men who deserved the dignity of a portfolio, like Norman Judd, William Dayton, Cassius Clay, were rewarded when they crossed the ocean as diplomats. David Davis went to the Supreme Court.

The President-elect had to consider many other things in addition to the bargains in launching his Administration. His Cabinet had to consider geography, custom, the fact that he was elected by a sectional, minority vote, the prominence of other Party leaders who, like Seward, had been given no option on a Cabinet position. When Lincoln's key appointments finally emerged, an admirable job of compromising appeared.[4] Novel though the task was with Lincoln, he carried it through with an understanding which presages his success as President through his characteristic of rising to the occasion.

Lord Charnwood, in his famous biography, pauses in his cosmopolitan admiration of Lincoln to deplore at considerable length the fact that he rose to the Presidency through methods known in political cliché as "corrupt bargains." [5] Realistically considered, all those bargains constituted no approach to "the indistinct and dangerous borderland of political corruption." Rather, Lincoln and his sup-

[1] Whitney, p. 86. G. P. Orth to S. Colfax, Nov. 20, 1860. This letter says that Indiana deserves a place in the Cabinet, that Colfax should have it. Thus it shows that the bargains were not generally known even to active Republican politicians. Godlove P. Orth MSS., Indiana State Library.

[2] Julian, *Political Recollections,* p. 183. Charles A. Dana; in Rice, *Reminiscences of Lincoln,* pp. 363–365.

[3] Hollister, *Colfax,* p. 147n.

[4] Herndon and Weik, *Lincoln,* Vol. II, pp. 181–184. D. Lamon, *Recollections of Lincoln,* pp. 27–28. Gideon Welles MS in *Magazine of History,* Vol. XXVII (Extra number 105), pp. 22–33. Welles, *Lincoln and Seward,* pp. 33–38. H. C. Whitney, *Lincoln the President,* pp. 1–4. Lincoln to C. B. Smith, May 26, 1860, in E. Hertz, *Lincoln,* Vol. II, p. 773. L. Swett, in Barnes, *Memoir of Thurlow Weed,* pp. 293–294.

[5] Lord Charnwood, *Lincoln,* pp. 162–167.

porters merely followed the course which is "necessary to every practical leader in an imperfect world." No surrender of ideals was involved.[1]

An indispensable factor in both the main phases of the struggle was the force of outside pressure. As President, Lincoln liked to tell as one of his stories how the shouting hosts in the Wigwam made him President.[2] The astonishing solidarity for Lincoln among the anxious hosts at Chicago militated against Seward, and acted at the same time as an influence of prime importance for Lincoln. Without it, he could not have won.[3] Henry J. Raymond, seeking an ignominious reason for Seward's defeat, wrote [4]: —

I have said . . . that the final selection of Lincoln . . . was a matter of accident. . . . Down to the time of taking the first ballot, there had been no agreement among the opponents of Seward as to the candidate upon whom they should unite. The first distinct impression in Lincoln's favor was made by the tremendous applause which arose . . . upon the presentation of his name as a candidate. . . . The arrangements for the Convention were in the hands of Mr. Lincoln's friends, and they had been made with special reference to securing the largest possible concourse of his immediate neighbors and political supporters. It was easy to see that the thundering shouts which greeted every vote given for him impressed what Mr. Greeley calls "the ragged columns forming the opposing host," with the conviction that he was the only man with whom Mr. Seward could be defeated. Vermont . . . was the first to catch the contagious impulse; and throughout the second ballot the efforts of other states to resist the current which deluged the Convention from without were but partially successful. On the third ballot the outsiders had it all their own way. . . . The final concentration upon Lincoln was then mainly, in my judgment, a matter of impulse.

There are two notable dissents from the view that the uncerebral force of noisy enthusiasm helped make Lincoln President. James Ford Rhodes wrote [5]: —

[1] J. G. Randall, "Has the Lincoln Theme been Exhausted?" *American Historical Review*, Vol. XLI, pp. 293–294. John W. Bunn, in I. N. Phillips, *Lincoln — By Some Men Who Knew Him*, pp. 153–154.

[2] *Magazine of History*, Vol. XLII (Extra number 165), p. 22.

[3] J. G. Blaine, *Twenty Years*, Vol. I, p. 169. N. B. Judd, in Rankin, *Intimate Character Sketches*, p. 200.

[4] In Parton, *Greeley*, p. 446. Also Barnes, p. 276.

[5] *History of the United States*, Vol. II, pp. 424–425.

In many contemporaneous and subsequent accounts of this convention,
it is set down as an important fact, contributing to the nomination of Lincoln, that on this day the Lincoln men out-shouted the supporters of Seward.
One wonders if those wise and experienced delegates interpreted this
manipulated voice as the voice of the people. . . . That a convention composed of such men — men who had looked behind the scenes and understood the springs of this enthusiasm — should have had its choice of a candidate dictated by the cheers and shouts of a mob, is difficult to believe.

Rhodes forgot that these shouting thousands in the Wigwam constituted an absolutely new force in conventions. Convention managers
had not yet learned, in 1860, how to take the new phenomenon.

Carl Schurz, writing his recollections long after, reflected that: —

Much has been said about the superior volume and fierceness of the shouting for Lincoln in the packed galleries and its effect upon the minds of the
delegates. But that is mere reporter's talk. The historic fact is that, as the
Convention would not take the risks involved in the nomination of Seward,
it had no other alternative than to select Lincoln as the man who satisfied the
demands of the earnest anti-slavery men without subjecting the party to
the risks thought to be inseparable from the nomination of Seward. That the
popular demonstrations for Lincoln in and around the Convention were, indeed, well planned and organized, is true. But they were by no means a
decisive factor. Without them the result would have been the same.[1]

In short, the Convention was sure to act sensibly by choosing the
best man for the task! For a man who knew American conventions
as well as Schurz did, and who usually interpreted public events with
great perspicuity, this view is a surprising lapse into ingenuousness.

When all this has been said, it is proper to assign credit to the
man who was, more than any other, although he served indirectly,
Lincoln's Warwick. This man, for all his prominence in American
history, rarely has been noticed in that connection. His name was
Stephen Douglas.

[1] Schurz, *Reminiscences*, Vol. II, pp. 184–185.

☆　　　☆　　　☆　　　☆

Bibliography

I

SOURCE MATERIALS

The following list of sources is given to include important facts concerning materials which do not appear in footnote citations. Newspapers, therefore, have not been listed because no additional facts about them are of value, though newspapers have been one of the supremely important sources, the above pages representing grist winnowed from tons of old journals.

Adams, Charles Francis, *Address on the Life, Character, and Services of William H. Seward*. Delivered by Invitation of the Legislature of the State of New York, in Albany, April 18, 1873. New York, 1873.

Arnold, Isaac N., *The Life of Abraham Lincoln*. Chicago, 1885.

Baker, George E. (ed.), *The Life of William H. Seward, with Selections from His Works*. New York, 1855.

Bancroft, George, *Abraham Lincoln — A Tribute*. New York, 1908.

Barrett, Joseph H., *Abraham Lincoln and His Presidency*. 2 vols. Cincinnati, 1904.

Bartlett, D. W., *The Life and Public Services of Hon. Abraham Lincoln*. New York, 1860.

Bates, Edward, *The Diary of Edward Bates, 1859–1866*. Howard K. Beale, ed. Washington, 1933.

Bigelow, John, *Retrospections of an Active Life*. 5 vols. New York, 1909–1913.

Blaine, James G., *Twenty Years of Congress: From Lincoln to Garfield*. 2 vols. Norwich, Conn., 1884–1886.

Bonham, Jeriah, *Fifty Years' Recollections with Observations and Reflections on Historical Events*. Peoria, 1883.

Boutwell, George S., *Reminiscences of Sixty Years in Public Affairs*. 2 vols. New York, 1902.

Bromley, Isaac H., "The Nomination of Lincoln." *Scribner's Magazine*, Vol. XIV, new series, pp. 644–656.

> Grandiose reminiscence.

Browne, Robert H., *Abraham Lincoln and the Men of His Time*. 2 vols. Chicago, 1907.

> Pious, ponderous, erratic, yet containing much interesting reminiscence.

Browning, Orville Hickman, *The Diary of Orville Hickman Browning*. Theodore C. Pease and James G. Randall, eds. 2 vols. Springfield, Ill., 1925–1933.

Carpenter, Frank B., "How Lincoln Was Nominated." *Century*, Vol. XXIV, pp. 853–859.

> A detailed account of Pennsylvania in the convention, not entirely reliable, by a noted Lincoln writer.

Carr, Clark E., *The Illini*. A Story of the Prairies. Chicago, 1904.

> An absorbing book of fictionized history.

Chittenden, L. E., *Personal Reminiscences*, Including Lincoln and Others, 1840–1890. New York, 1893.

Clay, Cassius Marcellus, *The Life of Cassius Marcellus Clay*. Memoirs, Writings, and Speeches, Showing His Conduct in the Overthrow of American Slavery, the Salvation of the Union, and the Restoration of the Autonomy of the States. Cincinnati, 1886.

Cleveland, H. I., "Booming the First Republican President. A Talk with Abraham Lincoln's Friend, the Late Joseph Medill." *Saturday Evening Post*, Vol. CLXXII, pp. 84–85.

> To be used with caution.

Coleman, Mrs. Chapman, *The Life of John J. Crittenden*. 2 vols. Philadelphia, 1871.

Conkling, Clinton L., "How Mr. Lincoln Received the News of His First Nomination." *Transactions,* Illinois State Historical Society, 1909.

Dittenhoefer, Abram J., *How We Elected Lincoln.* New York, 1916.

Dodge, Grenville M., *Personal Recollections of President Abraham Lincoln, General Ulysses S. Grant, General William T. Sherman.* Council Bluffs, 1914.

Dudley, Thomas H., "The Inside Facts of Lincoln's Nomination." *Century,* Vol. XL, pp. 477–479.

Errett, Russell, "The Republican Nominating Convention . . . of 1860." *Magazine of Western History,* Vol. X, pp. 361–365.

Foster, Lillian, *Way-Side Glimpses.* New York, 1860.
    A most interesting travel book.

Gibson, Charles, "Edward Bates." *Missouri Historical Society Collections,* Vol. II, pp. 52–56.
    By Edward Bates's campaign manager.

Greeley, Horace, *The American Conflict.* 2 vols. Hartford, 1864–1866.
——, *Recollections of a Busy Life.* New York, 1868.

Gresham, Otto, *The Greenbacks, or, The Money That Won the Civil War and the World War.* Chicago, 1927.

Halstead, Murat, *Caucuses of 1860.* A History of the National Political Conventions. Columbus, Ohio, 1860.

Herndon, William H., and Weik, Jesse W., *Abraham Lincoln: The True Story of a Great Life.* 2 vol. ed. New York, 1908.
——, *Herndon's Life of Lincoln.* The History and Personal Recollections of Abraham Lincoln, as Originally Written by William H. Herndon and Jesse W. Weik. Paul M. Angle, ed. New York, 1930.

Herriott, F. I., "Memories of the Chicago Convention of 1860. Being Interviews with General Grenville M. Dodge of Council Bluffs and Judge Charles C. Nourse of Des Moines." *Annals of Iowa,* Vol. XII, pp. 446–466.

Hertz, Emanuel, *Abraham Lincoln, A New Portrait.* 2 vols. New York, 1931.
    As a collection of Lincoln letters, valuable. As a portrait, hero-worship.

Howells, W. D., and Hayes, John L., *Lives and Speeches of Abraham Lincoln and Hannibal Hamlin.* Columbus, Ohio, 1860.

Photostats of corrections made by Lincoln during the campaign of 1860, in Illinois State Historical Library.

Ingersoll, L. D., *The Life of Horace Greeley, Founder of the New York Tribune,* with Extended Notices of Many of His Contemporary Statesmen and Journalists. Chicago, 1873.
Ponderous work containing much valuable original material.

Julian, George W., *Political Recollections, 1840 to 1872.* Chicago, 1884.

Koerner, Gustave, *Memoirs of Gustave Koerner.* Thomas J. McCormick, ed. 2 vols. Cedar Rapids, Iowa, 1909.

Lamon, Dorothy (ed.), *Recollections of Abraham Lincoln, 1847–1865, by Ward Hill Lamon.* Chicago, 1895.
Valuable but not wholly reliable.

Lamon, Ward H., *Life of Abraham Lincoln; From his Birth to his Inauguration as President.* Boston, 1872.
Ghost-written by Chauncey F. Black, this is fascinating volume.

Lincoln, Abraham, *Complete Works of Abraham Lincoln.* Gettysburg edition, 12 vols. John G. Nicolay and John Hay, eds. New York, 1905.
——, *New Letters and Papers of Lincoln.* Paul M. Angle, ed. New York, 1930.
——, *Uncollected Letters of Abraham Lincoln.* Gilbert A. Tracy, ed. Boston and New York, 1917.
——, and Douglas, Stephen A., *Political Debates Between Hon. Abraham Lincoln and Hon. Stephen A. Douglas, in the Celebrated Campaign of 1858, in Illinois.* Columbus, Ohio, 1860.

McClure, A. K., *Abraham Lincoln and Men of War-Times.* Philadelphia, 1892.
——, *Colonel Alexander K. McClure's Recollections of Half a Century.* Salem, Mass., 1902.
——, *Our Presidents and How We Make Them.* New York, 1902.

Oldroyd, Osborn H., *The Lincoln Memorial: Album-Immortelles.* Springfield, Ill., 1890.

Palmer, John M., *Personal Recollections of John M. Palmer.* Cincinnati, 1901.

Parton, James, *The Life of Horace Greeley, Editor of the New York Tribune.* New York, 1868.

Phillips, Isaac N. (ed.), *Abraham Lincoln, By Some Men Who Knew Him.* Bloomington, Ill., *c.* 1910.

Piatt, Donn, *Memories of the Men Who Saved the Union.* New York and Chicago, *c.* 1887.

Pierce, Edward L., *Memoir and Letters of Charles Sumner.* 4 vols. London, 1878–1893.

Pike, James S., *First Blows of the Civil War.* New York, *c.* 1879.

Proceedings of the First Three Republican National Conventions. C. W. Johnson, compiler. Minneapolis, 1893.

Procter, Addison G., *Lincoln and the Convention of 1860.* Chicago Historical Society, 1918.

Putnam, George Haven, *Abraham Lincoln, the People's Leader in the Struggle for National Existence.* New York, 1909.

Rankin, Henry B., *Intimate Character Sketches of Abraham Lincoln.* Philadelphia, 1924.
——, *Personal Recollections of Abraham Lincoln.* New York, 1916.

Raymond, Henry J., *The Life and Public Services of Abraham Lincoln, Sixteenth President of the United States; Together with His State Papers, Including His Speeches, Addresses, Messages, Letters, and Proclamations, and the Closing Scenes Connected with His Life and Death.* New York, 1865.

Rice, Allen Thorndike (ed.), *Reminiscences of Abraham Lincoln by Distinguished Men of His Time.* New York, 1889.

Schurz, Carl, *Reminiscences of Carl Schurz.* 3 vols. New York, 1908–1909.
——, *Speeches, Correspondence, and Political Papers of Carl Schurz.* 6 vols. Frederic Bancroft, ed. New York, 1913.

Seward, Frederick W., *Seward at Washington, as Senator and Secretary of State.* 2 vols. New York, 1891.
    A surprising work by Seward's noted son. Thorough, brilliantly written, absorbing.

Sheahan, James W., *The Life of Stephen A. Douglas.* New York, 1860.

Sparks, Edwin Erle (ed.), *The Lincoln-Douglas Debates of 1858.* Springfield, Ill., 1908.

Stanton, Henry B., *Random Recollections.* New York, 1887.

Stoddard, William O., *Abraham Lincoln: the True Story of a Great Life.* New York, 1885.

    Not so true.

——, *Lincoln At Work.* Boston and Chicago, *c.* 1900.

Villard, Henry, *Memoirs of Henry Villard.* 2 vols. New York, 1904.

Ward, William Hayes (ed.), *Abraham Lincoln.* Tributes from His Associates, Reminiscences of Soldiers, Statesmen, and Citizens. New York, *c.* 1895.

Welles, Gideon, *Diary of Gideon Welles.* 3 vols. Boston and New York, 1911.

——, *Lincoln and Seward.* New York, 1874.

——, "Nomination and Election of Abraham Lincoln." *The Galaxy,* Vol. XXII, pp. 300–308, 437–446.

Whitney, Henry C., *Life on the Circuit with Lincoln.* Boston, 1892.

——, *Lincoln the Citizen.* New York, 1907.

——, *Lincoln the President.* New York, 1909.

Wilson, Henry, *History of the Rise and Fall of the Slave Power in America.* 3 vols. Boston and New York, 1872–1877.

    The "how I won the war" theme ponderously developed.

Wise, John S., *The End of an Era.* Boston and New York, 1902.

Manuscript Collections

Chase MSS., Historical Society of Pennsylvania. Papers of Salmon Portland Chase.

Chase MSS., Library of Congress. Papers of Salmon P. Chase.

Fell MSS., Illinois Historical Survey, Urbana, Ill. Papers of Jesse W. Fell, photostats.

McLean MSS., Library of Congress. Papers of John McLean.

Schurz MSS., Library of Congress. Papers of Carl Schurz.

John Sherman MSS., Library of Congress.

Trumbull MSS., Library of Congress. Papers of Lyman Trumbull.

Washburne MSS., Library of Congress. Papers of Elihu B. Washburne.

Welles MSS., Library of Congress. Papers of Gideon Welles.

II

SECONDARY MATERIALS

Angle, Paul M., *Lincoln, 1854–1861.* Being the Day-by-Day Activities of Abraham Lincoln from January 1, 1854 to March 4, 1861. Springfield, Ill., 1933.

Angle, Paul M., *"Here I Have Lived."* A History of Lincoln's Springfield, 1821–1865. Springfield, Ill., 1935.

Bancroft, Frederic, *The Life of William H. Seward.* 2 vols. New York, 1900.

Baringer, William Eldon, "Campaign Technique in Illinois — 1860." *Transactions,* Illinois State Historical Society, 1932.

Barler, O. L., *A Study of Abraham Lincoln.* Beatrice, Neb., 1903.

Barnes, Thurlow Weed, *Memoir of Thurlow Weed.* Boston, 1884.

Barton, William E., *The Life of Abraham Lincoln.* 2 vols. Indianapolis, *c.* 1925.

——, "The Lincoln of the Biographers." *Transactions,* Illinois State Historical Society, 1929.

——, *President Lincoln.* 2 vols. Indianapolis, 1933.

Basler, Roy P., *The Lincoln Legend.* A Study in Changing Conceptions. Boston and New York, 1935.

    Stimulating and valuable literary criticism.

Beveridge, Albert J., *Abraham Lincoln, 1809–1858.* 2 vols. Boston and New York, 1928.

Bishop, Joseph Bucklin, *Presidential Nominations and Elections.* A History of American Conventions, National Campaigns, Inaugurations, and Campaign Caricature. New York, 1916.

Bissett, Clark Prescott, *Abraham Lincoln, A Universal Man.* San Francisco, 1923.

Brooks, Noah, *Abraham Lincoln and the Downfall of American Slavery.* New York, 1908.

    By a man who knew Lincoln well, much better than he knew Clio. The book might justifiably be called "Variations on a theme by J. G. Holland."

Browne, Francis Fisher (ed.), *The Everyday Life of Abraham Lincoln.* New York, *c.* 1913.

Carnegie, Dale, *Lincoln the Unknown.* New York, 1932.

    Fascinating biography for the general reader.

Carr, Clark E., *Stephen A. Douglas, His Life, Public Services, Speeches, and Patriotism.* Chicago, 1909.

Chadwick, French Ensor, *Causes of the Civil War, 1859–1861.* New York, 1906.

Charnwood, Godfrey Rathbone Benson, 1st Baron, *Abraham Lincoln*. New York, 1917.

Church, Charles A., *History of the Republican Party in Illinois, 1854–1912*. Rockford, Ill., *c.* 1912.

Clark, L. Pierce, *Lincoln, a Psycho-Biography*. New York, 1933.

Coffin, Charles Carleton, *Abraham Lincoln*. New York, 1893.

Cole, Arthur Charles, *The Era of the Civil War*. Centennial History of Illinois, Vol. III. Springfield, Ill., 1919.

Cortissoz, Royal, *The Life of Whitelaw Reid*. 2 vols. New York, 1921.

Currey, J. Seymour, *Chicago: Its History and Its Builders*. 5 vols. Chicago, 1912.

Curtis, Francis, *The Republican Party. A History of its Fifty Years' Existence and a Record of its Measures and Leaders, 1854–1904*. 2 vols. New York, 1904.

   Eulogistic anniversary work.

Davis, Granville Daniel, "Factional Differences in the Democratic Party in Illinois, 1854–1858." MS. doctoral dissertation, University of Illinois Library, 1936.

Davis, J. McCan, *How Abraham Lincoln Became President*. Springfield, Ill., 1909.

Dennett, Tyler, *John Hay, From Poetry to Politics*. New York, 1934.

Dodd, William E., *Lincoln or Lee*. New York, 1928.

Dodge, Daniel Kilham, *Abraham Lincoln, Master of Words*. New York, 1924.

Duis, E., *The Good Old Times in McLean County, Illinois*. Bloomington, Ill., 1874.

Eggleston, Percy Coe, *Lincoln In New England*. New York, 1922.

Fessenden, Francis, *Life and Public Services of William Pitt Fessenden*. 2 vols. Boston and New York, 1907.

Field, Henry M., *The Life of David Dudley Field*. New York, 1898.
   Magnifies Field's part in the nomination.

Fite, Emerson David, *The Presidential Campaign of 1860*. New York, 1911.
   Vivid, but rather old-fashioned in interpretation.

Fuess, Claude Moore, *Carl Schurz, Reformer*. New York, 1932.

Going, Charles Buxton, *David Wilmot, Free-Soiler*. A Biography of the Great Advocate of the Wilmot Proviso. New York, 1924.

Gresham, Matilda, *Life of Walter Quintin Gresham*. 2 vols. Chicago, 1919.

Valuable reminiscence, erratic history.

Hamlin, Charles Eugene, *The Life and Times of Hannibal Hamlin*. Cambridge, 1899.

Hanaford, Phebe A., *Abraham Lincoln: His Life and Public Services*. Boston, 1883.

Hapgood, Norman, *Abraham Lincoln, the Man of the People*. New York, 1900.

Hart, Albert Bushnell, *Salmon Portland Chase*. Boston and New York, 1899.

Herriott, F. I., "The Conference in the Deutsches Haus, Chicago, May 14–15, 1860. A Study of Some of the Preliminaries of the National Republican Convention of 1860." *Transactions*, Illinois State Historical Society, 1928.

——, "Iowa and the First Nomination of Abraham Lincoln." *Annals of Iowa*, Vol. VIII, pp. 81–115, pp. 186–220, pp. 44–466, Vol. IX, pp. 45–64, 186–228.

Exhaustive research by a historian's historian.

——, "Republican Presidential Preliminaries in Iowa — 1859–1860." *Annals of Iowa*, Vol. IX, pp. 241–283.

——, "The Republican State Convention, Des Moines, January 18, 1860." *Annals of Iowa*, Vol. IX, 401–446.

Holland, Josiah G., *Life of Abraham Lincoln*. Springfield, Mass, 1866.

An absorbing book, by far the best of the early biographies.

Hollister, O. J., *Life of Schuyler Colfax*. New York, 1886.

Hubbart, Henry Clyde, *The Older Middle West, 1840–1860*. New York, 1936.

Irelan, John Robert, *History of the Life, Administration, and Times of Abraham Lincoln*. 2 vols. Chicago, 1888.

Johns, Jane Martin, "The Nomination of Abraham Lincoln to the Presidency, an Unsolved Psychological Problem." *Journal*, Illinois State Historical Society, Vol. X, pp. 561–567.

——, *Personal Recollections of Early Decatur, Abraham Lincoln, Richard J. Oglesby, and the Civil War*. Decatur, 1912.

Johnson, Allen, *Stephen A. Douglas: A Study in American Politics*. New York, 1908.

Julian, George W., *The Life of Joshua R. Giddings*. Chicago, 1892.

Levy, T. Aaron, *Lincoln the Politician*. Boston, 1918.
In the Fourth of July manner.

Lewis, Lloyd, *Myths After Lincoln*. New York, c. 1929.
Most fascinating of all Lincoln books.

Lincoln Lore. Bulletins of the Lincoln National Life Foundation, Ft. Wayne, Ind. Louis A. Warren, ed.

Ludwig, Emil, *Lincoln*. Boston, 1930.
Here many Lincoln writers meet in pleasant literary atmosphere.

Macartney, Clarence Edward, *Lincoln and His Cabinet*. New York, 1931.

Macy, Jesse, *Political Parties in the United States, 1846–1861*. New York, 1911.

Masters, Edgar Lee, *Lincoln the Man*. New York, 1931.
An interesting diatribe which falls by its own contradictions.

Merriam, George S., *The Life and Times of Samuel Bowles*. 2 vols. New York, 1885.

Milton, George Fort, *The Eve of Conflict: Stephen A. Douglas and the Needless War*. Boston and New York, 1934.

Minnigerode, Meade, *Presidential Years, 1787–1860*. New York, 1928.

Morehouse, Frances Milton I., *The Life of Jesse W. Fell*. University of Illinois Studies in the Social Sciences, Vol. V, No. 2. Urbana, 1916.

Morse, John T., Jr., *Abraham Lincoln*. 2 vols. Boston and New York, 1893.

Newton, Joseph Fort, *Lincoln and Herndon*. Cedar Rapids, Iowa, 1910.

Nicolay, Helen, *Personal Traits of Abraham Lincoln*. New York, 1912.

Nicolay, John G., and Hay, John, *Abraham Lincoln: A History*. 10 vols. New York, c. 1886.

Oberholtzer, Ellis Paxson, *Abraham Lincoln*. Philadelphia, 1904.

Oldroyd, Osborn H., *Lincoln's Campaign, or The Political Revolution of 1860*. Chicago, 1896.

Page, Edwin L., *Abraham Lincoln in New Hampshire*. Boston and New York, 1929.

Pearson, Henry Greenleaf, *The Life of John A. Andrew*. 2 vols. Boston and New York, 1904.

Pratt, Harry Edward, "David Davis, 1815–1886." MS. doctoral dissertation, University of Illinois Library, 1930.

——, "David Davis, 1815–1886." *Transactions*, Illinois State Historical Society, 1930.

Ray, P. Orman, *The Convention That Nominated Lincoln*. Chicago, 1916.

Rhodes, James Ford, *History of the United States from the Compromise of 1850 to the McKinley-Bryan Campaign of 1896*. 8 vols. New York, 1920.

Roberts, Octavia, *Lincoln in Illinois*. Boston and New York, 1918.

Robinson, Luther Emerson, *Abraham Lincoln as a Man of Letters*. New York, 1923.

Roll, Charles, "Indiana's Part in the Nomination of Abraham Lincoln for President in 1860." *Indiana Magazine of History*, Vol. XXV, pp. 1–13.

Rothschild, Alonzo, *Lincoln, Master of Men*. A Study in Character. Boston and New York, 1906.

Ryan, Daniel J., "Lincoln and Ohio." *Ohio Archaeological and Historical Quarterly*, Vol. XXXII.

Salter, William, *The Life of James W. Grimes*. New York, 1876.

Sandburg, Carl, *Abraham Lincoln: The Prairie Years*. 2 vols. New York, 1926.
>   A magnificent work of biographical art, but not a history.

Scott, Franklin William, *Newspapers and Periodicals of Illinois, 1814–1879*. Springfield, Ill., 1910.

Seitz, Don C., *Horace Greeley, Founder of the New York Tribune*. Indianapolis, 1926.
>   A fascinating biography.

——, *Lincoln the Politician*. New York, 1931.
>   Interesting and valuable, but journalistic.

Sellers, James L., "James R. Doolittle." *Wisconsin Magazine of History*, Vol. XVII, pp. 168–178, pp. 277–306, pp. 393–401.

——, "The Make-Up of the Early Republican Party." *Transactions*, Illinois State Historical Society, 1930.

Shaw, Albert, *Abraham Lincoln*. Vol. I: *His Path to the Presidency*. Vol II: *The Year of His Election*. New York, 1930.

These first two volumes of a "Cartoon History" of Lincoln are interesting but unauthoritative. Valuable chiefly for their profuse contemporary illustrations.

Smith, Donnal V., "Salmon P. Chase and the Election of 1860." *Ohio Archaeological and Historical Quarterly*, Vol. XXXIX.

Smith, William Ernest, *The Francis Preston Blair Family in Politics*. 2 vols. New York, 1933.

Snider, Denton Jaques, *Abraham Lincoln*. An Interpretation in Biography. St. Louis, c. 1908.

A forgotten provincial philosopher nebulously limns Lincoln in terms of the "Folk-Soul, World-Mind, World-Spirit."

Starr, John W., Jr., *Lincoln and the Railroads*. New York, 1927.

Stearns, Frank Preston, *The Life and Public Services of George Luther Stearns*. Philadelphia, 1907.

Stephenson, Nathaniel Wright, *Lincoln*. Indianapolis, c. 1924.
——, *Abraham Lincoln and the Union*. New Haven, 1921.

Steiner, Bernard C., *Life of Henry Winter Davis*. Baltimore, 1916.

Stevens, Frank E., "Life of Stephen Arnold Douglas." *Journal*, Illinois State Historical Society, Vol. XVI, pp. 247–673.

Stevens, Lucia A., "Growth of Public Opinion in the East in Regard to Lincoln Prior to November, 1860." *Transactions*, Illinois State Historical Society, 1906.

Tarbell, Ida M., *In the Footsteps of the Lincolns*. New York, 1924.
In the romantic mood.
——, *The Life of Abraham Lincoln*. 2 vols. New York, 1902.
The journalistic Lincoln.

Vannest, Charles Garrett, *Lincoln the Hoosier*. Abraham Lincoln's life in Indiana. St. Louis and Chicago, 1928.

Wakefield, Sherman Day, *How Lincoln Became President*. New York, 1936.

Weik, Jesse W., *The Real Lincoln*. A Portrait. Boston and New York, c. 1922.

White, Horace, *The Life of Lyman Trumbull*. Boston and New York, 1913.

re Republican policy, 87; helps
launch Bates boom, 202; analysis of
Republican possibilities, 205; sup-
ports Bates, 214; mentioned, 300.

Collamer, Jacob, one of the conven-
tion-eve "field," 218; in presidential
balloting, 283 ff.; mentioned, 237.

Collins, Wilkie, 191.

Columbus, Ohio, 93, 96; Lincoln's
speeches in, 97-102; mentioned,
131.

Commercial Register, Sandusky,
Ohio, reports Lincoln for President meeting at Mansfield, Ohio,
54 f.

Compromise of 1850, Douglas on, 34;
Lincoln on, 36.

Concord, N. H., 160.

Congress, Lincoln in, 7; Kansas battle in, 13; and slavery in territories,
106; assembling of (Dec., 1859),
129; disorder in, 134 f., 139; hears
of Lincoln's nomination, 295; Lincoln in, recalled at Chicago Convention, 299; mentioned, 71.

Conkling, Clinton L., 290.

Conkling, James C., addresses Lincoln Club, 145; confers with Lincoln *re* Chicago Convention, 289;
mentioned, 305.

Connecticut, 160 f.; Republican losses
in, 176; called "doubtful," 276.

Connecticut delegation, and Bates,
204, 233; in presidential balloting,
283 ff.

Constitution of U. S., and slavery, 13-
15, 38; slavery in, Lincoln *vs.*
Douglas, 28 f.; Douglas on sanctity
of, 37; and slavery, Lincoln on,
106; Lincoln's investigation of
slavery in, 155 f.

Cook, Burton C., considers joining
Wade faction, 220; at Chicago,
230; and Wigwam packing, 267;
and Lincoln claque, 278 f., 288;
mentioned, 310.

Cooper Institute, 153 ff.

Corwin, Thomas, as Republican possibility, 190; in McLean boom, 206;

at Chicago Convention, 258; presents McLean to Convention, 281.

Corwine, R. M., corresponds with
Lincoln, 174 f., 179; at Chicago
Convention, 255, 258, 284.

Council Bluffs, Ia., 91.

Council Bluffs (Ia.) *Bugle,* 92 f.

Council Bluffs (Ia.) *Nonpareil,* 92.

Crittenden, John J., Lincoln writes to,
49 f.; as Republican possibility, 70,
91, 121, 190; and Union Party, 242.

Curtin, Andrew G., fears Seward's
radicalism, 195; at Chicago, 224,
273 ff.; hails Lincoln's nomination,
303; mentioned, 332.

Curtis, George William, in Chicago
Convention, 261 f.; mentioned, 226,
265.

DALLAS, George M., 122.

Danville, Ill., 33, 145.

Danville (Ill.) *Republican,* nominates
Chase for President, Lincoln for
Vice President, 145.

Davis, David, dissents from Bancroft's interpretation of Lincoln, 3-
4; and Indiana deal, 179, 214 f.; on
Lincoln's presidential chances, 180;
made Chicago delegate, 186; leader
of Lincoln's Chicago forces, 193;
Convention strategy of, 208 f.;
opens Lincoln headquarters, 213;
tactics of, 230 ff.; attacks New
England delegations, 232 ff.; attacks "favorite son" states, 236 f.;
and New Jersey delegation, 238 f.;
and Pennsylvania deal, 239, 277;
character of, 239 f.; methods of, after opening of Convention, 251;
methods of, after second day, 266 f.;
in anti-Seward caucus, 270; visits
Weed, 320; seeks aid of Bates in
campaign, 320; rewarded by Lincoln, 335; mentioned, 68, 235, 332,
335.

Davis, Henry Winter, 195; in vice
presidential balloting, 297.

Davis, Jefferson, as Democratic pos-

Slavery, as menace to North, 7, 36, 102; Douglas's attitude toward, 12, 36, 38, 41; Lincoln's attitude toward, 10, 13-15, 32, 36, 74, 102, 158; and Kansas-Nebraska Act, 19; in Constitution, Lincoln *vs.* Douglas, 28 f.; and Freeport Doctrine, 24 f., 29; traditional American attitude toward, 38; and "squatter sovereignty," 39; forecast as leading issue of 1860, 53; and Republican doctrine, 61, 98; and Democratic Party, 65; and Ordinance of '87, 99 f., 105; and popular sovereignty, 98 ff.; and Dred Scott decision, 100 ff., 104 f.; Lincoln on Douglas as champion of, 102; Lincoln on its sole chance of victory in 1860, 104; and Northwest Territory, 105; and labor, 105, 108 f.; American tradition *re*, and Democratic Party, 111; Lincoln on, and American tradition, 123 ff., 155 f.; rising opposition to, 135, 139; as factor in Republican nominations, 208; in Republican platform, 259; in Charleston Convention, 322; in Republican campaign, 327.

Slidell, John, 70, 122.

Smith, Caleb B., and Lincoln deal, 214 f.; in anti-Seward caucus, 270; in Convention, 281, 297 f.

Smyth, Frederick, introduces Lincoln as next President, 160 and n.; mentioned, 332.

South, The, and Douglas, 24; and Freeport Doctrine, 65.

"Southern Rights," Republican "menace" to, 327 f.

Springfield, Ill., 5, 7; Lincoln and Douglas debate, 16 f.; Lincoln meeting, 43; Republican caucus of Jan., 1859, 68; Palmer-McClernand debate, 114 f.; Republican clubs in, 135 f.; caucus of Jan. 1860, 142 ff.; receives news of Lincoln's nomination, 304 f.; notification ceremony, 315 ff.; on election night, 328; mentioned, 58.

Springfield (Ill.) Republican Club, 114.

Springfield Library Association, Lincoln lectures to, 73.

Springfield, Mass., 177.

Springfield (Mass.) *Republican,* on Republican contenders, 79; on preconvention candidate situation, 221; mentioned, 199, 205.

Squatter Sovereignty, 38 f.

Stafford, E., 165.

State Rights, and slavery, 14.

Stephens, Alexander H., 70, 102, 122.

Stevens, Thaddeus, at Chicago, 277.

Stewart, J. G., 136.

Stoddard, William O., 80 ff., 129, 132, 140 f., 148, 166, 332.

Stone, W. M., 282.

Storrs, Emery A., 146.

Stuart, A. H. H., 122.

Stuart, John T., 242.

Sullivan, Ill., 33.

Sumner, Charles, as Republican possibility, 122, 191; mentioned, 228, 310.

Supreme Court of U. S., in Freeport Doctrine, 25; and "squatter sovereignty," 38; Lincoln on mistakes of, *re* slavery, 157.

Swett, Leonard, speaks at Clinton Republican celebration, 111; endorsed for Governor by *Central Illinois Gazette,* 132; in caucus of Jan., 1860, 142; in Decatur Convention, 185 f.; on Sewardism in Illinois delegation, 187; lieutenant of Chicago Lincoln forces, 193; on Indiana deal, 214 f.; on Lincoln strategy, 219; on success of stop-Seward strategy, 229; on tactics of Lincoln men, 230 f.; on Lincoln's restraining order, 266 f.; visits Weed, 320; mentioned, 227, 332.

Tariff, and Republican Party, 56, 61, 129; as 1860 issue, 111; and Chase candidacy, 201; and Lincoln, 244; in Republican platform, 260; in